The Social Neuroscience of Education

Norton Books in Education

The Social Neuroscience of Education
Optimizing Attachment and Learning in the Classroom

Louis Cozolino, PhD

Foreword by Daniel J. Siegel, MD

W. W. Norton & Company
New York • London

For information about permission to reproduce selections
from this book, write to Permissions, W. W. Norton & Company, Inc.,
500 Fifth Avenue, New York, NY 10110

For information about special discounts for bulk purchases, please contact
W. W. Norton Special Sales at specialsales@wwnorton.com or 800-233-4830

Manufacturing by Courier Westford
Book design by Paradigm Graphics
Production manager: Leeann Graham

Library of Congress Cataloging-in-Publication Data

Cozolino, Louis J.
The social neuroscience of education : optimizing
attachment and learning in the classroom / Louis Cozolino.
p. cm. — (Norton books in education)
Includes bibliographical references and index.
ISBN 978-0-393-70609-3 (hardcover)
1. Learning, Psychology of—Social aspects.
2. Learning—Physiological aspects.
3. Neurosciences—Social aspects. 4. Brain. I. Title.
LB1060.C696 2013
370.15—dc23
2012031666

W. W. Norton & Company, Inc.
500 Fifth Avenue, New York, N.Y. 10110
www.wwnorton.com

W. W. Norton & Company Ltd.
Castle House, 75/76 Wells Street, London W1T 3QT

1 2 3 4 5 6 7 8 9 0

In memory of Brendan A. Maher
. . . teacher, mentor, and friend

Contents

Part III
How to Turn Brains On

Part IV
Applying Social Neuroscience in Schools and Classrooms

Acknowledgments

I would like to thank Deborah Malmud, Andrea Dawson, and Sophie Hagen at W. W. Norton for their many years of professional and personal support on this and other projects. To my research team at Pepperdine University—Traci Bank, Dawn Mitchell, Nattha Tritasavit, Kayla Stinson, James Wylie, Mary Sanker, Maura Sauls, Philly Gizzo, Drew Schoentrup, and Trista Ng—who, word by word, helped me transform a staggeringly large set of disparate ideas into meaningful and (mostly) coherent prose. A special thanks goes to Megan Marcus, who has worked with me throughout the entire journey of creating this book and has now gone on to her calling of revolutionizing teacher training.

To my colleagues John Arden, Sam Crowell, Richard Hill, Angela Kahn, Zeb Little, David Meltzer, Hans Miller, Joseph Palombo, Renee Schwartz, Gloria Mucino, Jeff Weinberg, Sandy Shapiro, Dan Siegel, Stan Tatkin, John Watkins, and John Wynn for their ongoing friendship, inspiration, and good counsel, thank you. I would also like to thank my friends and colleagues at Pepperdine who get me through the day with smiles and generous hearts, especially Camille Andres, John Baker, Unique Banks, Robert deMayo, Rebecca Reed, Ramy Rizkallah, Cheryl Saunders, and Edward Shafranske.

Finally, and most importantly, I wish to express my gratitude to my family, who help it all make sense.

Foreword by Daniel J. Siegel, M.D.

You are about to dive into a powerful synthesis of the world of social neuroscience and the field of education by a master scholar, articulate writer, and superb teacher. Louis Cozolino has created a work that will both inspire and inform educators who teach across the lifespan, from preschool and secondary school to university and even adult education. Education is an art built upon the social relationship between teacher and student that harnesses the neural mechanisms of learning. Here in *The Social Neuroscience of Education* you'll explore the fundamental ways in which relationships and the brain interact to form the foundations of how we learn. You'll be offered memorable insights and practical applications that will enhance your teaching, so that your experience as an educator can become more interesting, more enjoyable, and more impactful.

Beginning with the way the human brain has evolved and exploring how an individual brain develops, the book reviews how the brain is inherently social. That's news for many educators—and for most scientists! It means that our relationships shape the way our brains function in the moment and grow throughout our lives. The brain learns within relationships—through emotional communication that supports a sense of safety and security, and through logical communication that conveys meaning and relevance. In many ways, the relationship between student and teacher parallels the attachment between child and parent. Here you'll be given the opportunity to understand the science behind these foundational relationships in our lives. You'll explore how these close relationships actually stimulate the brain to absorb experience, shape neural connections, and create the long-lasting memories that teachers hope to inspire in their students.

The book then offers you cutting-edge views into how stress and suboptimal attachment experiences inhibit learning. You'll explore how understanding the social brain helps us see bullying as a form of traumatic experience that shuts down learning; you'll see why, and how, the social setting in schools can establish the safety that all students deserve.

The interactions we have with others directly affect the receptivity of the brain to take in new experiences and learn from them. If we are not receptive, we cannot learn. This book gives a clear explanation of the way the brain becomes receptive—vital information for any educator. Teachers are the experiential sculptors who facilitate environments for students to become receptive, shaping the brains of our next generation of learners.

This process, as you know if you are an educator yourself, is one of the most rewarding, most challenging, and sometimes most overwhelming of life's callings. Naturally the huge undertaking that is the teaching profession is filled with deep satisfaction—and also significant risk of burnout. A prime goal of this book, therefore, is to help teachers understand their own brains, offering techniques for taking care of your own neural needs. Keeping your well-being in mind is essential to create the experiential conditions to inspire students to learn.

When we see the light of learning turn on in our students' minds, as teachers we are participating in the ancient tradition of human transmittal of knowledge from one generation to the next, forming educational relationships that shape how culture evolves. From our earliest days of childhood, exploring the nature of our social and physical worlds is part of our human legacy. Curiosity and creativity are a natural part of who we are. Learning is built upon these fundamental ways in which we want to know more, learn more, do more, and engage with our world.

We learn through emotional engagement in our educational experience—finding what is relevant to our personal lives, and what in our personal lives can be relevant to what we are learning. Part of this personal exploration of the larger world is expressed in play—and play has been shown to stimulate the neural mechanisms of both reward and learning. We find play in what we do with our bodies, engaging the world of objects and others. We also find play in what we do with our minds, sensing the new combinations in our mental experience of feelings, thoughts, perceptions, and memories, of language, ideas, patterns, and concepts. One way we pass on what we've learned is through relating what we've encoded in our memory to others, in the form of stories. It is these narratives that form the basis for our knowledge storage as well as how we make sense of the world. Here you'll learn to capture the power of play and of narrative to embrace these natural human propensities embedded in our brains that help us learn.

Throughout this book you'll find cutting-edge science mixed with pearls of wisdom ready to apply in the classroom. You'll find wonderful quotations woven throughout the text which themselves offer insights to help solidify your own learning as you move through these enticing chapters. In the final section, our able guide addresses ways in which we can inspire not only the acquisition of new information, but also the human capacity for compassion and wisdom. We can teach by example, and we can impart knowledge. One new and powerful idea is to teach students about the brain itself, gaining insight into the neural underpinnings of their lives. When students learn to understand their own brains, they are equipped to take responsibility for their own learning. Teaching often occurs within a group setting, and our author further suggests that teacher-as-tribal-leader offers an important perspective with which to view our roles in the classroom. We evolved in tribes, we grow in families, and we learn in groups.

Equipped with this exciting new and practical information, educators will find themselves well prepared to invigorate their classroom roles and to see how their work sculpting the next generation plays an essential role in the functioning of our communities. I hope you'll enjoy this fabulous book and learn from it as much as I have!

Daniel J. Siegel, MD
The Mindsight Institute

Introduction

Is Social Neuroscience Relevant to Education?

> *I am who I am because of who we all are.*
> —Martin Luther King Jr.

American public education was initially conceived of as a cornerstone of the new democracy. Its mission was to shape an informed electorate capable of understanding complex political issues and seeing through the manipulations of aspiring dictators. Through the years, the educational system came to serve more utilitarian needs as the American economic engine transitioned from agriculture to industry. The new mission was to prepare the children of farmers and immigrants to become the workforce of the factories and businesses of the 19th and 20th centuries.

Over the last 50 years, schools have become the battleground for the debate of social issues such as integration, the separation of science from religion, and women's rights. At the same time, the hopes that past generations placed in school as a means of economic opportunity have declined. In some quarters, the perception of public education has shifted from being a solution to social and economic problems to a problem in and of itself. This shift is reflected in the rise of home schooling, the growing number of private schools, and chronically high dropout rates. Many taxpayers no longer view public education as a worthwhile investment, making it increasingly vulnerable to continuous budget cuts and declines in quality. Schools are now the battlegrounds for their own survival.

The current failures of public education are certainly no one's fault—who becomes a teacher with negative intentions or to make a quick profit? The failures we are witnessing may be an inevitable result of a cumbersome and antiquated system serving a rapidly evolving culture. Given the rigidity of large bureaucracies and the present pace of cultural evolution, the term "educational system" may have become an oxymoron. The world in which American public education was shaped is gone, yet the system remains.

Three Major Challenges

> *Every great advance in natural knowledge has involved*
> *the absolute rejection of authority.*
> —Thomas Huxley

While the challenges of contemporary education are many, three stand out as particularly relevant to educating human brains. First, most schools are based on a model of industrial production where uniform materials are converted into a predetermined product. This model has proven itself over the last 150 years and works exceptionally well for making automobiles, washing machines, and chicken nuggets. Students, however, are not homogeneous raw materials. They come from all classes and cultures with a wide range of social, emotional, and cognitive abilities. They also present with a wide variety of individual needs that require teachers to possess considerable parenting, counseling, and interpersonal skills. Regardless of whether students are prepared or able to learn, or whether their teachers have the time, training, or resources to educate them, we measure success by standardized test performance—the quality control measure of the educational assembly line.

The second mismatch between the industrial model and educating human brains is that teachers are not interchangeable cogs in a factory machine. Mass production is based on assembly lines that require workers to engage in the rapid repetition of very specific behaviors. Teachers, like their students, are unique individuals. It is the nature and quality of teacher-student relationships that create the possibilities of learning. This is especially true for children with cognitive, emotional, and social challenges who require of their teachers a wider range of skills and greater flexibility in how a curriculum is delivered.

A third reason why the model of industrial production does not work is that we are uncertain of the final product. Education is supposed to prepare young people for the future—but what future? People in positions to make these decisions were educated before computers, the Internet, and an information-based economy. The world is changing so quickly that it is hard to know what knowledge and skills children will need to have 20 or 30 years from now. In the absence of clear goals, it is nearly impossible to gauge the validity of a curriculum or the relevance of test performance. When tests are the measure of quality, the good student is one who can store and recall facts with minimal distraction and complaint. They are rewarded for information retention and good citizenship, but is this a formula for future success?

Students and teachers are not uniform raw materials or assembly-line workers, but a diverse collection of living, breathing human beings with complex evolutionary histories, cultural backgrounds, and life stories. Teachers are people whose job it is to engage, attach, and teach other people in the real world. When you remove homogeneous products and clear outcomes, you need teachers who can bring their humanity to work, form secure attachments, and make decisions on an individual and moment-to-moment basis. When a teacher begins to think of his or her classroom as an assembly line, it's time to make chicken nuggets. For these and other reasons, the model of industrial education cannot hold.

If we are going to move forward, we will have to admit that a one-size-fits-all model of education is doomed to fail the majority of students and teachers. Let's also admit that while we have plenty of beliefs, dogma, and rhetoric about how to prepare students for the future, we have little solid information about how to do this successfully. We have no idea about whether to limit or encourage their access to social networking, computer games, television, and other forms of media. In the absence of real data, teachers and administrators rely on popular books by nonscientists who generally misinterpret the little data that do exist (Coch & Ansari, 2009; Goswami, 2006). The bottom line is that we don't know if these activities are hurting their cognitive and interpersonal development or better preparing them for the world ahead.

Will reading the great books, studying ancient philosophy, or knowing the nuts and bolts of mathematics be of any help to our children in the future? Should we foster open-mindedness and free-thinking, or push the accumulation of facts and the use of search engines? Perhaps the focus of education should be on social responsibility, empathy, and mindfulness, as multiculturalism becomes more of an everyday reality? Our feelings about these issues are as strong as our knowledge is weak—none of us really know the answers.

Many Cultures—One Classroom

A teacher is someone who talks in someone else's sleep.
—Anonymous

Since their creation, America's public schools have served as a tool of cultural homogenization. It was long-ago hoped that a successful school could carve and polish Native Americans, African Americans, Hispanics, Asians, and Europeans into "true" Americans, converting them to the dominant values and behaviors of the Northern European majority. This required a requisite level of cultural shame, abandonment of traditional values, and an idealization of becoming "Anglicized." In many ways, the culture has shifted from Anglocentrism to one of cultural pluralism, with the goal of being integrated, equal, and different. Pluralism, with all of its advantages, comes with a wide array of challenges.

Every school lives within an existing community connecting hundreds of families through their children. The strength of these connections depends on a sense of partnership resting on shared educational values and a commitment to learning. In a safe community with strong families that value education and support the schools, a competent teacher can do a good job. In a dangerous community with few resources, fragmented families, and indifference to education, it takes a hero to be a successful teacher.

In my own experience half a century ago in New York City, the two primary ethnic groups in my neighborhood—Southern Italian Catholics and Eastern European Jews—had very different views of education. For Jewish families, a "good" boy or girl excelled in school and went on to college. Grades were closely scrutinized and children were held accountable for their performances. On the other hand, most Italian parents were indifferent to grades and oblivious to the existence of college. Their concern was whether their children were being respectful and not embarrassing the family with bad behavior. A "good" Italian boy or girl dropped out of school to get a job to help support the family. My grandparents left school in the 6th grade, both of my parents after the 10th—I obviously come from a family of good Italian boys and girls. My interest in education was a cause of suspicion in my community and reflected badly on my parents. On the other hand, my academic interests were taken for granted by my Jewish friends and applauded by their parents.

If you looked at the ethnic composition of the classes in my school from the best to the worst, you would see that the first class was composed mostly of Jewish students with more educated parents and that the bottom class was composed primarily of Italians. Jewish students competed for the honor society while Italian students competed to be "cool." There was another more insidious stratification across the levels. Because we were tracked for 12 years as either smart or slow, academic or commercial, this label became a stable part of our self-concept and an integral aspect of the stories we told about ourselves.

Today's inner-city schools present a far harsher reality for African American, Hispanic, and Asian American students than anything I ever encountered. The drugs, violence, and lack of resources in today's schools would have seemed like an apocalyptic nightmare in the Bronx of the 1960s. Today, this nightmare is an everyday reality for thousands of schoolchildren and we are seeing the effects of these horrific environments on how these children think about themselves, their place in society, and their futures.

Is Science Relevant to Education?

An abundance of knowledge does not teach men to be wise.
—Heraclitus

Horace Mann, the founder of American public education, believed that pedagogy should be based on sound scientific principles. His science of choice was phrenology, which is the study of intelligence and personality based on the arrangement of the bumps on our heads. Thus began a long history of "science-based" (or, more accurately, pseudo-science-based) teaching.

The most recent trend of "brain-based learning" applies findings from cognitive neuroscience to the classroom. Many steps ahead of Mann's phrenology, it attempts to apply what laboratory scientists have discovered about learning and memory to classroom education. The problem is that science is complex, challenging to learn, and difficult to apply. The result is that a few principles are taken out of context, turned into a sound bite or a list of "Ten Important Scientific Facts," and come to nothing but a new set of clichés.

Most teachers are understandably skeptical and rightfully question the value of brain-based consultants who pepper standard educational dogma with words like *neuron, cortex,* and *synapse*. The fact is, there is no substitute for the instincts of a bright, dedicated, and caring teacher. On the other hand, a thorough knowledge of the nature, limits, and possibilities of students' brains couldn't hurt. While we are just at the beginning of attempting to apply neuroscience to education, it is hard to deny that the evolution and development of the brain is a potential treasure trove of information about where we have come from, what we are capable of, and how we learn. However, this knowledge must be well understood, integrated with what we know about social and emotional development, and made culturally relevant.

Various branches of science have demonstrated that, in general, students seem to learn better when information is presented in particular ways and at a certain pace. Proper nutrition does have a measurable impact on memory and learning, and physical activity does enhance learning. Adolescents have different biological clocks that affect their sleep-wake cycles and result in different learning abilities at different times of the day. These findings are based on some pretty solid science, and should be considered when making decisions about schedules, curricula, and teaching methods (Fischer & Daley, 2006).

Despite the potential benefits of these focused scientific findings, none address the failure of the system as a whole or have any chance of saving it. Renaming teaching as "brain-based education" while keeping the present model in place is like rearranging the deck chairs on the Titanic. This is because teaching is a social, interpersonal, attachment-based endeavor, ill matched to Western scientific methodologies applied within a model of industrial mass production.

What has been missed thus far in essentially all books on brain-based education is the recognition that the human brain is a social organ of adaptation. By an organ of adaptation, I mean that the brain has evolved to interact with and learn how to navigate its environment for the sake of survival. And by a social organ, I mean that humans have evolved to be linked to and learn from other brains in the context of emotionally significant relationships. Therefore, the brain has evolved to learn within a naturalistic setting in the context of meaningful group and interpersonal interactions. All too often, proponents of brain-based learning conceive of brains as living in a vacuum and assume that what we have learned in laboratories can be applied in classrooms. But our social brains reside within (and are regulated by) an interwoven matrix of relationships and are guided by the realities of day-to-day survival. In other words, our ability to learn is regulated by how we are treated by our teachers, at home and in the classroom.

What successful teachers do to stimulate minds and brains to learn is more important than scientific findings from laboratories. Teachers are the experts in this domain and scientists should pay attention to their work, figure out why they are successful, and explore what their successes tell us about how brains learn. What I am attempting to do in this book is to use findings from fields such as social neuroscience and social psychology to more fully understand why successful teachers are successful, which brain systems they are tapping into, and how they manage to stimulate neuroplasticity and learning. My main goal is to explore the humanity of the teacher and the quality of the teacher–student relationship as the scientific center of teaching.

The Social Brain

A kindergarten teacher is a person who knows
how to make little things count.
                                             —Anonymous

The conception of the brain as a social organ emerged during the 1970s as neuroscientists began to discover that our anatomy and biochemistry are deeply interwoven with our social relationships. Since then, scientists have been exploring the complex neural terrain activated during social interactions that allows us to communicate, form sustained relationships, and impact each other's brains (Karmiloff-Smith et al., 1995). Thinking of the brain as a social organ is supported by thousands of studies that attest to the influence of relationships on health, neuroplasticity, and learning.

Using evolution as an organizing principle, we begin with the assumption that our highly social brains have been shaped by natural selection to enhance survival. Cooperation-based survival is not unique to humans but is seen in such diverse settings as beehives, herds of impala, and penguin colonies. For 100,000 years, anatomically modern humans evolved in small tribal communities, held together by family relationships, cooperation, and bonding through shared knowledge and common rituals. Due to the fundamental interdependence of group members, individual brains slowly evolved into a nexus of social connectivity as natural selections shaped tribes into functioning macroorganisms.

We know that the expansion of the cortex in primates corresponds to increasingly larger social groups that, in turn, established the foundation for the development of language, problem solving, and abstract abilities. Our larger and more complex brains allow for greater flexibility in responses to challenging situations across diverse environments and provide the ability to process the vast amount of social information required for communication and group coordination. Deep into prehistory, early learning took place among caring individuals with a "curriculum" relevant to the day-to-day physical and social needs of the community: a far cry from the structure of most modern educational institutions.

By studying tribal communities existing today, we can see that pre-industrial social life is shaped by cooperation, equality, and servant-based leadership. Cooperation, grounded in kinship and common interests, is reinforced through obvious survival benefits, especially when resources are scarce or when faced with a common enemy. Equality and a sense of fairness within a tribe make each member feel valued and sustain their commitment to the tribe. With short life spans and dangerous environments, the decentralization of power also protects against the catastrophic loss of a single leader. Finally, leadership is not inherited but earned through skills and services provided to other members of the tribe. In essence, a leader's authority is based on his or her contribution to others and earned through attention to the well-being of the group. We will come to see in later chapters how this stance is used successfully in the classroom.

In contrast, leadership within industrial societies is based on competition for resources, individual success, and authority based on discipline, obedience, and power over others. Industrial societies are also characterized by larger groups, greater division of labor, and social hierarchies based on inequality and dominance. Most educational institutions organized in this fashion establish a fundamental conflict between the structure of schools and our primitive social instinct upon which the neuroplasticity of learning has been shaped back into prehistory.

While Western culture has changed a great deal during the last 5,000 years, the social instincts, physiology, and biochemistry of the neural networks that evolved for 100,000 years in the context of tribal life remain essentially unchanged. It is possible that a good deal of the anxiety and depression so common in modern society may be partly explained by the alienation of our tribal brains from our historical social environment. There is also considerable evidence supporting the idea that those who best avoid the downside of modern culture are those who join tribes. From churchgoers to sports fans to gang members, the drive to join some version of a tribe and the benefits derived from membership are undeniable. It appears that we do best when we keep at least one foot firmly planted in our tribal past.

The most successful modern institutions may well be those that have found ways to access and harness the instincts of our primitive social brains. Examples of this sort of hybridization are factories that are organized around small production groups for the purpose of enhanced identification with the product and improved quality control. Military hierarchies and sports teams encourage intense ritualistic bonding in small subgroups preparing for combat or competition. These accommodations to tribal instincts within large hierarchies have been referred to as "work-arounds" in management sciences and cultural anthropology (Richerson & Boyd, 1998).

The power and success of these creative uses of our ancient instincts within large organizations leave no doubt of their continued relevance to human experience. As you will see in chapters to come, teachers who are able to tap into the primitive social instincts of their students through attachment relationships and build tribal class-rooms succeed in seemingly impossible educational situations. Over and over again "tribal" teachers find ways to teach students thought to be "unteachable."

As a teacher and therapist, I am especially interested in how rela-tionships impact and reshape the brain throughout life. The thousands of hours I've spent interacting with students and clients have provided me with an intuitive sense of how and why learning takes place. I have watched as my focused attention, consistency, and caring have been absorbed like water at a desert oasis. I have experienced the gradual building of confidence and strength as my presence has been absorbed and used as a source of security, guidance, and emotional safety. I have also experienced how working with my students and clients has changed, inspired, and helped me to grow. The social nurturance of teaching and psychotherapy is most definitely a two-way street.

Relationships are our natural habitat. Teachers and parents usually grasp this fundamental human reality just as corporate leaders, politicians, and laboratory scientists often don't. A school system that treats students like commodities, raw materials, or experimental animals is doomed to failure: a failure we witness every day. A bright 10-year-old boy attending an excellent public school recently told me, "School is bad and learning is boring, it's just a fact, how can you question it?" If this boy thinks education is a waste of time, imagine how those who are less fortunate must feel.

In the chapters to come, we will explore classroom teaching from the perspectives of evolution, attachment theory, social and developmental psychology, and social neuroscience. We will find that the human brain has evolved as a social organ and that it is interwoven with the other brains and minds that surround it. Most important, our present focus is on how our ability to learn is interwoven with and dependent on the quality of our relationships not only with our teachers, but also with our families, friends, classmates, and community.

Looking Forward

> *Success is dependent on effort.*
>
> —Sophocles

The central scientific thread throughout the coming chapters is the invisible yet profound connection between our deep evolutionary history and the modern classroom. The central argument is that our

xxvi The Social Neuroscience of Education

ability to learn is interwoven within our brains and bodies with our physical, emotional, and social survival. We will explore how and why our brains became social organs and how they allow us to weave together our minds and hearts with those around us.

Most important for education, we will discover that the quality of our relationships with our teachers, families, friends, and communities is as important to learning as the curriculum, testing, and technologies which usually occupy our attention. We begin with three broad questions:

1. How has the brain evolved to learn?
2. What conditions optimize learning? and
3. Can teachers and administrators use these findings in our classrooms and schools?

Although placed in order from basic principles to application, each section in this book can be read separately depending on your interests and prior knowledge. The first section, "The Evolution and Development of the Social Brain," presents foundational research from the fields of evolution, neuroscience, epigenetics, and attachment. Although heavily weighted toward science, my goal is to provide a solid rationale for the power and importance of human relationships in the learning process and specifically for attachment-based teaching.

The second section, "How to Turn Brains Off," focuses on the impact of different forms of stress on neuroplasticity with a special emphasis on how negative social interactions close our minds and shut down our brains. The negative impact of stress on learning is explored through an examination of negative interactions at home, the social and biological aspects of bullying, and the causes and consequences of teacher burnout.

The third section, "How to Turn Brains On," shifts focus to those aspects of brain functioning that are programmed to stimulate learning. Emotional attunement between teachers and learners is highlighted, as well as the central role of storytelling in traditional and contemporary learning. Research has also found that exploration and play, usually consigned to less important after-school activities, are central aspects of natural learning that support a state of mind and body most conducive to neuroplasticity and learning.

The final section, "Applying Social Neuroscience to Schools and Classrooms," describes a variety of ways that the science of attachment and learning can be and has already been brought to life in schools. Teaching students about their brains is presented as a vehicle to explore how each of us learns while promoting central issues in education including prejudice, humility, and compassion. The value of simulating the social and emotional elements of tribal life within schools and classrooms will be highlighted through the work of a number of marvelous classroom teachers and administrators such as Marva Collins, Rafe Esquith, and Geoffrey Canada. Finally, a teacher's inner emotional journey is explored as the foundation for a satisfying career and for the successful creation of an attachment-based classroom.

I hope you enjoy this journey through the mind, the brain, and human attachment. If I am successful in my mission, the interweaving of these diverse topics will cultivate within you a deeper understanding of the science behind the art of teaching. And while you may find the science somewhat challenging, the reward will be a deeper understanding of classroom and learning dynamics that influence your methods and emotions. I think you will find that the science makes a strong case for placing the humanity of teachers and students and the quality of attachment relationships at the center of the wheel of education.

Part I

The Evolution and Development of the Social Brain

Chapter 1

Why the Brain Became a Social Organ

Education is cumulative, and it affects the breed.
—Plato

In Western cultures, we are taught to cherish our individuality and experience the world from the perspective of a unique and separate self. This philosophical belief leads us to think of people as isolated organisms, rather than embedded within communities. It also leads us to search for abstract and technical answers to everyday human problems. Our language, ideologies, and politics continue to promote this separateness despite our continued failure to solve our most challenging problems with individualistic strategies (DeVries et al., 2003; Hofer, 1987). This misguided approach has had disastrous results when it comes to raising and educating our children.

Take, for example, the way in which physicians responded to the high mortality rates of children in orphanages early in the last century. Assuming that microorganisms were to blame, doctors separated children from one another and kept handling by adults to a minimum in order to reduce the risk of infection. Despite these mandates, children continued to die at such alarming rates that both intake forms and death certificates were completed at admission for the sake of efficiency. It was only after attachment researchers suggested that the children be held and played with by consistent caretakers and allowed to interact with one another, that their survival rates improved (Blum, 2002). What better evidence is there that the brain is a social organ requiring positive human connection as much as food and water?

Educational experts are guilty of a similar myopathy when they focus on curricular content and test performance rather than the social world of students and teachers. By relying on models of mass production, we, just like the orphanage administrators, miss the interdependent nature of human brains. In the same way, applying "brain-based" strategies derived from research in cognitive psychology doesn't address the fundamental mismatch between the social and emotional environment of contemporary classrooms and the way our social brains have evolved to learn. It is time to rethink education from a social and interactive perspective.

One of the many challenges of translating scientific findings into classroom applications is the disparity of perspectives of scientists and teachers. Scientists are not particularly social people and scientific methods are biased toward studying individual organisms. It is often difficult for scientists to grasp the idea that individual brains do not exist in nature. As much as one may adhere to the notion of the isolated self, humans have evolved as social creatures and are constantly regulating one another's biology. Without mutually stimulating interactions, people (and neurons for that matter) wither and die. In neurons this process is called apoptosis (programmed cell death); in humans it is called failure to thrive, depression, or dying of a broken heart. While science has long appreciated the complexity of the brain, it is just awakening to the ways in which brains are woven together into families, communities, and tribes.

Relationships are our natural habitat. From birth until death, each of us needs others to seek us out, show interest in discovering who we are, and help us to feel safe. We all yearn to be understood, recognized, and appreciated. Regardless of age, it is vital for us to feel a part of, participate in, and contribute to our "tribe." The inabilities to connect, contribute to others, love, and be loved result in anxiety, depression, and alienation. This is just as true for principals, teachers, and school board members as it is for our students.

What is the best frame of reference from which to study a student's brain: the individual, the student-teacher interaction, peer relationships, the classroom, or the broader community? To all of these, the answer is yes; we stand to learn a great deal from considering all of these perspectives. I also believe that it is only when we understand each level from neurons to neighborhoods to culture, that we can even begin to gain a deeper understanding of the interwoven tapestry of biological, psychological, and social processes that shape us. Let's begin by thinking about the brain in a historical context.

Deep History

Those who have learned to collaborate and improvise most effectively have prevailed.
—Charles Darwin

The vast majority of what we consider to be our past consists of the written history of the lives and battles of brave, wealthy, and notorious men. Our knowledge of the everyday lives of average men, women, children, and slaves is mostly gleaned from the background information provided in these "heroic" documents. Prehistoric men are depicted as brutes who were trapped in a moment-to-moment struggle for survival, a struggle from which they were saved by civilization, rationality, and Judeo-Christian values. The general notion is that human history began with the written word while what came before were dark, animalistic, and unhappy times. Despite our awareness of these biases, we tend to trust these written accounts of the past more than other forms of information (Carr, 1962).

In reality, there is no clear dividing line between the animal and the human mind. There was no "first human" but a gradual evolution from one way of experiencing the world to another. Given the many similarities between our behaviors and those of "lower" mammals and primates, we can rest assured that our more primitive natures continue within us along with later evolving modes of behavior and thought. It is certainly true that within our brains are

conserved many of the structures and functions of our primate ancestors. We also retain many animalistic and tribal instincts from our
deep evolutionary history.

To appreciate more deeply how our brains learn, we have to
utilize a variety of disciplines, such as evolutionary biology, social
psychology, cultural anthropology, and genetics. Through these and
other scientific perspectives, we can learn about patterns of instinctual and unconscious behaviors as well as witness these in action
in a variety of living cultures. Through these windows, we receive
glimpses of emerging patterns of humanity through the thousand
generations that connect our written history to our ancient ancestry.

The Evolution of the Social Brain

*The very essence of instinct is that it's followed independently
of reason.*
                                            —Charles Darwin

Let's begin with the assumption that evolution has shaped our brains
into social organs because being communal enhances our survival. For
most of the last 100,000 years, it is believed that anatomically modern
humans lived in tribes of between 50 and 75 individuals. These small-
scale foraging communities were held together by family relationships,
shared rituals, and the necessity of cooperation for survival (Boehm,
1992; Richerson & Boyd, 1998; Rodseth, et al. 1991). It was within
this interpersonal environment that natural selection shaped our social
brains and our first set of social instincts. As highly social creatures,
our primary ecological niche consists of a matrix of relationships.

We know that the expansion of the primate's cortex correlates
with increasingly larger social groups. We also know that this is a
two-way street: Larger brains can process more complex social information, and, in turn, larger groups are able to provide more dedicated child care, stimulation, and challenge to the brain (Dunbar,
2002). Thus, the benefit of living in a tribe goes far beyond the safety
of numbers; it leads to increasingly larger social organizations and

the necessity for a second set of social instincts to hold together these ever-expanding and less manageable groups.

There are many interesting theories about how humans evolved to be the complex social creatures we are. The big story may go something like this:

- Larger group size enhanced the probability of survival, but required bigger and more complex brains to process social information, and so larger brains were shaped by natural selection.
- More complex brains required longer periods of development, resulting in prolonged periods of child dependency and the necessity of caretaking specialization.
- As the size of primate groups expanded, grooming, grunts, and hand gestures became inadequate, and were gradually shaped into words and other symbols.
- Complex social structures encouraged the development of more sophisticated communication, leading to the development of oral and written language.
- As social groups grew in size and language became more complex, an even larger cortex was needed to process the increasing information load.
- Language and culture provided the ability to record and accumulate history, expand information, and allow for the development of technology.
- The accomplishments of culture allowed for even greater group size, requiring more sophisticated brains and an expansion beyond primitive social instincts based on the functioning of small tribes.
- A second set of social instincts were shaped to allow for multiple levels of attachment and connection as civilizations grew in size and complexity.

Over vast periods of time, tribes were shaped into macroorganisms made up of extended family groups and characterized by consistent contact, high levels of interdependence, cooperation, and group solidarity. In the absence of outside authority, group norms were dictated by the demands of immediate survival and enforced by the mores of tribal culture (Eibl-Eibesfeldt, 2007; Milgram, 1983; Nuttin, 1996). Lacking a rigid hierarchy and assigned leaders, members of tribes worked together through cooperation and consensus building in reaction to everyday situations and in times of emergency such as war or famine (Boehm, 1992). It is likely that the most viable tribes were more egalitarian, flexible, and inclusive. These biases would improve a tribe's reaction to changing situations while maximizing the contributions of all of its members. Respect and leadership status would be earned through fairness, generosity, and attention to the other individuals in the tribe. In essence, members of the tribe control their leaders because power is not inherited or assigned but earned through service to others.

If these tribal values shaped the evolution of our social brains for much of our evolutionary history, we can expect that they remain at the core of our primitive social instincts. This may be why we are not able to tolerate more than minimal coercion or injustice and why openly unfair social arrangements are ultimately unsustainable because they create feelings of injustice and drive people to revolt (Kennedy, 1989). Perhaps contemporary humans have such a low tolerance for inequality because we were programmed long ago to champ at the bit of unfair and coercive social control long associated with tribal failure and death. To this day, highly functional and long-lived countries and institutions manage to create a sense of living under generally accepted customs and fair laws (Richerson & Boyd, 1998).

Thus, modern humans appeared to have two sets of layered social instincts. The first is a set of primitive instincts rooted in the blood connections of family and tribe, which we share with other social mammals and primates. The second is a modern addition that connects us in larger groups based on more abstract loyalties. The evolution of these modern social instincts depended on the emergence of cortical networks required for concepts (like America, Christianity, or democracy) that are too abstract to experience directly. In other words, we needed to be able to see beyond our immediate experiences and circumstances to affiliate with others outside of our small tribe.

Although reflecting different stages of our evolution, these two sets of social instincts are strongly interwoven. In fact, the emotional power of our loyalties to larger groups is based on the brain's capacity to link them to the survival reflexes of our primitive social instincts. This provides us with the motivation to fight and die for beliefs and principles, as we do for family and friends. In this way, the primitive biochemistry, neuroanatomy, and reflexes of the deep history of our social brains are utilized in the service of maintaining large, successful institutions in the contemporary world. We see this emerge spontaneously in cliques, clubs, gangs, fraternal organizations, support groups, and online chat rooms. I am also proposing that it is the ability of teachers and parents to connect these primitive social instincts with abstract concepts such as grammar, mathematics, and getting into college, that motivates children to study and stimulates their brains to learn.

Keep in mind that teaching in tribal societies is generally performed by biologically related, caring, and deeply invested elders, one on one or in small groups. In these naturally occurring, attachment-based apprenticeships, learning is interwoven with the behaviors and biochemistry of bonding. In tribal societies, teachers and students are bound together in affection, kinship, and mutual survival. Teachers are likely "elected" because members of the tribe gravitated toward them based on what they have to offer. Tribal teachers are also well aware that as they age, they become dependent on their students for sustenance and survival. The physical setting of the tribal classroom is the natural environment where students and teachers join together to gather food, solve physical and social problems, and defend the community against external attack. The curriculum is guided by the practical tasks of daily life and the evolving needs of the community.

The Last 5,000 Years

An unpopular rule is never long maintained.
                                                    —Seneca

To this day, many groups around the world adhere to traditional tribal structures and values. In contrast, the last 5,000 years of Western culture have seen a shift from tribal to agricultural to industrial based societies. But while 5,000 years may be a long period of time for a culture, it is the "blink of an eye" in terms of biological evolution. The disparity of our biological and cultural clocks has resulted in a dilemma: tribal brains attempting to navigate in an industrial world. In other words, we find ourselves embedded in cultures that are, in many ways, mismatched with our neuroanatomy, neurobiology, and basic social instincts. One has only to watch the news to see the myriad ways in which human beings struggle and often fail to cope with this mismatch. In one way or another, we are all a little like Crocodile Dundee in the big city or 5-year-olds on our first day of kindergarten.

In contrast to tribal life, industrial society is characterized by larger groups, division of labor, and constant contact with strangers. Table 1.1 highlights some of the basic differences between tribal and industrial societies. Equality is replaced with dominance hierarchies based on discipline, obedience, and a lack of concern for fairness. All of these trigger stress in a brain shaped by the biochemistry of attachment and primitive social instincts. In addition to these incongruences, we are also challenged by the complexity of both our physical and informational environments that have emerged from so many technological advances. These everyday stressors, along with a lack of social support, often outstrip our coping abilities with detrimental effects on our physical and emotional well-being.

Table 1.1
Characteristics of Tribal and Industrial Societies

Tribal Society	Industrial Society
Small groups	Large groups
Cooperation	Individualism
Equality and fairness	Dominance hierarchy
Democratic decision making	Imposed and enforced rules
Cohesiveness	Competition
Shared responsibilities	Unequal division of labor

Despite the realities of contemporary society, we retain our primitive social instincts. Perhaps the loneliness and shame so common in Western society today is the result of our tribal brains failing to cope with modernity. The drive to belong to a tribe and the intense loyalties that tribes engender is undeniable. The positive effects on health, well-being, and learning abilities are also undeniable benefits of tribal membership. This is why establishing a tribal classroom can be so beneficial to learning, especially for children without secure attachments and strong affiliations outside of the classroom.

Work-Arounds

*Only passions, great passions, can elevate the soul
to great things.*

Denis Diderot

Leadership within industrial societies is achieved through competition, individual success, and authority based on power. This hierarchical structure has been adapted within corporations, governments, public schools, and most classrooms. Unfortunately, hierarchical social organization has allowed for the accumulation of wealth, military power, and scientific knowledge at the expense of human connectedness. The tribal values of mutual respect, cooperation, and caring that shaped our social brains for countless generations have been largely factored out of the modern cultural equation. However, the most successful institutions are able to integrate the instinctual imperatives of our tribal brains into the structures of contemporary hierarchical organizations. The accommodations to tribal instincts within large institutions have been referred to as *work-arounds* (Richerson & Boyd, 1998).

Successful, complex institutions require effective work-arounds where our basic social instincts are utilized to personal and group advantage. In essence, we work around contemporary hierarchical structures to create groups within institutions that tap into and resonate with our fundamental social instincts. Large institutions, schools, and classrooms that incorporate work-arounds are buttressed by integrating tribal principles and activities into a large-scale industrial framework.

An example of a work-around is a factory organized around small production groups to enhance worker pride, group cohesion, and job satisfaction. Another is the way military organizations are made up of smaller fighting groups (squads and platoons) that emphasize intense fraternal bonding and loyalty to one another as brothers-in-arms (Luttwak & Horowitz, 1975). In a similar manner, large schools encourage a tribal spirit among members of sports teams while maintaining a hierarchical control and command over the school as a whole. It is easy to imagine that the emotions engendered in a squad of soldiers or a team of athletes bear a great resemblance to those in primitive groups of hunters and warriors. Is it possible to apply the principles of this type of tribal work-around to classrooms?

The tribal classroom is an example of a work-around where fostering bonding, attachment, and group cohesion is seen as the foundation for learning. The tribal classroom would be based on democratic leadership, cooperation, group cohesion, equality, fairness, trust, and strong personal relationships. (Fair rewards have actually been shown to result in more activation in the brain's reward centers than larger rewards that are unfair to others [Tabibnia & Lieberman, 2007].) Thus, while some educators have called attachment building in the classroom "optional," I would suggest that it is essential in order to optimize learning. I would go even further and say that it is absolutely essential for teaching students who are unable to navigate the industrial educational model due to trauma, social-emotional challenges, and cultural disconnections. In other words, we can help "unteachable students" to learn by tapping into their primitive social instincts that, in turn, stimulate their brains to learn.

The teachers and educators described later in this book have found ways to utilize primitive social instincts by summoning the power of the tribe. Taking a close look at the work of teachers who are successful with students whose brains have been previously shut off to learning reveals that the more the social milieu of the classroom matches the characteristics of tribal life, the better students and teachers perform. It appears that these teachers have figured out a way of creating a niche better suited for the human organism than the standard modern classroom.

Survival of the Nurtured

Life's greatest happiness is to be convinced that
we are loved.
                                                              —Victor Hugo

We have explored an idea of how our modern social instincts may have evolved as a latter variant of our primitive social instincts. But even our primitive social instincts have a more primitive origin in the neuroanatomy and biochemistry of mother-child bonding. As we have seen, increasingly sophisticated social groups allowed for task specialization such as hunting, gathering, and intensive caretaking. Caretaking specialization, in turn, allowed for longer postnatal development and brains built not by genetic preprogramming but by the impact of lived experience. Prolonged, intimate caretaking relationships are the cradle of the evolution of the human brain. Thus, not only are our primitive social instincts still accessible, so are our even more primitive drives for bonding and attachment. This means that a teacher can leverage both sets of instincts to stimulate neuroplasticity and learning.

As a highly mechanized and technical species, we no longer need to adapt to life on the savannah. As young children, our survival doesn't depend on how fast we can run, climb a tree, or tell the difference between edible and poisonous mushrooms. Rather, we survive based on our abilities to detect the needs and intentions of those around us. Our primary environment has become other people. If we are successful in relationships, we will get what we need to survive. Therefore, reading and reacting to other people's behaviors, emotions, and attitudes have been hardwired into our brains. We are not only wired to connect, but we are also wired to attune to, resonate with, and learn from others. In addition, we are also wired to need others to treat us with care and compassion. The Golden Rule—

"do unto others as you would have them do unto you"—is driven by a complex neurobiology embedded deep in our genetic history.

In contemporary society, the real challenges (besides achieving and maintaining connections with others) are multitasking, balancing the demands of work and family, information management, and coping with stress. We need to maintain perspective, pick our battles carefully, and remain mindful of our needs and limitations amid countless competing demands. What prepares us best for these challenges? In some ways, it is the same thing that prepared our ancient ancestors to survive in their world: the kind of early nurturance that drives the development and integration of the diverse systems within our brains. Optimal sculpting of key neural networks through healthy early relationships allows us to think well of ourselves, trust others, regulate our emotions, maintain positive expectations, and utilize our intellectual and emotional intelligence in moment-to-moment decision making. Decades of research findings across a variety of disciplines all point to the same conclusion: Those who are nurtured best survive best. It turns out that our emotional resilience and our ability to learn are inextricably interwoven.

When a parent, teacher, or institution abuses, neglects, or abandons a child, they communicate to the child that he or she is not a valued or accepted member of the family and tribe. Nonloving behavior signals to the child that the world is a dangerous place and warns him or her not to explore, take chances, or trust others. It also teaches him or her not to trust the information that others are trying to convey. Unnurtured children grow to have thoughts, states of mind, emotions, and immunological functioning that are inconsistent with well-being, enthusiasm, or curiosity. With all due respect to the old adage, what doesn't kill us, often makes us weaker.

We are beginning to understand how our brains link together, influence one another, and the power that each of us has to impact and heal the brains of others. This knowledge is vital to the process of teaching, and it needs to be integrated into our pedagogy, teacher training, and curricula. When a teacher is harsh, critical, dismissive, demoralized, or overly stressed, their students attune to and come to embody these antilearning states of brain and mind. But how is all of this conscious and unconscious information transmitted to students?

The Social Synapse

Facts are dumb until brought into connection with some general law.

Louis Agassiz

Individual neurons are separated by small gaps called synapses that are inhabited by a variety of chemical substances that participate in synaptic transmission. It is this synaptic transmission that stimulates each neuron to survive, grow, and be sculpted by experience. In a parallel mechanism, our social behaviors traverse the "social synapse." The messages we send one another are received by the senses and converted into electrochemical signals within the social networks of the receiver's brain. Because most interpersonal communication is automatic and unconscious, much of the transmission across the social synapse is unseen and taken for granted. These internal signals generate chemical changes, electrical activation, and new behaviors that, in turn, trigger new messages. This invisible linkage is vital in education because interactions in and out of the classroom either excite or inhibit the neural plasticity upon which learning depends.

The existence of a social synapse leads to the potential for another parallel between neurons and people. Neurons have two additional levels of communication beyond the synapse called the second and third messenger systems. The second messenger system consists of changes in the cell's internal biochemistry. The third system is the activation of mRNA and protein synthesis, which actually builds cellular structure and neural networks. In other words, when we interact, we are participating in the long-term construction of each other's brains. Thus, successful teaching involves a neurobiological process where teachers optimize plasticity and build new neural structures.

Before birth, genes serve as the template for the organization of the basic structure of the brain. After we are born, they contain the information for the ongoing construction and reconstruction of the brain by experience. The transcription process guides the creation of new protein structures that build the brain in reaction to environmental demands. Through this biochemical alchemy, experience shapes the architecture of our neural systems, making each brain a unique mixture of our shared evolutionary history and our individual experiences. Thus, our brains are built at the interface of experience and genetics, where nature and nurture become one (Crabbe & Phillips, 2003; LeDoux, 2003).

Like every living system—from single neurons to complex ecosystems—brains depend on interactions with others and the scaffolding of caretakers, loved ones, mentors, and teachers for their survival, growth, and well-being. Put in slightly different terms, teachers are neuroscientists who conduct experiments in the neuroplasticity of learning. But they are not detached observers; their personalities, enthusiasm, and spirit are all vital components of the neurobiological process.

The Child's Brain in the Classroom

Men of genius do not excel in any profession because they labor in it, but they labor in it because they excel.
—William Hazlitt

The brain has been shaped by evolution to adapt and re-adapt to an ever-changing world. In other words, the brain exists to learn, remember, and apply what has been learned. Learning and memory are dependent upon modifications of the brain's chemistry and architecture in a process called "neural plasticity." Neural plasticity reflects the ability of neurons to change both their structure and relationships to one another in reaction to experience (Buonomano & Merzenich, 1998; Trojan & Pokorny, 1999). We know that animals raised in enriched and more challenging environments have larger brains, longer neurons, and more synapses (Diamond et al., 1964; Guzowski et al., 2001; Ickes et al., 2000; Kempermann et al., 1998; Kolb & Whishaw,

1998). We also know that when adult humans engage in exploration, education, and challenging jobs, their brains become more complex, robust, and resistant to age-related diseases (Kessler et al., 2003; Scarmeas et al., 2004; Staff et al., 2004). Teachers use their personalities, interpersonal skills, and teaching methods to create enriched physical, conceptual, and social environments that stimulate neural plasticity, enhance brain development, and optimize learning.

The curriculum and social environment of a classroom have a synergistic impact on learning. Supportive, encouraging, and caring relationships stimulate students' neural circuitry to learn, priming their brains for neuroplastic processes. Studies with birds have demonstrated that the ability to learn their "songs" can be enhanced when exposed to live singing birds versus tape recordings of the same songs (Baptista & Petrinovich, 1986). Some birds actually require social interactions to trigger brain plasticity (Eales, 1985). Studies of high-risk children and adolescents who show resilience in the face of trauma and stress often report one or two adults that took a special interest in them and became invested in their success. This underscores the fact that, like birds, humans engage more effectively in brain-altering learning when they are face-to-face, mind-to-mind, and heart-to-heart with caring others. This is how learning occurs in tribes and in tribal classrooms, where teachers and classmates are able to become family.

The Core Elements of Social-Emotional Learning

The best teachers teach from the heart, not from the book.
—Horace Mann

Brains grow best in the context of supportive relationships, low levels of stress, and through the creative use of stories. While teachers may focus on what they are teaching, evolutionary history and current neuroscience suggest that it is who they are and the emotional environment in the classroom they are able to create that are the fundamental regulators of neuroplasticity. Secure relationships not only trigger brain growth, but also serve emotional regulation that enhances learning.

A low level of stress and arousal—where the learner is attentive and motivated to learn—maximizes the biochemical processes that drive neuroplasticity. The activation of both emotional and cognitive circuits allows executive brain systems to coordinate both right and left hemispheres in support of learning, affect regulation, and emotional intelligence. Let's begin with a brief summary of each of the central elements of social-emotional learning. This is just a preview—we will return to these ideas throughout the coming chapters.

Safe and Trusting Relationships

Those who trust us, educate us.
                                                    —George Eliot

It is becoming increasingly evident that facial expressions, physical contact, and eye gaze connect us in constant communication exchanges with those around us. It is within this interpersonal matrix that our brains are built, rebuilt, and regulated. A teacher's supportive encouragement properly balanced with an appropriate level of challenge activates dopamine, serotonin, norepinephrine, and endorphin production at levels conducive to learning (Barad, 2000; Huang et al., 1999; Kang & Schuman, 1995; Kilgard & Merzenich, 1998; Kirkwood et al., 1999; Tang et al., 1999). Through these and other biochemical processes, teacher-student attunement creates states of mind and brain that make students better able to incorporate, recall, and use new information.

From a neurobiological perspective, the position of the teacher is very similar to that of the parent in building a child's brain. Both can enhance a child's emotional regulation by providing a safe haven that supports the learning process. This "holding environment" optimizes neuroplasticity, allowing for new learning (Kegan, 2000). Among the many possible implications of this finding for the classroom is the fact that teacher-student attunement isn't a "nice addition" to the learning experience, but a core requirement. This is especially true in cases where children come to class with social, emotional, or intellectual challenges. The social brain takes into account both what we are learning and from whom we are learning it.

Low to Moderate States of Arousal

Education breeds confidence. Confidence breeds hope.
Hope breeds peace.

—Confucius

In the early part of the 20th century, experimental psychologists discovered that learning is maximized during low to moderate states of arousal and is turned off at high states of arousal. We now know that the brain shuts down plasticity in the absence of arousal to conserve energy and at high levels of arousal to divert energy toward immediate survival. In recent years it has been discovered that mild to moderate levels of arousal trigger neural plasticity by increasing the production of neurotransmitters and neural growth hormones, which trigger neural growth, enhance neural connectivity, and support cortical reorganization (Cowan & Kandel, 2001; Jablonska et al., 1999; Myers et al., 2000; Pham et al., 1997; Zhu & Waite, 1998). In other words, successful learning requires a minimum of anxiety.

Stress in the learning environment, traumatic memories from past experiences, or high levels of tension in a student's life outside of the classroom can all impair learning by inhibiting neuroplasticity. Negative attitudes and emotions about school are sometimes passed down from parents, siblings, and others in the student's life that can interfere with learning. When chronically stressed and traumatized learners are confronted with new learning, they are often unable to activate neuroplastic processes without emotional scaffolding. Effective teachers intuitively modify their approach to the materials in response to students with additional social and emotional issues that impede their learning. Through encouragement, not taking anger personally, and finding creative ways to approach difficult material, teachers can create emotionally supportive learning experiences, which can build confidence, reduce anxiety, and jumpstart neuroplastic processes.

Activating Thinking and Feeling

> *What a peculiar privilege has this little agitation of the brain that we call "thought."*
> —David Hume

Among the many evolutionary adaptations of the human brain is the differentiation of the left and right hemispheres. In the process of primate evolution, the left became increasingly specialized for linear processes such as language and rational thought, while the right grew dominant for strong emotional states and visual-spatial experience. Along the way, each hemisphere became able to inhibit the other. As I'm sure you know, strong emotions impair reasoning and problem solving, while intellectual defenses can cut us off from our feelings. With their ever-increasing functional divergence and inhibitory abilities, keeping the hemispheres well balanced and functionally integrated became a growing challenge.

The simultaneous activation of both affective and cognitive neural networks allows executive brain systems to enhance affect regulation and develop emotional intelligence. Encouraging critical thinking in emotionally salient situations allows both hemispheres to increase coordinated activities. In times of fear and anxiety, the verbal centers of the left hemisphere sometimes shut down, impairing the semantic and narrative aspects of learning central to academic success. Decreasing stress enhances hemispheric balance and allows for ongoing integration of thinking and feeling. In these ways, teachers help their students' brains to integrate the bodily and emotional functions of the right hemisphere with the social and language-oriented functions of the left hemisphere.

The Co-Construction of Narratives

> *A whole is what has a beginning and middle and end.*
> —Aristotle

A story well told contains conflicts and resolutions, gestures and expressions, and thoughts flavored with emotion. The convergence of these diverse functions within the narrative provides a nexus of neural network integration among left and right, top and bottom, and sensory, somatic, motor, affective, and cognitive processes in all parts of the brain (Siegel, 2012a). Stories are then transferred from brain to brain across the social synapse and serve to integrate the functioning of individuals within groups by teaching skills, transmitting values, and creating shared perspectives and goals. Given that the brain's evolution is intertwined with both increasing social complexity and the emergence of language, the co-construction of narratives has come to serve as an agent of both neural and social coherence.

In the classroom, narratives serve as a powerful memory tool and a blueprint for behavior and self-identity. Because narratives require the participation of multiple memory networks, stories can enhance memory by storing information across multiple regions of the brain. A learner's self-narrative, either good or bad, becomes a blueprint for thoughts, feelings, and behaviors that turn into self-fulfilling prophecies. Students with traumatic learning histories incorporate the negative evaluations of parents, teachers, guidance counselors, and other students into their self-references. When negative statements become part of the learner's self-narrative, they raise stress and diminish success. On the other hand, personal narratives of success reduce anxiety and enhance neuroplasticity. Editing negative self-narratives can be a central component of transforming a challenged learner into a successful student.

Interpersonal Neurobiology

I want you to be everything that's you, deep at the center of your being.
                                                    —Confucius

Along with social and affective neuroscience (Adolphs, 2003; Panksepp, 1998) and sociophysiology (Adler, 2002; Gardner, 1997), interpersonal neurobiology is among the emerging fields attempting to bridge the gap between the biological and social sciences. Interpersonal neurobiology ". . . explores the ways in which relationships and the brain interact to shape our mental lives" (Siegel, 2012b). As a synthetic and "consilient" field of study, interpersonal neurobiology utilizes many scientific perspectives from the social and biological sciences in an attempt to more fully understand the emergence of culture and mind from the interaction of biology and human connection.

At the core of interpersonal neurobiology is an attempt to understand how the brain is shaped by relationships and the application of this knowledge to education, counseling, and parenting. Our central questions include:

- How does the brain learn?
- How do relationships impact the brain?
- How do brains regulate one another during moment-to-moment interactions?
- How do teachers best activate and guide neuroplastic processes?
- What are the effects of stress on learning?
- How does the teacher-student relationship impact learning?

The first few years of life are a period of exuberant brain development, providing early experience with a disproportionate impact on neural development. We also know that the brain is capable of change at any time and that social interactions are a primary trigger of neural plasticity. Close connections with teachers, friends, spouses—in fact, any meaningful relationship—can activate neuroplastic processes and change the structure of the brain, for better and for worse. Due to the interdependence of interpersonal experiences and biological growth, we are particularly interested in the impact of significant attachment relationships on brain development.

The fact that the human brain has evolved into such a highly specialized social organ of adaptation is both good news and bad news. When good-enough parenting and other environmental factors combine with good-enough genetic programming, our brains are shaped in ways that benefit us throughout life. We are able to form meaningful relationships, deal with stress in a positive way, and be open to exploration and new learning. The bad news? Our brains are just as capable of adapting to unhealthy environments and pathological caretakers. This adaptation may help us to survive a traumatic household or neighborhood, but it may impede our ability to connect with our teachers, learn in the classroom, or form trusting relationships outside of the home later in life.

When children come to school, they enter with brains already shaped by their families, neighborhoods, and cultures. Because of this, thinking of home, community, and school as separate entities is an arbitrary and false abstraction. Certainly, an early childhood that teaches the lesson that the world is a dangerous place, that people are untrustworthy, and that there is no future, will not build a brain open either to teachers or new learning. A teacher can see a child's history reflected in his or her postures, attitudes, words, and spirits, and by the end of the first day of the new school year, has a pretty good idea of the challenges that lie ahead.

Chapter 2

How Brains Learn

One person cannot be skilled in everything, each has his own special excellence.

—Euripides

Just a few years ago, it was assumed that our brains finished growing by late childhood and started to decline around age 25. We now know that both of these ideas are far from true. As organs of adaptation, our brains have been shaped to adapt and re-adapt to changing environmental demands. As a social organ, our brains continue to mature in a manner designed to meet changing social roles throughout life. The truth is that our brains never stop maturing and possess the capacity for lifelong neural plasticity. This sustained plasticity serves the accumulation of information, the building of expertise, and the transmission of knowledge to the next generation. Instead of a tale of decline, we now see healthy brain aging as an evolving matrix of energy and information embedded in the context of social relationships. This new perspective is especially interesting when we consider the different ways we learn as we age. Let's take a look at the basic mechanisms of how the brain develops and learns. This will serve as a foundation for understanding the research in the chapters ahead. If you already have a solid knowledge of the basic elements of neuroscience, you may want to skip ahead to the next chapter.

Brain Basics

The brain is wider than the sky.
—Emily Dickinson

Half of the volume of our brains consists of neurons that receive, process, and transmit signals via chemical messengers and electrical impulses. We have an estimated 100 billion neurons with between 10 and 10,000 connections each, creating limitless networking possibilities (Nolte, 2008; Post & Weiss, 1997). When a neuron fires, information travels via an electrical charge down the length of its axon. Neurons, like people, must connect with others in order to survive. Neurons communicate with one another across synapses (the spaces between neurons) via chemical messengers called *neurotransmitters*. Most neurons develop elaborate branches called *dendrites* that form synaptic connections with the dendrites of other neurons. The relationships formed among neurons record our learning in memory. So when our students learn, the profiles and strengths of the dendritic connections are altered to store new information.

Neurogenesis, the birth of new neurons, occurs in the fluid-filled cavities within our brains called *ventricles*. These new cells migrate to areas involved with new learning, such as the hippocampus, amygdala, and cerebral cortex (Eriksson et al., 1998; Gould, 2007; Gould et al., 1999; Gross, 2000). During evolution, it appears that primates exchanged much of our capacity for neurogenesis for continually reshaping existing neural networks. In other words, instead of being replaced by new neurons as they are in many other animals, existing neurons are preserved, modified, and expanded in ways that support the retention of memory, deepen existing skills, and further the development of expert knowledge (Purves & Voyvodic, 1987).

As discussed earlier, neuroplasticity and neurogenesis are regulated by stress and relationships, making the social and emotional climate vital to successful classroom learning (Fowler et al., 2002).

The other half of the brain's volume is made up of approximately one trillion *glial cells* involved in the construction, organization, and maintenance of neural systems. More recently, it has become apparent that they are also involved in neural communication as well as the modulation of plasticity and learning (Allen & Barres, 2005; Pfrieger & Barres, 1996; Sontheimer, 1995; Vernadakis, 1996). *Astrocytes*, the most abundant kind of glia, participate in shaping synapses, regulating synaptic transmissions, and synchronizing synaptic activity (Fellin et al., 2006; Halassa et al., 2007; Newman, 2003). During our evolutionary history, the ratio of astrocytes to neurons has steadily increased, suggesting that our expanding cognitive sophistication is partly related to their participation in information processing (Nedergaard et al., 2003; Oberheim et al., 2006).

The two most basic divisions of the nervous system are the *central nervous system* (CNS) and the *peripheral nervous system* (PNS). The CNS includes the brain and spinal cord. The PNS comprises the *autonomic nervous system* and the *somatic nervous system*. The autonomic nervous system has two branches called the *sympathetic* and *parasympathetic* nervous systems. The sympathetic system controls the mobilization of the body in response to a threat while the parasympathetic system fosters the conservation of energy and bodily maintenance. Activation of the sympathetic nervous system in response to stress modulates the brain's ability to learn.

The brain is often thought of as being made up of three divisions— the brain stem, the limbic system, and the cerebral cortex—each with its own set of functions and responsibilities. The *brain stem*—the inner core of the brain—oversees the body's internal milieu by regulating temperature, heart rate, blood flow, and respiration. The brain stem is fully formed and functional at birth.

The *limbic system*, lying between the brain stem and the cortex, is involved with motivation, memory, and emotion. Throughout this book, you will notice repeated references to two limbic structures that are central to learning and memory. The first is the *amygdala*, a key component in neural networks involved in attachment and emotional regulation (Cheng et al., 2006; Phelps, 2006; Strange & Dolan, 2004). The amygdala is the structure primarily responsible for the activation of the sympathetic nervous system. The other is the *hippocampus*, which organizes explicit memory and the modulation of emotion in collaboration with the prefrontal cortex (Ji & Maren, 2007). Optimal learning requires the proper activation and balance of the amygdala and the hippocampus.

The outer layer of the brain, the *cerebral cortex*, processes sensory and motor information and comes to organize our experience of the world. As we grow, the cortex allows us to form ideas and mental representations of other people, the environment, and ourselves. As opposed to the brain stem, the limbic system and the cortex are experience-dependent, meaning that they are shaped through interactions with our physical and social environments.

During primate evolution, each side of the cortex and limbic system have developed specialized functions for skills like language, visual processing, and emotional regulation. Despite these differences, referred to as *laterality*, most brain functions are optimized by the interactive participation of both sides of the brain. The two hemispheres communicate with each other primarily via the *corpus callosum* consisting of long connective fibers that cross the midline (Myers & Sperry, 1985; Sergent, 1986, 1990).

The cerebral cortex is subdivided into four lobes: frontal, temporal, parietal, and occipital. Each is represented on both sides of the brain and specializes in certain functions. The *occipital* cortex comprises the areas for visual processing; the *temporal* cortex for auditory processing, receptive language, and memory functions; the *parietal* cortex for linking the senses with motor abilities and the creation of the experience of a sense of our body in space; and the *frontal* cortex for motor behavior, expressive language, and directed attention. The frontal and parietal lobes combine their processing to perform what is usually referred to as executive functions—the organization of space and time in the service of goal-directed behaviors.

Two additional cortical lobes, the *cingulate* and *insula*, are gaining increasing recognition as important areas involved in linking bodily and emotional processing with conscious experience. In years to come, it is likely that we will think of the brain as having six instead of four cortical lobes.

Brain Development and Neural Plasticity

All entities move and nothing remains still.
—Heraclitus

Experience sculpts the brain through the selective excitation and connection of specific neurons that come to form functional neural networks. As our brains develop, the number of neurons decreases while the surviving neurons continue to grow from what look like small sprouts into microscopic oak trees. The gardeners among us might enjoy the fact that this process of growth is referred to as *arborization*. Early in development, there is an initial overproduction of neurons that gradually decreases through the process of pruning or *apoptosis* where they are eliminated if they don't form functional relationships with other neurons (Purves & Lichtman, 1980).

Neurons have long projections called *axons* covered with *myelin*, an insulator that enhances the efficiency of their electrical conductivity. Because neurons myelinate as they develop, one way of assessing the maturity of a neural network is to measure its degree of myelination. Multiple sclerosis—a disease that breaks down myelin—results in a decrease in the efficiency of neural communication, negatively impacting cognition, affect, and the control of motor movement (Hurley et al., 1999). The *white matter* of the brain is white because myelin is white, while *gray matter* consists primarily of neuronal cell bodies.

Learning is believed to occur through changes in the connectivity among neurons in response to stimulation. Repeated firing of two adjacent neurons results in metabolic changes in both cells, resulting in an increased efficiency of their joint activation. In this process, called *long-*

term potentiation (LTP), or Hebbian learning, excitation between cells is prolonged, allowing them to become synchronized (Hebb, 1949). Underlying LTP is the constant reaching out of small portions of the dendrites in an attempt to connect with adjacent neurons. When these connections are made, neurons build more bridges between them. This is only one small piece of a vastly complex set of interactions involving the connection, timing, and organization of firing among billions of interconnected neurons (Malenka & Siegelbaum, 2001).

The Infant Brain

They may forget what you said but they will never forget how you made them feel.
—Anonymous

Anyone who has been pregnant can tell you that babies are physically active well before birth. And although their movements appear random, they are the brain's best guess at which will eventually be needed for survival. Through months of trial-and-error learning, these best guesses are shaped into purposeful and intentional behaviors that reflect the establishment of increasingly stable neural networks (Katz & Shatz, 1996; Shatz, 1990). As sensory systems mature, they also provide increasingly precise input to guide behavior and further elaborate the neural networks that control them. As positive and negative values are connected with certain perceptions and movements—such as the appearance of the mother followed by soothing contact—emotional networks integrate with sensory and motor systems to connect social and emotional meaning with behaviors.

Some newborn animals can stand and walk on wobbly legs within a few minutes of birth. Unlike us, they don't have the luxury of a gradual introduction to the world. These animals rely on preprogrammed brains driven by primitive instincts. From birth, they have to be ready to contribute to their own survival by avoiding danger and keeping up with the herd. Conversely, we humans are born premature and highly dependent newborns whose brains are shaped

through years of interactions with our caretakers and the environment. This extended period of postnatal brain development makes
ours the most dependent *and* adaptive brain on earth.

In contrast to the brain-stem and limbic structures, the cortex is
extremely immature at birth and continues to develop into adulthood.
Because of this developmental timing, brain-stem reflexes and limbic
activity organize much of the infant's early experience. The neonate
will orient to the mother's smell, seek the nipple, gaze into her eyes,
and grasp her hair. A good example of a brain-stem reflex is the Moro
reflex, by which the infant reaches out with open hands and legs
extended, putting the infant into a position conducive to grasping and
holding (Eliot, 1999). The child's reflexive orientation to the mother's
face and his or her spontaneous smiles are all triggered by brain-stem
reflexes to attract her attention and make her feel good. In fact, children born without a cortex or limbic system still smile (Herschkowitz
et al., 1997). These reflexes "jump-start" the attachment process by
connecting parent and child. During the early months of life, one of
the primary jobs of our cortex is to inhibit primitive reflexes in preparation for the development of later cortical control.

The growth of neurons and the development of increasingly
complex neural networks require large amounts of energy. Ever
notice how warm a baby's head is? All that heat is the result of energy
being utilized an eighth of an inch from your hand. Early sensitive
periods account for the higher level of metabolism in the brains of
infants compared to adults. It has been estimated that in rats' brains,
250,000 synaptic connections are formed every second during the
first month after birth (Schuz, 1978). Just imagine what the number
must be for humans.

Networks dedicated to individual senses develop before the association areas that connect them (Chugani et al., 1987). At the same
time the connective fibers, or white matter, that link them allow for
inter-network communication, coordination, and integration. The
growth and coordination of the different senses parallel what we also
witness in behavioral advances like hand–eye coordination and the
ability to inhibit incorrect movements (Bell & Fox, 1992; Fischer,

1987). As these networks grow and integrate there is a gradual synchronization of electrical brain-wave patterns.

As the brain develops, top-down neural networks provide the pathways for inhibiting reflexes and bringing the body and emotions under increasing cortical control. An example of this is the development of the fine motor movements between the thumb and forefinger required to hold a spoon. Primitive grasping reflexes only allow for the spoon to be held in a tight fist. The developing cortex enables the grasping reflex to be inhibited, while other networks dedicated to finger dexterity and hand–eye coordination mature.

It is clear from this example that a vital aspect of the development of the cortex is *inhibitory*—first of reflexes, later of spontaneous movements, and even later of emotions, impulses, and inappropriate behaviors. As we all know, the ability to inhibit motor movements, attention to distraction, and salient emotions is what allows us to sit still, focus, and learn in a traditional classroom. The developing brain has to achieve a fine balance of excitation and inhibition to optimize learning.

Another good example of brain maturation is our ability to swim. The newborn's brain-stem reflex to hold its breath and paddle when dropped into water is lost (inhibited by higher brain circuitry) just weeks after birth. The skills involved with swimming need to be relearned as cortically organized skills in years to come. Motor networks need to be taught body movements, as breathing becomes timed and synchronized with each stroke. We see the changes in motor control and posture as a child moves from being able to sit upright without help at about 6 months, to crawling at about 9 months, and then to walking without help by about 1 year. At 2 years, a child will walk up and down stairs; by 3 she can pedal a tricycle. As these skills are shaped, so, too, are the brain systems dedicated to balance, motor control, visual–spatial coordination, learning, and motivation. Children instinctually know they must learn though repeated trial and error, which is why our attempts to help them are often met with the impatient protest of "I do it!" This makes for years of frustrating but necessary spills and boo boos.

As the middle portions of the frontal cortex expand and extend their fibers down into the limbic system, children gradually increase their capacity to inhibit impulses, regulate their emotions, and self-soothe. In the same way that the cortex inhibits primitive brain-stem reflexes, it learns to modulate the amygdala's response to fearful situations. The growth, development, and integration of neural networks continue to be sculpted by environmental demands. In turn, neuronal sculpting is reflected in increasingly complex patterns of behavior and inner experience. When these systems are damaged or developmentally delayed, we witness symptoms related to deficits in impulse control, attention, and emotional regulation.

The Child's Brain

Give me the children until they are 7 and anyone can have them afterwards.
—St. Francis Xavier

Brain development, especially early in life, is highlighted by periods of exuberant neural growth and connectivity called *sensitive periods* (sometimes referred to as critical periods). Sensitive periods are triggered via the interaction of genetic timing and experience. Sensitive periods are times of rapid learning when thousands of synaptic connections are made each second (Greenough, 1987; ten Cate, 1989). The timing of sensitive periods varies across neural systems, which is one reason why different abilities appear at different ages. The extent of neural growth and learning during sensitive periods results in early experience having a disproportionate impact on the shaping of our brains. We don't know for sure how much flexibility each system has outside of its sensitive periods, but we all know from experience that it is easier to learn something new than to relearn something we have been doing wrong.

During the first year, relationships shape networks of attachment and emotional regulation, while year two ushers in an explosion of language development. Although the entire cortex is developing at a high rate, the right hemisphere has a relatively higher rate of growth during our first two years (Chiron et al., 1997). During this time, vital learning in the areas of attachment, emotional regulation, and self-esteem are organized in neural networks biased toward the right hemisphere. Somewhere around age 3, this higher rate of growth shifts to the left hemisphere.

Because parent-child relationships are the child's primary environment, these relationships shape networks dedicated to feelings of safety and danger, attachment, and the core sense of self. It may be precisely because there is so much neural growth and organization during sensitive periods that early interpersonal experiences may be far more influential than those occurring later. These early experiences shape our sense of self as well as our ability to relate to others. Children enter the classroom with unconscious templates of self-image and attachment that they project onto the teacher. Understanding the dynamics of these attachment schema can help teachers connect with students, especially those who have been primed to distrust and be fearful of others.

The Adolescent Brain

Small children disturb your sleep, big children your life.
—Yiddish proverb

A central dogma of 20th-century neuroscience was that the brain didn't change that much after childhood. But as researchers began to take a closer look at adolescent brains, they were amazed by the amount of neural change taking place. Not surprisingly, they found considerable plasticity from the onset of puberty into the early twenties. Once this was discovered, it became obvious that the upheavals of adolescence and early adulthood coincide with a previously unrecognized sensitive period of brain maturation in the prefrontal cortex (Blakemore, 2008; Nelson et al., 2005). It also demonstrates the power of scientific dogma to blind us to what is right in front of us.

Consider the challenges faced by adolescents. For most of our evolutionary history, humans had to mature and mate by their mid-teens. These challenges required a reshaping and reprioritizing of attachment bonds formed during infancy and childhood. Adolescents had to break from the values and structures of their family in order to become desirable to peers and potential mates. Simultaneously, they had to gradually transfer their sources of emotional security to new and genetically unrelated others. They were (and continue to be) faced with establishing a social identity, connecting with a peer group, creating new boundaries with their families of origin, and preparing to establish families of their own. This is another good example of how cultural changes have left brain evolution in the dust. Despite the fact that childbearing has been delayed into the 20s and 30s, the brain still expects this to happen at 12 or 13 years of age.

So while your teenagers may be making you crazy, keep in mind that adolescence is no picnic for them either. Radical upheavals in the brain parallel the sudden mood swings, intense emotions, and the feeling that you are alone in a vast and hostile world. The neural and social revolutions of adolescence are fraught with danger. Driven by rising hormones, dysregulated neural systems, and destabilized frontal lobes, judgment and perspective become less than stellar.

As frontal executive systems are reorganizing, many adolescents become intoxicated with a sense of power, invulnerability, and impulsivity. Reward systems, such as those mediated by dopamine, also destabilize during adolescence in order to allow for the creation of new attachments, behaviors, and goals. This search for purpose and meaning makes adolescents more vulnerable to good and bad social influences, peer pressure, and cults (Canetti et al., 1997; Dahl, 2004).

Adolescents also become vulnerable to risk taking, eating disorders, suicidal behaviors, and addictions (Chambers & Potenza, 2003; Rosenberg & Lewis, 1995; Spear, 2000; Steinberg, 2008; Teicher et al., 1995). Tobacco and alcohol companies are well aware of this vulnerability and spend vast amounts of money to convert teenagers into lifelong customers. Perhaps the postponement in modern culture of the historically relevant challenges of adolescents, such as mating, childbearing, and establishing an occupation, lead to confusion, emptiness, and psychological distress.

From adolescence through early adulthood, brain development is reflected in an increase in white matter in the frontal lobes, corpus callosum, and in circuits connecting the frontal and temporal lobes. These continued structural changes parallel advances in judgment, impulse control, and emotional regulation that are accurately reflected in the cost of car insurance from adolescence to young adulthood. Just as in early childhood, there is also a continual decrease of gray matter, telling us that individual neurons continue to be eliminated as the brain develops more processing efficiency. Table 2.1 outlines some of the structural changes that have been discovered to occur during adolescence.

Table 2.1
Structural Changes in the Brain During Adolescence

Increases in white matter in:	Results in enhanced:
Cerebral cortex	cognitive processing[1]
Broca's-Wernicke's circuits	language capacity[2]
Frontal-temporal-hippocampal circuits	planning, foresight, self-regulation[3]
Corpus callosum	hemispheric communication[4]
	cognitive and emotional integration[5]
	memory storage and retrieval[6]

Decreases in gray matter across the cerebral cortex impact:

the selection of functional and well-connected neurons[7]
the organization and shaping of neural networks[8]
enhanced processing efficiency[9]

During adolescence, the brain is on its way to peak performance in areas of motor coordination, sensory acuity, and reaction time. Historically, these abilities in males contribute to the tribe's survival through improved hunting, foraging, and fighting. In females, an increased focus on emotional connectivity, attachment, and communication supports the raising of children and bonding within the tribe. Changes in the brain during adolescence represent the adaptation of neural networks to new goals of reorganizing our social relationships, developing more efficient information processing, and preparing for having children of our own.

The Adult Brain

True wisdom comes to each of us when we realize how little we understand of life, ourselves, and the world around us.
—Socrates

For most of us, the hormonal, neural, and social upheavals of adolescence gradually settle down during our thirties. Overall, we see a more streamlined and efficient brain as we learn to better regulate our emotions in the service of reality-based problem solving. To this end, the prefrontal cortex continues to develop by pruning less efficient gray matter while increasing white matter connectivity (Sowell et al., 1999). The dorsal and lateral regions of the prefrontal cortex and the parietal lobes mature and interconnect with the rest of the cortex, supporting higher levels of abstract thinking. During young adulthood, especially in males, lateral specialization in the frontal lobes appears to reach its peak. This increasing specialization involves the active inhibition of less efficient brain regions that may slow cognitive processing (Luna & Sweeney, 2004; Pakkenberg & Gundersen, 1997).

These anatomical findings coincide with intelligence tests that show improvements in planning as well as spatial and long-term memory (Brown et al., 2005; Schweinsburg et al., 2005). Temporal lobe volume increases until age 30 and begins to decrease thereafter, reflecting the relatively early decline in our ability to recall new information (Sowell et al., 2002, 2003).

During midlife, the number of neurons within the cortex continues to decrease while subcortical structures stabilize and become more focused, specific, and efficient (Allen et al., 2005; Bartzokis et al., 2001; Good et al., 2001; Grieve et al., 2005; Jernigan et al., 2001; Pfefferbaum et al., 1994; Sowell et al., 2003; Tisserand et al., 2004). These structural changes reflect evolution's "choice" of speed over slow and measured consideration, a strategy that reverses later in adulthood as the brain adapts to social roles that require deeper and more complex processing. White-matter volume increases until at least age 50 and then begins to decline (Bartzokis et al., 2001; Davatzikos & Resnick, 2002; Ge et al., 2002; Guttman et al., 1998; Nusbaum et al., 2001; O'Sullivan et al., 2001; Pfefferbaum et al., 2000, 2005; Salat et al., 2005).

Increasing participation of multiple brain regions through adulthood appears to be an adaptive strategy embedded in our genetic blueprint. Slower, more inclusive processing as we grow older serves the kind of synthetic knowledge and problem-solving abilities traditionally embodied in tribal elders. In fact, when brain activity is measured by the complexity of electrical activity, there is a linear increase from childhood into the sixties—the highest age measured (Anokhin et al., 1996).

As we shift our focus from measures of overall volume to specific neural networks responsible for specific tasks, we find that aging is not uniform. As a rule of thumb, brain networks that evolved most recently and develop later in childhood are the most vulnerable to aging (Grieve et al., 2005; Whalley & Deary, 2001). For example, white-matter tracts connecting the frontal lobes with temporal and hippocampal structures show early signs of volume loss with corresponding decreases in short-term memory (Giannakopoulos et al., 1997; Head et al., 2005). This may be why no matter how wise we become with age, it is still harder to recall people's names, find where we parked the car, and remember that our glasses are on our heads.

The co-evolution of the human brain with caretaking, attachment, family, and culture strongly suggests that the life history of our brains has been guided by age-appropriate social roles. In fact, as many as 540 brain-related genes have been shown to have different activation patterns at different times of life (Erraji-Benchekroun et al., 2005). It is logical to assume that the expression of some of these genes may trigger the brain's adaptation to changing social roles over time.

Declines in explicit memory, attention, and the acuity of the senses stand in stark contrast to systems that specialize in attachment, emotional regulation, and problem-solving. The retention and even improvement of social judgment and empathy reflect the continued health and development of brain networks that have the orbital and medial regions of the frontal lobes at their apex (Happe et al., 1998). Solid social judgment relies on the accumulation of experience, slow consideration, and emotional maturity. Although there may be a decreased need for new learning and quick reactions as we age, sustained attachment and emotional stability seem to have been worthy of continued metabolic investment.

Natural selection may have made the "decision" to maintain brain structures dedicated to attachment, affect regulation, and caretaking in order for older adults to have a continuing investment in the social economy of their tribes. If social interactions and neuroplasticity are synergistic, it is clear why elders who become isolated are more likely to lose cognitive functions. On the other hand, those who remain connected and needed by others are far more likely to remain vital and alive. Isolation, lack of challenge, and understimulation are the enemies of a healthy brain at any age.

Chapter 3

How Relationships Build and Rebuild Brains

*To the soul, there is hardly anything more healing
than friendship.*
— Thomas Moore

Thus far, our central theme has been that the human brain is a social organ of adaptation; the brain is an organ that exists to learn. Every child is capable of learning even though many enter our classrooms with brains that have been turned off. The reasons for tuning out and turning off are most often a combination of cultural and personal experiences that pair classroom experiences with failure and shame. These psychological and biological factors are usually amplified by poor nutrition, an absence of health care, and inadequate sleep. Mix enough of these learning challenges together, and you will find children who appear unteachable, unreachable, and a waste of educational resources. Exposing closed minds and turned-off brains to knowledge can really be like talking to a wall.

Keep in mind that brains are naturally curious, programmed to explore, and thirsty for knowledge. These impulses are nurtured in a context of safety and become habits when associated with being rewarded by caring others. If a brain is unrewarded or punished for curiosity, it learns to hide, avoid risks, and stick with what is familiar and safe. Having an open or closed mind is something we learn from the emotions, attitudes, and behaviors of those around us.

Fortunately, the robust nature of the brain's adaptive capacity means that things that get turned off can get turned back on again. And because the brain is a social organ, relationships are usually the key to opening a closed mind and rebuilding the brain. The difficulty in turning the brain on to learning is proportional to the experiences that shut it off. Some kids only need to be given permission to think in new ways and try new things; others need to be brought along gradually and given lots of support to relearn how to learn. In this process, teachers literally build new brain structures that turn their students on to learning. But how do teachers build new brain structures?

Genetics and Epigenetics

When you teach your son, you teach your son's son.
—Talmud rabbinical writings

The science of genetics began with Abbot Gregor Mendel, who, in the garden of his ancient abbey, discovered many of the principles of inheritance that still hold true. It turned out that his discoveries with pea plants also apply to animals and humans because the underlying mechanisms of heredity, such as dominant and recessive genes, are the same for all complex life forms.

With the benefits of modern technology, Mendel's observations of the natural world were later understood to be the effects of template genetics, or the way in which genes and chromosomes combine to pass along traits from one generation to the next. We now know that our genetic information is coded in four amino acid bases (adenine, thymine, guanine, and cytosine), which flow from DNA to messenger RNA (mRNA) to protein structures. Although this understanding is a huge leap forward in our knowledge of the underlying processes of genetic transmission, only 2% of the genes were found to be directly tied to the construction of our bodies. The term used for the other

98% was "junk," thought to be the accumulated debris of millions of years of natural selection.

While the brain's general structure is shaped by template genetics, a large portion develops in an experience-dependent manner. The term *epigenetics* is used to describe the guidance of genetic expression by experience (in other words, experience determines which genes are expressed and which are not). More specifically, genetic expression is programmed by experience through the alteration of the chromatin structure of the double helix and the methylation of DNA, the process by which a methyl group is added to DNA (Szyf et al., 2007). In effect, the strands of genes are like immensely long keyboards, and experiences determine which notes will be played. It turns out that the nature and quality of intimate relationships impact this process.

This gets us back to the old nature-versus-nurture question: What do we inherit, and what do we learn from experience? Our best guess is that almost everything involves an interaction between the two. While we inherit a template of genetic material (genotype), what gets expressed (phenotype) is guided by how experience affects genetic expression. Experience can include anything from exposure to toxins, a good education, high levels of sustained stress, or a warm and loving environment. So while template genetics may guide the early formation of the brain during gestation, the regulation of gene expression directs its long-term development in reaction to its ongoing adaptation to the social and physical worlds.

An example of particular relevance to emotional development, learning, and education is the impact of early stress on the developing brain. Meaney and his colleagues (1996) have shown that early environmental programming of neural systems has profound and long-lasting effects on the hypothalamic-pituitary-adrenal (HPA) axis, which regulates an individual's responsiveness to stress. Research with rats has demonstrated that the stress of early maternal deprivation down-regulates brain health, learning, and the ability to cope with stress during adulthood (Karten et al., 2005; Mirescu et al., 2004). In interactions with students, teachers attempt to reprogram these neural systems in the context of physical safety, supportive relationships, and a stimulating learning environment. In this regard all teachers are neuroscientists attempting to use epigenetic processes to reshape the brains of students in ways that enhance their ability to think, learn, and act in more thoughtful and considerate ways.

To summarize, genes first serve to organize the brain and trigger sensitive periods, while experience orchestrates genetic transcription (epigenetics) in the ongoing adaptive shaping of neural systems, so that experience comes to shape the actual wetware of our brains. Our brains, in turn, organize other brains, allowing experiences to be passed through a group and carried forward across generations. While being embedded in a group comes with many challenges, it also comes with an ability to interactively regulate each other's internal states and assist in neural integration (Siegel, 2012a). At present, we lack the technology to study these epigenetic processes in humans in a noninvasive way; therefore, we rely on animal research to provide us with our fundamental knowledge.

How Experience Builds the Brain

All experience is an arch to build upon.
—Henry B. Adams

The epigenetic translation of experience into brain structure and environmental adaptation is a fascinating area of study with broad implications for the transformative power of relationships. This area of research is particularly relevant to teachers because of the many social and emotional parallels between the classroom and the family. In addition, many students spend more time in face-to-face interactions with their teachers than with their parents. I strongly believe that teachers shape the brains of their students by the same epigenetic mechanisms as parents. Let's take a closer look at these brain-shaping processes in action.

There is considerable evidence that mothers both pass on their genes (via DNA) and shape the way this DNA is expressed through their emotions and behaviors (Fish et al., 2004; Meaney & Szyf, 2005; Sapolsky, 2004). Thus, two parallel mechanisms of inheritance exist: (1) slow changes across many generations through natural selection and (2) rapid changes in gene expression in reaction to changes in the physical and social environments (Cameron et al., 2005; Clovis et al., 2005; Meaney & Szyf, 2005; Zhang et al., 2005). The classroom is just such an environment.

Epigenetic research has taken advantage of naturally occurring variation in the amount of maternal behavior in mother rats (dams) to explore the impact of their behavior on the brains of their pups. Mother rats instinctively lick, nurse, and retrieve their pups when they roll out of the nest. The amount of these three behaviors is then measured against specific aspects of the pups' brain development. Although this research is done, by necessity, with animals, two facts support applying these findings to humans. The first is that these biological and genetic mechanisms are conserved in evolution across species in the same way that the principles of genetics apply to all plants and animals. The second is that we have hundreds of studies with humans that demonstrate relationships between the quality of early experience and subsequent physical and emotional well-being which parallel the animal research.

Getting back to our rodent subjects, three different research methods have been employed to study the effects of maternal behavior on epigenetic expression. In the first model, the amount of maternal attention is measured and the brains and behaviors of pups that receive high and low levels of attention are compared. The second model examines the effects of maternal deprivation, while the third uses handling of the pups by human researchers as the experimental manipulation. Because it has been found that human handling stimulates more maternal attention, the first and third categories may be one and the same (Garoflos et al., 2008).

Results show that levels of maternal attention either stimulate or silence gene expression in domains of neural plasticity relevant to learning, the ability to cope with stress, immunological functioning, and the amount of attention females will come to give their own children in the future (Szyf et al., 2008). Neural growth is stimulated via the activation of neural growth hormones and mRNA expression; these processes are tied to the biochemistry of neuroplasticity and learning. Higher levels of maternal attention result in more benzodiazepine, oxytocin, and glucocorticoid receptors being formed in many regions of the brain, allowing for the dampening of fear and anxiety while increasing attention, curiosity, and exploratory behavior. Future maternal behavior is governed by the growth and activation of attachment centers and the regulation of oxytocin and estrogen receptors (Neumann, 2008). See Table 3.1 for some of the specific findings in each area of study.

Table 3.1
The Impact of Maternal Attention in Rats on Neural Growth and Plasticity

Neural Plasticity and Learning

Increased synaptic density, longer dendritic branching, and increased neuronal survival[1]

Increased neuronal survival in the hippocampus[2]

Fos expression (protein synthesis) in the hippocampus and the parietal and occipital cortex[3]

Increased brain-derived neurotrophic growth factor (BDNF) in the hippocampus[4]

Modulation of Arousal, Anxiety, and Fear

Increased medial prefrontal cortex (PFC) dopamine, increased startle inhibition, and decreased fear reactivity in response to stress[5]

Increased epigenetic expression of the glucocorticoid receptor gene promoter in the hippocampus[6]

Increased mRNA expression in the medial PFC, hippocampus, and amygdala[7]

Increased levels of benzodiazepine receptors in the amygdala and the locus coeruleus[8]

Modulation of Future Maternal Behavior

Enhanced metabolic activation in precentral medial cortex, anterior cingulate cortex, and lateral thalamus[9]

continued on next page

Table 3.1 continued

Elevated levels of estrogen mRNA and more maternal behavior later in life[10]

Increased levels of oxytocin and estrogen receptors in medial preoptic areas and increased maternal behavior when they have their own pups[11]

Less sexual behavior in females and females less likely to become pregnant after giving birth, allowing more time and attention to pups[12]

Overall, rat pups who receive more maternal attention learn better, remember more, are less reactive to stress, and are better able to continue learning at higher levels of arousal. Perhaps most important, they will suffer less from the damaging effects of stress hormones. This array of factors is what you might expect to see in humans who are considered "resilient" and able to thrive in the face of physical and emotional challenges. Finally, females growing up with more attentive mothers tend to be more attentive to their own offspring when they reach maturity. Although the biochemical and genetic mechanisms in humans between early attachment and later well-being are far more complex, the parallels are striking.

In regard to learning, maternal attention stimulates the production of neurotrophic growth factors that stimulate neural growth and enhance learning. While stress hormones inhibit the production of neurotrophins (and new learning), higher levels of neurotrophins appear to both buffer critical regions of the brain against stress and stimulate plasticity (Pencea et al., 2001; Radecki et al., 2005; Schaaf et al., 2000). And because the production of neurotrophins is under epigenetic control, physical, emotional, and interpersonal experience all influence their production (Berton et al., 2006; Branchi et al., 2004; Branchi et al., 2006). This means that the combination of positive attention and the stress reduction of secure attachments have a positive synergistic impact on brain growth and learning. These results suggest that interesting and relevant content presented in a safe and caring interpersonal context optimizes the brain's ability to learn and grow.

While more maternal attention results in increased growth and enhanced functioning, the stress of separation has the opposite effect. The same three areas that are up-regulated with more maternal attention are down-regulated by her absence. Deprivation of maternal attention down-regulates gene expression and impairs learning while increasing neural and glial death. Maternal separation increases vulnerability to stress by reducing GABA receptors in the locus coeruleus, resulting in more adrenaline and stress. In addition, fewer cortisol receptors in the hippocampus impair the inhibitory feedback to shut down cortisol production which further inhibits short-term memory and learning. See Table 3.2 for the specific findings of these studies.

Table 3.2
The Impact of Maternal Separation

Neural Growth and Plasticity

Increased neuronal and glial death[1]

Decreased neurotrophin levels in the ventral hippocampus[2]

Decreased glial density[3]

Modulation of HPA Activity

Reduced GABAA receptors in the locus coeruleus and decreased GABA receptor maturity[4]

Reduced benzodiazepine receptors in the central and lateral amygdala and increased mRNA expression in the amygdala[5]

Increased anxiety, fearfulness, and response to stress[6]

Increased long-term potentiation (LTP) and long-term depression (LTD) in amygdala-hippocampal synapses[7]

Decreased exploratory behavior, avoidance of novelty, and greater vulnerability to addiction[8]

Reduced gene expression[9]

Greater cortisol secretion in response to mild stress and increased startle response and startle-induced sounds[10]

Reduced somatic analgesia and increased colonic motility (mimicking irritable bowel syndrome in humans)[11]

Up-regulation of glutamate receptors[12]

continued on next page

Table 3.2 continued

Modulation of Future Maternal Behavior

Decreased synaptic density and cell survival in the medial prefrontal cortex[13]

Decreased activation in the bed nucleus of the stria terminalis and nucleus accumbens[14]

The evidence from the handling studies is essentially the same as for maternal attention in neural growth and the modulation of anxiety. Handled pups have more glucocorticoid (GC) receptors, lower cortisol levels, and greater brain activity reflective of less anxiety, helplessness, and fear. In turn, these pups are more resilient, more exploratory, and are better learners than their non-handled siblings. To whatever degree that researcher handling has a positive effect on the brain development of rats, it suggests that the brain may be capable of responding well to alternative forms of nurturance, even from a creature of a different species. There is also considerable evidence for the healthful effects of dogs, cats, and other human-animal relationships on well-being. If a human can do this for a rat, and dogs can do this for us, imagine what a caring and dedicated teacher is capable of doing for the brain of an anxious or traumatized child. See Table 3.3, for the findings on human handling for rats, parrots, and pigs.

Although the majority of this research has been done with rats, parallel findings have been observed in numerous studies with primates and humans. Rhesus monkeys deprived of maternal contact demonstrate reduced transcriptional efficiency of serotonin and its receptors in the brain, which can lead to negative emotional states of anxiety, dread, and depression (Bennett et al., 2002). We do know that low levels of maternal behavior in humans correlate with more fear, less positive joint attention, and higher levels of right hemisphere prefrontal activation, all of which are related to higher levels of stress (Hane & Fox, 2006). Low self-esteem is an interpersonal stressor that correlates with high levels of cortisol, decreased hippocampal volume, and deficits in short-term memory and learning (Pruessner et al., 2005).

Table 3.3
The Impact of Human Handling

Modulation of HPA Activity

Rat pups:
Increased concentrations of GC receptors in the hippocampus and
frontal lobes[1]

Increased GC receptor binding capacity in the hippocampus[2]

Increased corticotrophin-releasing factor (CRF) mRNA and greater
CRF levels[3]

Decreased inhibitory avoidance and increased object recognition[4]

Lower levels of stress in reaction to a predatory odor[5]

Increased neurotrophin-3 expression and neuronal activation in the
hippocampus and parietal lobes[6]

Low cortisol secretion in response to stress/high exploratory
behavior[7]

Protection against age-related neuroendocrine and behavioral decline
with age[8]

Decreased helplessness behaviors[9]

Baby pigs:
Lower basal and free plasma levels of cortisol[10]

Amazon parrots:
Decreased serum cortisol levels in response to stress[11]

Because of the obvious limitations to research with living human brains, we have to rely on samples of opportunity. One such study compared the brains of suicide victims with normal controls and found lower mRNA levels of BDNF and other brain-growth factors in the suicide victims. These data raise the possibility that early environmental programming may have made these individuals susceptible to chronic depression and suicide (Dwivedi et al., 2003). A more recent study of the brains of suicide victims found that those with histories of early abuse demonstrated decreased levels of glucocorticoid receptor mRNA and growth factor transcription when compared to those who had not been abused (McGowan et al., 2008; 2009).

These findings closely parallel the animal research and are supportive of the legitimacy of extrapolating findings with animals to humans.

These and other studies demonstrate that the reaction of the brain to maternal attention is not just a psychological theory, but a well-documented neurobiological phenomenon. The consistency of behavioral, emotional, and biological findings across species is too powerful to be discounted. In fact, over 900 genes have been discovered that are differentially expressed based on exposure to different levels of maternal behavior (Rampon et al., 2000; Weaver et al., 2006). There is no reason to believe that the maternal control of epigenetic expression has not been conserved and expanded in primates and humans. The way mothers and other important adults treat children is a way in which evolution has shaped genetic expression in the service of adaptation and survival. And there is reason to believe that teachers have a similar impact on biology and epigenetic expression.

Keep in mind that the amount of attention that a mother rat shows her pups exists in a broad adaptational context. Highly stressed mothers demonstrate lower rates of maternal behavior, which programs their offspring to have enhanced reactivity to stress, vigilance, and decreased exploratory behavior. This increases the probability of their short-term survival while simultaneously elevating the risk of physical and emotional pathology later in life (Diorio & Meaney, 2007). All of this suggests that the developing brain is woven into a matrix of interpersonal and environmental experiences that determine how the brain is built: The home, community, and classroom all have a hand in building the brains of children.

The fact that processes set in motion early in life can be modified by subsequent experience demonstrates the brain's ability to adapt to a changing environment. Chronic stress or trauma in adolescence can reverse the effects of positive attachment earlier in life, reshaping the brain to resemble one that was deprived of early maternal attention (Ladd et al., 2005). Fortunately, it has also been found that enriched social and physical environments can reverse the biological and behavioral effects of early deprivation and trauma (Bredy et al., 2004; Francis et al., 2002; Hood et al., 2003; Szyf et al., 2005; Weaver et al., 2005).

To summarize, insecure attachments, a dangerous environment, and chronic stress can create a perfect storm of biological and epigenetic consequences that can turn a brain off to learning. On the other hand, caring and supportive others can create a state of body and mind that primes our brains for curiosity, exploration, and learning. Have you ever tried to learn to do something new in the presence of a critical onlooker? And what about the demoralizing and depressing effects that indifferent and disrespectful students have on teachers? Teachers depend on a receptive audience to trigger their own positive biochemistry and brain growth.

Teachers don't burn out from working hard, but because they are frustrated, unappreciated, and hopeless about making a positive impact on their students. We often see that high-risk children and adolescents who eventually have successful lives describe with great affection the one or two people who took an interest in them—a mentor, a teacher, a ballet or karate instructor—someone who gave them time, believed in them, and encouraged their success. These reports should not be taken lightly; they reflect the biological reality that we learn better when we are face-to-face and heart-to-heart with someone who cares about us.

Chapter 4

Of Human Bonding

Education: n., the process of nourishing or rearing.
—The Shorter Oxford English Dictionary

The ways in which humans connect with one another can be studied from many perspectives. Sociologists and political scientists look at groups and nations, psychologists focus on dyads and families, while biologists explore the biochemistry of bonding and love. Most of the research on attachment has focused on the parent-child bond, a relationship that is particularly relevant to teachers. Teachers follow parents as authority figures and as a central source of nurturance. Parents shape the attachment schema that their children use to unconsciously guide their feelings, attitudes, and behaviors toward others and especially toward adults in positions of authority. While these schema are projected onto teachers, teachers also have the power to modify them.

Donald Winnicott

The art of motherhood involves much silent, unobtrusive self-denial, an hourly devotion which finds no detail too minute.
—Honoré de Balzac

Donald Winnicott, an English pediatrician and psychoanalyst, provided a helpful way of thinking about how early relationships shape the social brain. His work with mothers and children led him to coin terms such as *good-enough mothering*, *holding environment*, and *transitional object*—concepts that have become part of the basic lexicon of child development. Winnicott believed that to talk of an infant separate from its mother was a theoretical abstraction. What actually exists is a symbiotic infant–mother pair that shapes the neural networks of attachment, which continue to impact us throughout our lives.

According to Winnicott, the core of mothering is providing a *facilitating and holding environment* that requires both the mother's empathic abilities and respect for the autonomy of the child. A mother's devotion to her child allows her to offer an expanding scaffolding that constantly adapts to her child's changing needs and increasing abilities. The *good-enough mother*, in Winnicott's thinking, is a mother who does an adequate job in this difficult, complex, and constantly shifting dance of adaptation (Winnicott, 1962). A central component of development from Winnicott's perspective is the mother's ability to mirror her child. *Mirroring* is the process by which a mother attunes to her child's inner world and provides the child with the words and behaviors for self-expression. I'm certain that you are already seeing the parallels between an attuned parent and a gifted teacher.

In an appropriately attuned parent, a *graduated failure of adaptation* will parallel the infant's increasing abilities, frustration tolerance, and affect regulation. Winnicott used the term *impingement* to describe the impact of maternal misattunements on the child. These can take the form of not anticipating the child's needs, interfering with the need for quiet and calm, and even underestimating his or her abilities. Parents must eventually fail to adapt their children's needs in small ways to allow them to face the necessary challenges required for adequate development.

Minor impingements are challenges accompanied by levels of stress that the child is able to manage and master. Experiences with this sort of optimal frustration stimulate brain growth and promote neural network integration (Siegel, 2012a). *Major impingements* overwhelm the child's ability to cope and integrate experience in a cohesive manner, resulting in dissociated neural networks and functional disabilities. Gradual minor impingements push the infant and child to grow, whereas major impingements can result in derailment of positive adaptation and the solidification of defense mechanisms. Minor impingements are learning-enhancing experiences, whereas major impingements usually hamper a child's development.

One of Winnicott's most clinically useful concepts has been the idea of the development of a *true* and *false self*. Secure attachments and a sense of a safe world create the context for the development of the true self. The true self represents those aspects of experience that develop in the context of manageable (minor) impingements, support, and encouragement. Respect for the autonomy and separateness of the child motivates the parent to discover the child's interests, instead of imposing his or her own. The true self reflects our ability to tolerate negative feelings, integrate them into conscious awareness, and seek out what feels right for us in our activities, ourselves, and in our relationships with others. Winnicott's true self is obviously one in which neural network development has been maximized, affect is well regulated, and emotions and cognition are integrated. The true self reflects an open and ongoing dialogue among the heart, the mind, and the body.

Although we all need a false self or social face to cope with day-to-day life, an excess of stress can lead to a false self that is inflexible and maladaptive. For example, neglect, abuse, or continuous states of shame can overwhelm the child's natural development and lead to the dominance of emotional defenses. These stressful relationships will also inhibit neurogenesis and proper brain development (Stranahan et al., 2006). When self-involved or emotionally disturbed parents use children for their own needs, the child can become compulsively attuned to the parents, creating a false self designed to take care of the parents. Without appropriate assistance in developing his or her self-reflective capacity, children may never learn that they have feelings and needs of their own that can be taken care of by others.

John Bowlby

Come live in my heart, and pay no rent.

—Samuel Lover

While Winnicott worked with mother–infant pairs in his consulting office, John Bowlby observed primates in the wild and the behavior of children in orphanages. He was especially interested in mother–child bonds, the importance of exploratory behavior, and the impact of separation and loss on healthy development. His experiences led him to develop the concepts of *attachment figures*, *attachment schema*, *proximity seeking*, and *a secure base* (Bowlby, 1969).

Bowlby's work, which highlighted the importance of consistent caretakers to a child's sense of security, resulted in a major shift in the care of institutionalized children. To encourage bonding, children, who had previously been cared for by whoever was available, were now assigned specific caretakers. In addition, the role of nurses and caretakers changed from mere custodians into important attachment figures. Subsequently, Mary Ainsworth and her student Mary Main developed research methods to test Bowlby's theories. Decades of attachment research followed, providing us with some fascinating tools to study the sculpting of the social brain during childhood as well as the long-term impact of early experiences later in life.

Bowlby suggested that early interactions create an *attachment schema* that predicts subsequent reactions to others. Schema are implicit memories that organize within networks of the social brain, based on experiences of safety and danger early in life. A secure attachment schema enhances the formation of a neurochemical environment conducive to regulation, growth, and optimal immunological functioning. Insecure and disorganized attachment schema have the opposite effect, and these correlate with higher frequencies of physical and emotional illness (I will explore the biological processes involved in shaping the brain in a later chapter).

Bowlby believed the attachment schema to be a summation of thousands of experiences with caretakers that become automatic, unconscious predictions of the behaviors of others. Attachment schema become activated in subsequent relationships and lead us to either seek or avoid proximity and determine whether we are able to use relationships for physiological and emotional homeostasis. They shape our first impressions, our reactions to physical intimacy, and even whether we feel that relationships are worth having. Attachment schema are especially apparent under stress because of their central role in affect regulation. Teachers are faced with a classroom full of new attachment schema each fall.

Empirical research into attachment began with Ainsworth's naturalistic in-home observations of mothers interacting with their children (Ainsworth, 1978). These mothers fell into three categories: available and effective (free autonomous), dismissing and rejecting (dismissing), or anxious and inconsistent in their attentiveness (enmeshed/ambivalent). The belief was that these different caretaking styles would create differing coping and interpersonal styles in their children. The next step in this research was to determine whether the children of mothers in each category displayed differences in their attachment behaviors, especially under stress.

What Do I Do When I'm Afraid?

Men are swayed more by fear than by reverence.
                                                    —Aristotle

The method developed to study the children's attachment behavior was called the *infant strange situation* (ISS). This situation, which exposes a child to a stranger in the absence of the mother, was chosen because of Bowlby's observation that being left alone with a stranger evokes distress calls in young primates. This research was begun with a number of questions: How does a child use the mother when he or she is frightened and stressed? Does the child seek comfort from the mother or ignore her? Does the child soon feel safe and return to play or is he or she anxious, clingy, or withdrawn? These and other behaviors are thought to reflect the child's past experiences and future expectations of the mother's soothing capacity.

The actual ISS consists of placing an infant and its mother in a room, then having a stranger join them. After a period of time the mother exits the room, leaving the child alone with the stranger. A brief period follows before the mother returns. The child's *reunion behavior*, or how he or she responds to the mother's return, is used to determine the child's attachment style.

Four categories of the infants' reactions to their mothers' return have been derived from the ISS: *secure, avoidant, anxious-ambivalent*, and *disorganized*, which corresponded to the categories of maternal behavior originally derived from in-home observations. The general findings were as follows: Children rated as securely attached sought proximity with the mother upon her return, were quickly soothed, and soon returned to exploratory or play behavior. These children, comprising approximately 70% of the sample, seemed to expect that their mothers would be attentive, helpful, and encouraging of their continued autonomy. Securely attached children appear to have internalized their mothers as a source of comfort.

Avoidantly attached children tended to ignore their mothers when they returned to the room. They would glance over to her as she came in, or avoid eye contact altogether. These children tended to have dismissing and rejecting mothers and appeared to lack an expectation that she would be a source of soothing and safety. Avoidantly attached children behaved as though it was easier to regulate their own emotions than to seek comfort from their mothers, whose misattunement or dismissal might well compound their stress. Children rated as anxious-ambivalent sought proximity but were difficult to soothe and slow to return to play. Their slow return to play and emotional regulation may be a reflection of their mothers' anxiety and lack of internalized safety. These children tended to be clingy and engaged in less environmental exploration.

Finally, there was a group of children who engaged in odd behavior such as turning in circles or falling to the ground. They would freeze in place or be overcome by trancelike expressions. These children were included in a fourth category called disorganized attachment and often had mothers suffering from unresolved trauma. Parents of children in this category demonstrated frightened and frightening behavior to their children, creating an approach-avoidance conflict. The resulting inner turmoil deregulates the child to the point that his adaptation and coping skills—even his motor abilities—appear to become disorganized. Not surprisingly, children with avoidant and disorganized attachment schema are also shown to have higher levels of stress hormones and other biological markers of chronic stress (Spangler & Grossmann, 1993).

Secure and insecure attachment schema are quite different. Securely attached children do not produce an adrenocortical response to stress, suggesting that secure attachment serves as a successful coping strategy. On the other hand, those with an insecure attachment schema do show a stress reaction, demonstrating that insecure attachment is better described by a model of arousal rather than of successful coping (Izard, 1991; Nachmias et al., 1996; Spangler & Schieche, 1998). In other words, the behavior of insecurely attached individuals is an expression of arousal, anxiety, and fear. This may help us to be a bit more understanding of difficult students. What looks like disobedience usually masks anxiety, fear, and emotional dysregulation.

Attachment, Neural Integration, and Coherent Narratives

All men are children and of one family.
—Henry David Thoreau

The relationships discovered between parenting styles and children's attachment schema raised the question of whether parents' childhood experiences influenced their future parenting styles. While it was assumed that the parenting styles of adults are somehow shaped by childhood experiences, there was no empirical support for this transfer from one generation to the next. Because implicit memory is inaccessible to consciousness and explicit memories of childhood are shaped by complex cognitive and emotional factors, a measure was needed that could bypass the usual distortions of memory and all of our defense mechanisms. An extremely interesting research tool appears to have succeeded in this task.

The Adult Attachment Interview (AAI) (Main & Goldwyn, 1998) consists of a series of open-ended questions about childhood relationships and early experiences such as the following:

- "I'd like you to try to describe your relationship with your parents as a young child . . . if you could start from as far back as you can remember."
- "Choose adjectives that reflect your relationship with your mother, father, etc."
- "Which of your parents did you feel closest to and why?"

While the AAI is gathering information about what individuals remember of their childhoods, it also provides the data for a linguistic analysis of the narrative coherence. Coherence analysis is based on what are called Grice's maxims and includes an examination of both the logic and understandability of the narrative by using the following four principles:

- Quality: Be truthful, and have evidence for what you say.
- Quantity: Be succinct, and yet complete.
- Relevance: Stick to the topic at hand.
- Manner: Be clear, orderly, and brief.

Scoring takes into account the integration of emotional and experiential materials, gaps in memory and information, as well as the overall quality of the presentation (Hesse, 1999).

Siegel (2012a) proposed that the coherence of the AAI narrative parallels the level of neural integration attained during childhood, providing a window to early attachment experiences and emotional regulation. In essence, the AAI assesses how a person puts feelings into words, resolves traumatic experiences, and integrates the various networks of information processing across emotion, sensation, and behavior in making sense of his or her life. In this way, the AAI bypasses our defenses by examining the quality of the brain's synthesis of the various cognitive and emotional components of explicit and implicit memory.

Four categories emerge from the AAI that correspond to the findings of the in-home observations and the ISS. Mothers and fathers with securely attached children tended to have more detailed memories, as well as a realistic and balanced perspective of their parents and childhood. Adhering to Grice's maxims, they were able to describe these experiences in a way that was understandable and believable to the listener (Main, 1993). This *autonomous* group demonstrated an integration of cognitive and emotional memories, had processed their early negative experiences, and as a result, were more fully available to their children.

The second group of parents, associated with avoidantly attached children, demonstrated a lack of recall for childhood events and large gaps in memory for their childhoods. This lack of recall is believed to reflect a disruption of the integration of cognitive and emotional elements of autobiographical memory. They also demonstrated a *dismissing* attitude toward the importance of their early relationships, just as they were dismissive of their own children in the present. The narratives of these parents were incoherent due to both missing information and a tendency to either idealize or condemn their parents. A third group of parents, rated as *enmeshed* or *preoccupied*, tended to have anxious and ambivalently attached children. Their narratives contained excessive, poorly organized verbal output that lacked boundaries between the past and present. They appeared preoccupied and pressured, and had difficulty keeping the perspective and knowledge of the listener in mind.

Lastly, the *unresolved/disorganized* group had highly incoherent narratives disrupted by emotional intrusions and by missing or fragmented information. Their narratives not only reflected the disorganization of verbal and emotional expression, but also the devastating impact early stress had on the development and integration of their neural networks. The content of their narratives confirmed chaotic and frightening childhood experiences that we can assume were devastating to the integration and homeostatic balance of both body and brain. Table 4.1 provides a summary of attachment findings.

Table 4.1
Summary of Attachment Findings

In-Home Observations of Mothers	Infant Strange Situation	Adult Attachment Interview
free autonomous	**secure**	**autonomous**
emotionally available perceptive and effective	infant seeks proximity easily soothed/returns to play	detailed memory balanced perspective narrative coherency
dismissing	**avoidant**	**dismissing**
distant and rejecting	infant does not seek proximity infant does not "appear" upset	dismissing/denial idealizing lack of recall (LOR)
enmeshed/ambivalent	**anxious/ambivalent**	**enmeshed/preoccupied**
inconsistent availability	infant seeks proximity not easily soothed not quick to return to play	lots of output intrusions/pressured preoccupied idealizing or enraged
disorganized	**disorganized**	**unresolved/disorganized**
disorienting frightening or frightened	chaotic self-injurious	disoriented conflictual behavior unresolved loss traumatic history

In a later study, Fonagy, Steele, and Steele (1991) administered the AAI to expectant, first-time parents and had them come back to do the ISS with their children when the children reached their first birthdays. In 75% of these cases, the child's attachment pattern was predicted by the coherence of the parent's narrative evaluated many months before birth. Parents of infants who came to be securely attached were able to provide a fluid narrative of childhood with examples of interactions, had few memory gaps, and presented little idealization of the past. These parents did not seem to have significant defensive distortions and were able to express negative feelings without being overwhelmed; listeners tended to believe what they were saying. It is not a big stretch to see that these parents were best able to provide the kind of "good-enough" social environment that provided a balance between safety and challenge, attunement and autonomy.

We now have some evidence that parents' capabilities for attachment to their infants begin to take shape in their own childhoods. Their future skills as parents will depend on their empathic abilities, emotional maturity, and neural integration: in essence, how they were parented as children. Because attachment schema are part of implicit memory, these behaviors occur reflexively and unconsciously, connecting our childhood experiences across generations. In this way, a parent's unconscious is a child's first reality. These data may be particularly relevant for teachers because they suggest that a teacher's childhood and attachment schema will be reflected in the teacher's interaction with students. And to whatever degree the teacher–student relationship parallels the parent–child connection, a teacher's personal history will trigger feelings and behaviors in their students that will shape connections in the classroom.

Fortunately, negative events in childhood are not necessarily predictive of insecure attachment or future parenting styles. Processing early experiences and constructing coherent narratives are more accurate predictors of a parent's ability to be a safe haven for his or her children. This *earned autonomy*, through the healing of childhood wounds, appears to interrupt the transmission of negative attachment patterns from one generation to the next. Not surprisingly, parents' emotional self-insight gained through personal growth parallels their emotional availability to their children.

Maternal and paternal instincts—in fact, all caretaking behaviors including teaching—are acts of nurturance that depend upon the successful inhibition of competitive and aggressive impulses. Too often, however, inhibition is incomplete and some of us are unable to be *good-enough* parents. Nonloving behavior at home signals a child that the world is a dangerous place and tells him not to explore, discover, or take chances, impairing his ability to form secure attachments to teachers and classmates. Not only will these children struggle in school, they will grow to have thoughts, states of mind, and immunological functioning that are inconsistent with well-being, successful relationships, and long-term survival.

As we have seen, research strongly supports the theory that the brain is an organ of adaptation that is shaped by social interactions. When our early relationships are frightening, abusive, or non-existent, our brains dutifully adapt to these realities. Fortunately, there is reason to believe that these circuits of attachment and emotional regulation retain plasticity throughout life (Bowlby, 1988; Davidson, 2000; Kolb & Gibb, 2002; Maletic-Savatic et al., 1999). Research has revealed the broad tendency to move from insecure to secure attachment in the presence of secure others (Crowell et al., 2002). While social stress inhibits neural plasticity, social support, compassion, and kindness support positive neural growth (Czeh et al., 2007; Davidson et al., 2000). Regardless of the age of their students, teachers have the ability to stimulate neuroplastic processes and reshape brains in positive and more adaptive directions.

The Human Social Brain

Compassion is the basis of all morality.
—Arthur Schopenhauer

Our brains are crisscrossed with neural networks dedicated to receiving, processing, and communicating messages across the social synapse. These are the neural circuits that teachers use both to attach to their students and to stimulate curiosity, encourage exploration, and enhance learning. This section is a brief overview of the neural systems that are most vital to bonding, attachment, and stimulation of the brain. Some of the important brain regions, neural systems, and regulatory networks of our social brains are listed in Table 4.2 (also see Figure 4.1).

Table 4.2
Structures and Systems of the Social Brain

Cortical and Subcortical Structures

Orbital and medial prefrontal cortices (OMPFC)

Cingulate cortex and spindle (von Economo) cells

Insula cortex, somatosensory cortex, amygdala, hippocampus, hypothalamus

Sensory, Motor, and Affective Systems

Face recognition and expression reading

Imitation, mirroring, and resonance systems

Regulatory Systems

Attachment, stress, and fear regulation system	(OMPFC—amygdala balance)
Social engagement system	(the vagal system of autonomic regulation)
Social motivation system	(reward representation and reinforcement)

Cortical and Subcortical Structures

Let's start at the bottom and work our way up. The orbital and medial prefrontal cortices (OMPFC), the insula, and cingulate cortices lie buried beneath and within the folds of the later evolving cortex. This gives us the picture that the ability to bond and attach predates many of our higher cognitive and abstract functions. Some neuroanatomists see these contiguous structures as comprising a functional system called the basal forebrain, dedicated to the experience of self and others (Critchley, 2005; Heimer & Van Hoesen, 2006).

Resting above our eyes at the base of the prefrontal lobes, the OMPFC is a convergence zone for polysensory, somatic, and emotional information and is in the perfect position to synthesize information from both our internal and external worlds. The OMPFC allows us

Figure 4.1
The Orbital Medial Prefrontal Cortex–Amygdala Network

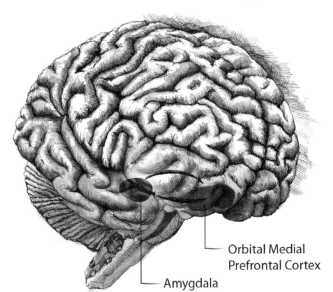

Orbital Medial
Prefrontal Cortex

Amygdala

to translate the punishment and reward values of complex social information, such as facial expressions, gestures, and eye contact, into meaningful information by associating them with motivations and emotions (O'Doherty, 2004; Tremblay & Schultz, 1999; Zald & Kim, 2001). In its position at the apex of the limbic system, the OMPFC's inhibitory role in autonomic functioning highlights its contribution to the organization of behavior, emotional regulation, and the attachment schema (see Figure 4.1) (Hariri et al., 2000; Price et al., 1996).

The cingulate cortex is a primitive association area of visceral, motor, tactile, autonomic, and emotional information (Kennard, 1955). It first appeared during evolution in mammals exhibiting maternal behavior, play, nursing, and social sounds (MacLean, 1985). The caretaking and resonance behaviors made possible by the cingulate cortex also provide an important component of the neural infrastructure for social cooperation and empathy (Rilling et al., 2002; Vogt, 2005). The anterior cingulate contains von Economo cells that appear to have evolved in humans, great apes, and whales to connect and regulate divergent streams of information (Nimchinsky et al., 1995, 1999). These cells may provide the neural connectivity necessary both for the development of self-control and the ability to engage in sustained attention to difficult problems (Allman et al., 2001, 2005).

The insula is sometimes described as the "limbic integration cortex" because of its massive connections to all limbic structures and its feed-forward links with the frontal, parietal, and temporal lobes (Augustine, 1996). In tandem with the anterior cingulate, the insula allows us to be aware of what is happening inside of our bodies and reflect on our emotional experiences (Bechara & Naqvi, 2004; Critchley et al., 2004; Gundel et al., 2004). Recent research suggests that the insula is involved with mediating the entire range of emotions from disgust to pain to love (Bartels & Zeki, 2000; Calder et al., 2003).

The somatosensory cortex, located along the front of the parietal lobes, processes information about bodily experiences. Along with the insula and anterior cingulate cortices, it contains multiple representations of the body that process and organize our experience of touch, temperature, pain, joint position, and our visceral state. These different processing streams combine to create our experience of our physical selves and participate in what we call intuition or "gut feelings," helping us to make day-to-day decisions (Damasio, 1994).

Moving to subcortical structures, we begin with the amygdala. As a primitive organ of appraisal, the amygdala closely monitors signals of safety and danger and mediates the fight-or-flight response via the autonomic nervous system (Davis, 1997; Ono et al., 1995; Phelps & Anderson, 1997). The OMPFC can inhibit the amygdala based on conscious awareness and feedback from the environment (Beer et al., 2003). By the same token, when we are frightened and our amygdala is activated, it inhibits the OMPFC and we have a difficult time being rational, logical, and in control of our thoughts and behaviors. Because the networks connecting the OMPFC and the amygdala are shaped by experience, our learning history of what is safe and dangerous, including our attachment schema, are encoded within the OMPFC-amygdala system.

The hippocampus is situated at the junction between the cortex and limbic system on both sides of the brain. In lower mammals like the rat, the hippocampus is a specialized spatial map of foraging territory. The human hippocampus, along with its adjacent structures, have come to be specialized in the organization of spatial, sequential, and emotional learning and memory (Edelman, 1989; McGaugh et al., 1993; Sherry et al., 1992; Zola-Morgan & Squire, 1990). In contrast to the early developing amygdala, the hippocampus is a late bloomer, continuing to mature into early adulthood along with other regions of the frontal lobe upon which it relies (Benes, 1989). Our lack of conscious memory for early childhood, known as childhood amnesia, is likely due to the slow development course of the hippocampus (Fuster, 1996; Jacobs et al., 2000; McCarthy, 1995).

The hypothalamus is a small and ancient structure that sits at the center of the brain below the thalamus and halfway between the cortex and the brain stem. It has extensive connections to the frontal lobes, limbic system, and brain stem. I include the hypothalamus as part of the social brain because it is centrally involved with the translation of conscious experience into bodily processes and thus, the transduction of early experience into the building of the brain and body. Its various nuclei organize many bodily functions such as temperature regulation, hunger, thirst, and activity level. The hypothalamus is also involved in the regulation of sexual behavior and aggression.

Sensory, Motor, and Affective Systems

The association region of the occipital lobe is dedicated to the identification of faces in the fusiform face area (FFA) (Gauthier et al. 2000; Halgren et al., 1999). These areas are interconnected with other clusters of cells responsible for monitoring eye gaze, body posture, and facial expression as the brain constructs complex perceptions and social judgments from basic building blocks of visual information (Jellema et al., 2000). In the temporal lobes, our senses are integrated, organized, and combined with primitive drives and emotional significance (Adams et al., 1997). Networks involved both in reading and identifying facial expressions are located in adjacent temporal regions (Desimone, 1991; Hasselmo et al., 1989).

Regions in the anterior (front) portions of the superior temporal sulcus (STS) integrate information about various aspects of the same person (form, location, and motion), allowing us to identify others from different angles, in various places, and while they are in motion (Jellema et al., 2004; Pelphrey et al., 2003; Vaina et al. , 2001). Mirror neurons in our frontal and parietal lobes become active when we witness others engaging in behaviors or when we ourselves engage in these actions. By bridging neural networks dedicated to perception and movement, mirror neurons connect the observed and the observer by linking visual and motor experience. It is hypothesized that mirror systems and resonance behaviors provide us with a visceral-emotional experience of what the other is experiencing, allowing us to know others from the inside out. They also provide us with the ability to learn by observation by converting watching into practicing within our brains.

Regulatory Systems

The body's regulatory systems are involved in the maintenance of internal homeostatic processes, balancing approach and avoidance, excitation and inhibition, and fight-or-flight responses with periods of rest and repair. They also control and modulate metabolism, arousal, and immunological functioning.

The Attachment, Stress, and Fear Regulation System

The hypothalamic-pituitary-adrenal (HPA) system regulates the secretion of hormones involved with the body's response to stress and threat. The immediate reaction to stress is vital for short-term survival, while the rapid return to normalization after the threat has passed is essential for long-term survival. Prolonged stress results in system damage and breakdown. The long-term effects of negative parenting experiences, failures of attachment, and early trauma are mediated via the HPA system. In turn, the activation of the sympathetic branch of the autonomic nervous system results in symptoms of anxiety, agitation, and panic. Throughout our lives, but especially during childhood, relationships with others regulate our stress and fear. A secure attachment indicates that we have learned to successfully utilize our relationships with others to quell our fears and modulate our arousal. The interconnections between positive relationships, stress, and learning are at the core of the power of attachment-based teaching.

The Social Engagement System

The tenth cranial nerve, also called the vagus, is actually a complex communication system between the brain and multiple points within the body, including the heart, lungs, throat, and digestive system. Its *afferent* (sensory) and *efferent* (motor) fibers allow for rapid continuous feedback between brain and body to promote homeostatic regulation and the optimal maintenance of physical health and emotional well-being (Porges et al., 1994). In the absence of external challenge, the vagus works to enhance digestion, growth, and social communication. When a challenge does arise, a decrease in vagal activation facilitates sympathetic arousal, high-energy output, and the fight-or-flight response. Between rest and all-out activation, the vagus allows us to maintain continued engagement by modulating arousal during emotional interpersonal exchanges.

The vagal system accomplishes this by modulating and fine-tuning sympathetic arousal. The development of this engagement system is likely dependent upon the quality of early attachment relationships that shape its structure and become translated into moment-to-moment somatic regulation. The vagal system also links facial, oral, and throat muscles involved in communication with internal organs and emotional processing, providing others with a moment-to-moment "read-out" of our internal state. The "tone" of the vagus refers to the vagal system's dexterity in regulating the heart and other target organs (Porges et al., 1996). Children with poor vagal tone have difficulty suppressing emotions in situations demanding their attention, making it difficult for them to engage with their parents, sustain a shared focus with playmates, and maintain attention on important material in the classroom. See Table 4.3 for more details.

Table 4.3
Correlates of High and Low Vagal Tone

Higher Vagal Tone Correlates With:	Lower Vagal Tone Correlates With:
• the ability to self-regulate	• irritability
• self-soothing capacity by 3 months of age	• behavioral problems at 3 years of age
• the range and control of emotional states	• emotional dysregulation
• more reliable autonomic responses	• distractibility
• suppression of heart-rate variability	• hyperreactivity to environmental and visceral stimuli
• positive social engagement	• withdrawal
• consistent caretaking/secure attachment	• impulsivity/acting out
• increased behavioral organization	• insecure attachment
• enhanced attentional capacity and the ability to take in information	

Vagal regulation allows us to become upset, anxious, or angry with a loved one without withdrawing or becoming physically aggressive. We can hypothesize that many who engage in domestic violence, child abuse, and other forms of aggressive behavior may not have had the kinds of early attachment relationships required to build an adequate vagal system. Thus, good parenting not only teaches appropriate responses in challenging interpersonal situations, but it also builds the vagal circuitry required to regulate our emotions and allow us to stay engaged in states of high emotion.

The Social Motivation System
Nelson and Panksepp (1998) postulate the existence of a *social motivation system* modulated by oxytocin, vasopressin, endogenous endorphins, and other neurochemicals related to reward, decreased physical pain, and feelings of well-being. While conserved from more primitive approach-avoidance and pain-regulation circuitry, the social motivation system extends into the amygdala, anterior cingulate, and OMPFC. These circuits and neurochemicals are thought to regulate

attachment, pair bonding, empathy, and altruistic behavior (Decety & Lamm, 2006; Seitz et al., 2006). It is the activation of these biochemicals that make it feel good to care for and be cared for by others. More importantly, they also decrease stress and promote learning.

The dopamine reward system of the subcortical area known as the ventral striatum is involved with more complex analysis of reward and social motivation. The ventral striatum becomes activated with an expectation of a social reward, such as when we anticipate being given candy or positive attention (Kampe et al., 2001; Pagnoni et al., 2002; Schultz et al., 1992). For example, once the cortex has determined that you find someone attractive, the ventral striatum becomes activated when he or she looks your way, giving the signal that the possibility for being rewarded with a desirable outcome has increased (Elliott et al 2000; Schultz et al., 1997; Schultz, 1998). The activation of the ventral striatum translates the anticipation of reward into a physical impulse to approach. In this way, those whom we find attractive actually exert what feels like a gravitational pull on us.

In just a few decades, we have come from the first articulations of the brain as a social organ, to a broad understanding of neural networks, regulatory systems, and biochemical processes that serve human relationships. It is very likely that there is more left to discover than we already know. What is certain is that the old notions of the brain as machines or computers are inadequate in the face of the social and emotional processes woven into the ways we process information. In the face of all of these findings, educational theorists need to address the essential inextricability of intellectual, emotional, and social processing that places secure attachment at the heart of learning.

Part II
How to Turn Brains Off

Chapter 5

What Is the Connection Between Learning and Stress?

I am not afraid of storms, for I am learning to sail my ship.
—Aeschylus

As organs of adaptation, brains serve survival in three fundamental ways. First, brains "appraise" the social and physical environments for positive and negative value: For example, is that a friendly dog? Should I talk to this stranger? Should I be walking this close to the edge of the cliff? Second, brains help us get to the things we want and away from things we wish to avoid by organizing our ability to walk and choose which direction to move in. Third, it learns and remembers our experiences of reward, punishment, success, and failure to apply to future situations. These three complex functions—appraisal, navigation, and learning (and the neural networks that organize them)—have co-evolved as an integrated and functional whole.

Our conception of classroom learning is usually distinct from our ideas about survival-based behavior. Thus, we tend to miss the fact that the neuroanatomy and neurochemistry of learning and memory are interwoven with the primitive survival circuitry dedicated to arousal, stress, and fear. This is why thinking and feeling are so intertwined, why plasticity turns off during high levels of anxiety, and why stressed brains are resistant to new learning. Thus, there is no cognition without emotion, and it is impossible to separate the internal experience of the learner from the material being learned.

At the core of the modern human brain lies the most primitive reptilian fight-flight circuitry. As the cortex evolved, these primitive regions became densely connected with the modern human brain. The result is that our unconscious sense of safety modulates everything from our ability to attend, concentrate and learn, while shaping our core beliefs about the world, the future, and ourselves. With the expansion of the cerebral cortex, abstract thinking, and imagination, we are now capable of being fearful of monsters living under our beds or an overwhelming fear of never finding love again after a breakup at 15.

Our experiences of anxiety and fear are the conscious emotional aspects of the brain's ongoing appraisal of threat. At its most adaptive, anxiety encourages us to not step off a curb without looking both ways and check to see if we signed our tax forms before sealing the envelope. At its least adaptive, anxiety inhibits learning, halts exploration, and keeps us from taking appropriate risks. Anxiety can be triggered by countless conscious or unconscious cues and has the power to shape our behaviors, thoughts, and feelings. Thus, what started out as a straightforward survival-based alarm system for reptiles and primitive mammals evolved into a potential nuisance for humans, one that needs to be carefully managed. For those of us who tend to be anxious, our alarm system is like having a smoke detector right over the toaster—we have to deal with lots of false alarms.

Just about any kind of stress triggers a range of physiological changes to prepare the body for fight or flight. Energy is mobilized through increased cardiovascular activity and muscle tone while being conserved via the inhibition of digestion, growth, and immune responses. A cascade of biochemical activations occurs in the hypothalamus, pituitary, and adrenal glands as well as increased levels of glucocorticoids, epinephrine, and endogenous opioids. The physiological consequences of stress are particularly relevant to learning because almost every one of them negatively impacts some aspect of attention, concentration, and memory.

As adults, we experience the effects of high levels of sympathetic arousal in situations such as automobile accidents, at crucial moments during sporting events, or during an especially heated debate. This same process may become activated in children and adolescents when they are called upon to speak in class, bullied in the playground, or overwhelmed by conflict at home. As social animals, other people are our primary sources of safety and stress. How others treat us has a direct and continuous impact on our sympathetic arousal. Because of the interwoven nature of arousal and plasticity, the regulation of anxiety through secure classroom relationships is one of the most powerful tools in a teacher's repertoire.

Multiple Memory Systems

No study, pursued under compulsion, remains in memory.
—Plato

Learning obviously depends on memory, and as we discussed earlier, memory systems have a deep and interwoven history with anxiety, fear, and survival. Although we tend to think of memory as a single function, we have a number of memory systems. The two broad categories of memory are the explicit and implicit systems. When we design a classroom curriculum, we are focusing on teaching information that will be stored in systems of explicit memory. However, sensory-motor, visceral, and emotional information is simultaneously encoded and stored outside of conscious awareness in systems of implicit memory. Implicit memory involves more subcortical and right hemisphere structures orchestrated by the amygdala. Explicit memory is organized by the coordination of multiple regions of the cortex and the hippocampus. Let's begin by focusing on explicit learning and the hippocampus.

The hippocampi are shaped like two seahorses on either side of the human brain at the base of the temporal lobes. They are essential structures for encoding and storing explicit memory and conscious learning (Zola-Morgan & Squire, 1990). The hippocampus also plays a central role in the organization of spatial and temporal information and participates in our ability to make inferences from previous learning in new situations (Edelman, 1989; Eichenbaum, 1992; Kalisch et al., 2006; O'Keefe & Nadel, 1978; Sherry et al., 1992).

The hippocampal connections with the cortex are noted for their slow maturation that continues into early adulthood (Benes, 1989; Geuze et al., 2005). The hippocampus is also extremely sensitive to the negative effects of stress hormones that cause dendritic degeneration, cell death, and inhibited functioning (Kim & Diamond, 2002; Watanabe et al., 1992). Chronically stressed children and adults have a smaller hippocampal volume, which correlates with deficits of short-term memory, learning, and increased vulnerability to future stress and trauma (Bremner et al., 1993; Gilbertson et al., 2002).

The amygdala, our central fear-processing hub, is located beneath the cortex on each side of the brain. As discussed earlier, the amygdala is our first executive center during both evolution and development, and it plays a central role in emotional learning throughout life (Berntson et al., 2007; Brodal, 1992; Elliott et al., 2008). As such, the amygdala is a central player in associating conscious and unconscious indications of danger with preparation for a survival response (Kukolja et al., 2008; Ohman et al., 2007). It has been conserved and expanded during evolution to process increasingly complex cognitive, sensory, and somatic input. The amygdala's central role in triggering the biochemical cascade of the fight-or-flight response makes it vital for processing memory, emotional regulation, and attachment.

The neural projections from the amygdala to numerous anatomical targets cause the multiple physical expressions of stress, anxiety, and fear (see Figure 5.1). For example, projections from the amygdala to the lateral hypothalamus result in an increased heart rate and higher blood pressure, while those projections to the trigeminal facial motor nerve result in fearful facial expressions (Baird et al., 1999; Davis, 1992). One important descending projection from the amygdala connects it to the locus coeruleus (LC), the brain's primary generator of norepinephrine—the chemical responsible for activating the sympathetic nervous system—which enhances focus on danger,

Figure 5.1
Some Targets of the Amygdala in the Fear Response

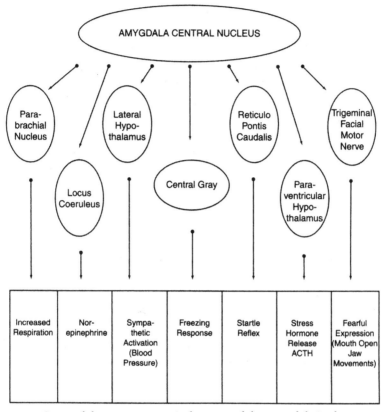

Some of the many anatomical targets of the amygdala in the
fear response, and their biological contributions.

while inhibiting activities such as paying attention in class or learning new information.

The biological link between prolonged stress and hippocampal atrophy appears to be mediated via the catabolic influence of stress hormones. Glucocorticoids (GC) such as cortisol are secreted by the adrenal glands to promote the breakdown of complex compounds so that they can be used for immediate energy. The first of these hormones was found to break down complex sugars, hence the name *gluco*corticoids. It was later found that they also block protein synthesis, inhibiting both new neural growth and the construction of proteins involved in immunological functioning. Overall, the mechanisms of long-term well-being are sacrificed for the sake of immediate survival. This makes great sense when stressors are short-lived. But when stress is chronic, high levels of cortisol put us at risk of physical illness and deficits in learning and memory. A number of roles of cortisol are seen in Table 5.1, along with its impact on the brain and its relationship to a variety of illnesses.

Table 5.1
Stress and the Hippocampus

Cortisol Helps to:

Break down fats and proteins for immediate energy

Inhibit inflammatory processes

Inhibit protein syntheses within the immune system (leukocytes, B and T cells, natural killer cells, etc.)

Suppress gonadal hormones, which support neural health, growth and learning

Chronic High Levels of Cortisol and Glucocorticoids Can:

Decrease plasticity[1]

Cause dendritic degeneration[2]

Cause deficits of myelination[3]

Propel cell death[4]

Inhibit neurogenesis and neural growth[5]

High Levels of Cortisol Can Correlate With:

Impaired declarative memory and spatial reasoning[6]

Compromised Hippocampi Result in:

Deficits of new learning[7]

Decreases in short-term and long-term memory[8]

The human brain is well equipped to survive brief periods of stress without long-term damage. In an optimal state, stressful experiences can be quickly resolved with good coping skills and the help of caring others. Working with rats and vervet monkeys, Sapolsky and his colleagues demonstrated that sustained stress results in hippocampal atrophy and a variety of functional impairments (Sapolsky, 1990; Sapolsky et al., 1990). Sapolsky's research is particularly important because it may help explain some of the negative long-term effects of childhood stress and trauma on adult cognitive and emotional functioning.

The focus on immediate survival supersedes all long-term maintenance akin to burning the furniture in order to stay warm through a long, cold winter. Thus, these biological processes need to be reversed immediately after the crisis has passed in order to allow the body to return to restoration and repair. It is apparent that this system was designed to cope with brief periods of stress in emergency situations, not to be maintained for weeks or years at a time. The consistent high levels of stress generated by modern society are poorly matched with our primitive stress systems. These findings would suggest that a child's ability to learn would certainly be handicapped by chronic stress.

Prolonged stress affects three major processes of the brain and body. First, it inhibits protein production in order to maintain higher levels of metabolism. Because proteins are the building blocks of the immunological system (leukocytes, B cells, T cells, natural killer cells, etc.), the suppression of protein synthesis diminishes our body's ability to fight off infection and illness. This is the primary reason for the high correlation between prolonged stress and disease. Second, sustained higher levels of metabolism continue to pump sodium into neurons, eventually overwhelming the cell's ability to transport it out again, resulting in the destruction of the cell. Third, because the building of neurons and dendrites depends upon the synthesis of protein, sustained levels of stress will inhibit brain growth and impair learning.

Although we like to think of childhood as a time of safety and innocence, many children grow up in a constant state of stress. Children who experience stress and trauma often perform far below their capabilities in situations requiring attention, concentration, and new learning. Stressors that are inescapable have a greater sustained cortisol activation and negative impact on the brain. Parental physical or mental illness, community violence, poverty, and many other factors are usually inescapable for a child. Visiting a child's home and getting to know the social and physical environment he or she lives in could go a long way in assessing stress levels and the impact the child's environment has on performance in the classroom. For students with a history of chronic stress and/or trauma, longer periods of relationship building and interventions focused on stress reduction may be necessary prerequisites for successful learning.

The Learning Power of Mild to Moderate States of Arousal

A cheerful mind is a vigorous mind.
                                        —Jean de la Fontaine

There are two circuits of sensory input that reach the amygdala in the human brain (see Figure 5.2). The first comes directly from the thalamus. The other circuit loops up through the cortex and hippocampus first before reaching down into the amygdala (LeDoux, 1994). The first system provides rapid responses for survival-related decisions based on a minimum of information. The slower second system adds cortical processing (context and inhibition) to appraise ongoing perceptions and behaviors. The amygdala's direct neural connectivity with the hypothalamus, limbic-motor circuits, and many brain-stem nuclei allow it to trigger a rapid survival response.

The relationship between the amygdala and hippocampus is extremely important for human learning. By accentuating small differences among inputs, the amygdala heightens awareness of specific aspects of the environment (orientation and attention) whereas the hippocampus inhibits responses, attention, and stimulus input (habituation) (Douglas, 1967; Kimble, 1968; Marr, 1971). The amygdala has a central role in the emotional and somatic organization of experience, whereas the hippocampus is vital for conscious, logical, and

Figure 5.2
Fast and Slow Fear Circuits

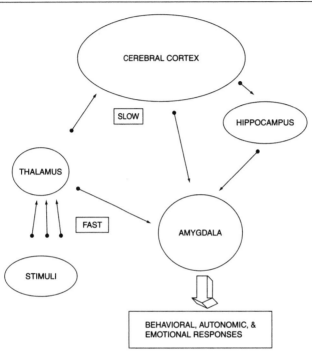

A depiction of the two pathways of information to the amygdala—one directly from the thalamus and the other through the cortex and hippocampus. (adapted from LeDoux, J. Emotion, memory and the brain. Copyright © 1994 by Scientific American, Inc. All rights reserved.)

cooperative social functioning (Tsoory et al., 2008). Anxiety, fear, and traumatic experiences lead to an increased influence of the amygdala in directing memory, emotion, and behavior. Their integration and balance impact emotional regulation, social relatedness, and our ability to succeed in the classroom.

We intuitively understand that students need to be both motivated and free from fear in order to learn. They need to have a bit of anxiety about grades to push them along, but not so much that they are frozen with fear (Anderson, 1976). Keeping students in a neuroplastic "sweet spot" of arousal is a core element in the art of teaching. In secure attachment, the child is able to use the parent as a safe haven and avoid experiencing autonomic activation in response to stress. A secure classroom allows students to cope with the stress of new learning and to regulate their fear of failure with the support of their teachers and fellow students.

The evolutionary logic of this link between learning and arousal probably goes something like this: When our needs for food, companionship, and safety are satisfied, and nothing interesting is going on, there is no reason to invest energy in learning. At the other extreme, dangerous situations call for immediate action and are no time to sit still and pay attention. At these times, cortical plasticity is shut down and all energy is diverted to bodily survival.

Robert Yerkes and John Dodson (1908) presented a classic paper on the formalization of the relationship between stress and learning. Their findings came to be known as the inverted-U learning curve. The initial hypothesis was that the more powerful shock a mouse receives as punishment for not learning, the more it would learn. Contrary to expectation, they found that mice learned to avoid a moderate shock faster than one of high or low intensity. They charted their finding on a graph with arousal on the x-axis and learning (performance) on the y-axis (see Figure 5.3). Over the years, this same phenomenon was

Figure 5.3
The Inverted-U Learning Curve

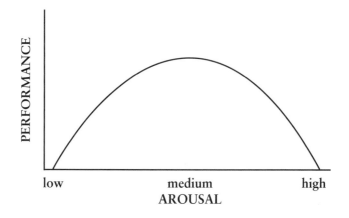

found to occur in many species (including humans) across an array of learning tasks (Broadhurst, 1957; Stennett, 1957). While this research took place long before we knew much about the amygdala and hippocampus, this same inverted-U pattern has been found to parallel the underlying biochemistry of learning in both structures (Baldi & Bucherelli, 2005).

Learning depends on building new dendrites and changes in neuronal connectivity. These processes, in turn, depend on the synthesis and modification of proteins guided by epigenetic transcription. Not surprisingly, the hormones secreted in response to stress (cortisol, norepinephrine, and endorphins) and neural growth hormones all modulate learning on this same inverted-U curve (Hardingham & Bading, 2003; Parsons et al., 2007). At mild levels of arousal, amygdala activation and sympathetic arousal facilitate hippocampal and cortical plasticity. It turns out, however, that plasticity is inhibited at moderate to high levels of arousal (Popescu et al., 2007).

At mild levels of arousal, amygdala activity enhances hippocampal processing by stimulating the release of moderate levels of norepinephrine and glucocorticoids (McGaugh, 2004; McGaugh et al., 1993). Through these chemical messages, the hippocampus is alerted to the importance of remembering what is being experienced and turns on long-term potentiation (LTP), neurogenesis, neural plasticity, and other biological processes involved in learning. When we are too anxious or afraid, the amygdala triggers high levels of norepinephrine and cortisol that inhibit hippocampal activation and new learning.

Hippocampal neurons require low levels of cortisol for stimulation and structural maintenance while higher levels of cortisol inhibit neurons' growth and other neuroplastic properties (Gould et al., 1990). Cortisol impacts learning and plasticity by regulating the protein synthesis required for dendritic growth and components of neural plasticity including LTP, long-term depression (LTD), and primed burst potentiation in this same inverted-U pattern (Diamond et al., 1992; Domes et al., 2005; Lupien & McEwen, 1997; Roozendaal, 2000). High levels of stress trigger the release of endorphins, which impede both protein synthesis and the consolidation of explicit memory. Table 5.2 lists a sample of neural processes that follow this pattern of biochemical activation and learning.

Table 5.2
The Inverted-U Curve of Learning and Arousal

Messenger RNA (mRNA) Expression[1]

Cortisol levels

Verbal memory[2]
Social memory[3]
Spatial memory[4]
Hip prime burst potentials[5]
LTP[6]

Norepinephrine levels

Olfactory plasticity[7]

Endorphin levels

Protein synthesis and memory consolidation[8]
Neural growth hormones[9]

Another limbic structure closely connected to the amygdala is the bed nucleus of the stria terminalis (BNST). Like the amygdala, it is connected upward to the prefrontal cortex, as well as down into the autonomic nervous system. Unlike the amygdala, the BNST is sensitive to abstract cues and is capable of long-term activation suggestive of its role in anticipatory anxiety (Davis, 1998; Kalin et al., 2001). It appears that the amygdala specializes in fear, while the BNST has evolved to deal with more complex anxiety triggers that emerged as our brains became increasingly capable of future-oriented thinking, such as "Will my friends still accept me if I don't get into honors English?" The BNST in rats has been found to grow in response to maternal responsibilities. The scaffolding caretakers create around their children involves a constant focus on potential dangers and future needs. Certainly many parents mention "constant worry" as one of the primary emotions of childrearing, even before their child arrives.

By regulating stress levels in the classroom through their interpersonal and pedagogical abilities, teachers are also manipulating the neuroplastic capabilities of their students' brains. Awareness of the challenges of each student and tailoring tasks and feedback to match their capabilities and emotional needs are elements of this process. Just as important are the nurturance of secure attachments and the safety of the emotional climate of the classroom. External demands to move the curriculum forward make it easy to place more emphasis on content than on the brains we are trying to teach. We are challenged to remind ourselves that learning is stimulated during times of exploration and adaptation and that brains are turned off by stress and anxiety. As teachers we can use these principles to optimize neural plasticity in the service of learning and to encourage positive brain change.

Learning Not to Fear

Laughter is the sun that drives winter from the human face.
—Victor Hugo

An unfortunate twist of evolutionary fate is that the amygdala is mature at birth while the systems that regulate and inhibit it take many years to mature. Thus, we enter the world totally vulnerable to overwhelming fear with no ability to protect ourselves. On the other hand, we are capable of attuning with caretakers who can regulate our anxiety and fear until our own brains are ready to take on the job. This is why we use proximity to our parents during the early years of life as our primary means of emotional regulation. The way our parents help us to regulate our anxiety and protect us from fear becomes the template upon which our attachment circuitry becomes organized.

Based on the different contributions to our survival, the hippocampus is constantly remodeled to keep up with new learning while the amygdala records and stores threats for future reference. Because the amygdala exhibits persistent dendritic modeling, we are unable to erase the painful or traumatic associations stored within it that lead many of us to be biased toward anxiety and fear (Rainnie et al., 2004; Vyas et al., 2003; Vyas & Chattarji, 2004). Getting past our fears and phobias appears to require the formation of new inhibitory neural connections from the cortex down to the amygdala. These connections are thought to prevent the amygdala from triggering the sympathetic nervous system and our experiences of anxiety, fear, and panic (Akirav & Maroun, 2007; Milad & Quirk, 2002; Ochsner et al., 2004; Rau & Fanselow, 2007).

Evidence for this includes the fact that this cortical-amygdala network exhibits a reciprocal activation pattern where more cortical activation results in less amygdala activation and vice versa. The severity of fear and anxiety is also positively associated with amygdala activation and negatively correlated with the size and responsivity of the orbital medial prefrontal cortex (OMPFC) capable of inhibiting it (Milad et al., 2005; Shin et al., 2006; Williams et al., 2006). It is within these descending networks from the OMPFC to the amygdala's central nucleus that the cortex carries out its inhibitory influences (Gottfried & Dolan, 2004; Quirk & Mueller, 2008).

Anxiety and depression are associated with a reduction in top-down control of cues for threat and negative emotions, respectively (Bishop et al., 2004; Brewin & Smart, 2005). These may be some of the reasons why our problem-solving abilities are degraded by fear while conscious preparation for a situation often lessens our fears (Schaefer et al., 2002). And while those of us with more attentional control will still have a bias to orient toward the threat, we will exert more top-down control as we become conscious of the stimulus (Derryberry & Reed, 2002). Overall, stress, anxiety, and fear are all enemies of learning. They impair cortical processing, problem solving, and the underlying biochemistry of neuroplasticity. Whatever teachers can do to minimize anxiety and stress in themselves and their students will enhance learning. A warm smile, a touch on the shoulder, and an occasional joke can go a long way.

Learning and Laughter

The shortest distance between two people is a smile.
—Anonymous

Everyday human interactions are punctuated with smiles, chuckles, and laughter. All forms of humor serve human bonding by communicating that we accept and care for each other. This is probably why possessing a sense of humor makes people more attractive and enhances feelings of intimacy and trust (Cann et al., 1997; Hampes, 1992, 1999). This may also be why "[he or she] makes me laugh" is a common response for females to the question of what they find attractive in their partners (Azim et al., 2005; Bressler et al., 2006). Humor evolved for many reasons, but it certainly serves the purpose of counteracting tension and stress. And while some feel that humor is antithetical to learning, consider the power of laughter and humor that has been revealed in scientific research.

Laughter becomes a regular part of mother-child communication by the second year of life (Meyer et al., 2007; Nwokah et al., 1994; Panksepp, 2007b). Even monkeys, great apes, and rats appear to laugh when they play or get tickled. Laughter is also contagious, so we tend to laugh more when watching a funny movie with a group or when a laugh track is added to a comedy soundtrack (Devereux & Ginsberg, 2001). In fact, a fit of laughter among teenage girls in Tanganyika spread throughout the entire community, closing schools for several months (Provine, 1992).

The vast majority of expressions of humor and lightheartedness are not reactions to jokes. Rather, they exist to encourage positive emotions that put us at ease (Provine, 2010). Humor helps people handle stress within relationships and communicate difficult information by lightening the mood. Many comedians and social critics such as Lenny Bruce, Mort Saul, and George Carlin brought difficult topics to public attention while making us laugh—an adaptive social strategy that expands the topics available for civic discussion (Reid et al., 2006).

In addition to its emotional value for relationships, understanding, appreciating, and generating humor are important exercises for the growing brain. To "get" a joke we have to both appreciate the juxtaposition of unexpected information and get an emotional jolt from our reward system. This is probably why so much of our humor centers on the violation of expectancies in which individuals are experiencing some kind of situational or social trouble (Deckers & Devine, 1981). Humor and laughter result in the widespread activation of brain regions (anterior cingulate, ompfc, and fronto-insular cortex) that are involved with both attachment and the recognition and resolution of novel and incongruent information (Forbasco, 1992; Iwase et al., 2002).

Whether one finds a particular situation or joke to be funny or offensive is modulated by the ompfc and hippocampus, suggesting that this system evaluates the contextual appropriateness of what is being experienced (Goel & Dolan, 2001). Further, the process of comparing expected with actual outcomes activates executive regions required for complex and abstract thinking, important aspects of social learning in children and adolescents (Moran et al., 2004). In support of this idea, listening to humorous material has been shown to enhance performance on tests of creativity and to broaden the scope of attention to environmental stimuli (Fredrickson & Branigan, 2005; Ziv, 1976). These findings suggest that humor may have co-evolved with our ability to navigate complex, changing, and problematic social relationships and that the laughter that peppers our interactions serves emotional regulation and social problem solving (Watson et al., 2007).

From a psychological perspective, humor has been shown to correlate with a sense of autonomy and self-efficacy by increasing one's perception of control over one's environment. In other words, if we can't control certain events in our lives, finding humor in our situation enhances a sense of perspective and control over the uncontrollable. Laughing with people is a good way to distance us from our common dilemmas (Goodman, 1992). "[Humor] is the healthy way of feeling a 'distance' between one's self and the problem, a way of standing off and looking at one's problem with perspective" (May, 1953, p. 61). Gaining emotional regulation through this distance helps us to apply problem-solving skills while providing a sense of empowerment and control (Sherman, 1998; Thorson, 1985; Wooten, 1996).

Humor in the Classroom

Play so that you may be serious.
—Anacharsis

If moderate to high levels of anxiety inhibit neuroplasticity, and if humor decreases anxiety, it stands to reason that humor could be used as a tool to enhance learning (Garner, 2006; Kher et al., 1999; Lomax & Moosavi, 2002; Schmidt et al., 2002). This may be especially true for students who tend to be frightened of particular subject matter or doubt their abilities to learn. Because humor is rewarding, the materials being learned will be paired with positive emotions, making it more likely to be returned to, repeated, and unintentionally rehearsed. Between teachers and students, humor expresses an interest in students and shows them that the teacher is human and sees them as human (Li & Balliet, 2009). It also serves to decrease social distance, thus enhancing compliance and participation. By the way, principals who share humor at school just happen to have teachers who report higher levels of teacher satisfaction (Hurren, 2006).

It turns out that while the amygdala triggers learning in both humorous and stressful situations, humor enhances emotional regulation and new cortical learning. Laughter also stimulates social-emotional connections from one person's right hemisphere to another person's right hemisphere (Coulson & Wu, 2005; Nelson, 2008; Samson et al., 2009; Sander & Scheich, 2005). Because understanding and appreciating humor rely on abstract and semantic networks on both sides of the brain, humor also supports lateral connectivity and integration (Bartolo et al., 2006; Cannon et al., 2007; Coulson & Van Petten, 2007; Goel & Dolan, 2001; Wild et al., 2003). Thus, humor serves the simultaneous functions of enhancing social connections, stimulating brain growth, and supporting neural network integration.

The effects of humor on learning depend on a variety of factors, including whether the humor is expected or unexpected, positive or negative, how the information is being presented, and who is presenting it (Takahashi & Inoue, 2009; Vecchio et al., 2009; Wanzer et al., 2010). Interestingly, if humor is expected, it becomes a distraction and impairs recall, making surprise a key element in the activation of plasticity (Kellaris & Cline, 2007). In the classroom, derogatory humor and sarcasm, especially from the teacher, can be harmful and impede learning (R. Berk, 2009; Frymier et al., 2008; Wear et al., 2009). Thus, the use and appreciation of humor is a complex neural task that supports both social and abstract intelligence.

Using positive humor in the learning environment has been found to correlate with increased memory for semantic information, resulting from increases in arousal, attention, rehearsal, enjoyment, and surprise (Kaplan & Pascoe, 1977; Morkes et al., 1999; Schmidt, 1994; Schmidt & Williams, 2001; Zillmann et al., 1980). Marketing experts, who have a huge stake in people remembering their messages, have found that advertising in a humorous manner increases memory for products (Duncan et al., 1984; Madden & Weinberger, 1982; Spotts et al., 1997; Strick et al., 2009). See Table 5.3 for some of the benefits of humor and laughter on various aspects of learning.

Table 5.3
The Benefits of Humor and Laughter for Learning

Improves memory recall[1]

Increases conceptual understanding[2]

Increases attention[3]

Stimulates brain regions important for complex and abstract thinking[4]

Activates brain growth hormones[5]

Increases reward value of materials[6]

Table 5.4
The Emotional and Physical Benefits of Humor and Laughter

Emotional

Reduces anxiety,[1] tension, and stress[2]

Reduces depression and loneliness[3]

Improves self-esteem[4]

Restores hope and energy[5]

Provides a sense of empowerment and control[6]

Physiological

Improves mental functioning through increased catecholamine levels[7]

Exercises and relaxes muscles[8]

Improves respiration by exercising the lungs and chest muscles[9]

Stimulates circulation by increasing heart rate and blood pressure[10]

Decreases levels of stress hormone[11]

Strengthens immunological functioning[12]

As students spend more time being entertained by a variety of media, the challenge of capturing and holding their attention also increases. Because teachers can never be as exciting as video games, or as tantalizing as Hollywood gossip, we have to capture students' attention in other ways. I've found that even the most ardent "gamer" responds to warmth, humor, and a compelling story. Just take a look at some of the research findings concerning the positive physical and emotional effects of humor and laughter (see Table 5.4).

One reason that humor and laughter feel so good is because they stimulate the brain's dopamine reward system (Mobbs et al., 2003). High levels of dopamine reduce anxiety, fear, and sadness, while increasing energy, self-esteem, and a sense of empowerment (Berk et al., 2001). Laughter also stimulates our brains to learn by increasing heart rate, depth of respiration, and blood pressure, and by activating muscles that secrete neural growth hormones (Fry, 1992). These physiological changes signal the brain to pay attention and learn.

Through its social and biochemical effects, humor plays an active role in healing social, emotional, and physical pain by enhancing mood and lessening anxiety and discomfort (Christie & Moore, 2005). Laughter helps us cope with stress by decreasing cortisol levels while making us more resistant to illness by stimulating the production of important components of our immunological systems such as T cells, natural killer cells, and B cells (Bennett et al., 2002; Berk et al., 2001; McClelland & Cheriff, 1997; Takahashi et al., 2001; Ziegler, 1995). So if you are tempted to think that laughing and joking around is "besides the point" when it comes to education, remember that laughter alters the expression of 23 separate brain-related genes (Hayashi et al., 2006). It is no wonder that many highly successful teachers blend stand-up comedy, drama, and performance art into their teaching style, with positive results.

Chapter 6

How Insecure Attachment Creates "Unteachable" Students

Be kind because everyone you meet is fighting a great battle.
—Philo of Alexandria

Over the years, I heard the label "unteachable" used to describe two groups of children: those with severe brain damage, and minority students failing to learn in inner-city schools. If we can manage to get past the pessimism and prejudice embodied in this label, there are a number of additional reasons to doubt its validity. The first is that the brain is wonderfully flexible and surprises even the savviest neurologists with its neuroplastic prowess. The second is that it takes no account of the genius that many teachers have demonstrated in reaching even the most difficult students. I believe that these students either lack the social skills, emotional resources, or behavioral abilities to sit in a classroom and learn, or they have yet to find the right teacher. I'm sure there were many who told Annie Sullivan that Helen Keller was unteachable.

There are an untold number of "unteachable" students who have been turned around with the kind of attention, care, and dedication they needed. Cognitive and social neuroscience are revealing that the brain is quite resilient and capable of reversing the effects of early negative experiences through positive ones. We see these processes in action in the teachings and writing of Marva Collins. Through her attachment-based teaching strategy, Collins has been successful with many children considered unteachable before entering her classroom.

Throughout her teaching career, Collins railed against prejudice, negativity, and the demoralization of both students and teachers. She came to believe that students would not learn in a system that accepted failure while paying no attention to the emotional well-being of the student. She realized that reaching and teaching students at greatest risk for falling through the cracks would take a caring and supportive environment that much more resembled a family than the schools she had spent her career teaching in.

When she could no longer stand to watch what she called the *institutionalization of failure,* she took $5,000 from her pension fund and opened Westside Preparatory School on the top floor of her Chicago brownstone. She accepted children who had been failing, were expelled, had dropped out, or were deemed unteachable by other teachers and administrators. She welcomed each new student with a frontal assault on shame by saying, *"Welcome to success and say goodbye to failure because you are not going to fail. I'm not going to let you fail. You are here to win, you were born to win, and if I have to care more about you than you care about you, then that's the way it will be"* (1992, p. 16, italics mine). By taking this hard-line yet loving stance, she at once established the expectations and values of her tribe of which each new student became a member.

Ms. Collins's message is as simple as it is profound: There are no miracles in successful education; it just requires endless commitment and determination. She recognizes the devastating effects of shame, rejection, and isolation reflected in the faces of the students who came to her for help. Her antidote to shame is love and total dedication to each student. Her philosophy of education is grounded in humanity, compassion, and an appreciation of the total child—a philosophy similar to many tribal cultures that see children as gifts from God, rather than as brains that must be filled with information.

While most teachers tend to focus on the bright students sitting up front, Ms. Collins is drawn to the "dirty little ones" who sit in the back of the class or stand by themselves on the playground. These are the children who are neglected or abused at home, don't get warm meals, and haven't learned to care enough about themselves to learn. She advises teachers to go to the back of the room and teach from where these children try to hide. Go to them on the playground and take their hand and find ways to connect them with the other students and the day's lessons. She encourages teachers to say something positive about each student every day.

Ms. Collins tells a story of a student who had never done well in school and seemed completely unmotivated to try. Day after day, she would sit down next to him and do his work for him, and then give him A's. Even his mother complained that something must be wrong with Ms. Collins's school if *her* son was getting A's. Ms. Collins's strategy was to get him accustomed to receiving A's, learn to be a proud student, and then let his pride and self-esteem motivate him to learn.

Discipline came in the form of loving lessons designed to teach and reconnect with her students instead of punishing them. She writes, "When you must reprimand your child, you do so in a loving manner. Don't ever try to degrade or humiliate him. His ego is a precious thing worth preserving. Try saying: I love you very much but I will not have that kind of behavior" (p. 196). She nurtured her emotionally wounded children back to intellectual health by caring for them as if they were her own, saying, "Great teachers don't send bad kids to the principal's office. They go up to the child, hug them and tell [them] that they care" (p. 36).

Collins believes that when children have communication skills and feel good about themselves, they have no reason to act out. On the other hand, acting out is a sign that something is wrong within a child who lacks a more direct means of expressing feelings. If these children are left on their own and then get into trouble, it is far more difficult to reach them if you have never touched them before. When children feel unloved and abandoned, they feel empty and filled with pain, rage, and violence. Ms. Collins's experiences have taught her that by loving students, and being available to work through problems with them, she eventually wears away their rebelliousness by removing the fear that drives it.

In Loco Parentis

One mother can achieve more than a hundred teachers.
—Jewish proverb

Marva Collins is a matriarchal elder who created a tribal school in her own home. She addressed the central issues of shame, self-esteem, and compassion by creating an environment conducive to learning for students who were not succeeding in the public school system. She was someone who could say to a child, Look, I love you but you have to get your act together. You're going to learn or you're going to die. Now, you take your choice. This is the message of the tribe: Learning is not optional, it is necessary for our survival. We are all depending on you and you must grow up and take responsibility for your life and the lives of others in the tribe.

She obviously considers herself a parent as well as a teacher and feels it is her responsibility to let her lesson go for a few minutes to find out what is bothering a child. Her method is to first empathize with the child so he doesn't feel alone and then make a commitment with him to solve the problem together. She believes that teachers should never say anything negative about their students, that students should be showered with compliments and encouragement, and that the classroom should be a place where students aren't afraid to make mistakes. Ms. Collins hit upon a basic neurobiological truth: When kids are too afraid to make mistakes, they are too afraid to learn. She wants all of her students to know that it takes more courage to take a chance and be wrong than to not try and play it safe.

She emphasizes physical contact and was not afraid to take a student's hand or give them a hug. She would sit next to a different child each day and grab the hand of a child standing off to the side and bring her into the group. She would reach out her arm, touch a student's face, lift his chin, and say, "Speak up, honey, you're brilliant." Ms. Collins encourages teachers to think of their classes as families and to establish a classroom climate of care and support. Her belief is that creating an exciting, stimulating, and emotionally safe classroom is the best way to gain and maintain attention. Perhaps her most important lesson is that teachers should always be rooting for their children to succeed, never laughing, ridiculing them, or saying anything negative.

In the midst of all this attention to the social and emotional elements of a successful classroom, she also emphasizes the importance of a combination of high standards and hard work. Lowering standards and allowing kids to slide only reinforce their beliefs in their own lack of worth. As in a real tribe, the stakes have to be high and each member needs to be held accountable. This is how we establish our feelings of membership and self-worth. It is in this process that we work against the internalized prejudices that poor and minority students have about their inability to learn. She states that "mediocrity, complacency, and a general lowering of standards are and have always been the antagonists of freedom in the saga of human life" (p. 53). She believes that poor minority children have fallen to the bottom because this was what was expected of them. And so we arrive back at this question: What creates an unteachable child?

A Classroom Full of Life Histories

> *The most useful piece of learning for the uses of life is to unlearn what is untrue.*
>
> —Antisthenes

When we scan the faces of new students each fall, we see in their faces and expressions a reflection of the ways in which their brains have been shaped to experience and cope with the world. Some are empty vessels eager for new learning while others are too terrified or numb to learn anything. One girl may seem off in another world, while the boy next to her is teasing the boy next to him, trying to provoke a fight. There are students in every class struggling with their sense of self-worth and lovability while there are others who already know they are worthless.

Children are born with millions of years of primitive self-centered instincts; they want to be the center of attention, win all the prizes, and be adored for everything they do. They want to fly like superheroes, be the most popular kid on the playground, and never have to wait their turn. On the other hand, most children have parents who want a respectful, hard-working, and well-behaved child. Gradually shaping a child's primitive narcissistic instincts into healthy and realistic self-esteem without crushing his or her spirit may be the central challenge of parenting.

This sort of socialization involves lots of no's, disappointments, power struggles, and time-outs. And although most children aren't harmed in this process, part of early life includes absorbing plenty of negative feedback. Problems in psychological and intellectual development occur when the normal egocentrism of childhood is met with prolonged and overwhelming experiences of shame. This can occur due to harsh parenting, an oversensitive temperament, or other interpersonal and environmental factors that overwhelm the child's ability to regulate their fear and anxiety. Understanding the power and impact of negative feedback, especially when it leads to a deep and abiding sense of shame, is central to successful teaching. Creating an optimal learning environment requires both a minimization of shame as well as the ability to uncover and heal emotional pain. This is clearly what Marva Collins witnessed in her classroom and what led her to create her own school where focusing on a child's emotional needs became interwoven into the classroom experience.

Because all healthy children are capable of learning, building unteachable children requires exposing them to criticism, fear, and abandonment in ways that create "core shame." To begin with, we need to distinguish core shame from appropriate kinds of shame and guilt that children need to experience. Appropriate shame and guilt emerge later in childhood with an understanding of other's expectations, an ability to judge one's behaviors, as well as the cortical development required to inhibit impulses. Appropriate shame and guilt support the development of conscience, deepen our empathetic abilities, and enhance our self-esteem as caring people (Greenwald & Harder, 1998; de Hooge et al., 2008).

We should reserve the term "core shame" to describe the process wherein some children come to experience themselves as fundamentally defective, worthless, and unlovable. Core shame is the polar opposite of self-esteem and creates "unteachable" students via a spectrum of defensive thoughts, feelings, and behaviors designed to protect them from pain—especially authority figures in a position to judge them. As Ms. Collins saw, to be successful with shame-based students, there is damage to undo before learning can take place. In fact, the most important gift any teacher can give to a child is to help him or her work past shame to a level of self-confidence that supports curiosity, exploration, and the joy of discovery. The main vehicle for this transformation is protection, compassion, dedication, and love.

The Origins of Shame

Owe no one anything except to love each other.
—Romans 13:8

During the first year of life, parent–child interactions are mainly positive, affectionate, and playful. The infant's limited mobility and skills keep him or her close to caretakers who provide for physical and emotional needs. As infants grow into toddlers, their increasing motor abilities and exploratory urges lead them to plunge head-first into danger. The unconditional affection of the first year gives way to loud and abrupt inhibitions designed to stop a child in its tracks. A chorus of "No's" replaces the smiles and soft tones! The child becomes accustomed to hearing "Don't" and "Stop!" and a shift in the use of his or her name from a term of affection to a command or warning, often with the addition of his or her middle and last names (Rothbart et al., 1989).

This parent-to-child warning mechanism, also seen in many animals, is designed to make children freeze in their tracks. It plays an important evolutionary role in protecting the young from predators and other environmental dangers. This freeze response is reflected within the autonomic nervous system by a rapid transition from sympathetic arousal to parasympathetic inhibition. Experientially, children are snapped from a mode of curiosity, exploration, and excitement to one of shutdown and withdrawal. As a result, the child stops, looks downward, hangs his head, and rounds his shoulders.

This state of submissive inhibition is essentially the same as when a dog hunches over, pulls his tail between his legs, and slinks away after being scolded for some canine faux pas. Similar postures occur in reaction to social exclusion, helplessness, and submission in virtually all social animals. It is a form of social communication that expresses what an adult might articulate as "you are the alpha and I am the beta," "please don't hurt me," and "okay, you're the boss." But for a child, it appears to be experienced more like "I'm not important, valuable, or lovable enough to be secure in my membership in the family"—an experience that feels life-threatening when your survival depends on your family's protection.

A parallel to these experiences may occur in early attachment relationships when an excited expectation of connection in a child is met with indifference, disapproval, or anger from a parent or caretaker. It has been hypothesized that these experiences of misattunement in the attachment relationship trigger the same rapid shift from sympathetic to parasympathetic control (Schore, 1999). Experientially, shame is a social emotion reflective of a fundamental sense of exclusion. While it may be difficult for adults to remember, toddlers expect their parents to be just as excited as they are about covering the floor with milk or flushing a smartphone down the toilet.

Negative parental reactions to their joy and enthusiasm can be experienced as painful rejection experiences that are translated to the developing psyche as shame, rejection, abandonment, and danger. And to whatever degree early relationships are characterized by these interactions, infants grow into more sensitive, fearful, and avoidant toddlers. These experiences are stored as visceral, sensory, motor, and emotional memories, creating an overall expectation of negative outcomes during future social interactions.

Because core shame is formed during a developmental period characterized by egocentrism, the loss of a parent through imprisonment, divorce, or even death is taken as rejection. During the first years of life, our parents don't leave a marriage or die from an illness; they abandon us because we weren't lovable enough for them to stay. Unable to connect our behaviors with our parents' reactions, early negative interactions are experienced as life-threatening, even though our parents may only be trying to protect us.

These ruptures of attunement and emotional connection happen between the best of parents and the healthiest of children. However, a child with a sensitive or anxious temperament may suffer greatly in the face of what appear to be normal, everyday parenting interactions. Differences in temperament and personality between parent and child can contribute to the development of core shame because they can result in so much misattunement. In other families, parents who were abandoned, neglected, or abused as children may use shaming and criticism as a predominant parenting style with their own children. This is quite common in rigid and authoritarian parents, religious cults, military families, or when there is mental illness in one or both parents. Children and adults who suffer with core shame usually feel like frauds and fear being uncovered for what they are.

Because shame is a powerful, preverbal, and physiologically based organizing principle, the overuse of shame as a disciplinary tool predisposes children to long-standing difficulties with emotional regulation and self-esteem (Schore & Schore, 2008). Chronically shaming parents have children who spend much of their time anxious, afraid, and at risk for depression and anxiety. On the other hand, attentive parents rescue children from shame states by reattuning with them as soon as possible after a rupture of connection. It is thought that repeated and rapid returns from shame states to reconnection and attunement result in rebalancing of autonomic functioning while contributing to the gradual development of self-regulation and self-esteem.

So what began as a survival strategy to protect our young has unfortunately become part of the biological infrastructure of later-evolving psychological processes related to attachment, safety, and self-worth. For social animals like ourselves, the fundamental question of "Am I safe?" has become interwoven with the question "Am I lovable?" Therefore, children riddled with core shame enter the classroom anxious and fearful, anticipating criticism, failure, and eventual exclusion. The defences designed to protect them from these painful emotions will also keep them from learning. In truth, every learning opportunity provides the possibility of failure, making the emotional cost of learning too high for many shame-based students.

Shame in the Classroom

Our sins are more easily remembered than our good deeds.
—Democritus

By the time we achieve self-awareness between 5 to 10 years of age, positive self-esteem or core shame have already been programmed as social and emotional givens. It is similar in many ways to booting up your computer and being presented with a desktop that has been organized by a Microsoft or Apple operating system. You accept it as the parameters of your computing universe, unaware of the thousands of lines of programming language required to generate the reality that has been created for you. In other words, basic self-esteem and core shame are programmed so early that although they are deeply known, they are never thought about or directly articulated. In the absence of conscious awareness, younger children associate shame with embarrassment, blushing, and ridicule, while older children will feel they are stupid and can't do anything right (Ferguson et al., 1991).

As children graduate into increasingly complex peer-group relations, core shame can come to shape their social life. As you might imagine, both victims and perpetrators of bullying are more likely to struggle with core shame. It becomes especially prominent during adolescence due to the heightened emphasis on being "cool," gaining acceptance into new groups, and dating (Anastasopoulos, 1997; Kaufman, 1974). Core shame distorts social cognition and can create the experience of rejection in neutral and even positive situations.

Consistent misperception of rejection and the negative distortion of social interactions create a vicious cycle that aversively impacts adolescents' popularity, social status, and ability to form relationships. Their lives become marked by chronic anxiety, depression, and exhaustion from their losing struggle to gain acceptance (Bradshaw, 1990).

In adults, core shame is acted out in the form of choosing abusive or nonsupportive partners, an absence of self-care, and unyielding perfectionism. You see expressions of core shame in an inability to tolerate being alone or in suicide attempts after a breakup. For people with core shame, even relatively minor abandonment is experienced as life-threatening because it triggers implicit memories of early and terrifying shame experiences. For some, any feedback suggesting that they are less than perfect triggers panic, making them unable to take risks, explore new ideas, or take instruction. Because not knowing something is intolerable, students with core shame have great difficulty dealing with the anxiety involved in uncertainty while working toward a solution.

When we are ashamed, our brains (like our bodies) close in and shut down. Most of the time, "unteachable" children suffer from disabling shame. Even the brightest students can have their cognitive and intellectual capacities negated by shame. At its heart, core shame is a sense of being a defective and fraudulent person who lives in fear of being exposed. Even though they have done nothing wrong, there is nothing they can do to make up for it (Kaufman, 1974). One of my students described it this way: "My shame makes it impossible for me to be loved because I can never believe someone could love me. And if they do, I can't possibly respect them because if they love me, their judgment must be seriously flawed."

Thus, establishing a healthy connection with a student flooded by shame is a necessary prerequisite to being able to stimulate his or her brain to learn. But as you can imagine, such a student will make a teacher run the gauntlet to prove that he is worthy of the student's trust. Both Ms. Collins and the other educators discussed in the chapters ahead have all reported being tested up to and often beyond their limits.

Because shame leads to anger and resentment, there is also considerable blame and hostility directed at others. Even a teacher's dedication and availability can be experienced as a threat. Bullies often act out their shame by victimizing others, while victims often accept the situation, because being victimized matches their sense of self-worth. Because the level of stress associated with chronic shame is so high, the negative effects on brain biochemistry result in chronic learning handicaps (see Table 6.1). As we will later explore in more detail, the stress created by shame inhibits the neuroplasticity that underlies new learning.

Table 6.1
Causes and Consequences of Shame

Psychological Effects

Depression[1]

Inferiority, low self-esteem, and self-efficacy[2]

Inappropriate self-blame[3]

Anger, hostility, and externalizing problems[4]

Envy and blame of others[5]

Biological Effects

Decreased immunological functioning[6]

Increased levels of cortisol[7]

Decreased neuroplasticity[7]

Family of Origin

Authoritarian and critical parents[8]

Childhood abuse and abandonment[10]

Parentification during childhood[11]

Memories of ignoring and abandoning mothers[9]

Feeling less favored than siblings[12]

Interpersonal Effects

Conflict avoidance[13]

Reflexive apologizing[15]

Reduced interpersonal problem solving[14]

Impact on School Performance

Reduced pride in response to success (girls)[16]

Maladaptive perfectionism[17]

Increased shame in the face of failure[16]

Fear of negative evaluation[18]

For those who suffer from core shame, early parental relationships are often described as having included constant criticism, abuse, and abandonment. Others describe dependent parents who, instead of parenting them, looked to their children for sympathy, guidance, and emotional support. In both cases, the absence of caring and competent parenting makes children extremely vulnerable to core shame. In their behavior with others, they are characterized as compulsive apologizers, desperately trying to avoid conflict and the anger of others, which feels inevitable and deserved. Praise bounces off them and usually goes unnoticed while anything that can be interpreted as criticism will be taken hard, triggering a fight-or-flight reaction. These students, who may be quite intelligent, won't try anything unless they feel certain of success. While serving to avoid failure, it also keeps them from taking on challenges and learning to regulate feelings of uncertainty on the way to mastery.

In the classroom, shame-based students often suffer from perfectionism and live in fear of negative evaluation from teachers and peers. Some develop a fear of being laughed at (gelatophobia) or of blushing (erythrophobia), which keeps them from raising their hand or speaking up in class. While the physiology, emotional expressions, and triggers for shame have cross-cultural commonalities, there are variations that emerge from different histories, morals, and customs (Bedford, 2004). Because of this, it is important to learn about what it means to have pride and keep "face" in someone's culture, subculture, or "gang" in order to be sensitive to the signs and symptoms of shame. In general, the more disrespect a group has had to endure within the broader culture, the more being respected is important to each individual.

Children with parents who have problems with addictions and/or the law may have core shame compounded by conscious shame of their family. Often, children are more deeply connected to parents who mistreat them, so don't assume that abused and abandoned children don't blame themselves for what has been done to them. A kind and attentive teacher may be attacked by a neglected student because being cared for activates her sadness about the parents she never had. Until a teacher is able to tame this reaction in a student, no good deed by the teacher will go unpunished.

Keep in mind that teachers are just as vulnerable to shame as their students. Children and adolescents are exceptionally good at detecting and exploiting the weaknesses and insecurities of others, especially those in a position to evaluate them. Your unexplored shame, fears, and vulnerabilities may become an Achilles heel and make it difficult to establish and maintain the position of a wise elder with challenging children and adolescents. We should all try to discover, explore, and heal our own brokenness before assuming a position of authority. Just as with students, emotional maturity and self-knowledge can make all the difference.

Radical Acceptance

Keep your gaze on the bandaged place. That's where the light enters you.

—Rumi

Through bonding, attachment, and compassion, teachers can create a tribal classroom that supports a sense of acceptance, inclusion, and security in each student. Tapping into the power of our primitive social instincts enables us to counteract the negative effects of core shame. Along the way, teachers are activating many of the same biological and neuroanatomical changes that occur during parenting. Because of this, *in loco parentis* is more than a legal term related to custodial responsibility; it also reflects a teacher's power to influence students' brains. Tribal teachers become loving and protective parents to their students, who in turn become caring and supportive siblings to one another. Attachment circuitry remains plastic throughout life and the teacher has the power to rewire earlier negative attachment experiences. It does take a village to raise a child and a teacher can create a village in the classroom.

The tribal teacher develops rapport and trust with students to create an emotional climate that is safe and supportive of new learning. The teacher becomes the students' secure base by expressing caring concern and a willingness to listen, and proving that he or she can be trusted. This secure attachment allows students to use teachers to help regulate their anxiety in the face of new challenges. The resulting emotional regulation in turn allows neural networks dedicated to new learning to stay active, engage, and grow. This is why the social agenda of the classroom must always be of equal importance to curricular content. Knowing the students' names when they show up to class means as much as the many hours of lesson prep time. Contrary to the assembly-line mentality of education, secure attachments provide a positive and cost-effective way of improving the performance of all students, especially those traditionally considered to be "unteachable" or at risk for failure.

Child Therapists

You, yourself, as much as anybody in the entire universe, deserve your love and affection.

—Buddha

A question that commonly arises among educators, adoptive parents, and legislators trying to decide where to direct funding is, "At what age do the negative effects of early abuse, trauma, and neglect become permanent?" Is there a critical period of brain development beyond which a child cannot form attachments and becomes unteachable no matter what resources are made available? Although I understand the desire for clear answers to complex social issues, these are moral rather than scientific questions. I am very skeptical of "experts" who think they have found scientific answers to moral questions like these. For one, the scientific data do not exist to answer these questions. The history of science has shown us that just when we think we know something, contradictory evidence comes to light that overthrows prior dogma. We also know that "science" has been used to justify everything from slavery to genocide. I think the best approach is to be compassionate, trust the power of neuroplasticity, and rely on our own ingenuity to discover new solutions to old problems.

An interesting and relevant example of this came from the primate laboratory of Harry Harlow, famous to all as the inventor of the wire monkey mother. To test the impact of maternal and social deprivation, Harlow isolated newborn monkeys for the first 6 months of life. Beyond minimal contact related to their basic needs, these young monkeys were left alone in a cage with only a few simple objects. Seeing these "isolate" monkeys is heartbreaking—they huddle in corners, rock, bite themselves, and stay curled up in a fetal position. It is as if they are trapped in a frightening autistic hell. Looking at the pictures can only make us hope that this research is no longer allowed.

When these isolate monkeys were introduced into a monkey colony at 6 months of age, they were understandably terrified. They didn't seem to understand what they were seeing, retreated from others, and did their best to avoid interaction. Based on this work, the assumption was that attachment circuitry had been hard-wired by 6 months, and it was too late for them to learn how to be social. But as with every "conclusion" in neuroscience, there is more to the story.

Harlow and one of his students, Steve Suomi, wondered if therapy could help these isolated monkeys overcome their fear and allow them to join the social world of the colony. But how do you do therapy with a young monkey? What could help to heal damaged neural systems of bonding and attachment? They finally came up with an idea; the therapists would be normally raised, 3-month-old monkeys, selected because they were smaller, craved playful contact, were less aggressive, and probably less threatening than same-aged peers (Harlow & Suomi, 1971).

Therapy consisted of three 2-hour sessions per week for 4 weeks—a total of 24 hours of "treatment." When the therapists arrived for the session, the isolate patients were terrified, retreated into a corner, and tried to soothe themselves by curling into balls, rocking, and shutting out their "therapists." The little monkeys were undeterred; they followed, touched, climbed on, and attempted to interact with their clients. The isolates tried to retreat as their anxiety increased but the little therapists followed. Again the therapists engaged, touched, climbed on, and got in the face of their clients. Apparently, when it comes to play and social engagement, a 3-month-old monkey can't take "no" for an answer.

As the sessions continued, the isolates gradually came to accept their therapists' interventions. These therapists interrupted autistic, self-stimulating behavior, and the isolates eventually began to initiate physical interactions. When these former isolates were introduced to the colony, they were able to find a role within the group and social hierarchy. Were they impaired? Most likely, as early deprivation often has a long-lasting impact, but it appeared to the researchers that they had attained a functional social recovery. Therapy was so successful that the authors stated, "By one year of age, the isolates were scarcely distinguishable from socially raised monkeys in terms of exploration, locomotion, and play" (p. 1537). These results surprised Harlow and Suomi because of their prior assumptions about critical periods.

This research should remind us to keep an open mind and encourage us to never give up on a child.

Chapter 7

How Bullying Impedes Learning

Intelligence plus character—that is the goal of true education.
—Martin Luther King Jr.

Research across many fields of study supports the fundamental notions that the brain is a social organ and that group membership is a fundamental human motivation (Baumeister & Leary, 1995). Despite the fact that our scientific methods most often study the isolated individual, social animals like ourselves can only be fully understood in a matrix of relationships. We have seen that the presence of an attentive mother builds young brains in ways that support learning, physical well-being, and the ability to form subsequent relationships. At the same time, children change their parents' brains by stimulating and building these same neural networks and emotional mechanisms. In fact, in primate species where the fathers do the bulk of infant caretaking, males achieve greater longevity through the positive biological impact of these loving relationships (Allman et al., 1998).

Social animals are linked together via social brain networks, and regulate each other's internal biochemistry, emotions, and behaviors. A good demonstration of this was seen when hunters attempted to decrease the danger of elephant stampedes by shooting the largest members of the herd. The result of this practice made herds far more dangerous. It turns out that the presence of the matriarch, who was usually among the largest of the group, down-regulated testosterone and aggression in the herd's adolescent males (Bradshaw et al., 2005). Thus, within a herd of elephants, the presence of the matriarch regulates the internal biology of the young males. So to study the hormonal activity and social behavior of a single elephant misses the homeostatic mechanism that exists within the herd.

In primate troops, the presence of safe older males allows the boys to practice aggression, learn how to use it, and understand its limitations (Adang, 2010). The same is true for human boys where the presence of the father and other male figures in the home correlates with better social adaptation later in life. Without the regulation of adults, adolescent males follow their testosterone-powered instincts in the absence of the modulating effects of a family structure to contain and direct their energies. We also observe that when human family and community structures break down, adolescents become increasingly aggressive and organize into destructive gangs.

It is clear that the people around us regulate our brains. Good relationships increase optimism, self-esteem, and well-being while supporting cognitive and emotional development. On the other hand, bad relationships impede social, emotional, and cognitive development, leading to decreased academic success. Teachers and administrators have the power to modulate the brains of students and direct their social instincts in the service of learning and emotional development. A focus on attachment-based education becomes increasingly important as we focus on students in failing schools within impoverished communities.

Positive Relationships

Children require guidance and sympathy far more than instruction.
—Anne Sullivan, the tutor to Helen Keller

Correlations between health and positive social connectedness are the most consistent and robust findings in the field of psychoneuroimmunology, the study of the connections among the mind, brain, and body. Social support not only has salubrious effects in itself, but it also buffers us against the negative effects of stress (Cohen & Wills, 1985). Being around supportive others reduces blood pressure, stress hormones, autonomic and cardiovascular reactivity, and the risk of illness (Edens et al., 1992; Gerin et al., 1992; Sachser et al., 1998; Spitzer et al., 1992). Social support also facilitates the production of T cells and natural killer cells that promote immune functioning. Positive relationships can buffer chronic and acute stress, thereby enhancing both health and longevity (Rowe and Kahn, 1997). See Table 7.1 for an overview of the positive physical and emotional benefits of social support.

Table 7.1
The Impact of Social Support on Physical and Mental Health

Positive Social Support

Cardiovascular Health	Immunological Functioning
General heart health[1]	Higher level of natural killer cells[4]
Lower blood pressure[2]	Lower urinary cortisol[5]
Lower cardiovascular reactivity to stress[3]	Improved immunological functioning[6]
General Health Status	**Mental Health**
Increased health status and well-being[7]	Better all-around mental health[11]
Decreased vulnerability to clinical illness[8]	Decreased depression and anxiety[12]
Decrease in symptom display[9]	Better emotional regulation[13]
Decreased risk of cancer recurrence[10]	Better sleep[14]

Negative Relationships

The strength of a nation derives from the integrity of the home.
—Confucius

Most of us are aware of the importance of positive relationships between teachers and students, which is why we pay so much attention to creating a warm and supportive classroom milieu. In contrast, we tend to be unaware of (or not attuned to) the impact of negative relationships that students suffer at home, on the schoolyard, or in the streets (Leff et al., 1999; Stockdale et al., 2002). The causes of this selective lack of attention are not known, although it has been suggested that adults need to idealize childhood and normalize the bullying many of us survived years ago. It could even be as simple as not seeing first hand what happens after class and students' tendency to not share their struggles (Fekkes et al., 2005). Many suffer abuse and bullying in silence, while only a few dramatic and lethal cases make the news (Leary et al., 2003).

While we have already focused on the impact of negative relationships with parents, we have yet to address bullying. Understanding bullying, identifying bullies and victims, and becoming involved in prevention will all support classroom learning. Bullies tend to keep silent for fear of reprimand while victims and bystanders remain silent out of shame and embarrassment. I remember a few incidents of bullying where I intervened, and more when I didn't. I remember the terror of being the target of a bully, and the shame of not doing anything to help others.

Bullying

All wars are civil wars because all men are brothers.
—François de Fenelon

Bullying has received increased attention during the last decade in the wake of the Columbine shootings and a number of bullying-related suicides. Described rightly as a "silent nightmare," bullying haunts schools, neighborhoods, and a surprising number of workplaces throughout the world (Smith, 1991). Prevalence estimates, ranging from 6% in Scandinavia to as high as 75% in the United Kingdom, reflect the fact that bullying is culturally modulated (Craig & Harel, 2004; Due et al., 2005; Glover et al., 2000). Attitudes about bullying vary greatly across cultures and among individuals, likely reflecting our own experiences with bullying while growing up. Many feel it is an inevitable rite of passage that helps children to develop character. In fact, Japanese teachers are encouraged not to intervene in bullying so children can learn to work out social problems, while adults in other countries encourage bullying (Pellegrini, 2002).

Bullying has a deep evolutionary history embedded in the establishment of social dominance and demonstrates a surprising degree of similarity across troops of monkeys, chimps, apes, and humans (Bjorkqvist, 2001). For social creatures like ourselves, part of our survival is forming alliances, gaining access to what we need, and finding our place in the social hierarchy. Bullying is just one part of this complex social dance. In other primates, bullying is displayed in behaviors like charging, pounding the chest, and bellowing for everyone to see. Bullying in humans is more complex and expressed through teasing, name calling, stealing, taunting, humiliating, spreading rumors, and social exclusion (Banks, 2000). It can even be highly organized in such practices as hazing and places such as military boot camps.

In social animals, displays of dominance are more likely to occur during the formation of new groups. In the same way, bullying is more likely to occur during periods of social transition, such as at the beginning of secondary school, when dominance hierarchies need to be reestablished. Most incidences of bullying are not dyadic phenomena but are public displays designed to be witnessed by others in the service of establishing and maintaining social dominance (Twemlow et al., 2004). On average, four peers witness episodes of adolescent bullying and 75% of the time they are either passive or participate in the bullying (O'Connell et al., 1999). Preteen bystanders are present around 86% of the time and intervene around 18% of the time (Atlas & Pepler, 1998; Hawkins et al., 2001; Salmivalli et al., 1996). Children who are considered to be different in some way are more likely to be bullied. They are easily identifiable targets, often suffer from low self-esteem, have difficulty defending themselves, and are less likely to be defended by others (Veenstra et al., 2010). Adolescent bystanders tend to identify with victims and have even been shown to experience vicarious trauma (Carney, 2000).

Mutual verbal abuse among men can certainly be seen in sports and in the military—think of the typical boot-camp experience or the pep talk from the coach before the big game. There may even be some truth in the fact that those who can successfully navigate bullying will be stronger for it. For example, verbally abused boys tend to experience an increase in testosterone, suggesting that confrontation may trigger some weaker or more introverted boys to behave in more aggressive ways (Vaillancourt et al., 2009). Historically, this may have served survival by stimulating testosterone in the faint of heart in preparation for hunting and combat. Unfortunately, the research suggests that being victimized by bullies is also predictive of psychological and physical problems that can last a lifetime.

Bullies and Their Victims

What the child says, he has heard at home.
—African proverb

Bullies are likely to have authoritarian parents who bully them and are unskilled at emotional communication (Ahmed & Braithwaite, 2004; Espelage et al., 2000; Kim et al., 2004; Rigby, 1994; Spriggs et al., 2007; Zimmerman et al., 2005). These findings parallel the animal literature where socially dominant animals tend to recreate their own biological and behavioral profile in their young. Bullying does not bode well for the bully either, who is at increased risk for future social and psychological problems. For many children, the act of bullying is a cry for help; it is an expression of fear, anger, or pain they are unable to express in words (Crick, 1996; Juvonen et al., 2003; Kaltiala-Heino et al., 2000; Kumpulainen et al., 1998). Bullies are just as likely to suffer from core shame as their victims.

Being victimized by bullies can have serious emotional and behavioral consequences, especially if the abuse is severe and/or chronic.

Studies have shown that victimization results in depression, anxiety, blunted emotions, sleep disturbance, and symptoms of posttraumatic stress disorder (PTSD). In fact, 17% of gay men, lesbians, and bisexuals who experienced chronic bullying during adolescence continue to experience symptoms of PTSD into adulthood (Rivers, 2001, 2004). Any and all of these symptoms will affect a child's ability to learn by creating stress and undermining attention, concentration, and memory. Being bullied will increase cortisol levels, impairing hippocampal functioning, short-term memory, and learning. Being bullied also increases the likelihood of becoming physically. This leads to greater social isolation as a result of greater amounts of time spent out of the classroom. Because of its prevalence and impact on the brain and body, the identification of bullying and proper intervention is a central issue in education.

Predator Stress

> *No one can keep a secret better than a child.*
> —Victor Hugo

Imagine how a bullied child might feel as he prepares to leave home to walk to school, knowing that he won't be safe again until he gets home that afternoon. He looks over his shoulder, jumps at any loud noise, and quickens his pace when bullies or gangbangers come into view. Although getting to class makes him feel a little safer, he has to be careful not to look "smart" or to "kiss up" to the teacher lest he attract attention. In a fundamental way, the victims of bullies are living the lives of animals of prey, constantly vigilant for stronger and more aggressive animals who can do them physical and emotional harm. And while the bodily changes that occur in victims of bullying have not been studied directly, we do know what happens in animals when exposed to predators.

In a typical study, a rat might be placed in a perforated Plexiglass chamber and "safely" exposed to the visual, olfactory, and acoustic stimuli of a cat. This parallels the experience of a young child walking through a dangerous neighborhood, being confronted by a bully, or being trapped in a home with abusive parents. Both the rat and the child will exhibit the behavioral and biochemical signs of fear and panic through startle, freezing, and retreat responses. The neurobiological processes of new learning decrease while the primitive brain takes over to prepare for the fight-or-flight response. Memory for objects, information, and physical space all become impaired, as do problem solving and abstract abilities. See Table 7.2 for a summary of the impact of predator stress on animals.

Table 7.2
The Impact of Predator Stress

Behavioral Changes

Freezing, inhibition of activity[1]

Retreat and avoidance responses[2]

Suppression of foraging, exploration, feeding, grooming, and childrearing[3]

Increases in fear, anxiety, startle responses[4]

Neurobiological Changes

Increases in cortisol levels[5]; levels of adrenocorticotrophic hormone[6]; and hypothalamic-pituitary–adrenal (HPA) sensitization[7]

Decreased prime burst potential[8]

Decreased pCREB (an indicator of metabolic activity) expression[9]

Decreased hippocampal spinogenesis[10]

Potentiation of right amygdala afference[11]

Increased right amygdala gene expression[12]

Inhibition of left amygdala afference[13]

Increased cFos (an indicator of protein synthesis) activation in defensive behavior circuitry[14]

Increased gene expression in the amygdala[15]

Decreased frontal acetylcholine, serotonin, and dopamine levels[16] with less hippocampal cell proliferation[17]

Cognitive Changes

Deficits in consolidation and retrieval of new memory[18]

Spatial working memory[19]

continued on next page

Table 7.2 continued

Short- and long-term spatial memory[20]

Memory for objects[21] and working memory[22]

Disruptions in Development

Pup survival[23]

Growth rate[24]

Normal development[25]

This research demonstrates that the biochemical and neurobiological effects of being exposed to predators negatively impact every level of functioning from emotional well-being to longevity. As you can see from Table 7.2, the effects of being preyed upon disrupt at least a dozen biochemical processes related to learning and memory, creating a profound handicap in the classroom and in life. We know that predatory stress triggers cortisol production and amplifies the effects of other stressors (Fox et al., 1997; Relyea, 2004; Sih et al., 2004). Children who are living in difficult family environments and/or who have experienced traumatic events demonstrate higher cortisol levels and are more likely to die at a younger age (Flinn, 2006). Not surprisingly, bullied students have higher anxiety and adrenocortical activity during the time preceding lunch as they brace themselves to leave the relative safety of the classroom (Carney et al., 2010).

As you know, kids experience extreme pressures to fit in, and those who don't are more likely to be bullied. Sadly, the children in most need of acceptance are also the most likely to be bullied. Kids who stutter, suffer from depression, have low self-esteem, and demonstrate poor social skills are like the lame members of the herd targeted by predators (Blood & Blood, 2004; Egan & Perry, 1998; Fekkes et al., 2006; Fox et al., 2005; Houbre et al., 2010; Johnson et al., 2002; Voss & Mulligan, 2000). Gay, lesbian, bisexual, overweight, and less physically attractive students are also common targets (Janssen et al., 2004; Rivers, 2004; Sweeting & West, 2001).

Table 7.3
The Result of Bully Victimization

Perceived by others to be at increased risk of depression and suicide[1]

Self-reported anxiety, depression, and suicidal ideation in girls[2,3]

Emotional problems[4]

Depression, anxiety, sleep disturbance, loneliness, and helplessness[5]

Anhedonia and psychosomatic illness[6,7]

Adolescent victims have an increased risk of negative mental health[8]

Negative symptoms are best predicted by chronic victimization[9]

The long-lasting negative effects of bullying are associated with a variation of a serotonin gene, suggesting an underlying biological vulnerability to both depression and negative social experiences (Sugden et al., 2010). In line with this data, victimization appears to be stable during development, with a small group of students serving as consistent targets of an array of bullies throughout their childhoods and adolescence (Hodges & Perry, 1999; Kuppens et al., 2008; Perry et al., 1988; Sourander et al., 2000). Boys and girls both bully and react to bullying in line with the usual gender role differences. Boys tend to suffer physical attacks while girls are more likely to experience relational victimization (Crick et al., 1999). Verbally victimized girls produce less testosterone and cortisol while verbally bullied boys produce more of both, meaning that girls tend to dissociate and become helpless while boys will more often mobilize for a fight (Vaillancourt et al., 2008, 2009).

Recent research shows that up to half of all children surveyed report at least one incidence of being cyberbullied via email, instant messages, or in chat rooms, and many do not know the identity of their perpetrators (Bond et al., 2001; Kowalski & Limber, 2007; Patchin & Hinduja, 2006; Rigby, 1997; Smith & Shu, 2000). While far less research has been done in the area of cyberbullying, the causes and consequences parallel face-to-face bullying except that it is even less likely to be shared with teachers and administrators (Agatston et al., 2007; Ybarra, 2004; Ybarra et al., 2007; Ybarra & Mitchell, 2004). This is especially unfortunate considering that absences, suspensions, and carrying a gun to school are linked to being harassed online (Ybarra et al., 2007).

As you might expect, those children likely to become bullies are also at risk for a variety of psychosocial and academic difficulties. They have a greater likelihood of being victims of abuse, poor attachment relationships, depression, and committing suicide. See Table 7.4 for a summary of the commonalities between bullies and their victims.

Table 7.4
Bullies and Victims

Of elementary students, 21% are both bullies and bullied[1]

A greater likelihood of having experienced physical, sexual, and emotional abuse in the home, and suffering emotional dysregulation[2]

Lower-quality attachment relationships[3]

Social adjustment problems at school and at home[4]

Victims have a dislike of school and see few constraints on bullying[4, 5]

Low levels of social acceptance and problem-solving skills[6]

At risk for depression and suicide[7]

Poorer psychosocial adjustment[8]

Some victims start picking on weaker peers[9]

Children with ADHD are at greater risk for bullying and victimization[10]

A child's reaction to bullying is moderated by biological and genetic factors as well as the quality of their social support (Benjet et al., 2010; Bollmer et al., 2005; Hodges et al., 1999; Kochenderfer & Ladd, 1997). A warm and supportive family environment helps to buffer victims from the impact of bullying (Bowes et al., 2010) and also reduces the risk that a victim will become a bully. In victims who go home to neglect or abuse, being bullied will have a negative synergistic effect with the social stress they already suffer.

Preventing Bullying

Only the educated are free.

—Epictetus

As we have seen, bullying is a manifestation of the primitive drive to establish dominance and is moderated by factors within the home and school. In the absence of established power structures, enforced rules, and adult guidance, kids naturally resort to more primitive strategies for establishing social structures. We have also seen that there are considerable differences in the prevalence rates of bullying across cultures. This strongly suggests that the existence of bullying can be modified by the culture of the classroom and the school. Research has shown that schools with positive discipline, more parent involvement, and high academic standards experience less bullying (Kuperminc et al., 1997; Ma, 2002; Stadler et al., 2010).

Bullying prevention can be integrated into a school's environment, culture, and value system. Children have been shown to respond to social norms that make bullying "uncool" and don't promote social advancement. If increased awareness and immediate intervention by school staff and parents become the norm, vulnerable students will not feel as different or alienated from others and will have a better opportunity to stay integrated in the group culture of the school. Responding to bullying within 1–2 minutes of seeing the incident and following up with separate meetings with both the bullied child and the bully have been shown to be useful. Alternative and anonymous methods of reporting bullying and other problems are helpful. The establishment of a group within the school to address bullying—consisting of parents, staff, teachers, and a student advisory board—can help provide suggestions and feedback.

When trying to inhibit primitive instincts, cortical activation is necessary to build new neural circuitry. Therefore, it is helpful to create explicit policies of what is to be expected of students. For example, not only should bullying be forbidden, but students should also know they are expected to be good citizens and not passively stand by as a peer gets bullied. Rules should be posted publicly and discussed, and clear consequences should be established for breaking the rules. Teachers can also allow time to discuss bullying on a regular basis and can integrate themes that deal with bullying into the curriculum. In a popular bullying intervention program, Olweus (1991) has suggested the following rules be posted for all to see:

- We will not bully others.
- We will try to help other students who are bullied.
- We will make a point to include students who are easily left out.
- If we know someone is being bullied, we will tell an adult at school and an adult at home.

Successful intervention programs generally include clear guidelines, rules, and procedures for before, during, and after incidents. They utilize staff, parents, and faculty to create, implement, and maintain the program. Most programs increase vigilance and supervision in areas outside of the classroom (Astor et al., 2005). Primary prevention programs that involve all students, not just affected ones, are considered the best defense against bullying (Elinoff et al., 2004). It may also be helpful to offer at-risk students workshops in social skills, assertiveness training, problem-solving strategies, and/or anger management programs.

These programs have been shown to create attitude change in pupils and the community, a willingness to report bullying events, and a respect for personal space (Glover et al., 2000). Participants experience greater bystander responsibility, perceived adult responsiveness, and less acceptance of bullying (Frey et al., 2005). Psychoeducational interventions aimed at teachers have also been shown to be successful for increasing teachers' use of intervention strategies, teacher self-efficacy, and reduced classroom bullying (Newman-Carlson & Horne, 2004). Another intervention program that modified the school environment, educated students, and trained teachers found a reduction in aggression and victimization among younger students and a reduction in victimization among the older students (Orpinas et al., 2003). The take-home message is that bullying and victimization no longer have to be included among the facts of school life. And although the establishment of social hierarchies through aggression and social exclusion may be embedded within our deep evolutionary history, the expansion of mindful awareness allows us to progress beyond these primitive instincts.

Chapter 8

Why Teachers Burn Out

A good teacher is like a candle—it consumes itself to light the way for others.

—Anonymous

Up to this point we have focused on the importance of addressing the primitive social instincts of students to stimulate and enhance learning. As you will see in the pages to come, the research on teacher burnout suggests that primitive social instincts and the effect of negative relationships are also at work in teachers. We will see that the more a school resembles a bureaucratic hierarchy with rigid authority structures and undemocratic policies, the greater the chance of teacher burnout. On the other hand, the more that a principal can establish a sense of tribe among faculty and staff, the more teachers will feel satisfied, thrive, and stay in the profession.

Teachers are special people who work to make a difference in the world. However, this doesn't protect them from normal emotions and basic human needs. Just like their students, when they feel thwarted, isolated, or bullied, they become ashamed, demoralized, and hopeless. As teachers burn out, their tolerance, concern, and care for their students decline and student achievement falls (Black, 2001). As this downward spiral gains momentum, teachers may develop callous and cynical attitudes toward students, parents, and their colleagues and grow increasingly ineffective (Jennings & Greenberg, 2009). Burnt-out teachers and unteachable students share high levels of stress and lack a sense of purpose for being in the classroom (Brouwers & Tomic, 1999; Glickman & Tamashiro, 1982).

Like everyone else, teachers need to know that they are needed, wanted, and are making an important contribution to those around them. Not surprisingly, when they feel effective, valued, and able to participate in opportunities to learn, teachers report much greater job satisfaction. The correlates of burnout, on the other hand, read like a perfect storm of assaults on self-esteem and emotional well-being. Chronic stress, inadequate support from administrators, challenging students, and a lack of adequate preparation have all been found to be major contributors of burnout. The findings summarized in Table 8.1 point out how the idealism that brings many into teaching may be overwhelmed by the challenges and limitations inherent in educational systems.

Table 8.1
Teacher Burnout: Systemic Factors

Lack of adequate resources and facilities[1]

Unreasonable time demands[2]

High-stakes testing and accountability[3]

Large classes and schools[4]

Excessive paperwork[5]

Lack of advancement opportunities[6]

Low participation in decision making[7]

Low organization efficacy and high rigidity[8]

Practical factors contributing to burnout include larger and more chaotic classrooms, combined with student apathy and the stress of high-stakes testing. Just as you would expect, consistently low student achievement despite sustained teacher effort contributes to demoralization. Dealing with verbal abuse, student disrespect, and concerns for one's physical safety promotes emotional exhaustion and increases the odds of burnout. These negative factors are all amplified in poor, inner-city schools with the greatest disparity between needed and available resources (Abel & Sewell, 1999; Goodman, 1980; Hanushek, 2002; Konert, 1997; Lopez, 1995; Rollefson, 1990).

The quality of school management contributes to burnout if it is experienced as overly rigid and poorly managed, and results in unnecessary paperwork and red tape. The chances of burnout increase when teachers are cut out of decision making, lack advancement opportunities, and have little control over what they do. Like everyone else, teachers struggle to focus on their work and stay sane in poorly managed organizations. Principals who are good managers and effectively define and communicate the mission of the school promote job satisfaction and decrease burnout (Vernadine, 1997). See Table 8.2 for a summary of the psychological and social correlates of burnout.

Table 8.2
Teacher Burnout: Psychological and Social Correlates

Low self-awareness[1]

Low self-management skills[1]

Low salary, low status, feeling unappreciated[2]

Lack of collegiality and support[3]

Negative student behavior and fear of violence[4]

Student apathy, indifference, absences[5]

Low student achievement[6]

Single and divorced teachers[7]

Part-time teachers/feeling isolated from colleagues[8]

Low religiousness[9]

Low involvement in activities[10]

Low openness to change[10]

Passive, immature psychological defenses[11]

External locus of control[12]

The reality is that teachers need compassionate and caring administrators, parents, and staff almost as much as children need these qualities in their teachers. The fact that teachers are adult professionals makes little difference when it comes to the basic social instincts to connect, belong, and feel valued. As you might expect, isolation, poor staff relations, and a lack of support from colleagues and administrators are highly predictive of burnout. Part-time teachers who feel isolated from their colleagues and receive less support are more likely to experience burnout as are those who are single, divorced, or lack solid social connections outside of work. Collegiality, positive collaborations, and coworker support allow teachers to cope with daily struggles by promoting personal and professional satisfaction. A flexible interpersonal context with more collaboration among teachers and administration also supports morale and success.

Personal experience and research findings both support the view that it takes considerable strength of character, self-esteem, and determination to be a successful teacher. This ability to thrive under high levels of stress (a trait some call "hardiness") includes a preference for novelty, a low degree of feeling alienated from others, and an internal locus of control (Maddi & Hess, 1992; Rich & Rich, 1987).

Being a good teacher is also not about intellectual horsepower. In fact, those who see teaching as an intellectual activity or who have high IQs and college GPAs are more likely to leave teaching (Borg et al., 1991; Byrne, 1994; Darling-Hammond & Sclan, 1996; Lamude et al., 1992; Quartz & TEP Research Group, 2003; Whiteman et al., 1985). In addition, teachers with the highest levels of commitment and idealistic expectations when they enter the profession are more likely to burn out or leave the field (Freudenberger, 1974; Maslach et al., 2001; Miech & Elder, 1996).

Teachers who succeed, especially in more difficult schools and in challenging classrooms, need to be up to the fight. Those who succeed adapt to these situations, work hard to change them, and utilize others to cope with stress and take on the problems (Brownell et al., 1994). A teacher's ability to communicate, be assertive, maintain good relationships, and impact the culture and policies of the school are all predictive of lower levels of stress and a greater sense of accomplishment (Friedman, 2003). In other words, they are able to summon the energy from within and gain the support from others that allows them to create a sustained and sustaining tribe.

Hardiness is not learned in school: It arises from strength of character, which is likely the result of the nurturance that a person experiences during development (Maddi & Kobasa, 1984). Teachers with inadequate social support and fragile defenses face situations that provoke emotions they have difficulty managing. For example, teachers who cope by avoiding negative emotions in challenging situations report higher levels of stress and burnout (Chang, 2009; Griffith et al, 1999; Mearns and Cain, 2003). Those who are passive, dependent, or utilize rigid coping strategies also have a higher likelihood of burnout. A passive coping style, a tendency to blame external factors for their difficulties, and unrealistic expectations of others all predict leaving the profession.

Stress and poor emotion management rank as the primary reasons teachers become dissatisfied and leave teaching (Darling-Hammond, 2001; Montgomery & Rupp, 2005). Teachers who stayed had a higher sense of self-efficacy, more active and direct styles of coping, and had sought out help and additional training in order to guarantee success (Brownell et al., 1994). See Table 8.3 for some of the correlates of teacher burnout.

Table 8.3
Correlates of Teacher Burnout

Burnout Correlates With:

Increased:
Blood pressure and heart rate[1]
Gastroenteritis, migraine, irritability, and depression[2]
Absenteeism and intention to leave teaching[3]
Cynicism[4]
Student apathy and misbehavior[5]

Decreased:
Physical and mental health[6]
Quality of personal life[7]
Effort and dedication to teaching[8]
Tolerances, sympathy, and caring for students[9]
Student performance[10]

Having a conceptual framework for dealing with challenging classrooms and topics provides more practical tools while decreasing anxiety and other negative emotions. The more time that teachers can devote to proactive classroom management and teaching strategies, the less stress they experience from discipline problems and work overload (Ben-Ari et al., 2003). Successful teachers feel competent, satisfied with their work, and less stressed, and are ultimately less prone to burnout.

Teachers feel most committed to their schools when they see their work as meaningful with positive and observable results (Farber, 1984; Ma & Macmillan, 1999). A lack of perceived efficacy, defined as the extent to which the teacher believes he or she has the capacity to affect student performance, correlates with both the degree of burnout and the likelihood of leaving teaching (Bergman et al., 1977; Brissie et al., 1988; Glickman & Tamashiro, 1982). Despite life being more stressful, Israeli teachers experience lower levels of burnout when compared to American teachers. This was hypothesized to be the result of the higher existential significance attributed to the work of being a teacher in Israel (Pines, 2003). This would certainly parallel the traditional significance of teaching within subsistence tribes.

The Need for Broader Teacher Training

Treat people as if they were what they ought to be, and
you help them become what they are capable of becoming.
                    —Johann Wolfgang von Goethe

Despite the fact that they will be called upon to be counselors, social workers, and parents, traditional training programs prepare aspiring teachers only as instructors. Once on the job it is clear that students require much more of them than they have been prepared for. Teachers often aren't sure who they are supposed to be for the students. This role ambiguity can be a cause of emotional exhaustion and negativity toward students, colleagues, and administration (Crane & Iwanicki, 1983). This is why so many teachers feel inadequately prepared by their training—a reason often given for leaving the profession. The majority of special education teachers report that they left college unprepared to meet the learning needs of diverse students, to balance the demands they had to face, and to cope with the poor working conditions they discovered in the field.

These findings strongly suggest that teachers need to be better prepared by their training programs to understand and deal with the social, emotional, and practical issues they will encounter. It might also be a good idea to screen aspiring teachers for psychological defenses, coping strategies, and emotional strengths and weaknesses. The research in teacher burnout could then be used to either guide them into an area where they have the highest likelihood of success or to try and help them acquire the coping and social skills they will need to succeed prior to being placed in a classroom.

The teachers' perceived ability to respond to students' human needs has been shown to have a high correlation with perceived effectiveness as instructors (Brouwers & Tomic, 2000). In another study, teachers' perceptions of how students view them had a stronger connection to burnout than the perceptions of parents or principals (Friedman & Farber, 1992). When teachers feel ineffective in reaching their students on a personal level, they are at risk for feeling helpless, incompetent, and unfulfilled. In my opinion, this constellation of facts suggests that teacher training should include a strong emphasis on the social and emotional skills required to be a successful teacher and a well-balanced human being.

Teachers Need a Tribe

Few things help an individual more than to place
responsibility upon him, and let you know you trust him.
—Booker T. Washington

As discussed in an earlier chapter, many aspects of our educational systems are a poor fit for our social brains. All of the elements involved in the creation of a tribal classroom to promote learning also need to be applied in the creation of a positive work environment for teachers. Large groups, administrative hierarchies, and a lack of democratic input from teachers all conspire against the utilization of our primitive social instincts. Just about every correlate of teacher burnout is related either directly or indirectly to the negative effects of social and emotional disconnection. For just as students will turn off in a classroom misaligned with their social brains, teachers will burn out if the organizational culture of the school is not supportive of their basic social needs.

Let's revisit the aspects of tribal life we explored when looking at the deep history of the brain and apply them to the creation of a tribal school. As a reminder, tribes are characterized by smaller, cohesive groups that stress cooperation and shared decision making. The social and emotional background of the tribe is a sense of shared values, responsibilities, and reward where leadership is based on service to the group. In contrast, modern groups are larger, organized in hierarchical structures, and characterized by unequal division of labor. The social structure is one of individualism, competition, and control via power. As we discussed earlier, the ability to create tribal workarounds within large groups taps into primitive social instincts that allow for more emotional stability and higher levels of performance.

Research shows that, despite enjoying rewarding contact with colleagues, teachers do not usually experience a "psychological sense of community" at their schools (Sarason, 1974). In one study, 60.8% of teachers reported that they rarely or never feel a sense of community (Farber, 1984). Keep in mind that the correlates of teacher burnout include isolation, feeling incapable of eliciting support from others, and being unable to master the social environment (Brouwers et al., 1999; Dussault et al., 1999; Ma & Macmillan, 1999; Rosenholtz, 1989).

The activation and utilization of primitive social instincts are a big part of the success of smaller schools and one of the reasons why small schools demonstrate better academic performance, greater student participation in extracurricular activity, and less teacher burnout (Green-Reese et al., 1991). While some of this may be tied to other variables, it is certainly more difficult to create and sustain a sense of community as we move away from the size of traditional tribes that allowed for greater intimacy, familiarity, and personal interactions. Wherever and whenever possible, smaller schools should be considered advantageous for both students and teachers.

Tribal Schools Need Chiefs

Teachers teach because they care. Teaching young people is what they do best. It requires long hours, patience, and care.
—Anonymous

A humanitarian orientation to discipline in the classroom, one we assume to be more similar to tribal organization, delegates authority to students, encourages independent decision making, and provides an abundance of positive attention and praise. This form of discipline has been found to correlate with less teacher stress and a greater sense of personal accomplishment in their work (Delaney et al., 1997). This orientation is contrasted with custodial discipline that attempts to control through coercion, punishment, and the use of public embarrassment (Willower et al., 1967; Woolfolk et al., 1990). This same social structure at the school level will have similar positive effects on teacher morale, dedication, and performance.

Administrators can strive to create flexible, collaborative, and inclusive school cultures that harness primitive social instincts, dramatically improving teacher morale and performance (Ma & Macmillan, 1999). School cultures that mimic tribal life through collegiality and collaboration produce greater teacher satisfaction, feelings of involvement, and success (Hargreaves, 1994; Leithwood et al., 1998; Taris et al., 2004).

As a "chief" in the classroom, teachers expect to give. As a member of the faculty, the expectation is to be provided for. Studies indicate that most teachers passively await the support they long for from principals (Brouwers et al., 1999). Research shows that a great deal of burnout is due to the perceived disparity between the energy and effort teachers put into schools and what they get back from the "system." When teachers give significantly more than they get, they have higher levels of emotional exhaustion and difficulties on the job (Taris et al., 2004; van Horn et al., 1999).

Being invited into administrative decision making reduces stress, increases job satisfaction, and reduces role ambiguity (Brissie et al., 1988; Jackson, 1983; Levitov & Wangberg, 1983). Unfortunately, many principals fail to create this sense of fairness and present teachers with a lack of input, unsuccessful administrative processes, and organizational rigidity (Blasé & Roberts, 1994; Ma & Macmillan, 1999). One study showed that 87% of teachers felt administrative meetings were unhelpful in solving their problems (Farber, 1984). Does this sound familiar? Stress and burnout increase when teachers feel that demands are high, yet their ability to make changes to enhance success is low (Karasek, 1979).

Negative Emotions and Conflict

The art of living is more like wrestling than dancing.
—Marcus Aurelius

Success triggers joy, pride, and excitement, while frustrations and failures result in irritability, sadness, and disappointment (Friedman, 1995; Isenbarger & Zembylas, 2006). Teachers who experience more positive emotions related to their work are more resilient, intrinsically motivated, and better able to cope with the complex demands of teaching (Fredrickson, 2001; Sutton & Wheatley, 2003). Despite this, negative emotions are an inevitable consequence of all human relationships. Negative emotions are unavoidable and sometimes even desirable. The problem is not that they exist, but there is the question of what to do with them. Because teachers strive to behave in a professional manner with students, parents, administrators, and colleagues, it is sometimes difficult for teachers to know how to deal with negative feelings. But, as we saw earlier, avoiding negative emotions increases both stress and burnout.

Teachers generally believe that regulating and controlling their emotions makes them more effective teachers and keeps students from being contaminated by their negative feelings (Sutton, 2004). In fact, it is often considered taboo for teachers to express negative emotions at school (Carson et al., 2006; Montgomery & Rupp, 2005). It appears that it is essential for teachers to develop close relationships either within or outside their profession that provide an outlet for the negative emotions that are not shared during working hours. Principals and other administrators also need to explore ways in which negative emotion can be expressed in safe and constructive ways.

Although we usually focus on bullying in children and adolescents, adults also experience bullying, especially in the workplace. While there are no studies on adult bullying in school settings, research shows that 25% of employed adults report workplace bullying (Hoel & Cooper, 2000). Victims report that they are criticized, ostracized, and made to feel that their work is judged unfairly. Projects can be sabotaged, information withheld, and attempts at accomplishing goals thwarted. Given the prevalence of workplace bullying, it would make sense that bullying is occurring among members of the faculty, staff, and administration in schools.

Workplace bullying has been shown to result in less work satisfaction and symptoms of anxiety, depression, and poor physical health, similar to what child and adolescent victims experience. To whatever degree a teacher feels bullied, he or she is all the more likely to be isolated, separated from the group, and unable to use naturally occurring social resources in the service of his or her professional and personal well-being. Table 8.4 summarizes some of the research findings on bullying in the workplace.

As with student bullying, problems among faculty and staff can also be a cry for help. Frustrations and other negative emotions in the classroom may be taken out on other adults. Just as with children and adolescents, some teachers may be easy targets of scapegoating because they stand out in some way, have lower status, or are less able to defend themselves. A teacher who feels like he is failing in his

Table 8.4
Workplace Bullying

Twenty-five percent of people report being bullied in the workplace[1]

Seventy-four percent of bullies were managers and/or supervisors[2]

Sixty-six percent of victims report being bullied for at least a year

Fifty-four percent of victims report that information that they needed to do their jobs was withheld from them[2]

Bullying correlated with poor mental health and low organizational satisfaction[2]

Bullying was associated with negative individual and organizational outcomes[2]

Psychiatric symptoms, PTSD, and psychosomatic problems result from bullying at work[3, 4, 5]

Thirty-eight percent of staff experienced bullying and 42% witnessed the bullying of others[6]

Bullied staff reported lower job satisfaction and greater stress, anxiety, depression, and the intention to leave[6]

Thirty-seven percent of young doctors reported being bullied during the last year[7]

Eighty-four percent of young doctors reported at least one incident of bullying, with black and Asian doctors reporting at much higher rates[7]

Forty-four percent of nurses reported being bullied during the last year[8]

Bullied nurses reported lower job satisfaction, greater anxiety, greater depression, and the propensity to leave their jobs[8]

Bystanders of workplace bullying experience higher levels of stress[9]

Victims of bullying experience unfair judgment of their work or offensive treatment[9]

Victims of bullying tend to use sedatives and sleep-inducing drugs[9]

---

work may scapegoat or sabotage another teacher whom he sees as successful. In fact, most exceptional teachers report being the target of anger, jealousy, and even rage, which increased with their success. Thus, negative faculty interactions, intimidation, and bullying need to be monitored by administration and other faculty and made part of the tribal discussion.

While challenging, implementing a zero-tolerance program for bullying among students is far more straightforward than combating bullying among adults. Yet, if the principal is to truly be the tribal chief, he or she has to watch over and protect teachers as much as students if a positive tribal environment is to be created and maintained. It took us many years to take bullying among students seriously and it may take many more to clearly see the negative effects of workplace bullying on morale, professional performance, and emotional well-being. However, a principal who focuses on and intervenes in problems with teachers sends the message that he or she is watching, cares about their experiences, and takes responsibility for the tribe. This message goes to the heart of primitive social instincts and will support the success of the school.

While successfully teaching students requires that teachers create a tribal classroom, being a successful principal requires being able to build a tribal school. It is not surprising that school cultures that mimic tribal life, with collegiality and collaboration, produce teacher satisfaction and feelings of involvement (Hargreaves, 1994; Leithwood et al., 1998). Just as teachers can create environments where students' social natures are harnessed to their benefit, principals can create positive school cultures to dramatically impact teacher morale. Not only does positive social support decrease emotional exhaustion, cynicism, and negative affect, but it also increases professional efficacy.

We never outgrow needing to be seen, appreciated, and cared for.

Part III
How to Turn Brains On

Chapter 9
How Emotional Attunement Stimulates Learning

Learn from others what to pursue and what to avoid,
and let your teachers be the lives of others.
—Dionysius Cato

My freshman philosophy professor had a mad passion for Greek tragedy. He would rise from his seat with a majestic wave of his arm and say things like, "Through imitation, we get to experience the joys and sufferings of each character. They arouse our passions, fuel our desires, and make us face our worst nightmares. We leave the theater utterly exhausted having been broken like fools, victorious with our heroes, and awed by the gods."

Like Aristotle, when he spoke of imitation, my professor was not thinking about mimicking the words and actions of others, but *living through* the characters of a play. He believed drama, especially tragedy, provided a powerful means of vicarious learning through emotional identification with others. This is not mere speculation: It has been found that reading about a character's thoughts triggers brain regions in children that are recruited for thinking about their own thoughts (Saxe et al., 2009). For learning to be successful, it had to lead to catharsis—a self-purification through emotion—that forges character through moral insight and personal growth. It follows that the most notable characters would be those struggling with situations and emotions that embody central human experiences.

Like Greek theatergoers, children are constantly listening, watching, and resonating to the attitudes, beliefs, and weaknesses of those around them. The neurobiological mechanisms that make imitation and attunement possible have been shaped through thousands of generations of social evolution. They now have a broad bandwidth carrying a vast amount of information about everyone around us. Much of the learning that takes place through imitation and attunement occurs via automatic and lightning-fast activation within implicit social brain networks. The discovery of the underlying neurobiological mechanisms of these networks and the implications for classroom education are beginning to emerge. What we learn will be especially important for students who come to class with negative experiences and insecure attachments.

The Discovery of Mirror Neurons

Monkey see, monkey do.

—Anonymous

Until recently, the neurobiological mechanisms for reflexive imitation remained a mystery. The first clue was accidentally discovered 20 years ago in a research lab in Parma. Neurons in the cerebral cortex of primates were discovered to fire both when observing a researcher engage in a specific behavior and when the primate is engaged in the identical behavior (di Pellegrino et al., 1992; Gallese, 2001; Gallese et al., 1996; Gallese & Goldman, 1998; Jeannerod et al., 1995; Rizzolatti et al., 1999). These neurons were found to be so finely tuned that they fired only when a specific object was grasped by particular fingers in a certain way. Actions such as picking up a banana with the right hand at a certain angle, peeling it with the thumb and forefinger, or bringing it to the mouth, were found to activate specific neurons (Rizzolatti & Arbib, 1998).

The activity of these neurons is all the more interesting because they don't fire in response to the hand or the banana, or even to the two presented together. They only fire when the hand is acting on the banana in a specific manner toward a particular goal. Although these cells came to be named *mirror neurons*, their role goes far beyond imitation. They are also involved in the planning and execution of actions in time and space as well as predicting the behavior of others—two essential abilities for survival. The most powerful implication of these neurobiological findings for education is that we evolved to learn from important others as we observed their activities. This learning is stored in networks containing nonverbal and largely unconscious procedural memories that convert vast amounts of sensory, motor, and somatic information into complex behaviors.

It is likely that mirror systems evolved as a way for social and skill-based behaviors to be automatically transferred from one animal to another across the social synapse. When one primate watches another performing an action, such as breaking the hard shell of a nut between two rocks, the motor circuits in the observer's brain needed to perform the same action are activated. The brain automatically connects these behaviors with the attainment of a goal, serving to motivate and reinforce the behavioral sequence leading to it. In this way, our brains actually practice doing what we are watching others do and we become motivated to imitate in order to attain the same reward. Thus, mirror neurons link visual and motor programs, turning observation into rehearsal. This is how a new skill learned by a member of a primate troop will quickly spread throughout the troop.

Since the discovery of mirror neurons in monkeys, imaging studies have demonstrated that analogous areas in the human brain are activated by observing, executing, and imagining hand actions (Bonda et al., 1994; Buccino et al., 2004; Decety & Chaminade, 2003a, 2003b; Nishitani & Hari, 2000). The overall pattern of brain activation depends on the task, whether it is observed, performed, or imagined, or if it involves emotion (Fadiga et al., 1995; Grafton et al., 1996; Ohnishi et al., 2004; Rizzolatti et al., 1996). For example, when humans observe hand movements, subcortical motor areas involved in learning new motor behaviors such as the basal ganglia and cerebellum become activated. But when asked to imagine performing the same movements, activation patterns shift to the frontal and parietal lobes that guide behavior (Decety & Chaminade, 2003a). Thus, there is little doubt that this elegant and sophisticated system for learning through the linking of minds and bodies has been conserved and expanded through primate and human evolution.

Mirror Neurons: Where Are They and What Do They Do?

There are two ways of spreading light: to be a candle or the mirror that reflects it.

—Edith Wharton

Mirror neurons lie at the crossroads of sensory, motor, somatic, and executive networks, allowing them to interweave inner and outer experiences with goal-directed behaviors (Iacoboni et al., 2001). Multiple maps of our bodies, the space around us, and the actions and reactions of others come together to allow us to navigate our physical and social environments. These networks serve as hubs of implicit and procedural memory that automatically guide our behavior based on past learning. For example, these systems allow us to sit down at a computer and record our thoughts without having to consciously remember how to type.

Thus far, mirror neurons have been discovered in the frontal and parietal lobes. The frontal lobes, especially in the left hemisphere, ground us in time through action plans and means-ends (causal) relationships. The parietal lobes, especially in the right hemisphere, construct a three-dimensional internal space where our real and imagined actions take place. Since our actions contain both purpose and context, human experience emerges from within the interwoven matrix of "space-time" constructed by the joint contributions of these two executive networks. Many of the mirror neurons found thus far in monkeys focus on actions of the mouth and hands, suggesting that their original purpose may have involved getting food to the mouth and eating. It appears that these same systems were likely conserved and utilized in the evolution of gestures, sound communication, and language. Table 9.1 lists the locations and functions of the mirror neuron systems that have been discovered thus far.

Table 9.1
Locations and Functions of Mirror Neurons

Frontal Lobe, Specifically the Inferior Frontal Gyrus

Dorsal: motor actions of the hand[1]

Ventral: ingestive (85%), chewing/sucking; communicative (15%), lip movements/licking

Posterior: orofacial and orolaryngeal movements

Functions:

imitation[2] and gestures[3]

integration of somatic, sensory, and motor systems with planning and motivation

sequencing of motor goals and anticipation of the consequences of actions[4]

action understanding and action monitoring

semantic representation of action

expressive language

Parietal Lobe, Specifically the Inferior Parietal Lobe

Functions:

synthesis of visual-spatial organization and somatosensory information

pragmatic analysis of objects[5]

linking objects, actions, and goals[6]

global representation of action patterns of motor behavior and limb position[7]

Basic Imitation

We are what we repeatedly do.

—Aristotle

Within hours of birth, newborns begin to imitate the faces of the adults around them. When adults open their mouths, stick out their tongues, or make happy or sad faces, babies reflexively imitate their actions (Field et al., 1982; Meltzoff & Moore, 1992). These imitative behaviors jumpstart motor programs and link us to the minds of others (Rizzolatti et al., 1999). The seemingly simple act of imitating the lip movements of another person involves the activation of many neural networks that progress around our cortex from the occipital lobes (vision), to the superior temporal sulcus (specialized perception of faces), to the inferior parietal lobe (three-dimensional spatial representation), to the primary motor cortex (initiation of the physical movement) in steps lasting 30–80 milliseconds each (Nishitani & Hari, 2002; Nishitani et al., 2005).

All of these steps along the way to "simple" imitation don't even include subcortical processes contributing to the somatic, emotional, and motivational components of perception (Carr et al., 2003; Cheng et al., 2007; de Vignemont & Singer, 2006). By 18 months, children advance beyond imitation to where they can understand the goal of an action without seeing it completed. This ability implies that frontal, parietal, and mirror systems are making predictions about the future based on current information (Leslie et al., 2004; Meltzoff, 1995). Thus, simple imitation is not so simple after all.

Reflexively looking up when we see others doing it, yawning in response to the yawns of others, and unconsciously crossing our arms when the person we are talking to does the same are all examples of imitation that continue throughout life (Platek et al., 2003). Why has evolution selected the automatic imitation of facial expressions, gestures, and actions? The most likely explanation is that imitation is central to learning, interpersonal attunement, and group coordination. It links us across the social synapse, allowing for the creation of larger organisms like couples, families, and tribes. "Child's play," once thought to be unrelated to brain development, is now understood to be essential in the development of these procedural learning networks.

From Imitation to Gestures and Language

Originality is nothing but judicious imitation.
—Voltaire

As the size of primate groups expanded, so did the size of the neocortex and the capacity for increasingly complex and abstract forms of social communication (Dunbar, 1992). Given their functions and locations related to obtaining and ingesting food, mirror systems were likely later recruited for the development of facial gestures and verbal communication (Rizzolatti et al., 1996; Wolf et al., 2001). The fact that mirror neurons are found in Broca's area (related to speech and language) highlights their involvement in the recognition and expression of phonetic gestures and the actual mechanics of spoken language (Gallese et al., 1996; Liberman & Mattingly, 1985; Petitto et al., 2000; Rizzolatti & Arbib, 1998). Some have hypothesized that mirror neurons were vital to the evolution of language by connecting individuals through grasping, sharing, and using objects together. This evolved into hand gestures, and then into the symbolic code of language (Arbib, 2002). Even the use of the word "grasp" meaning "to understand" may reflect the action-based origin of abstract thought and the primitive linkage between the somatic and the semantic.

Given that mirror neurons can trigger chains of logically connected neurons, any single action can come to represent a chain of actions connected to a goal. In this way, a gesture can become a "prefix" for a set of movements and intentions that can evolve into a symbol for communication (Rizzolatti & Arbib, 1998). In a chimpanzee, this prefix might be a scream that mimics the reaction to seeing a snake, signaling other members of the troop to scurry up a tree. For the troop, the gesture comes to represent both the danger and the required action. Millions of years may have shaped this gesture into a vocalization, and then an imitation of the snake's hissing sound, and finally, just the use of the word "snake."

Fast-forward to another evolutionary epoch. A human teenager spots a friend on a passing escalator. She can hold her hand to her head, extending fingers to her mouth and ear to let him know that she wants him to call her. If she shakes her hand rapidly with emphasis and widens her eyes, she also lets him know that she wants this to happen, *Oh my God! Really, really soon!* Thus, the gesture of an action (talking on the phone) becomes a prefix of a set of actions and an intended outcome. If you pay close attention to people's gestures while they are talking, it becomes clear that gestures continue to be a vital part of the organization and expression of our thoughts and desires.

There is considerable neurobiological evidence in humans that our gestures and words are linked. The observation of hand movements, even in imagination, results in the activation of Broca's area, as does the attempt to use a paralyzed hand (Bonda et al., 1994; Chollet et al., 1991; Parsons et al., 1995). This may explain why it is easier to follow speech when we can see the speaker's lips and also why lip reading is even possible (McGurk & MacDonald, 1976). In the other direction, verbal expressions related to physical actions activate motor areas that are linked to what is being described (Nyberg et al., 2001). For example, listening to speech activates our tongue muscles, aiding us in learning to speak and understanding what we are listening to (Fadiga et al., 2002).

Our ubiquitous use of physical metaphors to describe our inner experiences betrays the sensory-motor core of our emotional experience and abstract thought. We continually use and easily understand verbal expressions like she's *devastatingly* beautiful; he's *strikingly* handsome; she'll *knock you off* your feet; he *bowled* me *over*; she's a *bombshell*; or he *blew me away* without any trouble (Johnson, 1987). It is our shared visceral and physical experiences that make these metaphors meaningful to others. Neuroscience has also shown us that human reason is not derived from abstract logic but emerges from somatic and emotional experiences within our social and physical environments (Damasio, 1994; Greenspan & Shanker, 2004; Immordino-Yang & Damasio, 2007; Lakoff, 1990). All of these scientific findings help us to understand why teachers who stimulate all facets of their students' minds, brains, and bodies are often so successful.

Emotional Attunement and Contagion

A sense of security is something your children catch from you.
—Anonymous

Over the course of the brain's deep history, the functions of mirror neurons expanded to serve the demands of increasingly complex social interactions. Connecting neural networks dedicated to imitation and mirroring with those responsible for social and emotional processing paved the way for interpersonal attunement and the eventual emergence of empathy (Rizzolatti & Arbib, 1998; Rizzolatti et al., 1999). The linkage of mirror systems to the structures of the basal forebrain (insula, anterior cingulate, ompfc, and amygdala) allows us to map what we see others experience onto our own nervous systems (Leslie et al., 2004). In this way, those around us are able to "touch" us through our bodies and emotions (Wild et al., 2001). While our motor networks practice what we see being done by others, our emotional networks resonate with what we see is being felt by others. This emotional resonance then becomes the core of empathy.

When we look at another's face, muscles in our own face become activated in imitation of the perceived expressions (Lundqvist & Dimberg, 1995). These muscles send signals to our internal organs to stimulate physical states similar to those being experienced by those we are seeing. Seeing a child cry makes us reflexively frown, tilt our heads, say "aawwhhhh," and feel sad with them. Watching a defeated athlete walk slowly off the field not only leads us to feel sad, but it may also trigger memories of personal defeat and loss. In these and countless other ways, mirror neurons, and the neural systems they connect, bridge the gap between sender and receiver, enhancing emotional attunement and sympathetic understanding (Wolf et al., 2001). Individuals with Asperger's Syndrome and autism lack these abilities, creating severe social and emotional handicaps. See Table 9.2 for a list of the structures believed to be linked by mirror neurons and the functions these connections allow us to perform.

Mothers rely on mirror systems to stay emotionally attuned to their children. When mothers are asked to sing to their infants, attuned mothers will sing less playfully to distressed children, while less attuned mothers will not adjust to their children's emotional states (Milligan et al., 2003). Mother–child emotional resonance correlates with the child's later functioning, including spending more time in social engagement, better emotional regulation, engaging in

---

Table 9.2
Mirror Neurons Link Multiple Brain Regions and Neural Networks

Motor Components

Premotor cortex: motor representation of motor actions

Motor cortex: generation of action—motor sequences

Cerebellum and basal ganglia

Sensory Components

Superior temporal sulcus: facial expressions[1]

Somatosensory cortex: integrating the sensory, visceral, and motor aspects of experience

Occipital lobe: fusiform face area (FFA) face recognition[2]

Emotional/Motivational Components

Amygdala: fear/emotion, valence/salience

Insula: disgust,[3] somatic-visceral representation

Anterior cingulate: physical pain,[4] social exclusion[5]

---

more symbolic play, higher verbal IQ, and an increased ability to comment on his or her feelings and inner experience (Feldman et al., 1997; Feldman et al., 1999; Penman et al., 1983).

Emotional attunement also has a downside; it makes us susceptible to being "infected" by the feelings of others. Fears, anxieties, and phobias can all be passed from one person to another, especially from parents and other adults to children, via facial expressions and bodily postures as well as words, deeds, and beliefs (Hornik et al., 1987; Mineka & Cook, 1993; Platek et al., 2003; Walden & Ogan, 1988). Unfortunately, this also occurs in the classroom where even a teacher's personal biases and unconscious prejudices can have a powerful impact on students' academic performance and emotional well-being. A teacher's stress, fatigue, and anger will also resonate within her students via these same mirror systems. Parents are often surprised by how much their children are aware of their negative experiences because they have never been verbally shared. This is because they are unaware of how much they are sharing without words via these powerful and primitive resonance systems.

Luckily for us, the opposite is also true. There are people who display courage in the face of danger, behave in life-affirming ways, and inspire us to go beyond our assumed limits. Think of the young man standing in front of the advancing tanks in Tiananmen Square, Rosa Parks refusing to surrender her seat on a bus, or Winston Churchill's speeches during the bombing of London. Our bodies attune to their actions and words, sending "chills up our spines" or "warming our hearts," making us reconsider our acceptance of the status quo or fight on in the face of fear and exhaustion. This reaction to the inspirational behavior of others is another aspect of emotional contagion that serves group coherence and survival.

The discovery of mirror neurons may prove to be a milestone in the exploration of the social brain. They provide us with a brain-based mechanism for what we already know to be true—that brains are linked across the social synapse into dyads, families, and tribes. One of the many ways in which we impact the brains of others is by the expectations we have of their abilities. Our expectancies often unwittingly affect others via our conscious beliefs, behaviors, assumptions, and predictions. Optimism, encouragement, and giving someone the benefit of the doubt have been shown to positively impact performance. Just as significantly, negative biases, prejudices, and disapproval can impede learning and impair performance.

The interpersonal power of expectations is especially important when we are turned to for assistance and guidance. Research has shown that teachers can positively influence the learning, health, and well-being of their students by having positive and optimistic views of their abilities and potential. Every educator can learn to harness the power of positive expectancies in the service of maximizing their students' ability to learn. Just as a mother can make a boo-boo feel better by kissing it, so, too, can a teacher shape students' learning with compassionate actions, positive attitudes, and kind words.

Expectancy Effects in Medical Practice

Cure sometimes, treat often, comfort always.
                                        —Hippocrates

Mirror neurons allow us to both understand and influence each other's emotional and bodily states in profound ways. They also play a role in what is called the placebo effect. The term placebo, Latin for "I shall please," reflects the idea that responding to an inactive treatment results from the patient's desire to live up to the doctor's expectations. The placebo effect is the impact of a positive expectation of a cure based on what the doctor leads the patient to believe. The definition of the placebo effect has more recently been expanded to include the effects of sugar pills and other "nonactive" treatments in contrast to active chemical compounds or interventions. Because expectancy effects involve the influence of the mind on the brain and body, they are also modulated by cultural beliefs. For example, ill Chinese Americans born during inauspicious years have significantly shorter life spans; an effect that is proportional to how strongly they hold to traditional cultural beliefs (Phillips et al., 1993).

Drugs become less effective the longer they are in use, as doubts about the drug are made public. As a result, the placebo effect in medical research is always greatest when the drug is initially introduced onto the market (Shapiro, 1960). Doctors who show confidence and enthusiasm versus skepticism and doubts regarding the efficacy of a drug also inspire their patients to take the treatment for a longer time (Fisher et al., 1964). Until modern times, medicine men and women, shamans, and witchdoctors have understood and utilized this phenomenon in their roles as tribal healers (Frank, 1963). In contrast, placebo effects are seen as a nuisance in Western science, while the patients benefiting from them are seen as weak-minded, impressionable, or "fakers." Moerman and Jonas (2002) suggest renaming the placebo effect as "the meaning response," reflective of the fact that the impact of treatment is mediated via the meaning assigned to it by the doctor and patient.

Modern technological medicine has led to a decline in the use of the placebo effect as the role of the doctor has shifted from healer to technician. This is especially ironic given that placebo-control groups are a staple of the research upon which doctors' clinical decision making is supposedly based. The work of successful teachers has repeatedly demonstrated that the same expectancy effects significantly impact their students' expectations of themselves as learners. Perhaps when we get to the point where we are better able to specify and measure the neuroanatomical and biochemical mechanisms of positive human interactions, the human factors will gain more respect in the fields of education and medicine.

Expectancy Effects in the Classroom

Knowledge is learning something every day.
Wisdom is letting go of something every day.
                                                    —Anonymous

Teachers, like doctors, are human beings first and objective professionals second. Despite our training and conscious intentions, prejudices, distortions, and states of mind all influence how we relate to others, utilize training, and perform our jobs. Research has shown that despite a conscious desire to be free of bias, our brains unconsciously distort information in countless ways. The unfortunate fact is that teachers react differently to students if they are attractive or unattractive, male or female, tall or short, black or white, fat or skinny. These reactions aren't character flaws but simply the way our brains operate. Character does come into play in the process of recognizing these biases and becoming actively committed to changing them.

Research has shown that middle-class teachers have lower academic expectations for children from lower-income families. Mexican students with lighter skin are often seen as higher achievers than those with darker skin (Jacobson, 1966). When teachers score exams of allegedly brighter children, their responses are evaluated as having a higher intellectual quality than the same work thought to have been done by a "dull" child (Cahen, 1966). Although many biases are mediated by culture, the fact that bias exists is a consequence of having a brain that has evolved to react in a stereotyped manner in order to make quicker decisions based on minimal information. Again, this is not a character flaw, it is just the way our brains have evolved to process information.

Both research and classroom experience demonstrate that teacher expectation is an active agent in student achievement. In addition to emotional resonance and attunement with each student, expectations are also transmitted via social comparison and students' perceptions of teacher behaviors toward achievers (Brattesani & Weinstein, 1980; Weinstein et al., 1982; Weinstein & Middlestadt, 1979). Student perceive teachers giving low achievers more direction, negative feedback, and rules to follow. High achievers, on the other hand, are seen as receiving more opportunities and choice of tasks. These teacher behaviors communicate the implicit judgments of expectations of student achievement, thereby influencing the motivation and self-image of all the students in the class (Braun, 1976; Brophy, 1982; Brophy & Good, 1974; Good, 1980).

In the Pygmalion study, Robert Rosenthal and his colleagues administered traditional IQ tests to students under the guise of the "Harvard Test of Inflected Acquisition." The experimenters suggested to the teachers that this test would indicate which students would blossom in the upcoming year and which would fall behind. Twenty percent of the students were randomly selected as the "bloomers" and this list was distributed to teachers. The results of the study found that after 8 months the randomly chosen bloomers showed greater gains in total IQ and reasoning as compared to the control group. In addition to gains in the IQ measure, these students were also rated as more intellectually curious, better adjusted, happier, and less needy of approval than the students in the control group.

While the study generated a flood of justifiable criticism based on the use of IQ as one of the dependent variables (Jensen, 1969; Thorndike, 1968), it has been successfully replicated using measures of student–teacher interactions and achievement scores supporting Rosenthal's basic hypothesis of the social and emotional effects of positive teacher expectancy (Baker & Crist, 1971). These effects exist because teachers and students are mammals, primates, and human beings with mirror neurons and social brains.

The Neurobiology of the Placebo Effect

They can because they think they can.

—Virgil

Expectancy/placebo effects are examples of the top-down (cortical) modulation of mood, emotion, neurochemistry, and immune activity (Beauregard, 2007; Ochsner et al., 2004). The placebo and teacher expectancy effects rely on the ability of the prefrontal cortex to associate positive social experiences with good feelings and an optimistic state of mind. As we have already seen, the neural circuitry that organizes our emotional experiences connects to the networks that control our somatic and physical selves. In other words, the infrastructure of our conscious processing is interwoven with the circuitry that organizes our physical behaviors and experiences.

Based on their associated evolutionary history, social and emotional pain are mediated by the same neural systems that regulate physical pain. Key neurochemicals in pain modulation are the beta-endorphins, also called endogenous (internally generated) opioids. These are the chemicals that result in a "runner's high" and provide us with a buffer against physical pain when we are injured or in life-threatening situations. One theory of the expectancy/placebo effect is that support and optimism trigger the endorphins that make us feel (and actually become) physically and psychologically better.

A study by Wager and colleagues (2004) provided evidence for this hypothesis with findings of placebo-induced decreases in anticipatory responses in the amygdala and temporal poles (Ochsner et al., 2004; Petrovic et al., 2005; Phelps et al., 2001; Wager et al., 2003). Other brain regions involved in both the expectancy and placebo effects are the anterior cingulate, insula cortex, and thalamus, all rich in μ-opioid receptors that are stimulated by endorphins. The activation of these μ-opioid receptors has been linked to the downregulation of pain, decreased stress responses, and fewer stress hormones. The experimental administration of opioids to subjects during brain scans is associated with decreased activity in brain areas that process pain, while administering an opioid-blocking chemical (naloxone) decreases the effects of placebo analgesia (Levine et al., 1978; Wager et al., 2004). Behaviorally, endorphin activation assists in the adaptation and response to novel and emotionally salient stimuli, which helps us to stay calm and focused in the face of stress (Benedetti et al., 2005).

Because the expectancy effect and opioid analgesia share a common neural pathway, we are capable of opioid self-administration through positive thinking; we also stimulate opioid production in others through providing supportive and caring actions and expressions (Pariente et al., 2005). This is the biological foundation for the well-worn phrase "students may not remember what you said, but they will remember how you made them feel."

Like soothing touch, a soothing facial expression or a kind word communicated in an attuned emotional state has a positive effect on our internal biochemistry. Some evidence for this has been found when arousal (measured by skin conductance) was monitored simultaneously in clients and therapists during sessions. During states of matched arousal, there were significantly more positive social and emotional interactions than when they were out of sync (Marci et al., 2007). Why wouldn't this same process occur in the classroom? After all, therapy is simply a one-on-one teaching relationship focused on personal growth.

In addition to the opioid system, the expectancy effect likely activates the dopamine and serotonin systems, both of which are involved in reinforcing learning and prosocial behavior. These reward systems are triggered by loving touch, caring looks, and the anticipation of positive connections and feelings (Esch & Stefano, 2005; Fricchione & Stefano, 2005). This is the reason why holding someone's hand when we are scared makes us feel less afraid. And the better we feel about the relationship, the greater the soothing effect (Coan et al., 2006). Given that fear activation inhibits neuroplasticity and learning, a comforting relationship with a teacher may be exactly what an anxious child needs to open his or her brain to learning.

From Expectancy to Academic Self-Concept

When we are tired, we are attacked
by ideas we conquered long ago.

—Nietzsche

A student's self-concept as a learner is shaped by experience and is stored in both implicit and explicit systems of memory. Students construct their academic self-concept based on how they believe their parents, teachers, and peers appraise their academic ability (Harter, 1990; Skaalvik, 1997a; Sullivan, 1947). Someone with a history of academic success may see a failing grade or teacher negativity as an aberration and shrug it off, while someone with a history of failure would experience it as an affirmation of inadequacy. Students tend to work up or down to the level of perceived expectation and come to see their academic abilities as their teachers see them (Bong & Skaalvik, 2003; Bressoux et al. , 2006; Trouilloud et al., 2006). Perceived competence has been found to be a central element of self-concept (Shavelson and Bolus, 1982; Wigfield et al., 1997).

A teacher's unspoken beliefs about students, a class, and their own career will get communicated across the social synapse and influence learning outcomes. In the process, teacher expectations and emotions become woven into the fabric of students' academic self-concept and their broader sense of self (Trouilloud et al., 2002). A negative academic self-concept has been correlated with a self-defeating attitude, performance avoidance, anxiety, and a lack of self-esteem (Skaalvik & Skaalvik, 2000). See Table 9.3 for the correlates of academic self-concept.

Unfortunately, the students most likely to receive negative teacher expectancy are those at the greatest risk for academic failure. Students

---

Table 9.3
The Correlates of Positive Academic Self-Concept

Academic achievement[1]
Intrinsic motivation[2]
Internal locus of control[3]
Engagement and persistence[4]
Students' effort ratings[5]
Persistence after failure[6]
Help-seeking behavior[7]
Course selection[8]
Goal setting and mastery goal orientation[9]

---

with poor prior academic achievement, low self-concept, African American ancestry, and lower socioeconomic background have all been shown to be more vulnerable to the effects of teacher expectations (Brattesani et al., 1984; Jussim et al., 1996; Madon et al., 1997; McKown & Weinstein, 2002). To make matters worse, these same students are more likely to be in classrooms that test teacher competence, morale, and emotional well-being due to larger numbers of students and minimal resources (Finn, 1972; Jussim et al., 1998). These are precisely the students who most need and benefit from positive emotions and expectations from their teachers. Think back to Marva Collins who told students they were brilliant and refused to let them fail. Mirror neurons that allow for emotional attunement and learning through social imitation have as much power for good as for harm.

Buffering Students From Our Biases

Despite our best intentions, we all have unconscious beliefs that guide our behaviors, emotions, and thoughts. We have biased perceptions of the rich and poor, the strange and familiar, the red, black, brown, yellow, and white. So what can we do to minimize our all-too-human limitations? We can increase classroom autonomy by offering choices, encourage independent problem solving, and involve students in decision making. All of these actions promote intrinsic motivation, self-determination, and the students' ability to discern the causes of their successes and failures (Deci et al., 1991; Reeve, 2002; Reeve et al., 1999). Classrooms with these attributes have been shown to buffer students from unconscious teacher prejudice and negative expectancies.

Students in more autonomous classrooms, even when labeled with low expectations, are more likely to interpret a teacher's negative expectations as feedback and respond with increased effort (Koestner & Zuckerman, 1994). Those with an authoritarian teaching style may have a greater need for control and find it difficult to establish an autonomous classroom. Those who are least comfortable with student autonomy may be precisely those who need to shift their classroom environments to protect students from conscious and unconscious biases.

Bong and Skaalvik (2003) have recommended several teaching strategies, based on the findings of Schunk and colleagues, that have been shown to enhance students' perceptions of self-efficacy and academic performance. Table 9.4 contains a summary of these findings.

Table 9.4
Enhancing Student Self-Efficacy and Academic Performance

Provide students with proximal rather than distal goals[1]

Combine process goals with progress feedback[2]

Furnish feedback for effort associated with students' progress[3]

Prompt students to self-evaluate[4]

Have peers who have desired attributes to serve as teaching and learning role models[5]

Variations in teacher expectation may be less visible in open classrooms than in traditional classrooms. Open classrooms that facilitate student choice of activity, curriculum, and physical space were found to have less negative and public evaluations when compared to traditional classrooms (Blumenfeld et al., 1979; Horowitz, 1979; Weinstein et al., 1982). Negative feedback in the form of marks or reading grade placement has less of an effect on young children's academic expectations and self-concept (Entwisle & Hayduk, 1978; Stipek, 1977). This finding suggests that expectations are not communicated by grades but are transmitted via social interactions.

Finally, we have to accept the fact that the human brain is an imperfect organ that attempts to make the fastest conclusions based on the least amount of information. The unconscious and automatic impulses that served us well in the simpler environments of our evolutionary past are a huge shortcoming in our pluralistic and complex society. Accepting this reality instead of denying our limitations not only allows us to be open to new learning, but also provides our students with a model of openness, humility, and tolerance. This openness, combined with exposure to differences in others, is the best way to bring our brains out of the primordial forest and into the 21st century.

Chapter 10

Why Exploration Is So Important

The great man is he who does not lose his child's heart.
—Mencius

Over the last half-century, the term "plastic" has become synonymous with both flexibility and strength. Like plastics, our brains walk the line between these two equally important properties. The brain has to be stable enough to learn, remember, and use stored information across multiple situations while remaining flexible enough to store new information while modifying old learning. In other words, brains have to be rigid enough to maintain integrity and flexible enough to be adaptive.

Yeats once likened teaching to lighting a fire and he was more correct than he knew. Neurons are excitable cells that fire in response to being stimulated by other neurons. Neurons that fire together form functional connections that lead to new learning. The term "neural plasticity" refers to the ability of neurons and neural networks to be born, grow, and change the way they relate to one another in response to experience (Buonomano & Merzenich, 1998).

Plenty of evidence suggests that neuronal changes are key to learning. Portions of the cortex involved in sensory and motor functions reorganize in response to changing use during skill learning and after brain injury (Braun et al., 2000; Elbert et al., 1994; Karni et al., 1995). For example, violinists have larger motor areas dedicated to the fingers of the left hand than do nonstring players (Elbert et al., 1995), while Braille readers demonstrate a similar expansion in sensory regions dedicated to touch (Sterr et al., 1998a, 1998b). Even cab drivers show larger hippocampi because they rely so heavily on visual-spatial memory organized and stored in these brain regions (Maguire et al., 2006).

Because of their early maturation, sensorimotor areas were thought to have the earliest sensitive periods and the most permanent neural organization. However, the extensive plasticity discovered in these regions suggests that executive and association areas of the frontal and parietal lobes (characterized by their adaptation to change) should demonstrate even more flexibility (Beatty, 2001; Dalla et al., 2007; Gould et al., 1999; Hodge & Boakye, 2001; Mateer & Kerns, 2000). In fact, research has found a continual increase in white-matter volume in the frontal and temporal lobes well into the fifth decade of life, which enables our brains to pull together information stored in various regions of the brain (Bartzokis et al., 2001).

The activation and organization of the cortex appears capable of continual change in adaptation to changing environmental demands. This means that the brain is capable of greater and faster functional reorganization than previously thought (Polley et al., 1999; Ramachandran et al., 1992). Our ability to learn new skills and information throughout life is clear evidence for ongoing neural plasticity. The fact that grandparents fall in love with their grandchildren shows that our attachment circuits also remain plastic into our senior years. The study of neural plasticity and its speed, degree, and nature are vast new scientific frontiers with profound implications for education, medicine, and many other fields (Classen et al., 1998; Johansson, 2000). Exploration occurs in order to expose us to new challenges that the brain evolved to learn from.

Enhancing Plasticity

Tell me and I forget. Show me and I remember.
Involve me and I understand.

—Chinese proverb

It has been known for decades that enriched, stimulating environments have positive impacts on neural growth and learning. Rats raised in complex and stimulating environments show an array of neuroanatomical changes reflective of increased plasticity and brain growth (see Table 10.1). Enrichment in these animal experiments included the presence of colors, sounds, physical obstacles, and cognitive challenges—in essence, a stimulating classroom environment. Enriching environments enable mammals to build more complex and resilient brains that contain more neurons, more synaptic connections, and longer dendrites. In addition, the physiological and metabolic support systems for neural connections and growth are enhanced. Although the brain is not a muscle, it responds like a muscle by growing when stimulated and shrinking when unstimulated.

Table 10.1
The Impact of Enriched Environments on Experimental Animals

Increases in:

weight and thickness of cortex[1]
weight and thickness of hippocampi[2]
length of neuronal dendrites[3]
synapses among neurons[3]
activity of glial cells[3]
levels of neural growth hormones[4]
levels of neurotransmitters[5]
level of vascular activity[6]
level of metabolism[6]
amount of gene expression[7]
levels of nerve growth factor[8]

The effects of environmental stimulation on brain growth are so robust that they even counteract the effects of malnutrition. Malnourished rats reared in enriched environments have larger brains than less-stimulated, well-fed rats, despite the fact that their body weight is significantly less (Bhide & Bedi, 1982). Although controlled studies of nutritional and environmental deprivation are not possible with humans, some naturally occurring situations offer insights into the power of environmental enrichment. A study of Korean children adopted by families in the United States found that environmental enrichment counteracted the effects of their early malnutrition and deprivation. These children eventually surpassed Korean averages for height and weight, while their IQ scores reached or exceeded averages for the American children they grew up with (Winick et al., 1975).

Placing adult rats in enriched environments has been shown to ameliorate the effects of damage to their nervous systems and genetically based learning deficits (Altman et al., 1968; Kolb & Gibb, 1991; Maccari et al., 1995; Morley-Fletcher et al., 2003; Schrott et al., 1992; Schrott, 1997). In a postmortem study of the brains of older adult humans, a positive relationship was found between the length of dendrites in areas of the brain dedicated to language and the subjects' level of education (Jacobs et al., 1993). When our brains are faced with a challenging environment, they respond by growing more dendrites, synapses, and connections in order to process the additional information. In this way, brains are a physical manifestation of the energy of life.

Intellectual Challenge and Brain Health

Do not go where the path may lead, go instead
where there is no path and leave a trail.
—Ralph Waldo Emerson

A source of information about brain health and neuroplasticity comes from studying older adults. For example, a large minority of older adults appears to be better able to cope with the effects of age, brain injury, and disease than others. In fact, a quarter of older individuals presenting no symptoms of Alzheimer's disease while alive show significant Alzheimer's-related brain pathology upon autopsy (Ince, 2001; Katzman et al., 1989). This means that there was something about their brains that allowed them to function normally despite having the disease. It is believed that the cognitive declines associated with even healthy aging are related to the gradual degeneration of dendrites, neurons, and the biochemical mechanisms that support neural health and plasticity (Jacobs et al., 1997; Morrison & Hof, 2003).

One theory for explaining this unusual finding is called the cognitive reserve hypothesis that posits that the more intellectual challenge we encounter, the more neural structure, greater complexity, and more resilience to the negative effects of brain damage and aging we experience. Put another way, the more neural material you have built throughout life, the more you can afford to lose and still process information in a competent manner (Richards & Deary, 2005; Stern et al., 1992).

People with more cognitive reserve have had a higher-quality education and more complex job challenges than those with lower reserve (Stern et al, 2005; Whalley et al., 2004). One study demonstrated that individuals with more education had a significantly greater amount of plaques and tangles but functioned as well as others with a less advanced disease (Alexander et al., 1997). Some feel that people with high reserves are born that way, which is why they attain higher levels of educational and occupational status. Others feel that we earn our level of cognitive reserve through exposure to environmental stimulation. Support can be found for both perspectives and most likely, both are true for different people. For example, studies have found that expected age-related intellectual decline can be halted or reversed in many older adults by increasing their environmental and social stimulation (Schaie & Willis, 1986). The logical explanation would be that these experiences stimulate biological processes that enhance plasticity, creating more robust, complex, and flexible brains.

Frontal-lobe functions such as verbal fluency, controlled processing, and the abstract thinking demanded by high-complexity occupations appear to contribute most to cognitive reserves (Ardila et al., 2000; Le Carret et al., 2003). These are precisely the challenges that teachers work so hard to present to students in the classroom. Unfortunately, being a teacher or college professor does not protect against cognitive decline, although it probably slows down some of its manifestations (Christensen et al., 1997).

Novelty

> *Learning is, by nature, curiosity.*
>
> —Philo

Curiosity, the urge to explore and the impulse to seek novelty, plays an important role in survival throughout the animal kingdom. The degree of exploration exhibited by each species depends on factors such as the availability of food and the presence or absence of predators (Mettke-Hoffman et al., 2002; Whishaw et al., 2006). As environments change, the instincts and reflexes of animals can be gradually reshaped. Some animals, like squirrels and rabbits, are easily startled and usually run away when approached. However, after many generations of campus life and familiarity with humans, rabbits bask in the sun next to students at the University of Victoria and squirrels in Central Park will share your bench while waiting for a piece of a warm pretzel.

Human animals are generally considered to be exploratory creatures and we are rewarded for our curiosity by the generation of dopamine and endogenous opioids, which are stimulated in the face of something new (Deak et al., 2009; Katz & Gelbart, 1978; Wittman et al., 2008). These human adventures, paralleling gene mutations, guide many of us to think outside the box or go off on an adventure. This drive provides the possibility of new discoveries, expanded territories for our species, and the creation of new ideas, tools, and technologies. The willingness of individuals to search for new sources of food, mates, and habitats provides any group of animals with a distinct survival advantage. Humans have explored and inhabited most of the world, and we have now turned our attention to the depths of the oceans, the moon, and neighboring planets.

Like other animals, each of us varies in our comfort with novelty and our desire to explore the unknown. Some of us like nothing better than to jump out of airplanes or to get lost in a strange country. Others are happy to stay close to home. How we experience novelty depends a lot on temperament and whether it is rewarding or anxiety-provoking for us (Santillan-Doherty et al., 2010; Taghzouti et al., 1986). The answer to this question will determine if you have a brain prepared to learn new things or if you fall into safe, repetitive patterns of thinking and behavior. Not surprisingly, the same underlying biochemistry that modulates exploratory behavior also regulates the brain's ability to learn (Isaacson et al., 1978; Matzel et al., 2006).

Our brains have evolved to be especially attuned to detecting and evaluating the unexpected. While we habituate to the mundane and expected, any novel event triggers an orienting response and a cascade of biochemical and neural activations that heighten attention and enhance memory (Ranganath & Rainer, 2003). Some parts of our novelty-detection system are triggered by sounds, while other parts detect novel objects or new arrangements of familiar objects (Perez-Gonzalez et al., 2005; Pihlajamaki et al., 2003, 2004). One study found that the best-remembered parts of a lecture were extraneous statements, suggesting that the memory system is alerted when a teacher strays from the expected material (Kintsch & Bates, 1977).

Brain-stem and subcortical structures play a leading role in the rapid detection of environmental novelty. The cortex becomes involved a few hundred milliseconds later, first in shifting attention to the new information, then in the cognitive processes involved in comprehending what is being experienced, and finally in memory storage (Berns et al., 1997; Blackford et al., 2010; Montag-Sallaz et al., 1999; Parkin, 1997; Petrides, 2007). The prefrontal cortex, hippocampus, anterior cingulate, and other regions are involved in the detection, processing, and habituation to novel events and material (Knight, 1996; Yamaguchi et al., 2004). These same brain regions are activated when novelty captures our attention as well as when we make a conscious choice to examine new objects or situations (Barcelo et al., 2006). It is important for teachers and parents to know that new learning appears to depend on periods of slow waves and REM sleep in order to be consolidated into long-term memory (Ribeiro et al., 2004).

The instinct to orient to the unfamiliar and the exploratory impulse appear early in life. By 4 months of age, infants begin to prefer unexpected sounds to familiar ones, with a similar shift for visual objects between 7 and 11 months (Colombo & Bundy, 1983; Shinskey & Munakata, 2010). Young rats also demonstrate greater novelty preference and exploratory behavior than adults (Stansfield & Kirstein, 2006). For most children and adolescents, social investigation is preferred to environmental exploration and, as you might have predicted, girls show a greater preference for social investigation than boys with no evidence of habituation (Deak et al., 2009). See Table 10.2 for an overview of the research on the neurobiology of novelty.

Table 10.2
The Neurobiology of Novelty

Reward
Novelty triggers dopamine production in animals[1]
Novel experiences increase life satisfaction[2]
Engagement in spontaneous inquisitive exploration (piglets)[3]

Stress
Novelty triggers a cortisol response (monkeys)[4]
Handled animals had lower stress and more exploration (rats)[5]
Exposure to novelty triggers more grooming behavior (rats)[6]
Reduced fear to subsequent objects and human
    handling (Amazon parrots)[7]

Learning
Novelty leads to dopamine that stimulates hippocampal plasticity (rats)[8]
Novelty stimulates hippocampal LTP (rats)[9]

continued on next page

Table 10.2 continued

Novelty acquisition correlates with hippocampal long-term depression (LTD) (rats)[10]

Novelty enhances hippocampal protein synthesis (rats)[11]

Novelty enhances learning of familiar material presented with it (humans)[12]

Novelty triggers gene expression in a variety of brain regions (rats)[13]

Certain combinations of novel objects and environments trigger enhanced learning (rats)[14]

Novelty triggers long-term memory by modulating the phosphorylation state of CREB in the hippocampus[15]

Enhanced information processing[16]

Novelty triggers ACH release in the cortex and hippocampus[17]

Development
When separated from their parents in infancy, marmosets were less mobile and emitted fewer contact calls[18]

Human Neurobiology
More right hippocampal activation in response to novel stimuli[19]

Novelty activates right limbic regions along with temporal and parietal regions bilaterally[20]

More left hippocampal response to semantic novelty[21]

Right frontal specialization in processing cognitive novelty[22]

Comfort with novelty correlates with greater hippocampal neurogenesis[23]

Some groups of neurons in the hippocampus and amygdala fire for familiar objects and situations while others fire for novel stimuli[24]

Novelty triggers dopamine production, which may enhance memory and slow down age-related memory deficits[25]

Anxiety is the enemy of curiosity, exploration, and new learning. In general, inhibited and anxious children show greater amygdala response, and they tend to grow up to be adolescents and adults who avoid exploration and novelty (Schwartz et al., 2003). Fear of novelty in infant rats has also been found to predict levels of stress hormones and shorter life spans (Cavigelli & McClintock, 2003). Early experience has a large impact on emotional regulation, anxiety, and exploratory behavior. Rats who receive more maternal attention show higher levels of exploration and novelty seeking while maternal deprivation and social isolation result in increased anxiety and a fear of novelty (Champagne & Meaney, 2007; Denenberg & Grota, 1964; Hall et al., 2000). On the other hand, early exposure to novelty decreases defensive reactions to novel situations in adulthood and enhances a number of brain-based processes, including spatial memory, social memory, hippocampal LTP, and increased right hippocampal volume in adulthood (Blanchard et al., 1974; Tang et al., 2006; Tang et al., 2003; Tang & Zou, 2002; Verstynen et al., 2001).

With younger children, a common challenge is to get them to overcome their fear of the new. During adolescence, the challenge is to temper their attraction to risk taking and novelty seeking, tendencies in line with the evolutionary significance of separating from parents, taking on new challenges, and establishing new social ties (Kelley et al., 2004). In both instances, the challenge is to stimulate cortical activation in the face of more primitive instincts to leap before you look.

Anxious and traumatized people often develop what is called neophobia, or the fear of anything new. Staying in the same place and doing routine things to avoid surprises will minimize fear and anxiety. This is a state of mind and body diametrically opposed to exploration and novelty seeking. If the classroom has been a place of consistent failure, shutting down may be a student's only defense against shame and humiliation. It is with these students that teaching and emotional nurturance need to become interwoven. Because little cognitive and intellectual learning can take place when someone is in a state of high anxiety, one of the key factors in successful teaching for such a student will be the reduction of anxiety-based avoidance responses.

Anxious and traumatized students find it difficult to use their imagination, to role play, or to discuss hypothetical situations. This aspect of neophobia makes them appear more concrete and less intelligent.

Anxious students usually need transitional stages of exposure to novelty that allow them to slowly downregulate their anxiety. While throwing some beginners into the deep end of a pool will help them learn to swim, just as many become frightened enough to never want to swim at all. Like all other learning, the brain needs to be in a mild state of arousal to activate neoplasticity. In high states of arousal, fear creates traumatic learning which inhibits the type of exploration and flexible learning we strive to stimulate in the classroom.

Chapter 11

How Play Became Nature's Pedagogy

Study forced on the mind will not abide there. . . .
Train your children in their studies not by compulsion
but by games.

—Plato

Humans are a playful species, as are marsupials, birds, turtles, lizards, and fish (Burghardt, 2005). We choose to play not because we have to but because it's rewarding and fun. For most of us, play conjures up images of children running, jumping, and laughing. But what exactly is play and what relationship does it have to learning?

A stumbling block to grasping the importance of play in Western educational theory is our tradition of idealizing rationality, memorization, and abstract thinking. Most of us were raised with the notion of learning as the "work" of childhood as opposed to a natural state of brain, mind, and body. In fact, the brain's evolution and development are based on the actions and reactions of the body. These physical and somatic experiences turn out to be the infrastructure for our rational and abstract capabilities. Although little formal study has been dedicated to the relationship of play to learning, it appears that play can be utilized as a teaching tool to enhance motivation and learning (Mann, 1996). It appears that learning while playing is rooted in our deep history.

Early evolutionary theorists felt it unnecessary to study play because it appeared to have no role in survival. They now believe that the adaptive function of play must be in proportion to the amount of energy it requires and the number of neurobiological systems that support it (Caro, 1988). It is now thought that play has many important roles in building skills required for adaptation and survival (Byers & Walker, 1995; Pellegrini et al., 2007). Seagulls purposely drop and catch objects in a manner that simulates the skills they need to hunt, while dolphins create rings of bubbles to swim through in order to perfect the accuracy of their swimming (Gamble & Cristol, 2002; McCowan et al., 2000). Many animals, including humans, engage in rough-and-tumble play to test their strength and establish social hierarchies.

Play is thought to have evolved in mammals along with the emergence of maternal behavior, nursing, and social vocalizations, pointing to its importance in forming bonds and sustaining ongoing attachment relationships (MacLean, 1985). From the early months of life, a game of peek-a-boo brings joy to both children and adults by stimulating the biochemistry of attachment, well-being, and reward. Play among males and females serves as a means of rehearsal for later courtship and mating behavior (Pellis, 1993; Pellis & Iwaniuk, 1999). Throughout life, playful actions are experienced as expressions of positive feelings, safety, and togetherness (Hannikainen, 2001). The play that animals engage in is moderated by factors such as the amount of social contact, the availability of food, and their familiarity with the environment. Just like learning, play only occurs in the absence of danger, when food is available, and when the physical and social environments are conducive to well-being.

Within the brain, play behavior is organized within the basal ganglia and cerebellum as well as cortical and subcortical regions dedicated to sensory, motor, and emotional behavior. A game such as Simon Says stimulates all of these brain regions, providing the opportunity to practice and improve inhibitory motor control while building cortical executive networks. Play is reinforced within these neural networks through the activation of dopamine, endorphins, and serotonin. The stimulation of these biochemicals associates play with social connectivity, feelings of well-being, and a sense of accomplishment. The types and amounts of rough-and-tumble play are modulated within each species by neurochemicals such as testosterone and adrenaline and specific aspects of their social structure (Vanderschuren et al., 1997).

With the emergence of language in humans, physical play was reshaped into word games, debate, arguments, and verbal banter. All this verbal play strengthens the organization of mental structures, while sustaining interest and excitement about remembering and learning (Singer & Lythcott, 2002). Although imaginative behavior seems disconnected from physical activity, the two are inextricably interwoven evolutionarily and neurobiologically. We know that imagining behavior helps subsequent performance just as our abstract and imaginative processes are replete with physical metaphors. For example, we "try on" new ideas or "explore" novel solutions, while the use of imagination can certainly be considered a form of mental play.

Freud saw play as the first crucible of self-expression while Bettelheim (1987) felt that children's play helps us learn how they see the world. Play provides learning experiences that result in expanded behavioral repertoires in social animals and expanded abstract abilities in humans (Baldwin & Baldwin, 1974). As children age, we witness that the level of abstraction involved in play grows in sophistication (Elder & Pederson, 1978).

Play and Social Learning

Children's playings are not sports and should be deemed their most serious actions.
—Montaigne

Most male animals engage in play fighting, referred to as rough-and-tumble play (RTP). RTP builds strength, stamina, and the skills needed for hunting and protection (Barber, 1991; Bell et al., 2009). On a group level, RTP enhances group coordination among animals that hunt in packs and serves as a context for learning turn taking, sharing, and developing a sense of fairness (Bekoff, 2001; Pellis & Pellis, 1991). RTP also stimulates all of the actions of fighting in the absence of physical injury, distress, or regret and allows for skill building and social bonding (Boulton & Smith, 1992). The positive emotions generated during RTP inhibit aggression against those whom you are attached to and may need on your side in real-life battles. The exaggerated moves, fakes, and attempts at deception may all be related to predicting, anticipating, and thwarting the behaviors of other players (Smith, 1982; Spinka et al., 2001). Football, rugby, and many other sports are obvious descendants of more primitive survival-based activities.

Tickling is a mock attack on vulnerable parts of the body that tests one's strength and methods of escape in a friendly manner. Like play, tickling is also shared by other species. As hard as it is to believe, rats have been found to emit ultrasonic sounds in anticipation of play, suggesting that they also find play both desirable and rewarding (Knutson et al., 1998). These vocalizations can be increased by tickling an area of the rats' bodies that is a target point for play, like the nape of the neck (Panksepp, 2007b). Because they occur only in response to positive and playful social interactions, rats appear to be laughing when they are enjoying themselves.

Play appears to be necessary for the normal development of social communication and the appropriate use of aggression (van den Berg et al., 1999). Play fighting helps to establish a dominance hierarchy in a controlled manner while modulating aggression (Drea, 1996; Smith et al., 1999). Playful approaches of a subordinate animal to a dominant one serve to maintain friendships while participation in RTP enhances likeability (Pellis, 1993, Smith & Lewis, 1985). Children are usually able to differentiate RTP from real fighting via facial expressions, verbalizations, and inferences about intent (Costabile et al., 1991; Smith & Lewis, 1985). Boys are generally much more aware of the importance of RTP in establishing a dominance hierarchy while girls are much more likely to see it as simple play (Pellegrini, 2003).

I received a lesson in establishing dominance many years ago. I spent a week on a reservation in southern Arizona with some very interesting people, one of whom owned an even more interesting Alaskan albino wolf. After a few days, it became clear that the wolf was not just a big dog—he was stronger, more agile, and more intelligent than any dog I had ever encountered. He understood very complex commands and was able to jump to the top of a six-foot wall and quickly walk along it without a slip. When he became too warm, he could dig down many feet until finding a temperature that suited him. One such den had actually undermined the foundation of his owner's house.

One day, we pulled onto the campus of the University of Arizona in Tucson with the wolf in the back of a pickup truck. When the wolf jumped from the cab, a dog of about the same size ran up to him and they immediately began to sniff each other in all the appropriate places. Within seconds they had darted from the sidewalk into a large grassy area surrounded by hedges. They both took off at full speed and when they got to the hedge, the dog crashed out of control into the bushes while the wolf gracefully sprang over them onto the far wall. The dog, composing itself, shot once again across the courtyard with the wolf in pursuit. In no time, the wolf was on the dog's tail. He subtly tripped the dog, which again went rolling in a cloud of dust. The dog jumped up, shook off the dust, and headed straight for us. It arrived at our feet simultaneously with the wolf, rolled on its back, and bared its neck to the wolf. In under a minute, we had witnessed the establishment of the dominance hierarchy of a new pack. These two could now cooperate and get along clearly, each knowing who was boss.

Play serves many important roles in social learning and the solidification of group structure (Parrott & Gleitman, 1989; Poirier & Smith, 1974). As a fan of sports radio, I listen to endless discussions about the relative merits of players, teams, and how they match up against one another. Common topics include relative strengths, skill sets, and how the athletes' emotional maturity impacts their performances and abilities to play well with others. Because sports are so popular, I have to assume that the interest, intensity, and emotion we invest in them is somehow connected with our deep history.

It certainly appears that athletes and sports fans are engaging in the same interpersonal and abstract processes involved in organizing hunting or warrior parties. Bats and balls have replaced spears and swords, and man-made rules are substituted for the variables encountered in nature or on the battlefield. But the same mental and social skills required for survival during most of our evolutionary history are all employed in sports. Perhaps this is why guys who play ball on the weekends are called weekend warriors and why teams are said to battle, fight it out, and clash with one another.

Our natural interest in play can also serve as a platform for acquiring new skills. I first learned how to calculate averages and percentages by figuring out baseball statistics in elementary school, making my interest in sports a motivational tool for skills in other areas of learning. I am also able to recognize the thousands of faces I saw on baseball cards half a century ago and even remember a lot of the players' names. Table 11.1 summarizes some of the research findings from a variety of studies on learning, play, and the brain.

Table 11.1
Learning, Play, and the Brain

The amount of play is regulated by endorphins, dopamine, and serotonin.[1,2,3,4]

The frequency of play correlates with cerebellum size across species.[5]

Early social isolation results in an increase of play during adolescence.[6]

Social isolation increases play fighting.[7]

Play deprivation brings about a rebound when play is reintroduced.[8]

RTP is regulated by testosterone and adrenaline.[9]

RTP stimulates neuroplasticity in the amygdala, the dorsolateral prefrontal cortex, and in many other areas of the brain.[10]

Play stimulates the growth of the medial portions of the prefrontal cortex.[11]

Social play correlates with prolonged development and proximity.[12]

The amount of play correlates with brain size in rodents, marsupials, and primates.[13]

Species with more postnatal development play more and engage in more complex play.[14]

Adult-on-adult play fighting correlates with larger amygdala and nonvisual cortices.[15]

As we can see from the research, play enhances sensorimotor development, social-emotional skills, abstract thinking, problem solving, and academic achievement (Hofferth & Sandberg, 2001). It also suggests that the dichotomy that exists in our culture between education and play may have little grounding in our evolution or neurobiology (Burghardt, 2005). Whether we call it learning or play, we have a natural drive to engage in some endeavor in a productive and meaningful way that stimulates our brain to be "turned on and tuned in." In the recording studio, on a ballfield, or in the classroom, attaining and maintaining this state of mind is the goal of most teachers in the service of creating lifelong learners. The best way to teach the brain of a student may be to wrap lessons in play.

The Acting and Reacting Brain

Earlier we discussed how the brain came to be a social organ by evolving within a matrix of others. We now take another step back into our deep history to explore an even more fundamental reality, the fact that we live in a three-dimensional world as we move through time. The most basic role of a nervous system is to react to the physical environment in ways that support survival. And although we in the West tend to think of our minds as separate from our brains and bodies, the infrastructure of our brains and our abilities to think are grounded in physical experience. As we gradually unravel the mysteries of brain functioning, we face the challenge of figuring out how the brain has adapted to both physical space and the passing of time. As we do, we see more clearly the fundamental unity of mind, brain, and body.

Mirror neurons reveal an intricate, interdependent relationship between the frontal and parietal cortices and how our brains process the dimensions of time and space. Among other things, the frontal lobes specialize in sequencing cause-and-effect relationships and connecting them to future goals. The parietal lobes organize and interconnect spatial maps of the body and the environment. Together, the frontal and parietal lobes construct our experience of space and time, allowing us to navigate the physical world. In fact, neural circuits that connect and coordinate the frontal and parietal lobes may function together to organize executive functioning in ways that were previously attributed only to the frontal lobes.

The implications for education include a deeper appreciation of the sensorimotor contribution to conceptual and abstract learning. Even when we engage in imaginative processes, we are still relying on images of three-dimensional space, which activate and involve parietal regions. This neurological reality parallels discoveries in modern physics that space and time are inextricably interwoven.

Table 11.2
General Functions of the Prefrontal Cortex

Orbital and Medial Regions

attachment[1]	estimating reward value and magnitude[8]
social cognition[2]	sensitivity to future consequences[9]
thinking about a similar other[3]	achieving goals[10]
self-referential mental activity[4]	stimulus of independent thought[11]
appreciating humor[5]	inhibitory control in emotional
encoding new information[6]	processing[12]
sensory-visceral-motor	decisions based on emotional
integration[7]	information[13]

Dorsal and Lateral Regions

cognitive control[14]	voluntary suppression of sadness[19]
directing attention[15]	learning motor sequences[20]
organizing temporal experience[16]	decisions based on complex information[21]
organizing working memory[17]	thinking about a dissimilar other[22]
organizing episodic memory	the integration of emotion
(right brain)[18]	and cognition[23]

Neural fibers that connect the middle portions of the frontal and parietal lobes serve the integrative function of linking the right and left hemispheres, limbic and cortical structures, as well as anterior and posterior regions of the cortex (Lou et al., 2004). This may give rise to a global workspace or "central representation," allowing for sustained focus, conscious working memory, and self-reflection (Baars, 2002; Cornette et al., 2001; Edin et al., 2007; Sauseng et al., 2005; Taylor, 2001). They also work together to analyze the context and location of specific aspects of the environment and interrupt ongoing behavior in order to direct attention to new targets (Corbetta & Shulman, 2002; Peers et al., 2005).

Research suggests that the parietal lobes participate in the creation of internal representations of physical objects as well as the actions of others (Shmuelof & Zohary, 2006). In other words, they allow us to internalize others by creating representations of them in the three-dimensional spaces of our imaginations. This allows us both to learn from others and to carry the memories of others within us when they are absent. Frontal-parietal networks may be primarily responsible for the construction of the experience of self and others (Lou et al., 2005). These inner "objects," as described by psychotherapists, likely contribute to emotional regulation and a sense of continuity of self through time (Banfield et al., 2004; Tanji & Hoshi, 2001). See Table 11.3 for a summary of what is known about the functions of the parietal lobes.

Table 11.3
Specific Functions of the Parietal Lobes

Hemispheric Function

Left	Right
Verbal manipulation of numbers[1]	Analysis of sound movement[2]
Mathematics[3]	General comparison of amounts[4]
Multiplication[4]	Attention[5]
Motor attention[6]	Own-face recognition[7]

Bilateral Findings

Visual-spatial workspace[5]

Visual-spatial problem solving[5]

Visual motion[8]

Construction of a sensorimotor representation of the internal world in relation to the body[9]

Internal representation of the state of the body[10]

Verbal working memory[11]

continued on next page

Table 11.3 continued

Retrieval from episodic memory[12]

Ordering of info in working memory[13]

Controlling attention to salient events and maintaining attention across time[14]

Preparation for pointing to an object[15]

Grasping[16]

Movement of three-dimensional objects[17]

A sense of "numerosity" defined as nonsymbolic approximations of quantities[18]

Processing of abstract knowledge[19]

Perspective taking[20]

Processing of social information[21]

As we discussed earlier, Western thought is characterized by equating intelligence with abstract thought as opposed to emotional judgment, physical abilities, and introspection. Contrary to popular belief, studies of primate brain evolution suggest that it is the expansion of the parietal and not the frontal lobes that is the benchmark of the transition to the human brain (von Bonin, 1963). Could the fact that we don't generally think of the parietal lobes as a component of the executive brain reflect a cultural bias toward thinking over lived experience?

The emergence of self-awareness was likely built in a stepwise manner during evolution through a series of overlapping "maps," first of the physical environment, then of the self *in* the environment, and later of the self *as* the environment. The emergence of imaginal abilities allows us to create an increasingly sophisticated inner topography grounded in the structure of our physical environments.

The imaginal workspace afforded by the combination of good frontal and parietal functions allows for the creation of an inner reality organized by and grounded in both space and time. Within this inner world we can imagine ourselves, experiment with alternative perspectives and emotions, and rehearse for future actions in the external world (Knight & Grabowecky, 1995). Our ability to be "mindful" relies on learning how to use these frontal-parietal capacities as we build and elaborate the architecture of our mental experiences. Without the ability to reflect on, imagine alternatives to, and sometimes cancel automatic responses, there is little freedom beyond simple reactions to the environment (Schall, 2001).

Navigating Physical and Social Space

It is better to travel well than to arrive.

—Buddha

Our usual focus on teaching conceptual and abstract information makes it easy to discount the role of the body in learning and neuroplasticity. Yet the evolutionary history of all learning is grounded in the navigation of space with a body. This may be why the hippocampus, which serves as a cognitive map of the environment in mammals, is the portal to all explicit learning in humans. It is also why using the large muscles in our legs results in the secretion of neural growth hormones that cross the blood–brain barrier and trigger plasticity and learning. Our muscles have evolved to tell the brain to pay attention and learn while we are moving around.

Knowing where to go and how to get there requires at least two interwoven spatial maps: one for physical environments and another of our bodies. The hippocampus organizes a spatial map of the environment, and this map grows and shrinks based on the navigational demands placed on it. At the same time, the parietal lobes, which evolved from the hippocampus, construct maps of the body and the body in space to allow for goal-directed navigation (Maguire et al., 1998). We witness the development of these neural networks in a child's sensorimotor development through learned behaviors such as walking, throwing a ball, or being able to open a box of cookies.

Another central aspect of living is navigating our many interpersonal relationships. The sensory, motor, and spatial components of our attachment systems become interwoven with our experiences of self, other, and the physical environment. Think for a moment about how we describe our interpersonal emotions—we *fall* in love, *fly* into a rage, or have a hard time *handling* what a loved one has told us. Even the words bonding and attachment evoke an image of the joining together of two separate objects in space. Attachment schema are not abstract concepts; they are stored in systems of procedural memory and are manifest in our musculature, postures, gaits, and interpersonal stances. People can tell us they love us but we also have to feel it in our hearts. We learn to love with our brains and bodies and to store these experiences within our implicit procedural memory.

Procedural Memory

Memory is the mother of all wisdom.

—Aeschylus

Procedural memory is a primitive form of memory we share with all other mammals. It does not involve or require conscious awareness or self-reflection. Procedural memory is a subcategory of implicit memory that involves the storage of sensorimotor, visceral, and emotional experiences that allow us to engage with our physical and social worlds. Physical abilities such as walking down stairs, serving a tennis ball, or brushing your teeth would all be examples of procedural memories. Once we get to the stairs, walk onto the tennis court, or look at ourselves in the bathroom mirror, these behaviors go on automatic pilot and free us to think about other things. In fact, consciously thinking about doing things stored in implicit memory can impair performance. Golfers spend a lifetime perfecting their swing while simultaneously trying to empty their minds.

A basic biological strategy is to approach or avoid the things around us depending on their value to us. We approach what we need, what feels good and what reduces anxiety, while avoiding what is frightening or causes us pain. Our movements by definition are goal-oriented and the neural networks controlling movement, motivation, and goals have evolved in an interwoven fashion (Rizzolatti & Sinigaglia, 2008). As we navigate our worlds, our brains automatically generate myriad options, paths, and potential strategies designed to get us what we need based on a combination of present realities and past experience. In other words, when we encounter something or someone in our environment, our brains activate preexisting procedural memories that allow us to engage with it. These systems create *affordance*, or our ability to engage meaningfully with the objects and people around us. An affordance is neither objective nor subjective; but emerges from the interaction between self and world (Heft, 1989; Kytta, 2002).

A familiar example might be when you are sitting in a café talking with a friend and the waiter sets before you a cup of coffee, sugar, cream, and a spoon. Your implicit procedural memory allows you to use your hands automatically to engage these objects such that you are able to mix your personal blend of ingredients while not missing a word of the conversation. This is a complex goal-directed task that allows you to utilize the environment (affordance) with minimal conscious attention. At the same time, your abilities to use language, read facial expressions, and empathetically attune allow you to establish affordance with your friend.

In his study of how English children interact with natural environments, Moore (1986) discovered that children tend to focus on specific features with which to interact. Some examples were relatively smooth surfaces for *running*, things for *climbing* (trees), places for *hiding* (bushes), slopes for *sliding* down, obstacles for *jumping* over, and objects for *throwing*. This suggests that children naturally generate affordance categories, making connections between objects and what to do with them. It is not coincidental that the salient environmental features related to their play are also those that were historically relevant for survival—to hunt for food and escape from danger.

We can easily expand the idea of procedural learning to attachment relationships. Imagine sitting with a new friend and his 3-year-old son, paying special attention to their many interactions. When you first enter the house, the child holds his father's leg, leans into it, and rolls around the back so as to watch you from a safe vantage point. A little later he presents his finger, which he has pinched in the door of a toy car, for his father to kiss. At another point, he sneaks up from behind with a pillow and hits his father on the head as an introduction to some rough-and-tumble play. Still later, he finishes his juice box and hands it to his father with the words "all done." These interactions demonstrate the boy's ability to successfully use his father for safety, solace, stimulation, and service. These affordances are driven by mutual instinct and emotion, and they are reinforced through decreases in anxiety and increases in positive feelings.

Based on experiences like these, this child will likely enter school with the expectation of similar positive and useful connections with his teacher. He may assume that the teacher will also be a source of safety, solace, stimulation, and service and he will then build on the affordances he has developed at home. In interacting with the teacher, he will learn affordance strategies for the classroom such as raising his hand, sharing with his classmates, and approaching his teacher for comfort.

Thus, when a child has had positive and rewarding experiences with parents and other authority figures, she is more likely to be able to use her teacher as a source of emotional regulation and learning. This ability is reflected in a relaxed body, leaning toward the teacher when something interests her, curiosity, and optimism about being a successful learner. In turn, this state of mind optimizes neural plasticity and learning in the student and promotes enthusiasm in the teacher. The opposite stance would be seen in the anxious or traumatized learner who experiences the teacher as a threat and lacks the skills and affordance patterns to utilize the materials placed in front of her. As we know, many children enter school without many of the affordance skills required to successfully utilize teachers and classrooms. In many instances, affordance needs to be taught before content to establish the possibility of learning.

Why students succeed or fail in school is strongly determined by whether they possess affordance patterns that match the context and climate of the classroom. Culture, language, and the values in their families are parts of this, as are the social and emotional factors necessary for neural plasticity. A child from the Sahara Desert who is flown to the English countryside may have the affordance for a tree as a source of shade rather than as something to climb. This would have to be demonstrated and learned over time. In a similar way, we shouldn't assume that when presented with rows of desks, books, and a smiling face at the front of the room, a student sees and experiences the same thing we would if we were in his seat. While this disconnection is more obvious for a recent immigrant, it is less obvious when the disconnection has an invisible emotional cause. Because a lack of affordance is often tied to neglectful or traumatic attachment experiences, anxiety and fear usually go hand-in-hand with learning difficulties. In these cases, building affordance patterns needs to precede attention to the curriculum.

In our old way of thinking, perception was the emergence into consciousness of what was impinging on our senses. We now know that perception involves the active construction of experience within our brains. Thus, to perceive is to shape the current situation based on past learning. Affordance is the flip side of ergonomics, the study of how usable the tools in our environment are to us. Affordance determines our mind's ability to grasp the tools and opportunities in front of us. Therefore, physical activities, expressive movements, and social interactions as play are all necessary for optimal learning. An elementary schoolteacher with a profound understanding of these principles was Albert Cullum.

Albert Cullum

We are most nearly ourselves when we achieve
the seriousness of the child at play.
　　　　　　　　　　　　　　　　—Heraclitus

Over the course of his long career, Albert Cullum, an actor turned elementary school teacher, wove his loves of theater and teaching into a living classroom experience. As a teacher in a middle-class suburb, he did not face the challenges of poverty or community violence. As he saw it, his enemies were complacency, mediocrity, and a blind acceptance of the status quo. He faced these challenges by making education a sensory, motor, and emotional experience through the skills he learned on the stage. While initially drawn to the classroom to be a star, his goal became to make a star of each of his students.

Early on, Cullum realized that when play becomes the modus operandi of the classroom, disciplinary problems decrease while attention and learning increase. He felt that it was the nature of children to learn through active and imaginative play, which, in turn, stimulated enthusiasm, imagination, and openness to new ideas. He structured all of his learning activities to channel his students' youthful energy toward productive ends. Cullum used the works of Shakespeare and Shaw as vehicles to teach language, history, and human values, while encouraging self-expression and personal transformation.

Cullum's use of plays to teach elementary school was something many of his colleagues believed impossible. In an era characterized by "Dick and Jane," Cullum opted for Romeo and Juliet, Macbeth, and King Lear. He presented his students with highly challenging content while communicating a message of confidence and faith in their intelligence, maturity, and capabilities. Cullum found that when he presented even his youngest students with a worthy challenge they rose to the occasion, bonded more closely with one another, and gained self-confidence. The engagement with the material via performance led to an embodiment of knowledge and made each student a hero by being a cast member of a timeless story.

His classroom was always filled with the kind of noise you hear at a birthday party with children playing, laughing, moving, and touching everything around them. He created a learning environment that activated both explicit and implicit memory systems by blending history, art, music, literature, and math into fun, tactile, and emotionally engaging activities. Mr. Cullum was always in the middle of the fun. Never quite getting over being an actor, he would teach about the geography of Canada and Alaska while wearing a bear costume. His lessons were never dull or passive experiences.

When they weren't "swimming" down the Mississippi River they created out of construction paper that flowed through the classroom, students were taking part in the math Olympics, geography races, or art shows.

Cullum assumed that a sense of safety and belonging were essential elements of successful education. He endeavored to communicate love, compassion, and respect to his students, and he saw these qualities carried into their relationships with one another, in ways that transcended age, race, and status. As the sole African American student in one of his classes stated at a reunion decades later, "I felt as though my classmates loved me. I felt as though my teacher loved me." As an expression of his caring, Cullum established a democratic classroom environment to maximize the sense of investment and pride in being a member of the group.

Into his senior years, Cullum retained the rare ability to see the world through the eyes of a child. As a professor of aspiring teachers at Boston University later in his career, he engaged his students in ways that helped to remind them of the world of children and to rediscover the child within. In order to transform what he described as a "cancer of mediocrity" that he saw undermining his profession, Cullum believed that teacher training should include guided self-development and ever-deepening personal awareness. Much of Cullum's success lay in his ability to give voice to the perspective of children, his sense of accountability for his students' education, and his revolutionary curricula and teaching methods. By becoming fully engaged in the way children learn—through movement, emotions, activities, and play—he felt that teachers could open the floodgates to learning. To see him in action, see the documentary film *A Touch of Greatness*, filmed partly by his friend, director Robert Downey, Sr.

Chapter 12

Why Stories Are Essential for Learning

*If history were taught in the forms of stories it would
never be forgotten.*

—Rudyard Kipling

Through countless generations, humans have gathered to share stories. Whether it be tales of brave ancestors, strategies for a successful hunt, or fun ways to pass the time with friends and family, the stories of a tribe are a repository of shared knowledge and a matrix of culture. Stories connect us to one another, help to shape our identities, and serve to keep our brains integrated and regulated. The human brain co-evolved with storytelling, narrative structure, and the tale of the heroic journey as told in cultures throughout the world. Stories are, in fact, so ubiquitous in human experience that we hardly notice their existence.

Discounted by many educators as unworthy of the classroom, storytime is enjoyed by children but left behind to get on with the business of "serious" learning. Like our primitive social instincts, storytelling has a deep evolutionary history that has been woven into the fabric of our brains, minds, and relationships. The central role of storytelling in contemporary tribes attests to its early origins and central role in memory storage, emotional regulation, and social cohesion. Through the seemingly profound transformations from oral to written to digital-based record keeping, we have never lost interest in stories, especially about each other. Just think of all the energy we invest in gossiping across every new medium of communication.

By allowing for the articulation of personal experience and shared values, stories connect families, tribes, and nations, generate culture, and link us to a group mind. These connections, in turn, support the functioning and well-being of each individual brain. It is very likely that our brains have been able to become as complex as they are precisely because of the power of narratives to guide and organize our thinking. It is as if each of us has an external neural circuit existing in the stories of the group mind that helps us to regulate internal neural functioning.

Stories are a central aspect of personal identity and, in many ways, we become the stories of our experiences and aspirations. Identity has even been defined by philosopher Daniel Dennett (1991) as the "center of narrative gravity" of the stories we tell about ourselves. As children we are told who we are, what is important to us, and what we are capable of. We then tell them to others and eventually to ourselves. The impact of stories on the formation of self-identity makes them powerful tools in the creation and maintenance of the self (Bruner, 1990). These stories become organizing principles that serve to perpetuate both healthy and unhealthy aspects of self-identity. Positive self-narratives aid in emotional security and minimize the need for elaborate psychological defenses (Fonagy et al., 1991), while negative self-narratives perpetuate pessimism, low self-esteem, and decreases in exploration and learning.

Memory and Learning

The mind is everything. What you think you become.
—Buddha

Every culture has stories, myths, and fables born before the written word and passed down through the generations via storytelling and song. The Vedic song poems of ancient India were memorized, sung, and preserved by a class of scholars dedicated to the preservation of ancient wisdom. The accumulation and advancement of knowledge was completely dependent on the compulsion to hear and tell stories and on the brain's ability to remember and repeat them. This is probably the reason why our brains have evolved to possess a limitless storage capacity for stories and songs.

Memory experts use this evolutionary legacy to recall large amounts of unconnected information by placing them in a narrative. They may picture a room and place each of the items they are trying to remember in a different location. For recall, they go back to the visual image of the room and visualize each item where they placed it. This is not superhuman, they have simply learned to use the deep well of contextual and narrative memory we all share.

I am a terrible speller and completely depend on spellcheck. I can, however, spell "Mississippi" and "encyclopedia" because when I was young, Disney cartoons placed the spelling of these words in songs. And I doubt that anyone from my generation can spell "respect" without hearing Aretha Franklin's voice in their heads. It is also true that most of us can hear the first few notes of thousands of songs we learned years ago and almost immediately recognize them and be able to sing along. The words and notes seem to be waiting in our brains even though it may have been decades since we last heard them. These are all contemporary holdovers of the brain's evolutionary past and of our historic dependence on stories and songs.

Another window into our deep history is in the way elders and children relate to stories. It has always been the job of elders to tell stories, passing them on to the younger members of the tribe. Most of us have older relatives who tell the same story again and again as if they have never told us before. As we grow older, we also tend to tell more stories from long ago as the distant past becomes increasingly salient with advancing age.

Now think of who likes to hear the same stories again and again and again in exactly the same way. In fact, they will even correct you if you get a word or fact wrong. If you guessed young children, you are right! They demand that you tell them the same story every night for days, weeks, or months before they are ready to move on to the next one. What we are likely witnessing in these parallel processes is a genetically programmed process in both the older adult and child to transfer the stories, knowledge, and wisdom across the generations. The impulse to repeatedly tell and listen to stories appears to be a lock-and-key mechanism of intergenerational information transfer which fits into the child's impulse to hear them.

Stories and Neural Integration

Anyone who says they have only one life to live must not know how to read a book.

—Anonymous

As the human brain evolved, an increasing number of specialized neural networks emerged to handle the vast amount of information required for complex social interactions, abstract thinking, and imagination. This increasing complexity eventually allowed for the emergence of language, storytelling, and narrative structure. Keeping this ever-growing bureaucracy of neural networks integrated, balanced, and running smoothly became ever more challenging. My suspicion is that over time, language came to organize and integrate brain systems in order to allow for the emergence of even more neural complexity. Through language, individual brains gradually became able to use the minds of others through shared stories to aid in neural integration, emotional regulation, and enhanced executive functioning.

Although stories appear imprecise and unscientific, they serve as powerful organizing tools for neural network integration (Oatley, 1992; Rossi, 1993). A story that is well told, containing conflicts and resolutions and thoughts flavored with emotions, will shape brains and connect people. The structure of any story contains two basic elements: The first is a series of events grounded in the passage of time, and the second is some emotional experience giving the story relevance and meaning. In order to tell a good story, the linear linguistic processing of the left hemisphere must integrate with the emotional, sensorimotor, and visual information centers in the right hemisphere. Thus, a coherent and meaningful narrative provides the executive brain with a template for the oversight and coordination of the functions of the two hemispheres. In fact, the coherence and understandability of the personal narratives we generate are highly related to the security of our attachment relationships, self-esteem, and emotional regulation.

A good indicator of the power of stories is reflected in the faces of the listeners. Have you ever noticed what happens when you transition from talking about facts to telling a story? Eye contact locks in, distractions decrease, and a series of expressions reflect the events and emotions that run through the story. You can see the unfolding drama reflected in the eyes, faces, and bodies of your listeners. Listening to stories is a basic form of learning that goes back long before the invention of reading, writing, or arithmetic; stories contain all of the elements required to stimulate neuroplasticity and learning.

Emotional Regulation

When I approach a child, he inspires in me two sentiments: tenderness for what he is, and respect for what he may become.
—Louis Pasteur

During the first 18 months of life, the brain's right hemisphere experiences a sensitive period of development as the physical and emotional aspects of interpersonal experiences begin to take shape. These early experiences, vital to our future relationships and emotional health, are stored in systems of implicit memory. As the left hemisphere enters its sensitive period during the middle of the second year, spoken language begins to slowly take shape and integrates with the emotional aspects of communication already organized in the right. As the cortical language centers mature, words are slowly joined together to make sentences, which are later used to express increasingly complex ideas.

When a child is 4 to 5 years old, her brain has matured to the point where words and feelings can begin to be linked in meaningful ways. Putting feelings into words and placing them in the context of ongoing experience gradually result in the ability to regulate anxiety and fear through the inhibitory regulation of the amygdala (Hariri et al., 2000; Johnstone et al., 2007; Lieberman et al., 2007). Putting feelings into words and sharing them with others are learned abilities that are modeled on the skills and encouragement of others. Parents who lack these abilities or don't talk to their children about feelings deprive their children of a valuable source of emotional regulation.

Having an articulated personal story helps us remember where we come from, where we are, and where we are going. In other words, our stories ground us both within the present and in the flow of our histories. This blueprint helps us to avoid feeling lost or overwhelmed by the present while reducing the anxiety and stress of uncertainty about the future. Because creating a narrative activates frontal functioning that downregulates amygdala activation, they create a sense of control and reduce our anxiety. In a similar manner, believing you are an efficacious person stimulates frontal activation and soothing biochemistry that actually makes you a more efficacious person (Maier et al., 2006).

Writing about your experiences in diaries and journals supports similar top-down emotional regulation as telling your story to others (Dolcos & McCarthy, 2006). In a large series of studies, James Pennebaker and his colleagues had people journal about emotional issues of personal importance, especially experiences related to close personal relationships. These studies revealed increased well-being, including a reduction in physical symptoms, physician visits, and work absenteeism (Pennebaker, 1997; Pennebaker & Beall, 1986; Pennebaker et al., 1988).

Putting feelings into words results in a cascade of positive physiological, behavioral, and emotional effects, such as boosting immunological health (greater T-helper response, natural killer cell activity, and hepatitis B antibody levels) and lowering heart rate (Christensen et al., 1996; Petrie et al., 1995; Petrie et al., 1998).

Secure Attachment and Integrated Narratives

The best way to know life is to love many things.
—Vincent van Gogh

Narratives begin to be co-constructed in parent–child interactions early in life. This process is continued at school with teachers, peers, and in an ever-broadening array of social situations throughout life. When verbal interactions include references to sensations, feelings, behaviors, and knowledge, they provide a medium through which the child's brain is able to organize and experience the various aspects of its inner and outer experience in an integrated and coherent manner. The set of narratives we call autobiographical memory can enhance self-awareness while increasing our ability to self-soothe and solve problems.

From primitive tribes to modern families, co-constructed narratives are at the core of human-group interactions. Caretakers, teachers, and children weave a complex tapestry of associations as they narrate shared experiences and co-construct their worlds. As mentioned earlier, the repetition of stories also helps children to develop and practice recall abilities and to have their memories influenced and shaped in relationships (Nelson, 1993). This mutual shaping of memory between children and adults can serve both positive and negative ends. Positive outcomes include teaching the importance of accuracy of memory, imparting cultural values, and shaping a child's self-image.

When caretakers are unable to tolerate certain emotions, they will be excluded from family narratives or shaped into distorted but more acceptable forms. The narratives of their children will come to reflect these unconscious and conscious editorial choices. Whatever is excluded from the narrative during childhood will be more difficult to comprehend and cope with in the years to come. At the extreme, a parent can be so overwhelmed by the emotions related to unresolved trauma that his or her narratives become disjointed and incoherent. Parental narratives, both coherent and incoherent, become the blueprint for the organization and integration of their children's neural circuitry (Siegel, 2012a). There also appears to be a causal relationship between the complexity of children's narratives and their attachment security.

Securely attached children generally engage in self-talk during toddlerhood and more spontaneous self-reflective remarks at age 6. They tend to make comments about their thinking process and their ability to remember things about their history (Main et al., 1985). These processes of "mind," which insecurely attached children often lack, reflect the utilization of narratives for metacognition (thinking about thinking) that allows for a higher level of self-reflection. What we are witnessing reflected in their language is the internalization by children of both their parents' self-regulatory mechanisms and the degree of parental neural integration. As you might expect, children who are abused are usually insecurely attached, and less able to metacognize and engage in self-reflection (Beeghly & Cicchetti, 1994; Fonagy et al., 1991).

When an adult's inability to verbalize internal and external experiences leaves the child in silence, the child's capacity to use language to integrate his brain and organize conscious experience is left undeveloped. The only available option for expression may be acting out painful feelings or converting them into physical illnesses, depression, or anxiety. When children experience trauma in the presence of nonhealing adults, the stress of each new developmental challenge is multiplied. On the other hand, language and emotional attunement are central tools in the social-emotional learning process, creating the opportunity for neural integration, plasticity, and academic success.

If a child can learn to articulate her inner experience with the help of someone other than the primary caretaker, she may be able to earn a higher level of integration and security than would be predicted by her parents' social and emotional development. This can come from teachers who attune well to their students and assist them to articulate their feelings. All of this strongly suggests that teachers who can respect children's vulnerability and help them to express their thoughts and feelings in words can increase their ability to express, share, and regulate their anxiety while building positive self-narratives. There is no more important developmental or educational goal.

Expanding Self-Awareness

Meditation is participatory observation.

—Buddha

Like putting feelings into words, looking inward and becoming self-aware have to be learned. In exploring our inner worlds, we come to learn that our minds use language in different ways. In fact, through self-reflection, most of us become aware that we seem to shift among different perspectives, emotional states, and ways in which we talk to ourselves. I am aware of at least three kinds of language that arise during different states of mind: a reflexive social language, internal dialogue, and a language of self-reflection.

Reflexive social language (RSL) is a stream of words that appears to exist in order to maintain social connection. Primarily a function of the left hemisphere, RSL tracks the activities within the interpersonal world and is designed to "grease the social wheels." The verbal reflexes, clichés, and overlearned reactions in social situations of RSL provide a verbal web of connection with those around us. The best example is the obligatory "How are you? Fine, how are you? Fine. See you later." Most of us also experience this level of language whenever we automatically say something positive to avoid conflict, or tell others we are "fine," regardless of what's troubling us. The spontaneous clichés of RSL are as automatic to us as walking and breathing, serving the same purpose in human groups as grooming does in other primates.

In addition to RSL, we are also aware of the conversations that go on inside our heads. This *internal dialogue* is a private language that often departs in content and tone from what we express to others. While reflexive RSL is driven by social cooperation, internal dialogue is experienced as a single voice or a conversation often with a negative emotional tone. Internal language may have evolved on a separate track from social language to allow for social control and private thought programmed by early experiences. This automatic and sometimes compulsive flow of thoughts is most often driven by fear, doubt, and shame. Did I lock the back door? I'm so stupid! Do I look fat in these pants?

This inner voice is likely driven by the right hemisphere because it is both self-focused and usually negative in tone. Unfortunately, it is also a key way that right-hemisphere processing contributes to conscious awareness. It is the inner voice of our shadow that undermines our confidence and is the critical voice that gossips about others. RSL and internal dialogue both serve to maintain preexisting attitudes, behaviors, and feelings. RSL is an expression of how we have been taught to interact with other people while our internal dialogue reflects how we have come to feel about ourselves very early in life. We hear ourselves saying things to others that may or may not be true and we hear the voices echo the supportive or critical voices adults implanted early in life. So while RSL keeps us in line with the group, internal dialogue keeps us in line with the track our parents placed us on.

Although we seem to spend most of our time bouncing back and forth between RSL and internal dialogue, every once in a while we attain a state of mind that allows us to think objectively about both our RSL and internal dialogue. It is as if we find a quiet and safe place within us from which to reflect on our self free from a compulsive flow of words, thoughts, and actions. This third level of *self-reflective language* is a vehicle of thoughtful consideration. It employs our executive functions, language abilities, and imagination to allow us to be the executor rather than a witness of our lives.

Guiding students to become aware of these different kinds of internal language and states of mind supports an expansion of self-awareness, emotional regulation, and a skepticism toward "obvious" truths. Learning that we are more than other people's expectations and the voices that haunt us can provide hope and serve as a way to change our lives. This is especially important for children who lack parents capable of helping them build this awareness. As the language of self-awareness is expanded and reinforced, we learn that we are capable of evaluating and choosing whether to follow the expectations of others and the mandates of our childhoods, culture, and even the voices in our heads. Keep in mind that self-exploration can be unnerving for the beginner, triggering confusing thoughts and uncomfortable feelings. Thus, it is important to prepare students with what to expect and to provide a context through which their experiences can be understood, expressed, and received by others.

The Myth of the Hero and the Narrative Arc

Beware the barrenness of a busy life.

—Socrates

What makes for a good story? Why do people around the world gather together to listen to stories, watch television, and go to the movies? Why am I so compelled to watch movies like *Pretty Woman* or *A Few Good Men* over and over again? Any screenwriting class can teach you the formula for commercial success. Every story needs a protagonist (a hero) with whom the audience can identify. The hero simultaneously faces an external challenge and struggling with an inner wound that causes emotional pain. For the characters played by both Richard Gere and Tom Cruise, this pain comes from their estrangement from their fathers—a common dilemma of adolescent males who face the challenge of becoming an adult without adequate guidance and support. Not surprisingly, this is my story, too, and likely drives my fascination with this particular version of the heroic narrative. The challenge facing Gere is allowing himself to love, while for Cruise it is living up to his father's reputation.

At first, the hero avoids or fails the challenge, leading him to question his ability to succeed. The challenge is repeatedly resisted, questioned, and even rejected before it is eventually accepted. During the journey, the hero leaves behind old definitions of the self and travels into uncharted territory before discovering his own meaning and place in the world. Some inner transformation takes place that allows him to face his demons, succeed in his worldly challenge, and solidify his identity. Gere surrenders to his own vulnerability while Cruise faces his fears by confronting a particularly scary demon in the form of Jack Nicholson.

This narrative structure, seen in stories around the world and throughout time, has been called the Myth of the Hero (Campbell, 1968). It is the basic theme of ancient mythology, contemporary literature, and most children's stories. It is the adolescent struggle toward adulthood, the overcoming of fear after abandonment and trauma, and the striving for personal transformation and redemption. The universality of this story is likely the result of the commonality of brain evolution, shared developmental challenges, and the fundamental emotional similarities that are embedded in human experience. All humans share the fight for growth, survival, and actualization despite our superficial cultural differences. Table 12.1 outlines some common aspects of the heroic journey in more detail.

Table 12.1
Aspects of the Hero's Journey

The Journey Begins

The hero has an outer challenge to be faced and an inner brokenness to be healed.

Accomplishing these goals requires taking a journey to new and unknown places.

The journey offers a promise of growth and redemption.

Finding the Guide

The guide acknowledges and respects the brokenness and shame that lurk in the hero's shadows.

The guide sees beyond the hero's limitations.

The guide presents an invitation and a challenge to take the heroic journey.

Attaching to the Guide

The guide has something and believes the hero can have it, too.

The hero becomes aware that the guide sees something real in the world and in them.

The hero comes to gradually share the guide's vision.

continued on next page

Table 12.1 continued

The Challenge

The present system and the current self are insufficient and cannot save you.

One must venture forth beyond the safe and familiar confines of your life and beliefs.

Past rules will be broken in the cause of finding what can only be found elsewhere.

The Heroic Discovery

Limitations exist only in the mind.

Confronting fear and pain are gateways to new worlds.

Power is discovered in vulnerability; freedom is found in commitment.

Despite our desire to see childhood as a time of innocence and fun, many children are fighting a heroic battle for survival. Many of these children come to be designated as "unteachable" by experts, pundits, and even their own families. Although the causes of their external challenges may range from poverty and abuse to the indifference of privileged parents, their internal pain always stems from the shame of having been emotionally abandoned or the terror of feeling unsafe. These powerful negative emotions cast a shadow over their existence.

It is important to lose your innocence, but only in the context of a safe childhood, and gradually with the help of compassionate adults. Many of the children in our classrooms have lost their innocence—too early and with no signs of being rescued. Often, the people who should be helping them are preoccupied with their own pain. What is needed in these situations are healing environments for broken hearts and turned-off brains shut down by too much stress and too little comfort. These children need a healing environment with the guidance of a wise elder if they are to learn. An optimal classroom will be educationally stimulating and emotionally nurturing, in equal parts.

Filling a position once held by tribal elders, teachers can guide their students to become the heroes of their own stories. At the same time, teachers must also become heroes by overcoming prejudice, ignorance, and the bureaucratic status quo to make learning happen despite the forces that may be working against them. A demoralized or burned-out teacher will not be a wise and nurturing guide or be able to create and maintain a healing classroom environment.

Carl Jung said that the answers to our most important questions are to be found in the shadow. The shadow is the repository of our pain and shame; hidden within it is the pain of our families and the demons of our inner lives. The heroic teacher acknowledges the pain, suffering, hypocrisy, and lack of fairness in the world. Because you can't completely banish the shadow, you must learn to develop a relationship with it. If the shadow can be acknowledged and included as part of the emotional reality of the classroom, the teacher becomes transformed into a guide on the path to wisdom. Wisdom is knowledge mixed with compassion and presented in a manner that helps others to heal and grow. In others words, wisdom is knowledge in the service of others.

In order for teachers to become guides, they need to be familiar with their own shadows, which will allow their students to confront their own inner demons. Because a teacher who adheres to unfair rules will be seen as too insecure to be a guide, a heroic teacher must be brave enough to break the rules in service of his or her students. A successful guide snatches victory from the jaws of defeat, gaining freedom from determinism. The teacher invites the student to take a journey out of the narrow confines of his or her life into a new world beyond the limitations of the neighborhood, family, and culture.

Like the shaman, a teacher has to have a clear vision so that a student can come to believe that he or she sees something real that can be shared. The teacher's message must be "I know something you don't know, something you don't have, but I am committed to sharing it with you and bringing you on this journey." Teachers must tell stories of what is possible, stories that connect us to the unconscious, to our tribal histories and to each other. These stories will become the tribal glue of the classroom.

Everyone has a story but in the absence of self-awareness, our story is a simple chronology of events and external judgments. Teaching a meta-cognitive vantage point adds self-awareness and an objective distance that provides us with the ability to think about our story, reflect on our choices, and consider editing our thoughts, feelings, and behaviors. The narrative process allows us to separate the story from the self. It's like taking off your shirt to patch a tear and then putting it back on. When humans evolved the capacity to examine their narratives and see them as one option among many, they also gained the ability to edit and modify their lives (White, 2007).

Teachers hope to guide their students to the realization that they are more than characters in a story dictated by circumstance. We would love to instill in our students the belief that they can make choices, follow their passions, and become the authors of new stories—their own stories. Sometimes you have to make some suggestions about alternative narrative arcs and outcomes to get them started. If I focus on my work and study hard, could I get good grades? Could I graduate from high school, go to college, and get a good job? What if the suffering in my life has meaning? The remarkable heroic journey of a teacher and her students is embodied in the work of a high school teacher named Erin Gruwell.

Erin Gruwell

Prejudice is opinion without judgment.

—Voltaire

Erin Gruwell came to Wilson High School in Long Beach, California, as a student teacher from upscale Newport Beach. While Newport and Long Beach are only 30 miles apart, Gruwell found herself in another world. Although its reputation as a culturally diverse school initially drew Ms. Gruwell to Wilson, she soon learned that this "model of integration" consisted of separate and often hostile communities of Latinos, African Americans, and Asians (Gruwell, 2007, p. 4).

What Gruwell found in her classroom was very different from her own experience. The desks in her class were falling apart and etched with gang symbols, as were the textbooks. The students in her class were labeled as outcasts, learning disabled, and "behaviorally challenged." In other words, she had been given the bad kids: the students no one else wanted to teach. Gruwell soon realized that her students had more serious things to worry about than English literature. She discovered that some were traumatized by beatings from their stepfathers or grieving the loss of friends who had died in gang violence.

One of her students told her, "When you have nothing to live for, you look for reasons to die" (p. 48). Another student was given $25 to go to Target to buy school supplies. But because he didn't want to be called a "schoolboy" or a "sellout" by his buddies, he bought a handgun instead (p. 105). Gruwell realized her students needed first to be healed before they could learn. Her experiences inspired the "Freedom Writers," a program that allowed her students to journal about their unique stories, have their experiences known by others, and make sense and give meaning to their suffering.

Gruwell began by connecting her students' vulnerabilities and passions to relevant and realistic stories about tagging, living in the projects, and being incarcerated. She enticed them with questions like "what would happen if a Latina and an African American hooked up" as a parallel to Romeo and Juliet. Later, Gruwell took a leap to what she called "lessons that ignite a desire to go beyond the walls of the classroom." By exposing her students to the writings of people like Anne Frank, they came to realize that they, too, had stories to tell. A key element to her success is that she found ways to make education relevant to her students and to make her students' lives relevant to their education.

She recounted a particularly "teachable moment" when a student had drawn a caricature of another student, depicting him as having abnormally large lips. The note made its way around the classroom and eventually to the student it was portraying. With a fire inside she hadn't felt before, Gruwell grabbed the note, raised her hand in the air, and asked her students who had heard of the Holocaust. To her surprise, only a few students had. The drawing had reminded her of propaganda she had seen from Nazi Germany, where Jews were depicted as rats with long noses. It was then that she understood how her job was not only to teach the students English, but also to educate them about history, racism, and injustice. She took her class to the Museum of Tolerance. She found that they were able to relate to the pain and suffering of the Jews: being afraid to go outside their neighborhood, feeling ostracized from society, and having to overcome adversity. She states that this was when her journey truly began.

Ms. Gruwell wanted to give her students a way to share their own stories, so she gave them journals to write the story of their lives: their problems at home, the deaths of friends and family members to gang violence, and their encounters with racism. She shaped her lesson plans to show her students a way out of violence by teaching them to tell their stories. This proved to be her most successful tool—a way for her students to express themselves, be heard, and learn how to better listen to each other. She slowly came to realize that they were healing through writing. With their newfound love of writing, they wrote to Miep Gies (the woman who hid Anne Frank and her family) and to Zlata Filipovič (the teenage author of *Zlata's Diary: A Child's Life in Sarajevo*) and invited them to visit their school. Not surprisingly, they were well received by these kindred spirits.

In essence, Gruwell acted as a tribal chief who was bold enough to approach people in power in order to open doors for her students. She endured alienation, gossip, and criticism while staying true to her commitment to her students. One of her biggest accomplishments was to get the school administration to allow her to continue teaching the same group of students for two additional years: This feat breached all of the rules and outwardly acknowledged that she was succeeding with students where others had failed. She found that as her students acknowledged and shared their pain, the bond they created overcame the racial barriers dividing them. Gruwell was able to help her students make a shift from feeling indifferent and hopeless to empowered and capable. She showed her students that they could escape their traumatic pasts and rewrite the stories of their lives.

After countless journal entries and an ever-deepening appreciation of the power of the written word, they began to call themselves the Freedom Writers after the freedom riders of the 1960s who rode integrated buses across the South. With her encouragement, they transcribed their private prose into a book, *The Freedom Writers Diary: How a Teacher and 150 Teens Used Writing to Change Themselves and the World Around Them*. The positive reception to the book helped to give meaning to their personal struggles and gave them a way to inspire others to become the heroes of their own stories. During their final year at Wilson, the Freedom Writers received the Spirit of Anne Frank Award for "their commitment to combating discrimination, racism, and bias-related violence" (Gruwell & Freedom Writers, 2007, p. 3). As one of the students had written, "Historians say history repeats itself, but in my case I have managed to break the cycle because I am going to graduate from high school and go to college, an opportunity my parents never had" (Gruwell & Freedom Writers, 2007, p. 9).

Part IV
Applying Social Neuroscience
in Schools and Classrooms

Chapter 13

Information, Compassion, and Wisdom

A single conversation with a wise person is better than 10 years of study.
— Chinese proverb

Throughout this book we have explored the inextricable connectedness of the human brain, relationships, and shared culture. We now turn our attention to one of the social brain's highest accomplishments: the attainment and sharing of wisdom. Although wisdom has traditionally been associated with growing older, they are not synonymous, so age sometimes shows up all by itself. Aging is associated with wisdom only for those with higher levels of emotional development, moral reasoning, and a continued investment in other people (Pasupathi & Staudinger, 2001). Additionally, because wisdom reflects an integration of brain functioning, it appears to go along with the development of more mature psychological defenses, meaningful relationships, and life satisfaction (Ardelt, 1997, 2000).

The general view is that wisdom is attained through the accumulation of experience, reflection, and compassion. Wise elders serve as the "glue" for their families and communities, and they are sought out for their knowledge, guidance, and comfort. By both age and position, teachers are the wise elders of the classroom. Even teachers in their twenties seem ancient to elementary schoolchildren and a world away from adolescence.

Wisdom is a difficult accomplishment that requires a lifetime of dedication and attention. I suppose this is why it appears to be such a rare and valuable asset to any community. As a form of social intelligence, wisdom requires sustained and caring connections with others through continued contributions to a tribe and a deep sense of belonging. At the same time, the maturation of the brain allows for less impulsivity and emotional arousal which support more careful consideration of complex social situations. Healthy aging often brings an increasing sophistication of thought, a maturation of psychological defenses, increasing empathy, and a broadening perspective. Some of the elements which contribute to developing wisdom are summarized in Table 13.1.

Table 13.1
Factors Supporting the Emergence of Wisdom

Psychological
Lifetime learning, accumulated experience,
  and maintenance of old memories

Self-knowledge and increased perspective

A balance of inner awareness (mindfulness)
  and connection with others (sociality)

Social
Sustained social interactions and attachment to family

A respected place within the community

A set of contributions and social obligations to the community

Biological
Decreased anxiety and increased optimism

Increased cortical-network participation in
  complex social problem solving

Well-maintained social-brain networks in the
  service of sustained attachment

What Is Wisdom?

Wisdom is the daughter of experience.
                              —Leonardo da Vinci

Wisdom is a time-honored contribution to the tribe that arises through simultaneous biological, psychological, and social development. Although we know it when we see it, wisdom defies easy definition. In fact, each chapter of a popular book about wisdom edited by Yale psychologist Robert Sternberg (1990) contains a different definition. In the East, wisdom has traditionally focused on controlling one's thoughts, increasing self-awareness, and promoting social harmony (Takahashi & Bordia, 2000). Wisdom in the Western world was seen as good advice, codes of social behavior, and more esoteric knowledge related to the workings of heaven and earth. As the West became more scientific, wisdom became more closely associated with knowledge. After more than a century of increasing contact, Eastern and Western notions are blending together to create a view of wisdom as an embodiment of one's knowledge that is expressed in the context of compassionate relationships (Ardelt, 2004).

We tend to think of wisdom as being grounded in a deep experience of the emotional and moral self, combined with an abiding awareness of our common humanity. In essence, wisdom is the result of a synthetic or inclusive way of experiencing the world (Takahashi & Overton, 2002). And while knowledge gives you the capacity to understand what you are doing, wisdom helps you to attain a correct, prudent, and just application of that knowledge. This is probably why knowledge can be judged against objective standards, while wisdom is recognized in the hearts of listeners and acknowledged through group consensus (Staudinger & Baltes, 1996). Although no specific study has been done measuring brain activation while people are "acting wisely," it is safe to assume that we would see more diverse brain activation across systems dedicated to social, emotional, and intellectual functioning.

Who comes to mind when you think of a wise person? How about a caring grandfather, rabbi, minister, or guru? Perhaps a public figure like a politician, scientist, or celebrity? When a group of undergraduates were asked to name well-known "wise" individuals, their top ten choices were as follows: (1) Gandhi, (2) Confucius, (3) Jesus, (4) Martin Luther King Jr., (5) Socrates, (6) Mother Teresa, (7) Solomon, (8) Buddha, (9) the Pope, and (10) Oprah Winfrey (Paulhus et al., 2002).

This list is certainly an interesting and diverse mix of people from various cultures and historical eras. You may notice that Napoleon, Einstein, and Bill Gates are not on this list. Therefore, power, intellect, and wealth aren't synonymous with wisdom for these educated young adults. Similarly, we don't see the names of any presidents, generals, or Wall Street tycoons. Instead, those who were thought of as wise were known more for their insight, compassion, and courage than for their intellectual horsepower or business acumen. In fact, four of the first five on this list died for their beliefs.

In looking over this list, you may have an emotional reaction when thinking of one or more of these people. I certainly feel strong emotions when I think back to the speeches of Dr. King that I first heard as an adolescent trying to make sense of our society. I had an intuitive sense that what Dr. King was saying was at a deeper level of human significance than most everything else I was hearing in public discourse. He seemed to be looking beyond the current realities of life and pointing both to a deeper level of feeling and a higher way of thinking. As I listened, my breathing would grow deeper, my vision would appear to widen, and I would feel as if life were becoming clearer. Perhaps this kind of emotional and physical reaction to another human being is an aspect of how we identify wisdom: knowledge combined with an emotional message that stirs our hearts and fires up our brains.

Wisdom appears to bring together intellectual and emotional intelligence in ways that maximize affiliation, compassion, and our common humanity. These ten individuals perceived wisdom as emerging in the context of interacting hearts and minds coming together to solve human problems. I asked some of my graduate students what they thought the attributes of wise people might be and they came up with these three categories: (1) a broad perspective, (2) character, and (3) attitudes toward others. A broader perspective includes seeing beyond one's own biases and needs, knowing what is most important, and getting down to essentials. The type of character that contributes to wisdom is one that is grounded in strong moral principles and possesses the courage to stand up for those principles in the face of danger. Attitudes toward others included kindness, forgiveness, and empathy.

Attaining wisdom involves being able to see past the surface of things to deeper levels of meaning. Wise individuals also seem to transcend the notion of a single correct perspective, remain open to new learning, and recognize the inescapable distortions inherent in one's own perspective. A good example of this attitude comes from Michelangelo, who, in the ninth decade of life, wrote above his studio door *"Ancora Imparo"* (I'm still learning). The wealth of experience, deep consideration, and emotional regulation required to become wise comes as a result of gradual changes in neural processing, emotional maturity, and the accumulation of knowledge. These changes allow for a deeper, broader, and more profound comprehension of human experience.

The social science research suggests that wisdom during adulthood coalesces from a complex pattern of personality variables, life experiences, and inner growth (Staudinger, 1999). Those judged as wise have been found to excel in coping with existential issues and grasping the relativism of values (Baltes et al., 1995). They also tend to have good social abilities, a rich internal life, and are open to new experiences (Staudinger et al., 1998). Someone with wisdom is capable of sustaining his focus on a problem as he considers its multiple dimensions, meanings, and his personal responsibility in the matter at hand (Holliday & Chandler, 1986). Given that navigating complex and difficult relationships is one of life's most enduring challenges, most wisdom is expressed in how people interact with and treat one another. Looking back at our list of wise people, most could be considered social revolutionaries striving to uplift the oppressed and increase the common good.

The Maturation of Thought

> *The more you know, the less sure you are.*
>
> —Voltaire

Piaget's stages of cognitive development unfold as a consequence of normal brain development. He has described a progression from concrete to abstract thinking that follows a predictable course as cortical and subcortical neural networks mature and integrate. Wisdom, on the other hand, is not a natural consequence of the passage of time but a quantum leap from the linear unfolding of cognitive and emotional development. Clues about the attainment of wisdom appear to exist in the interwoven maturational processes of thought and emotion. That is, social emotional development appears to be a foundation for the eventual attainment of wisdom.

For adolescents and young adults, learning means to quickly gather information, organize talking points to present an argument, and then convince others. Because younger people tend to assume the existence of a single valid answer, a final solution is quickly decided upon based on the overt information, and then energetically defended. All of these tendencies are manifestations of the reflexive search for means-end connections characteristic of their stage of neurological and psychological development. And given that adolescents have been historically responsible for starting families, hunting, and fighting wars, this sort of impulsivity and quick decision making has a deep and important survival-based history. Table 13.2 contains a list of some of the factors typically found in the problem-solving strategies of less mature thinkers.

The way that adolescents and young adults think about problems is also tied to their primary developmental challenge of constructing a social identity. A central component in this process involves creating

Table 13.2
Characteristics of Less Mature Thinkers

A need for certainty and control

Limited recognition of complexity and an inability to incorporate opposites

A lack of openness to unconscious processes

The belief that all the important information to make a decision is apparent

Lower empathic abilities

Less mature psychological defenses

More denial, blame, and projection

Less humor, sublimation, and suppression

Adapted from Labouvie-Vief (1990)

idealized mental images of the self. As the young person is confronted with new and more attractive options, each one is "tried on" and, for a time, feels like the final and best one. As part of a search for absolute truths, adolescents and young adults hold themselves and others to high standards tied to abstract ideals. Many use their identification with these ideals to remain free from blame, avoid disagreements, and place responsibility for problems on others. This combination of factors often leads adolescents to feel disappointed in their parents for not living up to their newly discovered values and ideals. I imagine this may sound familiar to those with adolescent children or with memories of your own adolescence.

The next logical question to ask is whether there are ways that teachers can plant the seeds of wisdom. The answer may be in promoting ways of thinking that appear to be a part of the maturation of thinking. Younger minds tend to be drawn to the specific content of each situation, stimulating neural networks that deal with new information and are primed to absorb details from the world around them. Training in wisdom could include being encouraged to shift focus from specific details to general principles and broader perspectives. Games requiring taking the perspectives of others can also be helpful. As thinking matures, there is a parallel expansion of an awareness of the complexity of human experience and the limits of human understanding. At the same time, rapid decisions and a subsequent "hardening of the categories" give way to slower, deeper, and more flexible deliberation.

While the answers to complex problems often seem obvious to adolescents, experience teaches us that solutions to human problems are hardly ever simple or straightforward and that not all of the important information may be immediately apparent. The accretion of experience provides us with a framework that allows us to sit with ambiguity while we ponder complex problems. This requires an ability to keep in mind a broader time horizon and maintain a memory for the future. All of this higher order mental processing depends upon emotional regulation, impulse control, and tolerance for ambiguity and uncertainty. Emotional safety and a secure sense of identity help us to accept our own ignorance—a central component of wisdom. All of these aspects of the development of wisdom can be woven into every learning opportunity to support the deepening of consideration and the expansion of perspective. Table 13.3 lists factors typically found in more mature thinkers.

Table 13.3
Characteristics of More Mature Thinkers

Increased recognition of complexity and an ability to incorporate opposites

An understanding that not all of the important information is apparent

An increased openness to unconscious processes

More information gathering

Less concern about being in control

An ability to tolerate personal limitations and ignorance

More realistic expectations and forgiveness of others

Increased empathy and maintained connectedness

More mature psychological defenses

Less denial, blame, and projection

More humor, sublimation, and suppression

Adapted from Labouvie-Vief (1990)

It seems almost certain that the potential to become wise depends not only upon the maturation of thinking, but also upon the development of emotional intelligence. Because thinking is strongly influenced by emotion, our psychological development provides the necessary platform for the quantum leap from thought to wisdom. It is emotional intelligence that allows us to maximize our intellect in the service of others.

Thanks to denial and our other psychological defenses, most of us are able to cope with the reality of our vulnerabilities and mortality. The lucky ones among us have the luxury of confronting these existential realities gradually and in small doses. As we grow older, however, we start to gain an increasing recognition and acceptance of our frailty and the inevitability of death. When people are traumatized, especially early in life, their defenses and assumptions of safety are prematurely shattered. The unfortunate reality of modern life is that child neglect is common, parents are often stressed or absent, and violence is an everyday occurrence in many communities. In fact, the majority of inner city children know someone who has died a violent death. In these situations, the amygdala takes executive control of the brain and a child is at risk of lapsing into a state of chronic anxiety that can derail both the maturation of thinking and the potential for wisdom.

The silver lining is that traumatic experiences are also capable of enhancing self-discovery and often support the attainment of wisdom. Think back to the list of the ten wisest people mentioned earlier. Most of them found ways to transform their suffering into personal values and a code of behavior that included an active dedication to others. In fact, the central tenets of Buddhism are based on the belief that suffering and the alleviation of suffering are at the core of human existence. So while few of us would choose to suffer, the experience of suffering often has a central place in personal and cultural history. In order for this to occur, trauma and suffering need to be transformed into a meaningful process. The work of Erin Gruwell and her Freedom Writers is a clear example of this process. Teaching wisdom requires a consistent focus on alternative perspectives, the nurturance of compassion, and encouragement to look below the surface and beyond the horizon.

Wisdom, Prejudice, and the Brain

It is the mark of an educated mind to be able
to entertain a thought without accepting it.

—Aristotle

The central social and political issue of my lifetime has been racial prejudice. The struggle for racial equality by African Americans in the United States has resulted in the expression of profound wisdom and egregious stupidity. My generation has experienced school desegregation, the civil rights movement, and the election of the first African American president. We have struggled with the shame of slavery, disparities of socioeconomic status, and cultural differences that we can barely discuss out of fear of being politically incorrect. Through all of these challenges we struggle to be open-minded while maintaining an awareness of our limitations and the tenacity of the prejudices and fears with which we were raised. The issues involved in racial prejudice are central to educating our children and understanding how their brains work. This information can then be used to point their minds in the direction of wisdom.

The ubiquity and power of racial prejudice seem to support the belief that we are hard-wired to distrust and even hate those who are different from us. Imagining the lives of our tribal ancestors, we can easily see the survival benefit of an automatic system for rapid classification of unfamiliar others to avoid potential harm and exposure to new diseases (Schaller et al., 2003). The prejudice against darker skin color, even within dark-skinned communities, may also reflect our ancient fear of the dark and its association with danger (Uhlmann et al., 2002). To whatever degree this scenario of natural selection holds true, it would make sense that the social neuroscience of racial prejudice would be related to the activation of the primitive fear circuitry beneath the level of conscious awareness.

Because the brain is built at the interface of nature and nurture, our primitive instincts interact with the prejudice we experience within our cultures. Therefore, it is difficult to separate what the brain creates from how the brain is shaped by experience. Research with African American children in the 1940s showed that they would choose white dolls over brown ones, describing the brown dolls as "ugly" and "not pretty" or labeling them with racial epithets. White dolls were described as "good," "pretty," and "the best looking because they're white" (Clark & Clark, 1950). Given that our self-concept is infused with our place in the family, neighborhood, and the general culture, the prejudice we experience becomes woven into our developing sense of self. Thus, being the victims of prejudice creates a powerful inner disadvantage for children with darker skin, even among their own people (Sidanius et al., 2001).

In the exploration of the social neuroscience of racial prejudice, patterns of brain activation in African Americans and in Caucasian Americans have been compared when these groups were exposed to same-race versus other-race faces. A clear same-race advantage in recognizing and distinguishing between faces has been repeatedly demonstrated with greater activation in brain areas involved in facial recognition when looking at same-race faces (Brigham & Barkowitz, 1978; Golby et al., 2001; Malpass & Kravitz, 1969; Walker & Tanaka, 2003). As a result, Caucasians think about other Caucasians in far more complicated ways than they think about African Americans, resulting in much less cognitive processing and conscious consideration (Linville & Jones, 1980). The statement "they all look alike" may reflect an underlying truth of how we deploy our attention when looking at other-race versus same-race faces.

It has been demonstrated that African Americans are better at recognizing Caucasian faces than vice versa, which is likely due to greater exposure to Caucasian faces in the media (Golby et al., 2001). We do know that, through exposure and conscious attention to facial details, Caucasian adults can be successfully trained to distinguish among African American faces and that this learning process results in a decrease in implicit racial bias (Brigham & Barkowitz, 1978;

Lebrecht et al., 2009; Tanaka & Pierce, 2009). In other words, just focusing on and learning to distinguish among African American faces have been shown to have a diminishing effect on racism in Caucasians. The activation of conscious attention and awareness decreases amygdala activation and a fearful cognitive bias, just as learning about any fearful stimulus allows us to activate cortical circuits that regulate fear.

Assuming that fear was at the heart of prejudice, a second line of research directly explored amygdala activation in same-race and cross-race situations. It was found that when Caucasians and African Americans were shown pictures of other-race faces, they exhibited more amygdala activation and an enhanced startle response (Hart et al., 2000; Krill & Platek, 2009; Phelps et al., 2000). Although it takes approximately 500 ms for a visual stimulus to reach conscious awareness, information about race is coded in just 50 ms (Ito & Urland, 2003; Ito et al., 2004). This means that a person's race influences our eventual conscious perception of them before we are even aware of whom we are seeing. The rapidity of this response also results in the automatic and unconscious frontloading of all of our past biases into the experience of each new person.

This heightened fear activation influences our conscious cognitive processes in many ways. For example, individuals from other groups are more readily associated with aversive stimuli. This is the likely reason why African Americans are more readily misperceived as carrying weapons and their faces are more likely to be perceived as angry by Caucasian subjects (Hugenberg & Bodenhausen, 2003; Olsson et al., 2005; Payne, 2001). Other-race speakers are seen as more forceful or powerful than same-race speakers (Hart & Morry, 1996, 1997; Hass et al., 1991; Linville & Jones, 1980).

Interestingly, Caucasian students who rate higher on tests of social dominance perform better on tests when the tests are administered by African American teachers (Danso & Esses, 2001). It is likely that the African American testers presented an unconscious challenge to the Caucasian students, which led them to perform better. Both African Americans and Caucasians have greater amygdala activation to African American faces, which may be due to the consistent pairing of African American faces with criminal behavior by the media (Lieberman et al., 2005). The association of African American faces with criminal behavior is likely modulated in African Americans by their greater exposure to black faces.

Because fear conditioning does not require awareness, the brain's knee-jerk reaction to individuals of other races is unrelated to our conscious attitudes. This is why social psychologists have found that stereotypes are automatically activated and require conscious inhibition to produce low-prejudice responses (Devine, 1989). Once stereotypical attitudes and beliefs are inculcated, change requires "intention, attention, and time" (Devine, 1989; Phelps & Thomas, 2003). Because most children are exposed to some degree of racial prejudice, open discussion and increased interracial exposure can work against prejudice being turned into conscious beliefs and negative behaviors. In the same way, increased focus and awareness of the handicapped have also been found to decrease discrimination (Langer et al., 1985).

We know from studies of anxiety and fear that conscious labeling activates cortical neural networks that can regulate emotional activity. Verbal encoding of African American targets results in less amygdala activation in Caucasians, reflecting the ability of conscious processing to inhibit fear (Lieberman et al., 2005). Conscious processing is directly involved with the inhibition and control of automatic implicit processing. So when the same-race faces are presented for 500 ms, or the time it takes to be consciously aware of what is being presented, amygdala activation slows while frontal activation increases (Cunningham et al., 2004). In other words, people can learn to inhibit their primitive automatic responses and replace them with thoughts more reflective of equality. Via conscious effort, positive experiences, or consistent exposure, it is possible to create a break between reflexive prejudice and conscious experience (Devine, 1989).

Our response to people of other races is modulated by a variety of cognitive and emotional factors (Wheeler & Fiske, 2005). When Phelps and her colleagues (2000) showed pictures of well-known and well-liked African Americans to Caucasian subjects, amygdala activation was attenuated or even absent. These results suggest that exposure to and knowledge about a person of a different race can teach the brain not to be afraid. Segregation seems to perpetuate and enhance prejudice by keeping our brains from habituating to and learning about one another, leaving us to analyze the faces of people from other races with less efficient neural circuitry, and making us more vulnerable to cultural stereotypes and media representations.

Some research suggests that blacks prefer to interact with whites who exhibit more racial bias instead of those who make an effort to appear unbiased (Shelton et al., 2005). This suggests that honest communication may actually be the best route to working through and getting past prejudice. The greater the expectation of prejudice, the more likely it will be found. Self-perception of academic abilities combined with positive racial identity is correlated with engagement and achievement in school, despite the awareness of discrimination (Taylor et al., 1994).

So, while racist practices and beliefs remain a current reality, we can actively work against the corrosive effects of racism by supporting cultural pride, self-esteem, and increased integration and contact between people of different races. Issues of race also have the potential for stimulating the kind of self-awareness and perspective that could enhance and promote the development of wisdom inside and outside of the classroom.

Chapter 14

Teaching Students About the Brain

Science is organized knowledge; wisdom is organized life.
—Immanuel Kant

The human brain wasn't designed by an engineer to adapt to our current situation. Instead, it was shaped over millions of years of sequential adaptation in response to ever-changing environmental demands. The most primitive brains contained hundreds of neurons and performed a few basic tasks. Over time, brains grew in size and complexity; old structures were conserved and new structures emerged, expanding some of our abilities while diminishing others. This mixture of conservation, adaptation, and innovation has resulted in an amazingly complex brain, capable of everything from monitoring respiration to creating culture. Modern human brains now contain billions of neurons, trillions of connections, and seemingly infinite computational capacities.

This added complexity came with a cost. Not only do all of these systems have to develop and interconnect, but they also have to stay balanced and properly integrated for optimal performance. In addition, the way that brains process information is biased in order to lessen anxiety and increase efficiency. Despite the fact that most everything we "know" about our brains consists of educated guesses, there are a few guesses we can have some confidence in. This chapter contains a dozen potentially helpful things teachers should know about the workings of the human brain. You may even consider sharing some of them with your students.

1. The Brain Is a Social Organ of Adaptation

To be uncertain is to be uncomfortable,
but to be certain is to be ridiculous.
—Chinese proverb

Neurons are "excitable cells" that require sustained connection and mutual stimulation to survive. The electrical and chemical messages within and between neurons are gradually translated into patterns that come to represent learning. In a similar fashion, our brains require stimulation and connection to survive and thrive. A brain without connection to other brains and sufficient challenge will shrink and eventually die. The modern human brain's primary environment is our matrix of social relationships.

As we explored earlier, the human brain has been shaped into a social organ over thousands of years of primate evolution. We are now linked together via dedicated social brain networks, mirror neurons, primitive bonding instincts, neurochemistry, language, and culture. As a result, close supportive relationships stimulate positive emotions, neuroplasticity, and learning. On the other hand, abandonment and intimidation trigger anxiety, adrenaline, and cortisol, all of which inhibit learning. To fully understand how brains learn, they have to be explored as social organs of adaptation—a reality that makes the relationships within a classroom as relevant as the curriculum.

2. We Have Two Brains

Unity can only be expressed in the binary.
—Buddha

Many birds and fish have two identical hemispheres. Each "half brain" is complete and autonomous, allowing migratory birds to fly long distances and fish to sleep with one side of the brain at a time so that they can keep swimming. Over the course of primate evolution, the cerebral hemispheres have differentiated from one another and developed specialized functions and skills. This likely occurred because increasing social demands required more computational power and dedicated neural topography. In general, the left hemisphere has taken the lead on language processing, linear thinking, and pro-social functioning while the right hemisphere specializes in visual-spatial processing, strong emotions, and private experience.

It is believed that as the hemispheres differentiated, it became increasingly necessary for one hemisphere (the left) to take control of conscious processing in order to avoid conflicts in decision making. Meanwhile, the right hemisphere provides sensory, bodily, and emotional information to the left in the form of feelings and intuition (Nasrallah, 1985). While we are awake, the left hemisphere may or may not allow this input into conscious awareness. This filtration appears to support social coordination, sustained attention, emotional regulation, and the experience of having only one brain.

Neurological patients who experience damage to the nerve fibers connecting the two hemispheres sometimes demonstrate conflict between the two sides of their bodies (Jason & Pajurkova, 1992). The experience and behavior of such patients supports the idea of different "selves" in each hemisphere and their alternate ways of processing information. To be "of two minds" about something may be more than ambivalence; it may reflect the conflict inherent in having two brains in the same head with somewhat different agendas and processing styles. Recognizing that we possess two brains can go a long way in coming to accept and manage our internal conflicts, many of which are an artifact of the brain's evolutionary history.

While most tasks involve contributions from both hemispheres, each side provides its own specialties and expertise. For example, normal speech requires the semantic skills of the left hemisphere and the emotional and tonal abilities of the right. When people become either too emotional or too rational, there is an increased likelihood that the balance between left and right functioning in the prefrontal cortex has been disrupted. The common imbalance between affect and cognition in many of us may reflect this struggle for homeostatic balance among the hemispheres.

Good teachers intuitively grasp this in their students, and they will seek to balance the expression of emotion and cognition. We encourage overly rational students to be aware of and explore their feelings. On the other hand, we try to help anxious students develop the cognitive capabilities of their left hemispheres to regulate their emotions. In the face of trauma or sustained stress, the hemispheres come to function in a less integrated fashion, resulting in problems in emotional regulation and social connectedness. People with histories of childhood abuse and neglect have even been shown to have fewer connecting fibers in the corpus callosum that integrate the right and left hemispheres (De Bellis et al., 1999; Teicher et al., 2004).

3. Early Learning Is Powerful

In child's lunchbox, a mother's thoughts.
—Japanese proverb

By the time we are born, primitive brain structures responsible for physical, social, and emotional survival are highly developed. This means that early learning is primarily sensory, emotional, and motor, which is stored in systems of implicit (unconscious) memory. Much of our most important emotional and interpersonal learning occurs during our first few years of life, when our more primitive neural networks are in control. Self-awareness emerges years later as the cortex continues to mature, having already been programmed by early experience—which we automatically assume to be reality. As a result, a great deal of extremely important learning takes place before we are consciously aware that we are learning (Casey et al., 2005). For most of us, the early interactions that shape our brains remain forever inaccessible to conscious memory, reflection, or modification. This artifact of evolution, expressed in the sequential nature of our neural development, transforms the ups and downs of childhood into the core of our personalities, fears, and longings.

Early experiences shape structures in ways that have a lifelong impact on three of our most vital areas of learning: attachment, emotional regulation, and self-esteem. These three spheres of learning establish our abilities to connect with others, cope with stress, and feel that we have value. It is obvious that our dependency on early caretakers can influence us in both wonderful and perfectly terrible ways. We see this in abused and neglected children who often enter school with a variety of symptoms including anger, eating disorders, and depression, rendering them ill equipped to relax, open their minds, and learn.

Every time children behave in a way they (or we) don't understand, a teacher has the opportunity to engage in an exploration of their inner world. When painful experiences can be consciously thought about, named, and placed into a coherent narrative, children gain the ability to reintegrate dissociated neural networks of affect, cognition, and bodily awareness. This process creates the possibility of naming the pain, decreasing shame, and promoting healing. This raises the question as to whether teachers have to also be therapists. As we learn more about the workings of the brain, we discover that there is no meaningful way to separate cognitive from emotional learning. So while teachers don't necessarily have to also be therapists, we may have to shift our understanding of what it takes to be a successful teacher.

4. Conscious Awareness Is an Island in a Sea of Automatic Processing

*The key to growth is the introduction of higher
dimensions of consciousness into our awareness.*

—Lao Tzu

The vast majority of neural processing occurs in neural networks not involved in conscious processing. In fact, conscious awareness and explicit memory are but a small fraction of the vast amount of neural processing that occurs each millisecond. Think of how many things you do without having to think about them: breathing, walking, balancing, even constructing the syntax of a sentence, is handled automatically. You just have to think about what you want to say; you don't have to think about how not to say it.

Automatic unconscious processing is also much faster than conscious processing. Pulling your hand off of a hot stove, flinching when a ball is coming toward your face, or braking to avoid another car are all reflexes that happen long before we would be able to make a decision to do them. Natural selection has deemed conscious processing too slow for most things.

5. Unconscious Automatic Processing Is Very Fast

To be conscious that we are perceiving and
thinking is to be conscious of our own existence.
— Aristotle

In order to survive, animals have to be tough or fast. The tortoise and the hare are good examples of these different, yet equally viable, survival strategies. While our elaborate cortices separate us from both of their brains, further down, all of our brains are pretty similar. Our expanded cortex allows us vast flexibility in responding to situations compared to simpler animals. Of course, conscious awareness and thinking through options take time and, in some circumstances, a speedy reflex is far more adaptive.

The simultaneous need for both speed and response flexibility leads us to run on multiple clocks. We are consciously aware of time second by second while our brains process information in hundredths and even thousandths of seconds. The brain can function like a superhero that shifts into a faster time frame and moves within a world that appears to be standing still. Because of its incredible speed, it is able to process incoming information, analyze it based on a lifetime of experience, and present it to us in half a second. The brain then creates the illusion that what we are experiencing is happening right now and that we are making decisions based on our conscious thought processes.

While it takes approximately 500–600 milliseconds for neural activation triggered by experience to register in conscious awareness, subcortical brain regions can react to internal and external stimuli (a potential threat) in less than 50 milliseconds. This means that by the time we have become consciously aware of an experience, it has already been processed many times in our more primitive neural networks and triggered implicit memories organized by past learning. This unconscious backdrop shapes our conscious experience of "the present moment" before we experience it (Nomura et al., 2003; Wiens, 2006). In fact, 90% of the input to the cerebral cortex comes from internal neural processing, based on both species-specific memories (like fear of snakes) and past personal experience. Based on these neural realities, it is especially important to teach students to question their assumptions and the possible influences of past experiences and unconscious biases on their feelings and beliefs.

6. The Mind, Brain, and Body Are Interwoven

To keep the body in good health is a duty . . . otherwise we shall not be able to keep our mind strong and clear.
—Buddha

In the Western world, the connection between a healthy mind and body goes back to the Greeks who thought of them as conceptually identical. Neural networks dedicated to action, perception, and cognition evolved together and develop interdependently during our lifetimes. Physical activity exerts a stimulating influence on the entire brain that keeps it functioning at an optimal level. Just as the Greeks suspected, intelligence is a full-body proposition that includes physical activity, nutrition, and proper sleep.

The brain evolved to learn and solve problems while moving through a changing natural environment. This is why exploration, neural plasticity, attention, and memory are interwoven components of learning. Exercise activates learning as it elevates the respiration and blood flow feeding our brains. Exercise has also been shown to stimulate the birth of new neurons in the hippocampus and to pump more oxygen through the brain, stimulating capillary growth and frontal-lobe plasticity. Athletes possess more glial cells, which support efficient neural functioning as well as higher levels of endorphins, dopamine, serotonin, and norepinephrine aiding emotional well-being and learning.

When we walk, run, or exercise, the large muscles in our legs secrete neural growth hormones that cross the blood-brain barrier to support neuroplasticity and learning (Cotman et al., 2007; Tsatsoulis & Fountoulakis, 2006; van Praag et al., 2005). Through other biochemical mechanisms, exercise also relieves stress, elevates mood, and improves attention—which further enhance learning. This may be one of the reasons why physically fit children exhibit better concentration and attention and suffer from less depression, anxiety, and academic problems.

It has been repeatedly demonstrated that exercise stimulates a wide range of genetic transcriptional processes that support neurological and immunological functioning. The majority of exercise-stimulated transcription is dedicated to brain-based learning and neural plasticity including the stimulation of brain-derived neurotrophic growth factor (BDNF) and nerve growth factor (VGF). See Table 14.1 for an expanded list of the effects of exercise on brain functioning (based on neuroanatomical data from rodent studies).

Table 14.1
How Exercise Enhances the Biological Mechanisms
of Learning and Memory

Enhanced Mechanisms	Impact on the Neurobiology of Learning
Gene expression[1]	Increased neuroplasticity
Brain-derived neurotrophic growth factor (BDNF)[2]	Increased neuroplasticity
Insulin-like growth factor (IGF-1)[3]	Enhanced neural protection
Nerve growth factor (VGF)[4]	Enhanced neuroplasticity
Vascular endothelial growth factor (VEGF)[5]	Enhanced neurogenesis

continued on next page

Table 14.1 continued	
Hippocampal neurogenesis[6]	More available neurons
Long-term potentiation (LTP)[7]	Increased connectivity
Capillary growth[8]	Increased oxygen and glucose availability

Although the brain is only a fraction of our body's weight, it consumes approximately 20% of our energy. This energy investment in the brain demonstrates how central nutrition is to learning. For example, skipping breakfast has been found to correlate with decreases in neurotransmitter production, alertness, and cognitive speed (Bellisle et al., 2004; Dani et al., 2005; Kanarek, 1997; Molteni et al., 2002; Rampersaud et al., 2005). Because educating starving brains can be a losing battle, proper nutrition is a necessary ingredient in academic success (Dani et al., 2005; Ivanovic et al., 2000). See Table 14.2 for a few of the effects that diet can have on the brain.

Table 14.2
The Effects of Diet on the Brain

Chemical Compound	Impact on Neural Structures	Found in:
Antioxidants[1]	increased hippocampal plasticity enhanced dopamine functioning	blueberries, strawberries,
	reduction of neuronal lesions and inflammation	spinach, Concord grapes
Folic acid[2]	enhanced neuronal self-repair increased neural longevity	whole wheat, leafy greens,
		liver, oranges, and asparagus
Essential fatty acids[3]	maintenance and health of cell membranes proper central nervous system functioning	salmon, flax seed, soybean oil, and walnuts
Phytoestrogen[4]	increased vascular health and functioning hippocampal neurogenesis	broccoli, berries, and soy

Teaching about the interconnections among the brain, the body, and how we learn will provide students with important scientific knowledge, which could improve their academic performance and physical health.

7. Sleeping Is Vital to Learning

Sleep is the golden thread that ties health and our bodies together.
—Thomas Dekker

Sound and sufficient sleep is particularly important for learning and memory (Curcio et al., 2006; Medeiros et al., 2001; Perez-Chada et al., 2007; Walker et al., 2002). Sleep boosts cognitive performance and augments learning while sleep deprivation limits our ability to sustain vigilance and attention (Doran et al., 2001; Lim & Dinges, 2008). There is considerable evidence that dreaming involves the rehearsal and consolidation of recent learning into long-term memory while naps that include slow wave and REM sleep improve perceptual skills (Mednick et al., 2003).

Sleep deprivation has been shown to impair flexible thinking and decision-making involving innovation, revising plans, and effective communication (Curcio et al., 2006; Harrison & Horne, 1999, 2000). In fact, the more complex the subject matter, the more helpful sleep is (Peigneux et al., 2001). Table 14.3 includes some suggestions for better sleep that may be helpful for both teachers and students.

Contrary to popular belief, adolescents need almost as much sleep (9.25 hours) as children (10 hours), although the average teenager gets only between 6.5–7.5 hours. Between 1974 and 1993, total sleep time for adolescents decreased because of later bedtimes but unchanged waking hours (Iglowstein et al., 2003). Most teenagers try to "catch up" on their sleep on weekends, which serves only to further disturb their biological rhythms. Modeling on their parents, they also become dependent on hypercaffeinated "power drinks" to get them through the day.

Table 14.3
Suggestions for Better Sleep

Exercise daily.

Limit naps to 30 minutes in the early afternoon.

Increase exposure to sunlight, especially later in the day.

Check the effect of medications on sleep and avoid caffeine, alcohol, and tobacco after lunch.

Limit liquids, avoid heavy meals in the evening, and eat a light snack before bed (i.e., warm milk and a carbohydrate).

Go to bed and arise at the same time every day (consistent schedule).

Get in bed only to sleep and get out of bed if you are not able to sleep.

Create a good environment for sleep (quiet/dark/comfortable)

Develop a bedtime ritual (relaxation techniques/soft music/warm bath).

Avoid thinking about life issues or engaging in problem solving while trying to fall asleep.

Adapted from Wolkove et al., (2007)

One study found that more than half of students 13 years and older are sleep-deprived (Dexter et al., 2003). For some reason (most likely related to brain maturation), adolescent sleep-wake cycles appear to occur later in the day, making early-morning classes problematic. Besides lifestyle changes, adolescents also experience a phase shift in their circadian rhythm during puberty, resulting in their falling asleep at increasingly later times. Although the reason for the phase shift is unknown, it could be related to changes in light sensitivity or may reflect developmental changes in the prefrontal cortex.

A study published in 1998 found that adolescents are often "pathologically sleepy," with sleep patterns similar to patients suffering with narcolepsy. This may be one of the many reasons why teenagers are at the wheel in over 50,000 automobile accidents each year (Wolfson & Carskadon, 1998). Sleep deprivation is apt to exacerbate the irritability, depression, and behavioral problems that often occur during adolescence (Hofferth & Sandberg, 2001). Signs of sleep disorders in the classroom will include sleepiness, tardiness and absence, and caffeine dependency, as well as academic, behavioral, and emotional difficulties (Dahl, 1999). An awareness of these biological realities can lead to changes in personal habits, sleep hygiene, school start times, and parents being less likely to accuse their adolescents of being lazy.

8. Learning Can Be Enhanced: Lessons From Cognitive Psychology

Inspiration is the impact of a fact on a well-prepared mind.
—Louis Pasteur

Learning is enhanced through regularly reestablishing attention. Because our brains evolved to remain vigilant to a constantly changing environment, we learn better in brief intervals. This makes sustained attention a limited resource that needs to be used wisely. Learning and memory improve when information is presented in spaced intervals that allow for natural fluctuations in attention. This is likely one reason why variation in materials, breaks, and even intermittent naps facilitate learning (Bodizs et al., 2002; Mednick et al., 2002; Pezdek & Miceli, 1982). It is probably important to reestablish attention every 5 to 10 minutes and continue to shift the focus of attention to new topics.

Learning is enhanced through practice and repeated exposure. Because learning involves the strengthening of connections between neurons, repetition supports learning while the absence of repetition and exposure results in its decay (Atwood & Karunanithi, 2002). This has ramifications for how information is taught daily, weekly, and throughout the school year.

Learning is enhanced through multichannel processing. Given that visual, semantic, sensory, motor, and emotional neural networks all contain their own memory systems, multichannel learning increases the likelihood of both storage and recall (Benton et al., 1983; Posner, 1988; Schacter, 1992). Because we have an amazing capacity for visual memory, written or spoken information paired with visual information results in better recall (Kandel & Squire, 2000; Mayer et al., 1996). There is a greater likelihood that learning will generalize outside the classroom if it is organized across sensory, physical, emotional and cognitive networks (Gick & Holyoak, 1983; Meltzoff et al., 2009).

Learning is enhanced through conceptual processing. When problems are represented at higher levels of abstraction, learning can be integrated into larger schemas that enhance memory, learning, and cognitive flexibility (Anderson et al., 1996; Biederman & Shiffrar, 1987; Klahr & Carver, 1988; Mayer et al., 1996; Novick & Holyoak, 1991). Starting with major concepts and repeatedly returning to them during a lecture enhances both understanding and memory, a phenomenon that increases when students create their own categories and strategies of organizing information (McDaniel et al., 1988). Chunking material into meaningful segments makes it easier to remember, and improves test performance while increasing prefrontal activity (fMRI) during encoding (Bor et al., 2003).

Learning is enhanced through hypothesis testing and feedback. A primary way our brains evolved to learn is through trial-and-error exploration. This is true of learning and adapting to both our social and physical environments. Therefore, using what we learn to attempt to solve real-world problems and adjusting our behaviors or ideas based on the results augments the retention of skills and information.

Learning is enhanced by certain environmental conditions. While the body is regulating the brain, the environment is regulating the body. Therefore, inadequate school facilities, poor acoustics, outside noise, and inadequate classroom lighting all correlate with poorer academic performance (Cash et al., 1997; Nelson & Soli, 2000). Chairs with poor support hamper blood supply to the brain and impede cognition while temperatures above 74–77 degrees Fahrenheit have been shown to correlate with lower reading comprehension and math scores (Linton et al., 1994).

Learning is enhanced through music training. Listening to music evokes memory recall and visual imagery, and stimulates a wide range of emotions. It also results in increased complexity in the organization of white matter as well as a significant increase in regional cerebral blood flow over the posterior two-thirds of the scalp (Nakamura et al., 1999). These activations reflect the deep evolutionary history of music in the forming of social groups and the expansion of cognitive processes. The possibility that music stimulates neuroplasticity is supported by the fact that children with music training demonstrate better verbal memory than their nonmusical counterparts (Ho et al., 2003). Music training is also associated with math proficiency because it increases language skills, working memory, and the ability to represent abstract numerical qualities (Chan et al., 1998; Schmithorst & Holland, 2004).

9. Fear Is Tenacious

Fear defeats more people than any one thing in the world.
—Ralph Waldo Emerson

At birth, the executive center of our brain is the amygdala. Its first job is to figure out what is safe and what is dangerous. Although the amygdala eventually comes to share executive control with the prefrontal cortex, it remains capable of hijacking the brain in states of high anxiety, fear, and terror. One of the amygdala's most important jobs is to permanently remember any and all threats and to generalize these experiences to other similar signs of danger.

Evolution has shaped our brains to err on the side of caution and to trigger fear whenever it might be remotely useful. Fear makes us less intelligent because amygdala activation interferes with prefrontal functioning. Fear also shuts down exploration, makes our thinking more rigid, and drives "neophobia," the fear of anything new. Its tendency to both generalize and escalate its reaction is the reason a single panic attack outside the home can eventually lead to a generalized anxiety, fear of leaving the house, or full-blown agoraphobia.

Learning is inhibited when the amygdala pairs relationships with fear, pain, or shame. Openness and trust are fragile creatures, especially with teachers who are going to judge our work and assess our intelligence. Although students' chances of learning are dependent upon getting input from others, past negative relationships can make them keep others at arm's length. When people are hurt or afraid, caring relationships are not easily entered into or benefited from. With these students, teachers need to become amygdala whisperers by using their warmth, empathic caring, and positive regard to decrease amygdala activation and create a state of mind that increases neuroplasticity and learning.

10. Stress Impairs Learning

What doesn't kill you makes you weaker.
—Anonymous

For our primate cousins with smaller cortices and more straightforward environmental demands, danger is encountered and quickly resolved. In the daily struggle for survival, animals either escape or get eaten in relatively short order. But when you add a huge cortex capable of building culture and information superhighways, the human brain has to adapt to a world of constant challenge without clear resolution. A large cortex also adds a memory for the future and endless possibilities for anticipatory anxiety of dangers to come. In addition, we now have a vast imagination capable of creating frightening fantasies that our primitive brains are unable to distinguish from reality. And beneath it all, the primitive amygdala is always erring on the side of wariness and fear.

Stressful situations trigger the release of the stress hormone cortisol. Cortisol's motto is "live for today for tomorrow we may die." Stress hormones are catabolic, which means they break down complex biochemical compounds for immediate energy and inhibit protein synthesis upon which neural growth and our immune system rely. Thus, prolonged stress impairs our ability to learn and maintain physical health. Because chronic stress inhibits neural plasticity, success in school depends upon a student's ability to somehow decrease their stress. From specific stress-reduction techniques to the soothing effects of a supportive student-teacher relationship, stress modulation and academic success go hand in hand. The inclusion of stress-management techniques into the curriculum is an obvious application of neuroscience to education that can improve learning, emotional well-being, and physical health.

11. Our Brains Are Prone to Error

Men should strive to think much and know little.
—Democritus

One look around us makes it clear that precise thinking and self-insight do not appear to have exerted a strong pressure on natural selection. Defenses that distort reality in the service of decreasing anxiety are obviously more prevalent than good reality testing and exercising personal responsibility. Consider these three statements taken from actual auto accident reports: "The telephone pole was approaching. I was attempting to swerve out of its way when it struck the front end"; "My car was legally parked as it backed into the other vehicle"; and (my favorite) "A pedestrian hit me and went under my car." These are all perceptual distortions that reflect both egocentrism and decreased responsibility for negative occurrences.

At the same time, cognitive distortions tend to enhance social coherence by putting a positive spin on the behavior of those closest to us. This is most clearly seen in a mother's love. A judge once said that everyone he sends to prison has "a mother with an innocent child." Self-deception also serves a valuable purpose by increasing the likelihood of successfully deceiving others. If we believe our own fictions, we are less likely to give away our real thoughts and intentions via nonverbal signs and behaviors. When we are depressed, negative events carry more weight; when we are in love, our beloved's faults are impossible to see. Secure attachment and emotional regulation correlate with our ability to hear feedback, accept our own limitations, and use fewer reality-distorting defenses. In today's large social groups, self-insight, mindfulness, and recognition of our own limitations have become increasingly important to our survival as a species. Perhaps these hard realities will shape the future trajectory of brain evolution in the direction of emotional intelligence and mindful awareness.

12. We Analyze Others but Not Ourselves: The Primacy of Projection

Men use thought only to justify their wrongdoings,
and speech only to conceal their thoughts.

—Voltaire

If you put someone in a brain scanner and ask her to analyze other people, all sorts of networks become activated. The existence of these sophisticated neural systems reflects the millions of years of natural selection that have been refining our brains' ability to read, predict, and control the action of others. The dedication of so much neural activity to the actions, thoughts, and feelings of others reflects the importance of social and emotional awareness and understanding to our group survival.

If you put the same person in a scanner and ask her to think about herself, there is much less activity. It appears that evolution has not seen fit to invest anywhere near as much energy or neural architecture into self-awareness. In fact, some theorists believe that self-awareness is an accident of evolution and detrimental to survival because it leads us to hesitate and question our decisions. And while analyzing what is on the minds of others is reflexive and automatic, self-awareness requires concentration, effort, and runs the risk of triggering anxiety. Which do you think is going to be the norm?

It is abundantly clear that our brains have evolved to pay attention to the behaviors and emotions of other people. Not only is this processing complex, but it is lightning fast, shaping our experience of others milliseconds before we even become consciously aware of their presence. We automatically generate a theory of what is on their mind—our ideas about what they know, what their motivations may be, and what they might do next. As a result, we are as quick to think we know others as we are slow to become aware of our own motives and faults. In biblical terms, it is reflexive to attend to the mote in our brother's eye and not see the beam in our own.

Freud thought this process was a defense mechanism—a way of pushing unwanted feelings onto others. In fact, projection may be more of a by-product of how our brains interweave our automatic theories of others' minds with our understandings of ourselves. This may be why we so often see our own truths in what we think and feel about others before we realize that it applies to us. How many times have you heard yourself giving others advice that you should be taking?

A good way to compensate for this neural bias is to ask ourselves if the thoughts and feelings we have about others are, in fact, autobiographical. Taking our thoughts about others and trying them on for size has the potential to teach us about ourselves and increase our empathic abilities. Simple exercises that guide students to examine what and how what they think and feel about others may be true for themselves can open a window of self-awareness, empathy, and insight.

Chapter 15

Building Tribal Classrooms

Character is our destiny.

—Heraclitus

Throughout this book I have presented scientific evidence for the neuroplastic power of secure attachments in the context of natural learning environments. The basic premise is that the more the environment of a classroom parallels the interpersonal, emotional, and motivational components of our tribal past, the more our primitive instincts will activate the biochemistry of learning. Further, the benefits of these tribal "work-arounds" will be most significant for students whose cultural backgrounds and learning styles are especially mismatched with the modern industrial classroom. If the brain is a social organ of adaptation, then education should be an interpersonal process of social, cultural, and environmental exploration.

As a boy, I was a troubled and distracted student. Overwhelmed by stress at home and using most of my energy to cope with my anxiety, I had neither the support nor the motivation to be anything more than a mediocre student. I was, however, fortunate enough to cross paths with a handful of sensitive, caring, and stimulating teachers who encouraged me to follow my interests and passions. In their classes I somehow found algebra, social studies, and literature to be interesting and worthy of my attention and energy. Tests in these classes were transformed from inevitable sources of shame into worthy challenges and opportunities to make my teachers proud.

Despite my generally negative self-image as a learner, with these teachers I was open to and interested in learning. From an early age, it was clear to me that relationships have the power to heal and inspire. They also instilled within me the subversive idea that I might be capable of earning a living with my head instead of my hands. By the time my 10th-grade guidance counselor suggested that I switch from an academic to an "industrial" track and my father told me to forget about college and join the army, I was ready to prove them wrong. I rebelled with a vengeance, staying in school and eventually earning three graduate degrees.

Based on my own history, it is easy to see why teachers like Marva Collins, Albert Cullum, and Erin Gruwell are so close to my heart. They were subversives who stood up to the status quo and created new and more effective ways of teaching. And when we think of the brain as a social organ, it becomes clear that their success was grounded in their ability to simulate primitive social instincts in the context of an attachment-based classroom. If it weren't for heroic teachers like these, many of us would have achieved far less satisfying and productive lives.

In these final two chapters we will explore how some of the concepts from social neuroscience we have discussed have been embodied in the lives and teachings of a few exceptional educators. We will look at Joe Clark, Jaime Escalante, and Rafe Esquith, as their work exemplifies the importance of physical safety, emotional security, and ecologically relevant curricula. In the final chapter we will focus on the importance of smaller schools and classrooms and the value of integrating the schools with the community as demonstrated in the work of Geoffrey Canada and Steve Barr. Finally, we end with what may be the most important element of all: the emotional development and inner journey of the teacher in preparation for becoming a wise elder and tribal leader.

Physical Safety

I won't say ours was a tough school, but we did have our own coroner.

—Lenny Bruce

The central evolutionary driver of attachment and social connections of all kinds is assumed to be their survival value. In fact, the neural circuitry that assesses the environment for danger also serves as the infrastructure of attachment circuitry in social animals. Because of this, physical safety, attachment security, and learning have evolved as interdependent processes. This is why plasticity is maximized and children learn best when they feel protected and connected. The goal of attachment-based teaching is to have each child move from feeling vulnerable, frightened, and unimportant to feeling protected, cared for, and valued—a state of mind that optimizes learning.

Tribal educators foster an environment of safety by serving as protector and defender. They accomplish this by promoting security through structure, consistency, and vigilantly monitoring for any sign of potential danger. The chief is always ready to intervene if a member of his or her tribe is in danger. The message from tribal educators to each student is that if any child or adult is bothering you, let me know, because I am here to look after and protect you. The prototypic educator as warrior and tribal chief is Joe Clark.

Principal Clark

Good deeds are usually wrought at great risk.

—Herodotus

Moments before his first day as principal, Mr. Clark yelled to the teachers through his signature bullhorn, "Assume your positions!" In military fashion, the faculty lined up in preparation for the waves of students about to fill the hallways. This was very different from the first day of school a year earlier when a security guard had been stabbed for interfering with a drug deal. Mr. Clark was the new sheriff in town, charged with bringing law and order to a few square blocks of Patterson, New Jersey, called Eastside High: a school that had become synonymous with violence, drugs, and academic failure.

Selected by the district's superintendent based on his past success at a neighboring school, Clark came equipped with the fundamental belief that discipline is the essence of education. Clark ran a very tight ship and had zero tolerance for anything that compromised safety or learning. His radical enforcement of the rules was rooted in protecting the sanctity of Eastside as a vehicle of learning and self-growth. His goals were simple: Uphold the goals of education, inspire those who wanted to be inspired, and uplift the school and the community.

In his book *Laying Down the Law* (1989), Clark writes that before his arrival, the students had taken control: "They had the power, they set the tone, and the tone was chaos" (p. 47). He believed that if learning was going to take place, the "diseases of the ghetto" had to be cut out. Before the school year began, Mr. Clark had the graffiti covered, new desks installed, and plants, fountains, and couches added to make Eastside look more like a school than a prison. Trophies were taken out of closets, polished, and displayed and a dress code was implemented to support dignity, self-respect, and professionalism.

Mr. Clark immediately became notorious for expelling students who were wreaking havoc and making it impossible for others to learn. He tossed out the troublemakers and padlocked the doors to make sure that the students who wanted to learn and the teachers who wanted to educate them could get to work in an environment of peace and safety. He was unwilling to allow a small minority of students to poison the learning atmosphere for everyone else. Clark built stronger fences, fired incompetent security guards, and replaced them with strong and responsible adults who were dedicated to the goal of learning. By circumventing the rules (and in some instances the law) to create a safe learning environment, he risked both his job and professional reputation. Doing what he felt was right for his students at his own peril was exactly what is expected of a tribal leader.

Clark diligently watched over his students as a "surrogate father," patrolling the halls up to 20 miles a day to let everyone know he was on the job. During his first year as principal, he held back 400 students who were not working up to grade level. In response to the protest, he replied, "If you think getting left back is hard, try living as an illiterate" (p. 68). Like any good tribal elder, he wanted to instill important cultural values to shape good citizens, responsible adults, and nurturing parents of the next generation. To support these goals, he developed extracurricular programs to teach job and life skills because so many students had given up on their own parents and had no one else to turn to.

Mr. Clark knew that for his students to excel, his teachers needed to feel supported. He promoted teacher pride by encouraging them to ask for what they needed—a fresh coat of paint for their classrooms, new books, whatever would enhance the learning environment—and he always did his best to deliver. When teachers went on strike asking for more money, he kept anyone from crossing the picket line because he knew they deserved a raise. He made a point of telling his teachers that he didn't blame them for the problems of education, but he did point a finger at fellow principals who were afraid to assume the responsibility of making their schools orderly and safe for dedicated students and committed teachers. As Mr. Clark saw it, the essential equation for learning is that the student must be able to receive what the teacher is transmitting in the context of peace, order, and mutual respect.

Commentary

As a tribal leader, Mr. Clark is a board of education's worst nightmare, because his methods often disregarded protocol, due process, and the law in the service of the safety and education of his students. Historically, it is well within a tribal leader's role to disregard rules, beliefs, and past teachings in the service of the tribe's survival and advancement.

By expelling bullies and drug dealers from school and chaining the doors to keep them out, Clark sent the clear message to his students that he knew they were in danger and that it was his job to protect them. The tribal leader's commitment to group safety serves as a template for teachers and students to watch out for and protect one another. Grounded in the basic biochemistry of bonding and attachment, protecting your tribe is the essence of tribal cohesion and the key to its survival value.

Leadership through service was demonstrated by Clark's dedication and willingness to risk his job and reputation for his beliefs. By coming together against common enemies such as the drug dealers, gangbangers, and later the school board that threatened to fire him, he solidified his school as a group with mutual needs and a common goal. And although he seems to have violated the expectations of democratic participation in order to foster group cohesion, an embattled school in a dangerous neighborhood may require a warrior tribal leadership. Democratic decision making in a tribe is almost always waived in the face of danger (war, famine, etc.) to enhance coordination, efficiency, and survival against an outside enemy.

Emotional Security

Being loved gives you strength,
loving someone gives you courage.

—Lao Tzu

Our brains react in the same way to threats against the self as it does to threats against the body. Because of this, disrespect, shame, and humiliation shut down learning as quickly as physical attacks. Attachment-based teachers take this to heart and do whatever it takes to minimize shame in interactions with their students and in students' interactions with one another. In an optimal learning environment, there should be the same zero tolerance established for shaming as for bullying. Using fear, embarrassment, and shame to control students is a clear indication that a teacher is not viewing the classroom through the eyes of a student. Like a tribal chief, a teacher's authority will come to be recognized based on the respect and compassion shown to students.

In order to reach and teach a class, an attachment-based perspective calls on us to grasp the inner *and* outer worlds of students, including their interests, passions, needs, and vulnerabilities. Understanding the world from their point of view and striving to empathize with their philosophies and beliefs creates the possibility for emotional attunement and helping them to "feel felt" by their teachers. Grasping these dynamics lays the foundation for mutual compassion and an awareness of how to present information in ways that students can hear.

Building secure attachments is the gateway to emotional regulation, self-esteem, and learning. Because the same factors that make a healthy home are present in a tribal classroom, teachers have the opportunity to reparent their students and shape new attachment circuitry. Whether they are establishing consistency via norms, instilling the students with a curative sense of belonging, or unifying the class against a negative outside force, tribal teachers become loving and protective parents to their students, who in turn become caring and supportive siblings to one another. This emotional security creates a safe haven and secure base from which to explore, take risks, and build self-esteem as valued and valuable individuals.

Professor Jaime Escalante

If you desire ease, forsake learning.

—Nagarjuna

A native Bolivian and the son of two teachers, Jaime Escalante began teaching math at Los Angeles's Garfield High in 1974 (Escalante, 1990). He soon learned of the long-standing prejudices against his Mexican American students and of their poor self-image as learners. The culture of East Los Angeles and the low morale at Garfield High painted a picture of a bleak future and the irrelevance of education. Escalante preached to his students that only *ganas* (desire) was required to succeed—the moment-to-moment choice to work hard, persevere, and stand up in the face of adversity. He felt that a central aspect of his job was to bring out the ganas in each of his students. Mr. Escalante worked tirelessly before and after school, on weekends, and during summers alongside his students, never asking them to work harder than he worked himself.

Historically, a majority of Mexican American students have been considered "slow learners" or "retarded" in American schools without regard for their degree of acculturation or English-language skills. Blind to these deeply engrained prejudices, Mr. Escalante felt that all students perform up or down to the level of the expectations placed upon them. Because the only way out of their current life-styles of gangs, violence, and poverty was hard work, he had to build their self-esteem while maintaining high standards. Mr. Escalante's strategy was to be far more demanding than other teachers and require each student to sign a contract to solidify his or her commitment to working harder and putting in longer hours than had ever been expected of them before.

To enter his classroom each day, students had to turn in their homework, which was called the "tickets to the show." Once inside, students found that they had entered the math Olympics, engaging in warm-up routines where they would clap their hands and stomp their feet. His students wore special sports jackets, hats, and school t-shirts to psych them up to take exams. "Escalantes," the hodgepodge of sports slang, pop culture, and high school vernacular that constituted the language of the Escalante tribe, made no sense to outsiders. As insiders, the students knew they didn't need gangs or other surrogate families; they were members of the Escalante tribe.

Under Escalante, these "unteachable" Mexican American students excelled on the nationally administered AP Calculus test. Their performance was so good that the entire class was accused of cheating and forced to retake the test under official scrutiny. With both their intelligence and integrity under question, Escalante's tribe dug deep, bonded even more closely, and repeated their excellent performance on an alternate version of the exam.

While respect, discipline, and hard work were pillars of his classroom, Escalante believed that "students learn better when they are having a good time." Over the years, Escalante became part entertainer by engaging his class with humor and using a variety of games to stimulate interest and participation. He mixed jokes and card tricks with quizzes, lectures, and memorization drills. He even held up a small clown head as a reminder that they would end up working at Jack in the Box if they didn't do their homework. Through a flare for the unexpected and his proclivity for showmanship and improvisation, Escalante made math engaging and fun.

Escalante recognized the power of relationships to change lives and realized that for some of his students, he was the first person to show them love. He was seen as a father figure and, like a father, he stood up to and stood up for many angry and troubled kids. He once asked his students what they wanted from their parents. They told him peace at home, understanding, trust, and love. In reflecting on his years of teaching, he realized that these were the values that he had always held in his heart.

Commentary

If people did not do silly things,
nothing intelligent would ever get done.
                                                —Ludwig Wittgenstein

Due to their age, ethnicity, and income, many of the students with the most difficulty learning are those at the bottom of the social hierarchy. Their struggle with multiple layers of marginalization and disrespect makes the establishment of respect and empowerment all the more vital in these communities. A tribal teacher like Jaime Escalante recognizes the power of love, concern, interest, and a willingness to listen as central educational tools. When a student receives the same respect he is expected to give, he realizes that he, too, is a worthy and valuable member of the class. All of these practices support the creation of secure attachment and a tribal mind-set within each student.

Escalante shaped his class into a tribe by using a wide range of attachment-based practices. Like Joe Clark, he and his students faced the common enemies of poverty and prejudice in ways that solidified their bonds. The battle against the calculus exam and the subsequent fight with the testing board further deepened their sense of being a unified tribe. In the process of this heroic struggle, Escalante guided his students to build new identities as warrior-learners and provided them with the experience of hard work leading to success. This generates a revolutionary and heroic narrative that replaces one shaped by the hopelessness and shame of internalized prejudice.

Escalante was the tribal chief who gained authentic leadership through service and self-sacrifice. Mutual hard work, team spirit, and the secret language they shared supported group cohesion and a feeling of being a part of something both exclusive and special. His students formed a new gang with a strong leader and a shared goal of passing the big exam and attaining future success. Escalante's love of humor and turning learning into play decreased anxiety and supported the neuroplastic mechanisms of new learning. As a tribal leader, he made sure that his students knew he believed in them and fought to instill within them the pride and courage they needed to succeed.

Tribal teachers tap into their own primitive protective instincts that drive them to fight for their students and endure the negativity they may have to navigate to advocate for their tribe. The tribal teacher has the potential to create, and in fact be, a secure base at the center of a classroom family. For many students who lack this at home, the classroom may be their best and last chance to have this experience.

Ecological Relevance

> *The goal of life is living in agreement with nature.*
> —Zeno

The survival of a species is based on diversity, flexibility, and adaptation. Each tribe consists of individuals with different skills, special abilities, strengths, and weaknesses. Tribal life assumes this diversity and optimizes survival by finding ways for each individual to make a positive and important contribution. This allows each individual to be an integral component of the whole. This may be the reason why the "one-size-fits-all" model of contemporary education doesn't work for so many of our students. A natural learning environment needs to contain a range of learning modalities and specialty areas that parallel the breadth of student learning styles and specialized abilities.

You may have noticed that you almost never have to bribe boys to play video games or beg girls to be on a social media site. These modern contrivances are naturally compelling because they tap into genetically programmed and biologically reinforced instincts. Millions of years of evolution have shaped our brains to engage with the world in ways that support our gender-based social roles. In other words, our brains have evolved to attend to and learn those things that are personally, socially, and ecologically relevant. The flip side is that you are never going to stimulate a student's motivation or awaken a passion for learning with a rigid and irrelevant curriculum.

Not only is it unnatural and ineffective to teach the same material to all students at the same pace, but it can actually be damaging to many of the students' psyches and self-esteem. When a standard curriculum is presented in a fixed environment, the students for whom it is a bad match become bored and turned off to learning. When children are forced to read at times and in ways that they are not ready for, they experience shame instead of enjoyment and failure instead of accomplishment. Learning can become a dreaded activity and the experience of failure and indifference can generalize beyond the walls of the classroom.

As we discussed in an earlier chapter, culture was shared and transmitted through stories for countless generations before written language. Narratives, from both literature and personal experience, are emotionally engaging and memorable, and contain lessons about every possible human situation. In a very real sense, teaching through stories evokes the historical power of tribal elders and taps into a way of learning that our brains find most natural. Stories are also essential for all of us in becoming more mindful and self-aware. They allow us to question the world around us and create alternative narratives we can use to better regulate our emotions and guide our behaviors. Elementary school teacher Rafe Esquith uses multiple levels of narrative to build the external skills and internal strength of his students.

Professor Rafe Esquith

Judge a man by his questions rather than by his answers.
—Voltaire

Following his own passion for exploration and facing new challenges, Rafe Esquith creates a classroom environment buzzing with life. Because he believes that children learn best by being exposed to new situations, he fills each day with an orchestrated flow of stimulating learning opportunities. The constant newness is designed to capture and hold attention, enhance memory, and make learning dynamic, exciting, and fun. His fifth graders move from task to task in 30- to 60-minute blocks from learning algebra, to playing rock and roll, to reading *The Grapes of Wrath*. Later on, they may engage in book binding, designing string art, or weaving carpets before moving on to practicing for an upcoming performance or math exam. Esquith's orientation to discipline is to make learning so interesting that the worst punishment is to be banned from participation.

On the first day of class, Mr. Esquith tells his students that his purpose as a teacher is to guide them to explore their motivations, to think critically about issues of right and wrong, and to develop a personal code of behavior. He encourages them to see each moment as an opportunity to develop character and evolve as a person. Like Albert Cullum, Esquith uses the plays of Shakespeare to expose students to an array of human emotions, motivations, and behaviors. His goal is to present them with meaningful questions of values, ethics, and different ways of understanding success.

Another core element of his teaching method is a system of microeconomics where each student is assigned a job such as a banker, hall monitor, office messenger, clerk, or police officer. They receive monthly paychecks in exchange for fulfilling certain responsibilities associated with their jobs and earn bonuses when they do extra work.

Students pay rent on their desks, balance a checkbook, pay taxes, or suffer monetary consequences for being late or not doing their jobs. Purchases made with savings at the end of the school year reinforce the value of delayed gratification and hard work.

Because Esquith feels that books are a doorway to lifelong learning, he plans each reading lesson with the goal of matching the right book to each student's interests to provide the individual scaffolding needed to ensure success. Through this kind of care, he hopes to instill a love of reading that encourages students to become life long learners. He teaches his students that "failure is not trying" and celebrates mistakes as opportunities to try again.

A former student of Mr. Esquith had such a positive experience in his class that he registered it as a nonprofit organization and secured grants to support Esquith's work. These funds are used to buy equipment to record their plays and musical performances and to go on field trips that many students could not afford. These field trips, earned with many hours of additional study, are an integral component of the curriculum. Before going to a Dodgers game, for example, students have to learn the rules and history of baseball, and then play a game themselves. By the time they enter the stadium, they are probably more knowledgeable of the game than most fans. For a trip to Washington, D.C., students study about the Lincoln Memorial, review the inscription on the monument wall, and learn about the Civil War. Lessons about Native American culture are paired with camping trips to South Dakota, Montana, and Wyoming. Mr. Esquith's method of "going mobile" with his students is intended to broaden their horizons and stimulate their passion for exploration.

Another aspect of trip preparation is teaching students about airplane travel, restaurant etiquette, and hotel procedures. He teaches organization, planning, and awareness of others by assigning roommates months before and providing diagrams of the hotel rooms so they know where to put their belongings; he even has them coordinate their shower schedules. Mr. Esquith creates a matrix of experiences designed to build a sense of community that can serve as a foundation for exploration and discovery.

Despite the fact that many of his students come from impoverished backgrounds or speak little English, his assumption is that they are all capable of being successful in his class. Toward this end, he strives to make his classroom accessible to all learning levels and to weave language skills into every lesson. Like the other educators we have discussed, Esquith places high expectations on his students in the belief that true excellence takes sacrifice, hard work, and enormous effort. Simultaneously, his methods help make it possible to build the confidence necessary to face new challenges, endure negative feedback, and overcome other obstacles to learning.

Esquith has found that his students watch him very closely and that his actions are a powerful teacher. He certainly is a man on a mission, spending 12 hours a day, 6 days a week, 48 weeks out of the year in the classroom and offering free SAT classes on Saturdays for former students who are applying to college. He believes that kids do not mind having hard teachers if they are fair and hold themselves to the same standards they expect from their students. Beneath it all, Esquith's goal is to demonstrate how the classroom is like a family to which each member makes a variety of important contributions.

Commentary

> The best teachers teach from the heart, not from a book.
> —Anonymous

Given that stimulating environments build the cerebral cortex, Mr. Esquith's students must build plump and vibrant brains! The ongoing alternation of subject matter throughout the day supports sustained attention, while the mix of subjects stimulates cognitive flexibility, expression, and the use of multiple sensory modalities. He challenges them on almost every imaginable dimension, and the vast majority find it within themselves to rise to the occasion.

Because learning in tribes is driven by group survival, challenges that are both life-relevant and worthy of mastering are most likely to activate primitive social instincts. Therefore, the ecological validity of his assignments to the day-to-day lives of his students enhances their capacity to learn. Keep in mind that tribal expectations were high because failure was not an option. Therefore, worthy challenges and high expectations are signs of respect, while providing the support necessary to master the challenges placed before the students are indications of love and support. Both signify the social inclusion and acceptance that are the true opposite of shame. Teaching math in the context of balancing a checkbook, creating a personal budget, or even calculating sports statistics provides them with real-world skills that support the tangible value of their efforts in the classroom.

By focusing on the moral fortitude of the characters in plays and novels, Esquith evokes fictional role models who impart the importance of developing a personal code of behavior. In the process, students learn how to be accountable for their own actions and how to think independently. In the process of putting on plays, they learn about discipline, risk taking, and teamwork. The transmission of values through storytelling harken back to traditional modes of tribal education.

Tribal learning occurs in the context of modeling, daily activities, and ritual practices that involve all of the senses, the body, and our emotions. The tribal teacher uses movement, emotions, activities, and group projects to activate our natural learning instincts. By drawing on children's imagination, enthusiasm, and openness to new ideas, a tribal teacher can direct their energies into playful learning activities. Building attachment-based classrooms requires enough emotional security to be unafraid to experiment, go the extra mile, and make yourself vulnerable to students in the service of student learning.

Chapter 16

Teachers Within Classrooms
Within Communities

*It is time that villages were universities, and their elder
inhabitants the fellows of universities.*
　　　　　　　　　　　　　—Henry David Thoreau

In this chapter, we will explore three final contributions to attachment-based teaching and the creation of tribal classrooms. We will look at the value of smaller schools and classrooms that more closely parallel the setting of our social evolution. We will look at one way this is being accomplished by the Green Dot Schools of Steve Barr and colleagues. Next, we will look at schools in the context of community through Geoffrey Canada's model of the Harlem Children's Zone. We will conclude by focusing inward on the personal journey of the teachers to attain and sustain wisdom, and a heroic vision of our role in society.

Groups: Size and Continuity

One characteristic of tribal life is maintaining optimal group size for direct communication, interdependence, and mutual accountability.

We see these dynamics play out in the differences between social interactions in small towns and large cities. People in small towns are much more likely to know one another, say hello, and help each other in times of trouble. This dynamic is likely present because of the resemblance of small towns to the tribes of our evolutionary past that stimulate primitive social instincts. In line with this, small versus large groups enhance vigilance for threats and make it more likely that individuals will contribute to the common good (Isaac et al., 1994; Roberts, 1996). As social groups grow larger, the biochemistry of attachment appears to be supplanted by a state of mind and body that weakens primitive social instincts in the service of self-preservation. As this occurs, we see that people grow less attuned to, identified with, and empathetic toward one another.

The economy of scale within public education often leads to the creation of classrooms, schools, and educational bureaucracies that create a sense of alienation and a diffusion of responsibility. Administrators blame politicians, teachers blame administrators, and students and their parents blame everyone. Because the problems are innate to the structure itself, individuals are hard-pressed to create positive change. When group size is optimized for attachment in combination with physical and emotional safety, a classroom can become a secure base from which to think new thoughts, explore, and learn. Smaller classes and school sizes allow for more personal interactions, one-on-one and small-group activities, and a stronger sense of group identity, which enhance tribe building.

As a young New Yorker, Geoffrey Canada dreamed that someday Superman would come and fix his community. This is a telling statement from the mouth of a child about what it takes to change entrenched, rigid, and dysfunctional systems. As we have seen again and again, it takes heroic efforts and a thick skin to create a tribal classroom within the present industrial system. Although we tend to take large, cumbersome, and largely ineffective school systems as a necessary reality, some educators have created alternative structures that appear to work much better. One of these people is Steve Barr.

Steve Barr and Green Dot Schools

A society grows great when people plant trees
in whose shade they know they shall never sit!
                                        —Greek proverb

The educational strategist Steve Barr and his brother Mike were raised by a hard-working, single mom in Monterey, California. Steve, an athletic and popular kid, gained admission to a private high school and went on to college. Mike, overweight and socially reclusive, dropped out of his public high school and enlisted in the Navy. After college, Steve went on to become a successful campaign manager for a number of political candidates including Bill Clinton. Mike lost his leg in a motorcycle accident and later died of a drug overdose.

When Steve's mother died 3 years later, he decided to change his life. Barr told a reporter, "So there I was, at age 39 I had just buried my family. At that point I wanted to do something different with my life and the schools that had so failed my brother were a good place to start." In 1999, Barr moved to Los Angeles on a mission to change a public school system that had become notorious for being a collection of overcrowded and unsafe "drop-out factories." Working without a salary, he organized his ideas, networked with investors, and nurtured his dream into what eventually became Green Dot Schools.

A year later, Barr, along with Shane Martin (the dean of education at Loyola Marymount University) and a group of supporters opened Amino Leadership Charter High School. Amino in Spanish literally translates as "vigor" or "courage" (though Barr prefers the translation "get off your butt"). They started with five new teachers and a handful of basic policies. By the next year, students at Amino outperformed nearby Hawthorne High on every measurable academic standard. By 2010, Green Dot Schools had expanded to 19 campuses.

From the beginning, keeping schools and classrooms small was a central element of Barr's vision. Using California charter schools as a template, Green Dot Schools would be no larger than 560 students. Classes would also be kept small, with low student-teacher ratios and a curriculum geared toward college preparation. In traditional public school settings, it is easy for students to feel lost in the crowd and unaccountable to anyone for showing up and doing their work. A small school provides the necessary matrix of social relationships that support commitment and a sense of accountability, while stimulating neuroplasticity and learning. Instincts of social bonding are further enhanced by making entry into the school competitive and establishing the shared challenge of getting into college.

Incoming ninth graders are sent to mini-campuses and given extra attention. The purpose is to make sure that they are up to grade level and have the basic skills to succeed in high school. Each classroom is set up as an autonomous teaching environment where the teacher determines what material will be presented and through what techniques. This translates into more personalized education for the students and allows teachers to utilize their interests and strengths. Students, teachers, and administrators are all held personally accountable for student performance on grades, standardized tests, graduation rates, and college acceptance.

Teachers and principals are expected to form relationships with each student and his or her family. Julio Murcia, the principal of Animo Leadership High, is known for going out into the neighborhood and visiting the homes of current and prospective students. Mr. Murcia is visible every morning and afternoon in front of the school where students are dropped off and picked up, where he makes himself available to students, parents, and school staff. He feels that parental inclusion and a sense of consistency between school and home are paramount for success.

Commentary

It is not so much what is poured into the student,
but what is planted that really counts.
                                                                        —Anonymous

In comparison to the public schools that surround them, Green Dot Schools are characterized by smaller, safer, and student-centered programs. In keeping with our hypothesis about the tribal instincts of the social brain, smaller schools are more likely to be successful, especially with students who have greater social, emotional, and educational needs. Each student gets more one-on-one time and the chance for sustained and sustaining connections with teachers and peers.

From the teachers' perspective, the orientation toward smaller classes and academic freedom correlate with decreased stress, increased health, and a sense of personal accomplishment (Delaney et al., 1997). The fundamental ingredients of small school size and the focus on personal relationships among teachers, students, families, and community come together to create a tribal work-around within a big city. Barr's innovative business planning allows for the creation of a school that leverages social relationships in the service of learning.

There is also considerable evidence that supports the benefits of smaller schools (Barker & Gump, 1964; Berlin & Cienkus, 1989; Raywind, 1994). Multiple studies have also found that smaller schools improve attitudes, attendance, achievement, and graduation rates—especially for minority and inner-city students (Fowler, 1995; Lindsay, 1982; Rogers, 1987). Smaller schools have been found to enhance academic achievement, on-task behavior, participation in extracurricular activities, and positive relationships among students, staff, and faculty (Conant, 1959; Cotton, 1996; Fowler & Walberg, 1991; Lotan & Ben-Ari, 1994). Because parents who earn less tend to work longer hours, children at Green Dot Schools benefit from participating in extracurricular activities rather than being unsupervised in dangerous neighborhoods. Small cooperative classroom groups simulate the social context for tribal learning where students learn to communicate and collaborate with others.

We have all witnessed that when systems reach a certain size, attention and resources shift from their stated mission to maintaining the institution. There is a gradual diversion of time, energy, and capital away from the constituents and toward administrative and political functions. Smaller, decentralized schools tend to direct more of their resources to student needs versus those of the organization

(Berlin & Cienkus, 1989). Unlike a public school, where one-third to one-half of the budget goes to supporting district staff and headquarters, $.94 of every Green Dot dollar is used to provide resources for the classroom. In this way, Green Dot Schools have been able to follow the model of private schools—better-paid teachers, smaller campuses, and higher expectations (Fine, 2007). The central office and the growth of the Green Dot system are funded solely through outside donations and investment (McGray, 2009).

Geoffrey Canada and the Harlem Children's Zone

When you teach your son, you teach your son's son.
                    —Talmudic rabbinical writings

As anyone who has tried knows, teaching within a community that does not value education is a difficult and uphill battle. Valuing education can be so incongruent with the surrounding culture that students who are motivated to learn are bullied and considered sellouts if they read a book or answer a question in class. Teachers in these communities often find themselves in dangerous and impoverished schools with students who receive insufficient attention at home and who lack the preparation and motivation to learn. Expanding the scope of education beyond the classroom and individual school, Geoffrey Canada created a model of bringing educational values to an entire community.

Canada's vision of a broad community educational environment is manifest in what he calls the Harlem Children's Zone. He believes that for students to learn, the entire community must be contaminated with the value of education. He feels that when most of the kids in a neighborhood are involved in high-quality educational programs, the culture of that neighborhood begins to change. If children are exposed to people talking about going to college, it impacts children's beliefs about the world and what they can do in the future. In Canada's words, if this message spreads throughout the community, it won't seem unusual for kids to do their homework, "speak proper English," or do well in school (Tough, 2009, p. 125). This is why Canada frames his tribe in terms of a "zone" instead of a single classroom or school.

In contrast to the current model of education, Canada's vision is to support children and their families from gestation. It begins with a "baby college" where expecting and new parents learn basic parenting skills and are taught ways to give their children an advantage in school. Once their children are born, parents graduate into a weekly program to continue to learn about child discipline, health, and brain development. At age 4, their children can enter the Harlem Gems prekindergarten program and can later enroll in the Promise Academy. The "promise" is to get every student into college, providing that students and their parents make a total commitment to education. Over the years, parents interact, connect, and support each other with the common goal of educating themselves and their children.

Although the lack of material resources is a problem for poor parents, a larger problem is that they believe education is something that only takes place in school. Canada has found that only about one-third of the parents in his programs take responsibility for their children's education. Most lack what Canada sees as a middle-class value of creating learning experiences at home and doing everything they possibly can to give their children an advantage. Canada believes that these are not poor parenting skills or moral failures, but a natural consequence of their own childhood experiences, environment, and cultural history. As we all know, advantages and disadvantages of all kinds accumulate from generation to generation.

The development of adjunctive programs for parents is driven by research showing that a dearth of one-on-one interaction and a lack of exposure to reading materials put children at a decided disadvantage when they get to the classroom. Canada feels that while middle-class kids are reading the 800-page *Harry Potter*, those without access to books need to be stimulated every 15 or 20 seconds or they lose focus. For children to be successful, Canada feels that parents need to be connected to the school, be involved in their children's education, and continue the educational process after school and on weekends.

His teachers work hard to develop close relationships with parents and participate in a program to get fathers more involved. Parents are educated about the importance of reading to their children, the value of shared activities, and the importance of their involvement in their children's academic development. One of Canada's goals is to help the families of his students embrace proactive educational values while maintaining the positive values of their Harlem culture.

Commentary

> You can't hold a man down without staying down with him.
> —Booker T. Washington

At the heart of Harlem Children's Zone is the establishment of cultural values that enhance the long-term well-being and survival of the community. These values include the importance of higher education, personal responsibility, and hard work required to succeed in school. Canada's attempt to instill middle-class educational values clearly parallels the role of traditional tribal elders in guiding their tribe toward practices that enhance sustainability.

Research has consistently found that lower social and economic status is associated with lower cognitive abilities and achievement during childhood and beyond. Neurocognitive testing also reveals deficits in prefrontal executive functioning and left hemisphere language functions that appear to be interrelated (Noble et al., 2005). These data suggest that Canada's focus on language, reading, and sustained attention across various tasks may be the key to advancing problem solving and learning.

Canada believes that the way to accelerate kids who are far behind is to expose them to more instruction and immerse them in a well-run, disciplined, and demanding environment. Thus, he extended both the school day and the school year to provide more learning and less time to be unsupervised and on the streets. His students are divided into different achievement levels with lagging students required to be at school an hour earlier for remedial work. Others participate in after-school and Saturday classes to improve their test scores. In addition, the Harlem Children's Zone includes 40 tutors who work with 200 children from 4 to 7 pm Monday through Friday and from 9 am to 1 pm on Saturdays. Wearing a jacket and tie instead of a cape, Canada strives to be the mortal version of the Superman he has always waited for.

The Teacher

The most difficult thing in life is to know yourself.
—Thales

Although teaching may fit the definition of a profession, it isn't just another way to make a living. Those who aspire to become teachers usually have a passion and dedication which turns their work into a mission. A passion for teaching and compassion for others are not learned in school: They arise from the same complex dance of genes, temperament, and life experiences that have always drawn our ancestors to lives of service.

For most of our evolutionary history, being a successful teacher was a matter of life and death. The young *had* to learn the skills required for the survival of all. This may be why tribal teaching can look like performance art, demon possession, or a state of frenzy. Rafe Esquith says he teaches as if his hair were on fire, while Marva Collins calls on us to teach as if "Jesus himself" were in the classroom. To whatever degree enthusiasm, passion, and intensity can be brought into teaching, we tap into the primitive survival-based instincts that stimulate curiosity, motivation, and the biochemistry of learning in us and our students.

We may not all have it within us to teach like our hair is on fire and we vary in the degree to which we can risk our careers to reform education. Many even question the sanity of teachers who pour so much of their time and energy into their students. However, there is little doubt that the passion and excitement a teacher brings to the classroom has a positive impact on learning. Their hard work and love for what they do simultaneously expose students to the kind of effort it takes to succeed while demonstrating that they are worth the investment. Flowing in the other direction, the tribal teacher derives the energy, emotions, and health benefits that all social animals receive by caring for and dedicating themselves to others.

Unfortunately, being a good and caring teacher makes us vulnerable to our own insecurities. We long for our students' attention and enthusiasm, but often feel rejected, depressed, and angry when they refuse to engage with us. We want students to feel safe enough to take risks and explore yet are frustrated by their fears of evaluation, failure, and shame. Parents and administrators often take out their fears and frustrations on us, expecting us to single-handedly solve problems that are rooted in complex cultural and systemic issues. As we have seen from the research, the very elements that attract us to teaching also make us vulnerable to disillusionment, exhaustion, and burnout. When the going gets tough, it is the solidity of the teacher's inner world and the strength of his or her attachments that make the difference between enthusiasm and success, or failure and burnout.

The Challenge and the Journey

It is always the season for the old to learn.

—Aeschylus

Depending on the day, teaching can either be a treat or torture (Palmer, 1998). When it is a treat, we get lost in the reciprocal flow of ideas and intoxicated by enthusiasm. When it is torture, we struggle to understand why we aren't connecting with our students and feel like failures. On these days, the hard edge of reality holds a mirror to our souls in which we see reflected the broken places within us that are usually hidden from view. Like the heroes of mythology, the things we find in these shadows can either break us or serve as the grounds for progress. As screenwriters and novelists always say, *conflict reveals character.*

Although most people don't become teachers expecting to be heroes, many discover that this is precisely what is required to be successful. The basic elements of childhood that many of us take for granted, such as physical safety, secure attachments, and invested parents, are often absent in our students. New teachers soon learn that without a solid emotional foundation, there is neither discipline in the classroom nor openness to learning. When children are neglected, unloved, and unsafe, their brains get the message that adults are dangerous and they shut down input from anyone in authority. One or more traumatized, hurt, or neglected students in a classroom will do anything they can to undermine a teacher.

Students will scoff at our naïvety, optimism, and dedication. Lacking the ability to express their feelings directly, they often act out their fear, sadness, and shame through attacks, sabotage, and bullying. They'll place bets on how long we will take their abuse and compete with each other to break our spirit. In essence, they do to us what has been done to them—all the while hoping we are strong enough to stand up to them, fulfill our promises, and not abandon them.

Most teachers in these situations feel frustrated and hopeless, suffer a crisis of faith, and question whether they have what it takes to succeed. Many will require the kind of hero's journey we discussed in an earlier chapter. Instead of chasing a white whale or fighting a dragon, the tribal teacher fights the forces of the status quo, insecure attachments, and fear of humiliation. Because the strength for this heroic battle comes from deep within, I echo the voices of educators who have called for self-exploration and personal growth as a central focus of teacher training.

If we are to succeed as tribal teachers, we will be initiated through an inner journey of personal transformation that allows us to unhook from old beliefs and identities. In the process, new challenges will continue to emerge that require facing old fears and finding new courage. Those of us who come out on the other side will have a new vision of what it means to be a teacher, deeper emotional security, and the empowerment that comes with engaging in and surviving a worthy challenge.

Our inner journey provides the ability to see beyond misbehavior to the emotions lying below the surface. This added perspective allows us to move beyond doling out punishment to understanding, attunement, and attempting to heal the causes of suffering. We also have to gain enough confidence and security to remember how to play, have fun, and engage in the kind of self-care we need to stay balanced and healthy. In the midst of everyday life, we have to continually "re-remember" why we became teachers to help us maintain perspective and our sense of purpose. There is nothing easy about this, which is exactly why the journey can be so valuable.

A fundamental truth is that children need a family as a safe foundation from which to meet the challenges of life. Without this, their minds and brains can be closed to learning and the energy and resources poured into teaching fall on closed ears and shuttered hearts. By watching a teacher work to create a cohesive tribe in the classroom, students get to witness what real heroism looks like.

Why are passion and compassion the bedrock of successful teaching? The most fundamental answer is that we all need the same thing: to be loved, to be appreciated, and to contribute to the good of others. This is echoed in Freud's definition of mental health (the ability to love and work); at the core of Carl Rogers's formula for successful psychotherapy (warmth, acceptance, and unconditional positive regard); and what Jaime Escalante's students told him they needed most in life (peace at home, understanding, trust, and love).

Families, tribes, and classrooms, in fact every human group, can trace their origins back to nature's first experiments with attachment and bonding. As human beings, we need to connect with our students as much as they need to connect with us.

Credits

Table 2.1: [1] Giedd, 2004; Sowell et al., 2002; Pfefferbaum et al., 1994; [2] Paus et al., 1999; [3] Benes et al., 1994; [4] Giedd et al., 1996; [5] Thompson et al., 2000; [6] Rajapakse et al., 1996; [7] Giedd, 2004; [8] Gogtay et al., 2004; [9] Jernigan et al., 2001; Sowell et al., 2002; Spear, 2000; Thompson et al., 2000.

Table 3.1: [1] Bredy et al., 2003; Champagne et al., 2008; [2] Weaver et al., 2002; Weaver et al., 2006; [3] Menard et al., 2004; Garoflos et al., 2008; [4] Alonso et al., 2002; Bekinschtein et al., 2008; Monfils et al., 2007; Liu et al., 2000; [5] Menard et al., 2004; Zhang et al., 2005; [6] Weaver et al., 2004; [7] Caldji et al., 2003; [8] Caldji et al., 1998; Caldji et al., 2004; [9] Braun & Poeggel, 2001; [10] Champagne et al., 2003; [11] Champagne et al., 2001, 2003, 2006; [12] Cameron et al., 2008.

Table 3.2: [1] Zhang et al., 2002; [2] Marais et al., 2008; [3] Leventopoulos et al., 2007; [4] Caldji et al., 2000; [5] Hsu et al., 2003; [6] Rees et al., 2006; [7] Blaise et al., 2008; [8] Brake et al., 2004; [9] Kuhn & Schanberg, 1998; [10] Kalinichev et al., 2002; [11] Coutinho et al., 2002; [12] Weaver et al., 2006; [13] Ovtscharoff & Braun, 2001; [14] Akbari et al., 2007.

Table 3.3: [1] Meaney et al., 1988, 1991; McCormick et al., 2000, O'Donnell et al., 1994; Smythe et al., 1994; [2] Sarrieau et al., 1988; [3] Plotsky & Meaney, 1993; [4] Kosten et al., 2007; [5] Siviy & Harrison, 2008; [6] Garoflos et al., 2007; [7] Vallee et al., 1997; [8] Vallee et al., 1999; [9] Costela et al., 1995; Tejedor-Real et al., 1998; [10] Weaver et al., 2000; [11] Collette et al., 2000.

Table 5.1: [1] Krugers et al., 2006; [2] Watanabe et al., 1992; [3] Alonso, 2000; [4] Sapolsky, 1990; [5] Dranovsky & Hen, 2006; Kelly et al., 2000; Pham et al.,

2003; Prickaerts et al., 2004; [6] Kuhlmann et al., 1996, 2005; Newcomer et al., 1994, 1999; [7] West, 1993; Lupien et al., 1998; [8] Bremner et al., 1993.

Table 5.2: [1] Fujikawa et al., 2000; [2] Abercrombie et al., 2003; Andreano & Cahill, 2006; Domes et al., 2005; [3] Takahashi et al., 2004; [4] Conrad et al., 1999; Kerr et al., 1994; Park et al., 2006; Yau et al., 1995; [5] Diamond et al., 1992; [6] Pavlides et al., 1995; [7] Sullivan et al., 1989; [8] Introini-Collison & McGaugh, 1987; [9] Cowan & Kandel, 2001; Gould et al., 1997; Jablonska et al., 1999; Myers et al., 2000; Pham et al., 1997; Zhu & Waite, 1998.

Table 5.3: [1] Schmidt et al., 2002; [2] Lomax & Moosavi, 2002; Duncan et al., 1984; Spotts et al., 1997; Strick et al., 2009; [3] Kaplan & Pascoe, 1977; Morkes et al., 1999; Schmidt, 1994; Schmidt & Williams, 2001; Zillmann et al., 1980; [4] Forbasco, 1992; Moran et al., 2004; Iwase et al., 2002; [5] Bennett & Lengacher, 2006a & 2006b; Pearce, 2004; [6] Mobbs et al., 2003.

Table 5.4: [1] Cann et al., 1999; Garner, 2006; Kher et al., 1999; Liechty, 1987; Lomax & Moosavi, 2002; Nezu et al., 1988; Yovetich et al., 1990; [2] Celso et al., 2003; Goodheart, 1994; Lefcourt & Thomas, 1998; O'Connell, 1960; Pfeifer, 1992; Rosenberg, 1991; Wooten, 1996; [3] Danzer et al., 1990; Deaner & McConatha, 1993; Overholser, 1992; [4] Frecknall, 1994; Martin et al., 1993; Overholser, 1992; [5] Bellert, 1989; [6] Sherman, 1998; Thorson, 1985; Wooten, 1996; [7] Fry, 1984, 1986, 1992; Derks et al., 1991; Goldstein, 1976; Svebak, 1982; [8] Cousins, 1979; Cushner & Friedman, 1989; Kuhn, 1994; Paskind, 1932; [9] Fry, 1994; Fry & Rader, 1977; Lloyd, 1938; [10] Fry, 1994; Fry & Savin, 1988; Fry & Stoft, 1971; [11] Berk et al., 1988, 1989; Fry, 1984, 1992; Fry & Stoft, 1971; Milsum, 1985; [12] Bennett et al., 2002; Berk et al., 1984, 1989; Dillon et al., 1985; Lefcourt et al., 1990; McClellan & Cheriff, 1997; Tomasi, 1976.

Table 6.1: [1] Ashby et al., 2006; Tangney et al., 1992; [2] Ashby et al., 2006; Baldwin et al., 2006; Covert et al., 2003; Smith et al., 2002; [3] Gilbert & Miles, 2000; Lickel et al., 2005; [4] Bennett et al., 2005; Tangney et al., 1992; [5] Zaslav, 1998; 6 Dickerson et al., 2004; [7] Dickerson et al., 2004; Gruenewald et al., 2004; Mills et al., 2008; [8] Dutton et al., 1995; Mills, 2003; [9] Claesson & Sohlberg, 2002; [10] Stuewig & McCloskey, 2005; [11] Wells & Jones, 2000; [12] Gilbert & Gerlsma, 1999; [13] Lopez et al., 1997; Schmader & Lickel, 2006; [14] Covert et al., 2003; [15] Lickel et al., 2005; [16] Alessandri & Lewis, 1996; [17] Ashby et al., 2006; [18] Lutwak & Ferrari, 1997.

Table 7.1: [1] Cacioppo & Berntson, 2002; Uchino et al., 1996; [2] Hanson et al., 1988; Kamarck et al., 1990; Cacioppo & Berntson, 2002; [3] Lepore et al., 1993; [4,5] Kiecolt-Glaser et al., 1984; [6] Cohen, 2004; Cohen et al., 2003; House et al., 1988; Kiecolt-Glaser et al., 2002; Seeman, 1996; Thomas et al., 1985; Uchino et al., 1996; [7] Cutrona et al., 1986; Eng et al., 2002; Larson, 1978; Shye et al., 1995; Uchino et al., 1996; [8] Cohen et al., 2003; [9] Anson, 1989; [10] Cohen, 2004; [11] Seeman, 1996; [12] Cohen, 2004; Russell & Cutrona, 1991; Segrin, 2003; Vandervoort, 1999; [13] Cohen et al., 2003; [14] Cacioppo & Berntson, 2002.

Table 7.2: [1] Nanda et al., 2008; Perrot-Sinal et al., 2000; Takahashi et al., 2005; [2] Apfelbach et al., 2005; Brennan et al., 2006; [3] Creel et al., 2009; Morrow et al., 2000; McGregor et al., 2002; Blanchard et al., 1998; [4] Adamec & Shallow, 1993; Belzung et al., 2001; Campeau et al., 2008; Funk & Amir, 2000; McGregor et al., 2002; Zoladz et al., 2008; [5] Boonstra et al., 1998; Clinchy et al., 2004; Hubbs et al., 2000; Morrow et al., 2000; Scheuerlein et al., 2001; Sheriff et al., 2009; Zhang et al., 2003; [6] Apfelbach et al., 2005; [7] Figueiredo et al., 2003; Rosebook et al., 2007, [8] Mesches et al., 1999; [9] Adamec et al., 2003; [10] Diamond et al., 2006; [11, 13] Adamec et al., 2001; [12] Rosen et al., 2005; [13] Adamec et al., 2001; [14] Dielenberg & McGregor, 2001; [15] Nanda et al., 2008; Rosebook et al., 2007; [16] D. Smith et al., 2006; [17] Tanapat et al., 2001; [18] Park et al., 2008; [19] Diamond et al., 1999; El Hage et al., 2006; [20] Diamond et al., 2006; Woodson et al., 2003; [21] El Hage et al., 2006; [22] Morrow et al., 2000; Woodson et al., 2003; [23] Lordi et al., 2000; [24] Zoladz et al., 2008; [25] Apfelbach et al., 2005; Lordi et al., 2000.

Tables 7.3: [1] Carney, 2000 (United States); [2] van der Wal et al., 2003 (Netherlands/England); [3] Bond et al., 2001 (Netherlands/England); [4] Bond et al., 2001; Rigby, 2003 (England/Australia/New Zealand); [5] Graham & Juvonen, 1998; Due et al., 2005 (Australia/New Zealand); [6] Kumpulainen et al., 1998 (Netherlands); [7] Fekkes et al., 2006; Kumpulainen et al., 1998 (Netherlands); Lien et al., 2009; Nishitani et al., 2005; [8] Stadler et al., 2010 (Germany); [9] Dill et al., 2004; Rigby, 2000 (Australia/New Zealand).

Table 7.4: [1] Forero et al., 1999 (Australia); [2] Shields & Cicchetti, 2001 (United States); [3] Walden & Beran, 2010 (Canada); [4] Ahmed & Braithwaite, 2004 (Australia/Iceland); [5] Schnohr & Niclasen, 2006 (Australia/Iceland); [6] Andreou, 2001 (Greece); [7] Kaltiala-Heino, 1999; Hay & Meldrum, 2010 (Finland); [8] Nansel et al., 2001 (United States); [9] Baldry, 1998 (Italy); [10] Unnever & Cornell, 2003 (United States).

Table 8.1: [1] Brissie et al., 1988; Buckley et al., 2004; Lumsden, 1998; Rudd & Wiseman, 1962; [2] Lortie, 1975; [3] Darling-Hammond & Sykes, 2003;

[4] Coates & Thorsen, 1976; Green-Reese et al., 1991; [5] Farber, 1984; [6] Farber, 1984; [7] Schwab, Jackson, & Schuler, 1986; Smylie, 1999; [8] Blasé & Roberts, 1994; de Lange et al., 1993; Farber, 1982; Friedman, 2003; Ma & MacMillan, 1999.

Table 8.2: [1] Jennings & Greenberg, 2009; [2] Gritz & Theobald 1996; Henderson & Henderson, 1996; Rudd & Wiseman, 1962; Tye & O'Brien, 2002; [3] Brissie et al., 1988; Brouwers, Evers, & Tomic, 1999; Burke & Greenglass, 1993; Greenglass et al., 1996; Greenglass et al., 1997; Hargreaves, 1994; Leithwood, Leonard, & Sharratt, 1998; Maslach et al., 2001; Tapper, 1995; Youngs, 1978; [4] Blasé, 1986; Brissie et al., 1996; Dunham, 1977; Friedman, 1995; [5] Blasé, 1986; Gonzalez, 1997; Morton et al., 1997; Roy, 1974; [6] Blasé, 1986; Hoover-Dempsey, Bassler, & Brissie, 1988; van Horn, Schaufeli, & Enzmann, 1999; [7] Bauer et al., 2006; Gold, 1985; Maslach & Jackson, 1981; [8] Bauer et al., 2006; [9] Gonzalez, 1997; [10] Maslach et al., 2001; [11] Burke & Greenglass, 1995; Burke, Greenglass, & Schwarzer, 1996; Maslach et al., 2001; McCormick, 1997; Semmer 1996; Watson, Clark, & Harkness, 1994; [12] Anderson & Iwanicki, 1984; Friedman & Farber, 1992; McCormick, 1997; McIntyre, 1981; Semmer, 1996.

Table 8.3: [1] Griffith et al., 1999; [2] Belcastro, Gold, and Grant, 1982; Huberman, Grounauer, & Marti, 1993; [3] Burke et al., 1996; Schwab et al., 1986; Weisberg & Sage, 1999; [4] Maslach, 1976; [5] Borg et al., 1991; Byrne, 1994; Jenkins and Calhoun, 1991; Lamude et al., 1992; Whiteman et al., 1985; [6] Guglielmi & Tatrow, 1998; Kyriacou, 1987; [7] Pierce & Molloy, 1990; Schwab et al., 1986; [8] Farber & Miller, 1981; Haberman, 1995; Schwab et al., 1986; [9] Farber & Miller, 1981; [10] Blasé & Blasé, 1994; Young, 1979.

Table 8.4: [1] Hoel & Cooper, 2000 (UK); [2] Fox & Stallworth, 2005 (UK); [3] Matthiesen & Einarsen, 2001 (Norway/UK); [4] Matthiesen & Einarsen, 2004 (Norway/UK); [5] Tehrani, 2004 (Norway/UK); [6] Quine, 1999 (UK); [7] Quine, 2002 (UK); [8] Quine, 2001 (UK); [9] Vartia, 2001 (Finland).

Table 9.1: [1] Ferrari et al., 2003; [2] Heiser et al., 2003; [3] Cantalupo & Hopkins, 2001; [4] Chaminade et al., 2002; [5] Freund, 2001; Jeannerod et al., 1995; [6] Buccino et al., 2001; Carlage et al., 2003; [7] Iacoboni et al., 1999.

Table 9.2: [1] Desimone, 1991; Hasselmo et al., 1989; [2] Gauthier et al., 2000; Halgren et al., 1999; [3] Gallese et al., 2004; [4] Hutchison et al., 1999; Singer et al., 2004; [5] Eisenberger et al., 2003.

Table 9.3: [1] Marsh, 1992; Marsh et al., 1988; Marsh & Yeung, 1997a; Shavelson & Bolus, 1982; Skaalvik & Hagtvet, 1990; Skaalvik & Vals, 1999; [2] Gottfried, 1990; Harter, 1982; MacIver et al., 1991; Meece et al., 1988; Skaalvik, 1997b, 1998; Skaalvik & Rankin, 1996; [3] Bong & Skaalvik, 2003; [4] Skaalvik & Rankin, 1996; Skinner et al., 1990; [5] Skaalvik & Rankin, 1995; [6] Bong & Skaalvik, 2003; [7] Ames, 1983; [8] Marsh & Yeung, 1997b; [9] Skaalvik, 1997b, 1998.

Table 9.4: [1] Schunk, 1983; [2] Schunk & Swartz, 1993; [3] Schunk & Cox, 1986; [4] Schunk & Ertmer, 1999; [5] Schunk et al., 1987; Schunk & Hanson, 1985.

Table 10.1: [1] Bennett et al., 1964; Diamond et al., 1964; [2] Kempermann et al., 1998; Walsh, Budtz-Olsen, Penny, & Cummins, 1969; [3] Kolb & Whishaw, 1998; [4] Ickes et al., 2000; [5] Nilsson et al., 1993; [6] Sirevaag & Greenough, 1988; [7] Guzowski et al., 2001; [8] Torasdotter et al., 1998.

Table 10.2: [1] Bunzeck & Duzel, 2006; Krebs et al., 2009; [2] Buchanan & Bardi, 2010; [3] Wood-Gush & Vestergaard, 1991; [4] Hennessy et al., 1995; [5] Núñez et al., 1995; [6] Jolles et al., 1979; [7] Meehan & Mench, 2002; [8] Tran et al., 2008; 9 Straube et al., 2003; Tang & Zou, 2002; [10] Manahan-Vaughan & Braunewell, 1999; [11] Izquierdo et al., 2001; [12] Bunzeck & Duzel, 2006; [13] Handa et al., 1993; Zhu et al., 1995; [14] Kemp & Manahan-Vaughn, 2004; [15] Viola et al., 2000; [16] Kitchigina et al., 1997; [17] Acquas et al., 1996; [18] Dettling et al., 2002; [19] Martin, 1999; [20] Tulving et al., 1996; [21] O'Kane et al., 2005; [22] Goldberg et al., 1994; [23] Lemaire et al.,1999; [24] Rutishauser et al., 2006; [25] Duzel et al., 2010.

Table 11.1: [1] Calcagnetti & Schechter, 1992; Humphreys & Einon, 1981; [2] Vanderschuren et al., 1997; [3] Panksepp et al., 1979; [4] Homberg et al., 2007; [5] Barton, 2004; [6] Hole, 1991; [7] Beatty et al., 1982; Panksepp & Beatty, 1980; Thor & Holloway, 1983; [8] Holloway & Suter, 2004; Ikemoto & Panksepp, 1992; [9] Beatty et al., 1981; [10] Gordon et al., 2003; Gordon et al., 2002; [11] Bell et al., 2010; [12] Diamond & Bond, 2003; [13] Iwaniuk et al., 2001; Lewis, 2000; [14] Pellis & Iwaniuk, 2000; [15] Pellis & Iwaniuk, 2002.

Table 11.2: [1] Minagawa-Kawai et al., 2009; Nitschke et al., 2004; [2] Berthoz, Armony, Blair, & Dolan, 2002; Mitchell, Banaji, & Macrae, 2005; [3] Mitchell, Macrae, & Banaji, 2006; [4] Gusnard, Akbudak, Shulman, & Raichle, 2001; [5] Goel & Dolan, 2001; [6] Frey & Petrides 2000; Nobre, Coull, Frith, & Mesulam, 1999; [7] Ongur & Price 2000; [8] Bechara, Damasio, Tranel, & Anderson, 1998; Gallagher, McMahan, & Schoenbaum, 1999; Gehring &

Willoughby, 2002; Kringelbach, 2005; Krueger, Moll, Zahn, Heinecke, & Grafman, 2007; O'Doherty, 2004; [9] Bechara, Damasio, Damasio, & Anderson, 1994; O'Doherty, Deichmann, Critchley, & Dolan, 2002; [10] Matsumoto & Tanaka, 2004; [11] McGuire, Paulesu, Frackowiak, & Frith, 1996; [12] Dias, Robbins, & Roberts, 1996; Simpson, Drevets, Snyder, Gusnard, & Raichle, 2001; Quirk & Beer, 2006; [13] Malloy, Bihrle, Duffy, & Cimino, 1993; Teasdale et al., 1999; Beer, John, Scabini, & Knight, 2006; [14] Koechlin, Ody, & Kouneiher, 2003; [15] Dias et al., 1996; Fuster, 1997; Nagahama et al., 2001; [16] Knight & Grabowecky, 1995; [17] Rezai et al., 1993; Petrides, Alivisatos, & Frey, 2002; [18] Henson, Shallice, & Dolan, 1999; [19] Levesque et al., 2003; [20] Pascual-Leone, Wassermann, Grafman, & Hallett, 1996; [21] Kroger et al., 2002; Malloy et al., 1993; Teasdale et al., 1999; [22] Mitchell et al., 2006; [23] Gray, Braver, & Raichle 2002.

Table 11.3: [1] Dehaene et al., 2003; [2] Griffiths et al., 1998; [3] Molko et al., 2003; [4] Chochon et al., 1999; [5] Newman et al., 2003; [6] Molko et al., 2003; Rushworth et al., 2001; [7] Uddin et al., 2005; [8] Antal et al., 2008; [9] Grefkes & Fink, 2005; Wolpert et al., 1998; [10] Wolpert et al., 1998; [11] Jonides et al., 1998; [12] Wagner et al., 2005; [13] Marshuetz et al., 2000; Van Opstal et al., 2008; [14] Husain & Nachev, 2007; [15] Astafiev et al., 2003; [16] Mountcastle, 1995; [17] Orban et al., 1999; [18] Castelli et al., 2006; Fias et al., 2003; Lemer et al., 2003; [19] Fias et al., 2007; [20] Ruby & Decety, 2001; Vogeley et al., 2004, [21] Iacoboni et al., 2004; Jackson & Decety 2004.

Table 14.1: [1] Cotman & Berchtold, 2002; Nagahara & Handa, 1997; Neeper et al., 1995; Oliff et al., 1998; [2] Adlard et al., 2005; Berchtold et al., 2001; Farmer et al., 2004; Garza et al., 2004; Neeper et al., 1995; Oliff et al., 1998; Vaynman et al., 2003; Vaynman et al., 2004; [3] Carro et al., 2001; Trejo et al., 2001; [4] Neeper et al., 1996; [5] Fabel et al., 2003; [6] Rhodes et al., 2003; Uysal et al., 2005; van Praag et al., 2005; [7] Farmer et al., 2004; Orr et al., 2001; [8] Black et al., 1990; Swain et al., 2003.

Table 14.2: [1] Galli et al., 2002; Lau et al., 2005; [2] Duthie et al., 2002; Kruman et al., 2002; Mattson, 2003; Mattson et al., 2002; [3] Uauy & Dangour, 2006; [4] Franco et al., 2005; Zhao et al., 2002.

References

Abbott, D. H., George, L. M., Barrett, J., Hodges, J. K., O'Byrne, K. T., Sheffield, J. W., . . . Ruiz de Elvira, M. C. (1990). Social control of ovulation in marmoset monkeys: A neuroendocrine basis for the study of infertility. In T. E. Ziegler & F. B. Bercovitch (Eds.), *Socioendocrinology of primate reproduction* (pp. 135–158). New York, NY: Wiley-Liss.

Abbott, D. H., Keverne, E. B., Bercovitch, F. B., Shively, C. A., Mendoza, S. P., Saltzman, W., . . . Sapolsky, R. M. (2003). Are subordinates always stressed? A comparative analysis of rank differences in cortisol levels among primates. *Hormones and Behavior, 43*(1), 67–82.

Abbott, D. H., Saltzman, W., Schultz-Darken, N. J., & Tannenbaum, P. L. (1998). Adaptations to subordinate status in female marmoset monkeys. *Comparative Biochemistry and Physiology Part C, Pharmacology, Toxicology & Endocrinology, 119*(3), 261–274.

Abel, M. H., & Sewell, J. (1999). Stress and burnout in rural and urban secondary school teachers. *Journal of Educational Research, 92*(5), 287–293.

Abercrombie, H. C., Kalin, N. H., Thurow, M. E., Rosenkranz, M. A., & Davidson, R. J. (2003). Cortisol variation in humans affects memory for emotionally laden and neutral information. *Behavioral Neuroscience, 117*(3), 505–516.

Acquas, E., Wilson, C., & Fibiger, H. C. (1996). Conditioned and unconditioned stimuli increase frontal cortical and hippocampal acetylcholine release: Effects of novelty, habituation, and fear. *Journal of Neuroscience, 16*(9), 3089–3096.

Adair, J. G., & Epstein, J. S. (1968). Verbal cues in the mediation of experimenter bias. *Psychological Reports, 22*(3), 1045–1053.

Adamec, R. E., Blundell, J., & Burton, P. (2003). Phosphorylated cyclic AMP response element binding protein expression induced in the periaqueductal gray by predator stress: Its relationship to the stress experience, behavior and limbic neural plasticity. *Progress in Neuro-Psychopharmacology & Biological Psychiatry, 27*(8), 1243–1267.

Adamec, R. E., Blundell, J., & Collins, A. (2001). Neural plasticity and stress-induced changes in defense in the rat. *Neuroscience and Biobehavioral Reviews, 25*(7–8), 721–744.

Adamec, R. E., & Shallow, T. (1993). Lasting effects on rodent anxiety of a single exposure to a cat. *Physiology & Behavior, 54*(1), 101–109.

Adams, R. D., Victor, M., & Ropper, A. H. (1997). *Principles of neurology.* New York, NY: McGraw-Hill.

Adang, O. M. J. (2010). Exploring the social environment: A developmental study of teasing in chimpanzees. *Ethology, 73*(2), 136–160.

Adlard, P. A., Perreau, V. M., & Cotman, C. W. (2005). The exercise-induced expression of BDNF within the hippocampus varies across the life-span. *Neurobiology of Aging, 26*(4), 511–520.

Adler, H. M. (2002). The sociophysiology of caring in the doctor-patient relationship. *Journal of General Internal Medicine, 17*(11), 883–890.

Adolphs, R. (2003). Investigating the cognitive neuroscience of social behavior. *Neuropsychologia, 41*(2), 119–126.

Agatson, P., Kowalski, R., & Limber, S. (2007). Students' perspectives on cyber bullying. *Journal of Adolescent Health, 41*(6), S59–S60.

Aguinis, H., Simonsen, M. M., & Pierce, C. A. (1998). Effects of nonverbal behavior on perceptions of power bases. *Journal of Social Psychology, 138*(4), 455–469.

Ahmed, E., & Braithwaite, V. (2004). Bullying and victimization: Cause for concern for both families and schools. *Social Psychology of Education, 7*(1), 35–54.

Ainsworth, M. D. S. (1978). *Patterns of attachment: A psychological study of the strange situation.* Hillsdale, N.J.: Lawrence Erlbaum.

Akaneya, Y., Tsumoto, T., Kinoshita, S., & Hatanaka, H. (1997). Brain-derived neurotrophic factor enhances long-term potentiation in rat visual cortex. *Journal of Neuroscience, 17*(17), 6707–6716.

Akbari, E. M., Chatterjee, D., Lévy, F., & Fleming, A. S. (2007). Experience-dependent cell survival in the maternal rat brain. *Behavioral Neuroscience, 121*(125), 1001–1011.

Akirav, I., & Maroun, M. (2007). The role of the medial prefrontal cortex-amygdala circuit in stress effects on the extinction of fear. *Neural Plasticity, 2007*, 30873–30883.

Albeck, D. S., McKittrick, C. R., Blanchard, D. C., Blanchard, R. J., Nikulina, J., McEwen, B. S., & Sakai, R. R. (1997). Chronic social stress alters levels of corticotropin-releasing factor and arginine vasopressin mRNA in rat brain. *Journal of Neuroscience, 17*(12), 4895–4903.

Alessandri, S. M., & Lewis, M. (1996). Differences in pride and shame in maltreated and nonmaltreated preschoolers. *Child Development, 67*(4), 1857–1869.

Alexander, G. E., Furey, M. L., Grady, C. L., Pietrini, P., Brady, D. R., Mentis, M. J., & Schapiro, M. B. (1997). Association of premorbid intellectual function with cerebral metabolism in Alzheimer's disease: Implications for the cognitive reserve hypothesis. *American Journal of Psychiatry, 154*(2), 165–172.

Allen, J. S., Bruss, J., Brown, C. K., & Damasio, H. (2005). Normal neuroanatomical variation due to age: The major lobes and a parcellation of the temporal region. *Neurobiology of Aging, 26*(9), 1245–1260.

Allen, L. S., Richey, M. F., Chai, Y. M., & Gorski, R. A. (1991). Sex differences in the corpus callosum of the living human being. *Journal of Neuroscience, 11*(4), 933–942.

Allen, N. J., & Barres, B. A. (2005). Signaling between glia and neurons: Focus on synaptic plasticity. *Current Opinion in Neurobiology, 15*(5), 542–548.

Allman, J., & Brothers, L. (1994). Faces, fear and the amygdala. Nature, 372(6507), 613–614.

Allman, J., Rosin, A., Kumar, R., & Hasenstaub, A. (1998). Parenting and survival in anthropoid primates: Caretakers live longer. *Proceedings of the National Academy of Sciences of the United States of America, 95*(12), 6866–6869.

Allman, J. M., Hakeem, A., Erwin, J. M., Nimchinsky, E., & Hof, P. (2001). The anterior cingulate cortex: The evolution of an interface between emotion and cognition. *Annals of the New York Academy of Sciences, 935*, 107–117.

Allman, J. M., Watson, K. K., Tetreault, N. A., & Hakeem, A. Y. (2005). Intuition and autism: A possible role for von Economo neurons. *Trends in Cognitive Sciences, 9*(8), 367–373.

Alonso, G. (2000). Prolonged corticosterone treatment of adult rats inhibits the proliferation of oligodendrocyte progenitors present throughout white and gray matter regions of the brain. *Glia, 31*(3), 219–231.

Alonso, M., Vianna, M. R., Depino, A. M., Mello e Souza, T., Pereira, P., Szapiro, G., . . . Medina, J. H. (2002). BDNF-triggered events in the rat hippocampus are required for both short- and long-term memory formation. *Hippocampus, 12*(4), 551–560.

Altman, J., Wallace, R. B., Anderson, W. J., & Das, G. D. (1968). Behaviorally induced changes in length of cerebrum in rats. *Developmental Psychobiology, 1*(2), 112–117.

Ames, R. (1983). Help-seeking and achievement orientation: Perspectives from attribution theory. In B. DePaulo, A. Nadler, & J. Fisher (Eds.), *New directions in helping* (pp. 165–188). New York, NY: Academic Press.

Anastasopoulos, D. (1997). Shame in psychotherapy with adolescents. *Journal of Child Psychotherapy, 23*(1), 103–123.

Anderson, C. R. (1976). Coping behaviors as intervening mechanisms in the inverted-U stress-performance relationship. *Journal of Applied Psychology, 61*(7), 30–34.

Anderson, G. C. (1991). Current knowledge about skin-to-skin (kangaroo) care for preterm infants. *Journal of Perinatology, 11*(3), 216–226.

Anderson, J. R., Reder, L. M., & Simon, H. A. (1996). Situated learning and education. *Educational Researcher, 25*(4), 5–11.

Anderson, M. B. G., & Iwanicki, E. F. (1984). Teacher motivation and its relationship to burnout. *Educational Administration Quarterly, 20*(2), 109–132.

Andreano, J. M., & Cahill, L. (2006). Glucocorticoid release and memory consolidation in men and women. *Psychological Science, 17*(6), 466–470.

Andreou, E. (2001). Bully/victim problems and their association with coping behavior in conflictual peer interactions among school-age children. *Educational Psychology, 21*(1), 59–66.

Anestis, S. F. (2005). Behavioral style, dominance rank, and urinary cortisol in young chimpanzees (Pan troglodytes). *Behaviour, 142*(9), 1245–1268.

Anisfeld, E., Casper, V., Nozyce, M., & Cunningham, N. (1990). Does infant carrying promote attachment? An experimental study of the effects of increased physical contact on the development of attachment. *Child Development, 61*(5), 1617–1627.

Anokhin, A. P., Birbaumer, N., Lutzenberger, W., Nikolaev, A., & Vogel, F. (1996). Age increases brain complexity. *Electroencephalography and Clinical Neurophysiology, 99*(1), 63–68.

Anson, O. (1989). Marital status and women's health revisited: The importance of a proximate adult. *Journal of Marriage and the Family, 51*(1), 185–194.

Antal, A., Baudewig, J., Paulus, W., & Dechent, P. (2008). The posterior cingulate cortex and planum temporale/parietal operculum are activated by coherent visual motion. *Visual Neuroscience, 25*(1), 17–26.

Apfelbach, R., Blanchard, C. D., Blanchard, R. J., Hayes, R. A., & McGregor, I. S. (2005). The effects of predator odors in mammalian prey species: A review of field and laboratory studies. *Neuroscience and Biobehavioral Reviews, 29*(8), 1123–1144.

Arbib, M. A. (2002). Grounding the mirror system hypothesis for the evolution of the language-ready brain. In A. Cangelosi & D. Parisi (Eds.), *Stimulating the evolution of language* (pp. 229–254). London, England: Springer Verlag.

Archie, E. A., Morrison, T. A., Foley, C. A. H., Moss, C. J., & Alberts, S. C. (2006). Dominance rank relationships among wild female African elephants, Loxodonta africana. *Animal Behaviour, 71*(1), 117–127.

Ardelt, M. (1997). Wisdom and life satisfaction in old age. *Journals of Gerontology: Series B, 52*(1), 15–27.

Ardelt, M. (2000). Antecedents and effects of wisdom in old age: A longitudinal perspective on aging well. *Research on Aging, 22*(4), 360–394.

Ardelt, M. (2004). Wisdom as expert knowledge system: A critical review of a contemporary operationalization of an ancient concept. *Human Development, 47*(5), 257–285.

Ardila, A., Ostrosky-Solis, F., Rosselli, M., & Gomez, C. (2000). Age-related cognitive decline during normal aging: The complex effect of education. *Archives of Clinical Neuropsychology, 15*(6), 495–513.

Asbell, B. (1963). Not like other children. *Redbook, 65*, 114–118.

Ashby, J. S., Rice, K. G., & Martin, J. L. (2006). Perfectionism, shame, and depressive symptoms. *Journal of Counseling & Development, 84*(2), 148–156.

Astafiev, S. V., Shulman, G. L., Stanley, C. M., Snyder, A. Z., Van Essen, D. C., & Corbetta, M. (2003). Functional organization of human intraparietal and frontal cortex for attending, looking, and pointing. *Journal of Neuroscience, 23*(11), 4689–4699.

Astor, R. A., Meyer, H. A., Benbenishty, R., Marachi, R., & Rosemond, M. (2005). School safety interventions: Best practices and programs. *Children & Schools, 27*(1), 17–32.

Atlas, R. S., & Pepler, D. J. (1998). Observations of bullying in the classroom. *Journal of Educational Research, 92*(2), 86–99.

Atwood, H. L., & Karunanithi, S. (2002). Diversification of synaptic strength: Presynaptic elements. *Nature Reviews Neuroscience, 3*(7), 497–516.

Augustine, J. R. (1996). Circuitry and functional aspects of the insular lobe in primates including humans. *Brain Research Reviews, 22*(3), 229–244.

Aydin, N., Fischer, P., & Frey, D. (2010). Turning to god in the face of ostracism: Effects of social exclusion on religiousness. *Personality & Social Psychology Bulletin, 36*(6), 742–753.

Azim, E., Mobbs, D., Jo, B., Menon, V., & Reiss, A. L. (2005). Sex differences in brain activation elicited by humor. *Proceedings of the National Academy of Sciences of the United States of America, 102*(45), 16496–16501.

Baars, B. J. (2002). The conscious access hypothesis: Origins and recent evidence. *Trends in Cognitive Sciences, 6*(1), 47–52.

Bagwell, C. L., Newcomb, A. F., & Bukowski, W. M. (1998). Preadolescent friendship and peer rejection as predictors of adult adjustment. *Child Development, 69*(1), 140–153.

Baird, A. A., Gruber, S. A., Fein, D. A., Maas, L. C., Steingard, R. J., Renshaw, P. F., . . . Yurgelun-Todd, D. A. (1999). Functional magnetic resonance imaging of facial affect recognition in children and adolescents. *Journal of the American Academy of Child and Adolescent Psychiatry, 38*(2), 195–199.

Baker, J. P., & Crist, J. L. (1971). Teacher expectancies: A review of the literature. In J. D. Elashoff & R. E. Snow (Eds.), *Pygmalion reconsidered* (pp. 48–64). Worthington, OH: Charles A. Jones.

Baldi, E., & Bucherelli, C. (2005). The inverted "u-shaped" dose-effect relationships in learning and memory: Modulation of arousal and consolidation. *Nonlinearity in Biology, Toxicology, and Medicine, 3*(1), 9–21.

Baldry, A. C. (1998). Bullying among Italian middle school students: Combining methods to understand aggressive behaviours and victimization. *School Psychology International, 19*(4), 361–374.

Baldwin, J. D., & Baldwin, J. I. (1974). Exploration and social play in squirrel monkeys (Saimiri). *American Zoologist, 14*(1), 303–315.

Baldwin, K. M., Baldwin, J. R., & Ewald, T. (2006). The relationship among shame, guilt, and self-efficacy. *American Journal of Psychotherapy, 60*(1), 1–21.

Baltes, P. B., Staudinger, U. M., Maercker, A., & Smith, J. (1995). People nominated as wise: A comparative study of wisdom-related knowledge. *Psychology and Aging, 10*(2), 155–166.

Banks, R. (2000). *Bullying in schools.* Retrieved from ERIC database. (ED507154)

Baptista, L. F., & Petrinovich, L. (1986). Song development in the white-crowned sparrow: Social factors and sex differences. *Animal Behaviour, 34*(5), 1359–1371.

Barad, M. (February, 2000). *A biological analysis of transference.* Paper presented at the UCLA Annual Review of Neuropsychiatry, India Wells, CA.

Barber, N. (1991). Play and energy regulation in mammals. *Quarterly Review of Biology, 66*(2), 129–147.

Barcelo, F., Escera, C., Corral, M. J., & Perianez, J. A. (2006). Task switching and novelty processing activate a common neural network for cognitive control. *Journal of Cognitive Neuroscience, 18*(10), 1734–1748.

Barde, Y. A. (1989). Trophic factors and neuronal survival. *Neuron, 2*(6), 1525–1534.

Barker, R. G., & Gump, P. V. (1964). *Big school, small school: High school size and student behavior.* Oxford, England: Stanford University Press.

Barrientos, R. M., Sprunger, D. B., Campeau, S., Higgins, E. A., Watkins, L. R., Rudy, J. W., & Maier, S. F. (2003). Brain-derived neurotrophic factor mRNA downregulation produced by social isolation is blocked by intrahippocampal interleukin-1 receptor antagonist. *Neuroscience, 121*(4), 847–853.

Bartels, A., & Zeki, S. (2000). The neural basis of romantic love. *NeuroReport, 11*(17), 3829–3834.

Bartolo, A., Benuzzi, F., Nocetti, L., Baraldi, P., & Nichelli, P. (2006). Humor comprehension and appreciation: An fMRI study. *Journal of Cognitive Neuroscience, 18*(11), 1789–1798.

Barton, R. A. (2004). Playing for keeps: Evolutionary relationships between social play and the cerebellum in nonhuman primates. *Human Nature, 15*(1), 5–21.

Bartzokis, G., Beckson, M., Lu, P. H., Nuechterlein, K. H., Edwards, N., & Mintz, J. (2001). Age-related changes in frontal and temporal lobe volumes in men: A magnetic resonance imaging study. *Archives of General Psychiatry, 58*(5), 461–465.

Bauer, J., Stamm, A., Virnich, K., Wissing, K., Müller, U., Wirsching, M., & Schaarschmidt, U. (2006). Correlation between burnout syndrome and psychological and psychosomatic symptoms among teachers. *International Archives of Occupational and Environmental Health, 79*(3), 199–204.

Baumeister, R. F., Brewer, L. E., Tice, D. M., & Twenge, J. M. (2007). Thwarting the need to belong: Understanding the interpersonal and inner effects of social exclusion. *Social and Personality Psychology Compass, 1*(1), 506–520.

Baumeister, R. F., DeWall, C. N., Ciarocco, N. J., & Twenge, J. M. (2005). Social exclusion impairs self-regulation. *Journal of Personality and Social Psychology, 88*(4), 589–604.

Baumeister, R. F., & Leary, M. R. (1995). The need to belong: Desire for interpersonal attachments as a fundamental human motivation. *Psychological Bulletin, 117*(3), 497–529.

Baumeister, R. F., & Tice, D. M. (1990). Point-counterpoints: Anxiety and social exclusion. *Journal of Social and Clinical Psychology, 9*(2), 165–195.

Baumeister, R. F., Twenge, J. M., & Nuss, C. K. (2002). Effects of social exclusion on cognitive processes: Anticipated aloneness reduces intelligent thought. *Journal of Personality and Social Psychology, 83*(4), 817–827.

Beatty, J. (2001). *The human brain: Essentials of behavioral neuroscience.* Thousand Oaks, CA: Sage.

Beatty, W. W., Dodge, A. M., Dodge, L. J., White, K., & Panksepp, J. (1982). Psychomotor stimulants, social deprivation and play in juvenile rats. *Pharmacology, Biochemistry, and Behavior, 16*(3), 417–422.

Beatty, W. W., Dodge, A. M., Traylor, K. L., & Meaney, M. J. (1981). Temporal boundary of the sensitive period for hormonal organization of social play in juvenile rats. *Physiology & Behavior, 26*(2), 241–243.

Beauregard, M. (2007). Mind does really matter: Evidence from neuroimaging studies of emotional self-regulation, psychotherapy, and placebo effect. *Progress in Neurobiology, 81*(4), 218–236.

Bechara, A., Damasio, A. R., Damasio, H., & Anderson, S. W. (1994). Insensitivity to future consequences following damage to human prefrontal cortex. *Cognition, 50*(1–3), 7–15.

Bechara, A., Damasio, H., Tranel, D., & Anderson, S. W. (1998). Dissociation of working memory from decision making within the human prefrontal cortex. *Journal of Neuroscience, 18*(1), 428–437.

Bechara, A., & Naqvi, N. (2004). Listening to your heart: Interoceptive awareness as a gateway to feeling. *Nature Neuroscience, 7*(2), 102–103.

Bedford, O. A. (2004). The individual experience of guilt and shame in Chinese culture. *Culture & Psychology, 10*(1), 29–52.

Beeghly, M., & Cicchetti, D. (1994). Child maltreatment, attachment, and the self system: Emergence of an internal state lexicon in toddlers at high social risk. *Development and Psychopathology, 6*(1), 5–30.

Beer, J. S., Heerey, E. A., Keltner, D., Scabini, D., & Knight, R. T. (2003). The regulatory function of self-conscious emotion: Insights from patients with orbitofrontal damage. *Journal of Personality and Social Psychology, 85*(4), 594–604.

Beer, J. S., John, O. P., Scabini, D., & Knight, R. T. (2006). Orbitofrontal cortex and social behavior: Integrating self-monitoring and emotion-cognition interactions. *Journal of Cognitive Neuroscience, 18*(6), 871–879.

Bekinschtein, P., Cammarota, M., Katche, C., Slipczuk, L., Rossato, J. I., Goldin, A., . . . Medina, J. H. (2008). BDNF is essential to promote persistence of long-term memory storage. *Proceedings of the National Academy of Sciences of the United States of America, 105*(7), 2711–2716.

Bekoff, M. (2001). Social play behaviour: Cooperation, fairness, trust, and the evolution of morality. *Journal of Consciousness Studies, 8*(2), 81–90.

Belcastro, P. A., Gold, R. S., & Grant, J. (1982). Stress and burnout: Physiologic effects on correctional teachers. *Criminal Justice and Behavior, 9*(4), 387–395.

Bell, H. C., McCaffrey, D. R., Forgie, M. L., Kolb, B., & Pellis, S. M. (2009). The role of the medial prefrontal cortex in the play fighting of rats. *Behavioral Neuroscience, 123*(6), 1158–1168.

Bell, H. C., Pellis, S. M., & Kolb, B. (2010). Juvenile peer play experience and the development of the orbitofrontal and medial prefrontal cortices. *Behavioral Brain Research, 207*(1), 7–13.

Bell, M. A., & Fox, N. A. (1992). The relations between frontal brain electrical activity and cognitive development during infancy. *Child Development, 63*(5), 1142–1163.

Bellert, J. L. (1989). Humor: A therapeutic approach in oncology nursing. *Cancer Nursing, 12*(2), 65–70.

Bellisle, F., Clement, K., Le Barzic, M., Le Gall, A., Guy-Grand, B., & Basdevant, A. (2004). The eating inventory and body adiposity from leanness to massive obesity: A study of 2,509 adults. *Obesity Research, 12*(12), 2023–2030.

Belzung, C., El Hage, W., Moindrot, N., & Griebel, G. (2001). Behavioral and neurochemical changes following predatory stress in mice. *Neuropharmacology, 41*(3), 400–408.

Ben-Ari, R., Krole, R., & Har-Even, D. (2003). Differential effects of simple frontal versus complex teaching strategy on teachers' stress, burnout, and satisfaction. *International Journal of Stress Management, 10*(2), 173–195.

Benedetti, F., Mayberg, H. S., Wager, T. D., Stohler, C. S., & Zubieta, J. K. (2005). Neurobiological mechanisms of the placebo effect. *Journal of Neuroscience, 25*(45), 10390–10402.

Benes, F. M. (1989). Myelination of cortical-hippocampal relays during late adolescence. *Schizophrenia Bulletin, 15*(4), 585–593.

Benes, F. M., Turtle, M., Khan, Y., & Farol, P. (1994). Myelination of a key relay zone in the hippocampal formation occurs in the human brain during childhood, adolescence, and adulthood. *Archives of General Psychiatry, 51*(6), 477–484.

Bengtsson, S. L., Nagy, Z., Skare, S., Forsman, L., Forssberg, H., & Ullen, F. (2005). Extensive piano practicing has regionally specific effects on white matter development. *Nature Neuroscience, 8*(9), 1148–1150.

Benjet, C., Thompson, R. J., & Gotlib, I. H. (2010). 5-HTTLPR moderates the effect of relational peer victimization on depressive symptoms in adolescent girls. *Journal of Child Psychology and Psychiatry, 51*(2), 173–179.

Bennett, A. J., Lesch, K. P., Heils, A., Long, J. C., Lorenz, J. G., Shoaf, S. E., . . . Higley, J. D. (2002). Early experience and serotonin transporter gene variation interact to influence primate CNS function. *Molecular Psychiatry, 7*(1), 118–122.

Bennett, D., Sullivan, M., & Lewis, M. (2005). Young children's adjustment as a function of maltreatment, shame, and anger. *Child Maltreatment, 10*(4), 311–323.

Bennett, E. L., Diamond, M. C., Krech, D., & Rosenzweig, M. R. (1964). Chemical and anatomical plasticity of brain. *Science, 146*, 610–619.

Bennett, K. M. (2002). Low level social engagement as a precursor of mortality among people in later life. *Age and Ageing, 31*(3), 165–168.

Bennett, M. P., & Lengacher, C. A. (2006a). Humor and laughter may influence health. I. History and background. *Evidence-Based Complementary and Alternative Medicine, 3*(1), 61–63.

Bennett, M. P., & Lengacher, C. A. (2006b). Humor and laughter may influence health. II. Complementary therapies and humor in a clinical population. *Evidence-Based Complementary and Alternative Medicine, 3*(2), 187–190.

Bennett, M. P., & Lengacher, C. A. (2009). Humor and laughter may influence health. IV. Humor and immune function. *Evidence-Based Complementary and Alternative Medicine, 6*(2), 159–164.

Benton, A. L., Hamsher, K., Vamey, N. R., & Spreen, O. (1983). *Contributions to neuropsychological assessment.* New York, NY: Oxford University Press.

Berchtold, N. C., Kesslak, J. P., Pike, C. J., Adlard, P. A., & Cotman, C. W. (2001). Estrogen and exercise interact to regulate brain-derived neurotrophic factor mRNA and protein expression in the hippocampus. *European Journal of Neuroscience, 14*(12), 1992–2002.

Bercovitch, F. B., & Clarke, A. S. (1995). Dominance rank, cortisol concentrations, and reproductive maturation in male rhesus macaques. *Physiology & Behavior, 58*(2), 215–221.

Bergman, N. J., Linley, L. L., & Fawcus, S. R. (2004). Randomized controlled trial of skin-to-skin contact from birth versus conventional incubator for physiological stabilization in 1,200- to 2,199-gram newborns. *Acta Paediatrica, 93*(6), 779–785.

Berk, L. S., Felten, D. L., Tan, S. A., Bittman, B. B., & Westengard, J. (1984). Modulation of human killer cells by catecholamines. *Clinical Research, 32*, 32A.

Berk, L. S., Felten, D. L., Tan, S. A., Bittman, B. B., & Westengard, J. (2001). Modulation of neuroimmune parameters during the eustress of humor-associated mirthful laughter. *Alternative Therapies in Health and Medicine, 7*(2), 62–76.

Berk, L. S., Tan, S. A., Napier, B. J., & Eby, W. C. (1989). Eustress of mirthful laughter modifies natural killer cell activity. *Clinical Research, 37*, 115A.

Berk, L. S., Tan, S. A., Nehlsen-Cannarella, S., Napier, B. J., Lee, J. W., Lewis, J. E., & Fry, W. F. (1988). Humor-associated laughter decreases cortisol and increases spontaneous lymphocyte blastogenesis. *Clinical Research, 36*, 435A.

Berk, R. (2009). Derogatory and cynical humour in clinical teaching and the workplace: The need for professionalism. *Medical Education, 43*(1), 7–9.

Berlin, B. M., & Cienkus, R. C. (1989). Size: The ultimate educational issue? *Education and Urban Society, 21*(2), 228–231.

Berns, G. S., McClure, S. M., Pagnoni, G., & Montague, P. R. (2001). Predictability modulates human brain response to reward. *Journal of Neuroscience, 21*(8), 2793–2798.

Berntson, G. G., Bechara, A., Damasio, H., Tranel, D., & Cacioppo, J. T. (2007). Amygdala contribution to selective dimensions of emotion. *Social Cognitive and Affective Neuroscience, 2*(2), 123–129.

Berthoz, S., Armony, J. L., Blair, R. J., & Dolan, R. J. (2002). An fMRI study of intentional and unintentional (embarrassing) violations of social norms. *Brain, 125*(8), 1696–1708.

Berton, O., McClung, C. A., Dileone, R. J., Krishnan, V., Renthal, W., Russo, S. J., . . . Nestler, E. J. (2006). Essential role of BDNF in the mesolimbic dopamine pathway in social defeat stress. *Science, 311*(5762), 864–868.

Bettelheim, B. (1987). The importance of play. *Atlantic Monthly, 259*, 35–42.

Bhide, P. G., & Bedi, K. S. (1982). The effects of environmental diversity on well-fed and previously undernourished rats. I. Body and brain measurements. *Journal of Comparative Neurology, 207*(4), 403–409.

Bibancos, T., Jardim, D. L., Aneas, I., & Chiavegatto, S. (2007). Social isolation and expression of serotonergic neurotransmission-related genes in several brain areas of male mice. *Genes, Brain, and Behavior, 6*(6), 529–539.

Biederman, I., & Shiffrar, M. M. (1987). Sexing day-old chicks: A case study and expert systems analysis of a difficult perceptual-learning task. *Journal of Experimental Psychology: Learning, Memory, and Cognition, 13*(4), 640–645.

Bigler, E. D., Anderson, C. V., & Blatter, D. D. (2002). Temporal lobe morphology in normal aging and traumatic brain injury. *American Journal of Neuroradiology, 23*(2), 255–266.

Bishop, S., Duncan, J., Brett, M., & Lawrence, A. D. (2004). Prefrontal cortical function and anxiety: Controlling attention to threat-related stimuli. *Nature Neuroscience, 7*(2), 184–188.

Bjorkqvist, K. (2001). Social defeat as a stressor in humans. *Physiology & Behavior, 73*(3), 435–442.

Bjornebekk, A., Mathe, A. A., Gruber, S. H., & Brene, S. (2007). Social isolation increases number of newly proliferated cells in hippocampus in female flinders sensitive line rats. *Hippocampus, 17*(12), 1193–1200.

Black, J. E., Isaacs, K. R., Anderson, B. J., Alcantara, A. A., & Greenough, W. T. (1990). Learning causes synaptogenesis, whereas motor activity causes angiogenesis, in cerebellar cortex of adult rats. *Proceedings of the National Academy of Sciences of the United States of America, 87*(14), 5568–5572.

Black, S. (2001). Morale matters: When teachers feel good about their work, research shows, student achievement rises. *American School Board Journal, 188*(1), 40–43.

Blackford, J. U., Buckholtz, J. W., Avery, S. N., & Zald, D. H. (2010). A unique role for the human amygdala in novelty detection. *NeuroImage, 50*(3), 1188–1193.

Blaise, J. H., Koranda, J. L., Chow, U., Haines, K. E., & Dorward, E. C. (2008). Neonatal isolation stress alters bidirectional long-term synaptic plasticity in amygdalo-hippocampal synapses in freely behaving adult rats. *Brain Research, 1193*, 25–33.

Blakemore, S. J. (2008). The social brain in adolescence. *Nature Reviews Neuroscience, 9*(4), 267–277.

Blanchard, D. C., Cholvanich, P., Blanchard, R. J., Clow, D. W., Hammer, R. P., Jr., Rowlett, J. K., & Bardo, M. T. (1991). Serotonin, but not dopamine, metabolites are increased in selected brain regions of subordinate male rats in a colony environment. *Brain Research, 568*(1–2), 61–66.

Blanchard, R. J., Kelley, M. J., & Blanchard, D. C. (1974). Defensive reactions and exploratory behavior in rats. *Journal of Comparative and Physiological Psychology, 87*(6), 1129–1133.

Blanchard, R. J., McKittrick, C. R., & Blanchard, D. C. (2001). Animal models of social stress: Effects on behavior and brain neurochemical systems. *Physiology & Behavior, 73*(3), 261–271.

Blanchard, R. J., Nikulina, J. N., Sakai, R. R., McKittrick, C., McEwen, B., & Blanchard, D. C. (1998). Behavioral and endocrine change following chronic predatory stress. *Physiology & Behavior, 63*(4), 561–569.

Blasé, J. J. (1986). A qualitative analysis of sources of teacher stress: Consequences for performance. *American Educational Research Journal, 23*(1), 13–40.

Blasé, J., & Blasé, J. R. (1994). *Empowering teachers: What successful principals do*. Thousand Oaks, CA: Corwin Press.

Blasé, J., & Roberts, J. (1994). The micropolitics of teacher work involvement: Effective principals' impacts on teachers. *Alberta Journal of Educational Research, 40*(1), 67–94.

Blood, G. W., & Blood, I. M. (2004). Bullying in adolescents who stutter: Communicative competence and self-esteem. *Contemporary Issues in Communication Science and Disorders, 31*, 69–79.

Blum, D. (2002). *Love at Goon Park: Harry Harlow and the science of affection*. Cambridge, MA: Perseus.

Blumenfeld, P. C., Hamilton, V. L., Wessels, K., & Falkner, D. (1979). Teaching responsibility to first graders. *Theory Into Practice, 18*(3), 174–180.

Bodizs, R., Bekesy, M., Szucs, A., Barsi, P., & Halasz, P. (2002). Sleep-dependent hippocampal slow activity correlates with waking memory performance in humans. *Neurobiology of Learning and Memory, 78*(2), 441–457.

Boehm, C. (1992). Segmentary "warfare" and the management of conflict: Comparison of East African chimpanzees and patrilineal-patrilocal humans. In A. H. Harcourt & F. B. M. de Waal (Eds.), *Coalitions and alliances in humans and other animals* (pp. 137–173). Oxford, England: Oxford University Press.

Boivin, M., Hymel, S., & Bukowski, W. M. (1995). The roles of social withdrawal, peer rejection, and victimization by peers in predicting loneliness and depressed mood in childhood. *Development and Psychopathology, 7*(4), 765–786.

Bolger, K. E., & Patterson, C. J. (2001). Developmental pathways from child maltreatment to peer rejection. *Child Development, 72*(2), 549–568.

Bollmer, J. M., Milich, R., Harris, M. J., & Maras, M. A. (2005). A friend in need: The role of friendship quality as a protective factor in peer victimization and bullying. *Journal of Interpersonal Violence, 20*(6), 701–712.

Bond, L., Carlin, J. B., Thomas, L., Rubin, K., & Patton, G. (2001). Does bullying cause emotional problems? A prospective study of young teenagers. *British Medical Journal, 323*(7311), 480–484.

Bonda, E., Petrides, M., Frey, S., & Evans, A. C. (1994). Frontal cortex involvement in organized sequences of hand movements: Evidence from a positron emission tomography study. *Society for Neurosciences Abstracts, 20*, 152–156.

Bong, M., & Skaalvik, E. M. (2003). Academic self-concept and self-efficacy: How different are they really? *Educational Psychology Review, 15*(1), 1–40.

Boonstra, R., Hik, D., Singleton, G. R., & Tinnikov, A. (1998). The impact of predator-induced stress on the snowshoe hare cycle. *Ecological Monographs, 68*(3), 371–394.

Bor, D., Duncan, J., Wiseman, R. J., & Owen, A. M. (2003). Encoding strategies dissociate prefrontal activity from working memory demand. *Neuron, 37*(2), 361–367.

Borg, M., Riding, R., & Falzon, J. (1991). Stress in teaching: A study of occupational stress and its determinants, job satisfaction and career commitment among primary schoolteachers. *Educational Psychology, 11*(1), 59–75.

Boulton, M. J., & Smith, P. K. (1992). The social nature of play fighting and play chasing: Mechanisms and strategies underlying cooperation and compromise. In J. H. Barkow, L. Cosmides, J. Tooby, & D. Premack (Eds.), *The adapted mind: Evolutionary psychology and the generation of culture* (pp. 429–444). New York, NY: Oxford University Press.

Bowes, L., Maughan, B., Caspi, A., Moffitt, T. E., & Arseneault, L. (2010). Families promote emotional and behavioural resilience to bullying: Evidence of an environmental effect. *Journal of Child Psychology and Psychiatry, 51*(7), 809–817.

Bowlby, J. (1969). *Attachment.* New York, NY: Basic Books.

Bowlby, J. (1988). *A secure base: Clinical applications of attachment theory.* London, England: Routledge.

Bradshaw, G. A., Schore, A. N., Brown, J. L., Poole, J. H., & Moss, C. J. (2005). Elephant breakdown. *Nature, 433*(7028), 807.

Bradshaw, J. (1990). *Homecoming: Reclaiming and championing your inner child.* New York, NY: Bantam.

Brake, W. G., Zhang, T. Y., Diorio, J., Meaney, M. J., & Gratton, A. (2004). Influence of early postnatal rearing conditions on mesocorticolimbic dopamine and behavioural responses to psychostimulants and stressors in adult rats. *European Journal of Neuroscience, 19*(7), 1863–1874.

Branchi, I., D'Andrea, I., Sietzema, J., Fiore, M., Di Fausto, V., Aloe, L., & Alleva, E. (2006). Early social enrichment augments adult hippocampal BDNF levels and survival of BrdU-positive cells while increasing anxiety and "depression"-like behavior. *Journal of Neuroscience Research, 83*(6), 965–973.

Branchi, I., Francia, N., & Alleva, E. (2004). Epigenetic control of neurobehavioural plasticity: The role of neurotrophins. *Behavioural Pharmacology, 15*(5–6), 353–362.

Brattesani, K. A., & Weinstein, R. S. (1980). *Students' perceptions of teacher behavior: Their role in a model of teacher expectation effects.* Paper presented at the annual meeting of the Western Psychological Association, Honolulu, HI.

Brattesani, K. A., Weinstein, R. S., & Marshall, H. H. (1984). Student perceptions of differential teacher treatment as moderators of teacher expectation effects. *Journal of Educational Psychology, 76*(2), 236–247.

Braun, C. (1976). Teacher expectations: Socio-psychological dynamics. *Review of Educational Research, 46*, 185–213.

Braun, C., Schweizer, R., Elbert, T., Birbaumer, N., & Taub, E. (2000). Differential activation in somatosensory cortex for different discrimination tasks. *Journal of Neuroscience, 20*(1), 446–450.

Braun, K., & Poeggel, G. (2001). Recognition of mother's voice evokes metabolic activation in the medial prefrontal cortex and lateral thalamus of octodon degus pups. *Neuroscience, 103*(4), 861–864.

Bredy, T. W., Grant, R. J., Champagne, D. L., & Meaney, M. J. (2003). Maternal care influences neuronal survival in the hippocampus of the rat. *European Journal of Neuroscience, 18*(10), 2903–2909.

Bredy, T. W., Zhang, T. Y., Grant, R. J., Diorio, J., & Meaney, M. J. (2004). Peripubertal environmental enrichment reverses the effects of maternal care on hippocampal development and glutamate receptor subunit expression. *European Journal of Neuroscience, 20*(5), 1355–1362.

Bremner, J. D., Scott, T. M., Delaney, R. C., Southwick, S. M., Mason, J. W., Johnson, D. R., . . . Charney, D. S. (1993). Deficits in short-term memory in posttraumatic stress disorder. *American Journal of Psychiatry, 150*(7), 1015–1019.

Brennan, F. X., Beck, K. D., & Servatius, R. J. (2006). Predator odor exposure facilitates acquisition of a leverpress avoidance response in rats. *Neuropsychiatric Disease and Treatment, 2*(1), 65–69.

Brennan, P. A., Pargas, R., Walker, E. F., Green, P., Newport, D. J., & Stowe, Z. (2008). Maternal depression and infant cortisol: Influences of timing, comorbidity and treatment. *Journal of Child Psychology and Psychiatry, 49*(10), 1099–1107.

Bressler, E. R., Martin, R. A., & Balshine, S. (2006). Production and appreciation of humor as sexually selected traits. *Evolution and Human Behavior, 27*(2), 121–130.

Bressoux, P., Kramarz, F., & Prost, C. (2006). *Teachers training, class size, and student outcomes: Evidence from third-grade classes in France.* Unpublished manuscript, Cornell University, Ithaca, NY.

Brewin, C. R., & Smart, L. (2005). Working-memory capacity and suppression of intrusive thoughts. *Journal of Behavior Therapy and Experimental Psychiatry, 36*(1), 61–68.

Brigham, J. C., & Barkowitz, P. (1978). Do "they all look alike"? The effect of race, sex, experience, and attitudes on the ability to recognize faces. *Journal of Applied Social Psychology, 8*(4), 306–318.

Brissie, J. S. (1988). Individual, situational contributors to teacher burnout. *Journal of Educational Research, 82*(2), 106–112.

Brissie, J. S., Hoover-Dempsey, K. V., & Bassler, O. C. (1988). Individual situational contributors to teacher burnout. *Journal of Educational Research, 82*(2), 106–112.

Broadhurst, P. L. (1957). Emotionality and the Yerkes-Dodson law. *Journal of Experimental Psychology, 54*(5), 345–352.

Brodal, P. (1992). *The central nervous system: Structure and function.* New York, NY: Oxford University Press.

Bronson, F. H., & Eleftheriou, B. E. (1964). Chronic physiological effects of fighting in mice. *General and Comparative Endocrinology, 15*, 9–14.

Brophy, J. (1982). Research on the self-fulfilling prophecy and teacher expectations. In L. Shulman, *The self-fulfilling prophecy: Its origins and consequences in research and practice.* Symposium conducted at the meeting of the American Educational Research, New York, NY.

Brophy, J. E., & Good, T. L. (1974). *Teacher-student relationships: Causes and consequences.* New York, NY: Holt, Rinehart and Winston.

Brouwers, A., Evers, W. J. G., & Tomic, W. (1999). *Teacher burnout and self-efficacy in eliciting social support.* Retrieved from ERIC database. (ED437342)

Brouwers, A., & Tomic, W. (1999). Teacher burnout, perceived self-efficacy in classroom management, and student disruptive behaviour in secondary education. *Curriculum and Teaching, 14*(2), 7–26.

Brouwers, A., & Tomic, W. (2000). A longitudinal study of teacher burnout and perceived self-efficacy in classroom management. *Teaching and Teacher Education, 16*(2), 239–253.

Brown, S. (1998). Play as an organizing principle: Clinical evidence and personal observations. In M. Bekoff & J. A. Myers (Eds.), *Animal play: Evolutionary, comparative, and ecological perspectives* (pp. 243–259). Cambridge, England: Cambridge University Press.

Brown, T. T., Lugar, H. M., Coalson, R. S., Miezin, F. M., Petersen, S. E., & Schlaggar, B. L. (2005). Developmental changes in human cerebral functional organization for word generation. *Cerebral Cortex, 15*(3), 275–290.

Brownell, M. T., Smith, S. W., McNellis, J., & Lenk, L. (1994). Career decisions in special education: Current and former teachers' personal views. *Exceptionality, 5*(2), 83–102.

Bruner, J. S. (1990). *Acts of meaning.* Cambridge, MA: Harvard University Press.

Brunner, E. (1997). Stress and the biology of inequality. *British Medical Journal, 314*(7092), 1472–1476.

Buccino, G., Binkofski, F., Fink, G. R., Fadiga, L., Fogassi, L., Gallese, V., . . . Freund, H. J. (2001). Action observation activates premotor and parietal areas in a somatotopic manner: An fMRI study. *European Journal of Neuroscience, 13*(2), 400–404.

Buccino, G., Binkofski, F., & Riggio, L. (2004). The mirror neuron system and action recognition. *Brain and Language, 89*(2), 370–376.

Buchanan, K. E., & Bardi, A. (2010). Acts of kindness and acts of novelty affect life satisfaction. *Journal of Social Psychology, 150*(3), 235–237.

Buckley, J., Schneider, M., & Shang, Y. (2004). *The effects of school facility quality on teacher retention in urban school districts.* Retrieved from the National Clearinghouse for Educational Facilities website: http://www.ncef.org/pubs/pubs_html.cfm?abstract=teacherretention

Buhs, E. S., & Ladd, G. W. (2001). Peer rejection as an antecedent of young children's school adjustment: An examination of mediating processes. *Developmental Psychology, 37*(4), 550–560.

Buhs, E. S., Ladd, G. W., & Herald, S. L. (2006). Peer exclusion and victimization: Processes that mediate the relation between peer group rejection and children's classroom engagement and achievement? *Journal of Educational Psychology, 98*(1), 1–13.

Bunzeck, N., & Duzel, E. (2006). Absolute coding of stimulus novelty in the human substantia nigra/VTA. *Neuron, 51*(3), 369–379.

Buonomano, D. V., & Merzenich, M. M. (1998). Cortical plasticity: From synapses to maps. *Annual Review of Neuroscience, 21*, 149–186.

Burghardt, G. M. (2005). *The genesis of animal play: Testing the limits.* Cambridge, MA: MIT Press.

Burke, R. J., & Greenglass, E. (1993). Work stress, role conflict, social support, and psychological burnout among teachers. *Psychological Reports, 73*, 371–380.

Burke, R. J., & Greenglass, E. (1995). A longitudinal study of psychological burnout in teachers. *Human Relations, 48*(2), 187–202.

Burke, R. J., Greenglass, E. R., & Schwarzer, R. (1996). Predicting teacher burnout over time: Effects of work stress, social support, and self-doubts on burnout and its consequences. *Anxiety, Stress & Coping, 9*(3), 261–275.

Burmeister, S. S., Jarvis, E. D., & Fernald, R. D. (2005). Rapid behavioral and genomic responses to social opportunity. *PLoS Biology, 3*(11), e363. doi:10.1371/journal.pbio.0030363

Burmeister, S. S., Kailasanath, V., & Fernald, R. D. (2007). Social dominance regulates androgen and estrogen receptor gene expression. *Hormones and Behavior, 51*(1), 164–170.

Bush, E. (2001). The use of human touch to improve the well-being of older adults: A holistic nursing intervention. *Journal of Holistic Nursing, 19*(3), 256–270.

Byers, J. A., & Walker, C. (1995). Refining the motor training hypothesis for the evolution of play. *American Naturalist, 146*(1), 25–40.

Byrne, B. M. (1994). Burnout: Testing for the validity, replication, and invariance of causal structure across elementary, intermediate, and secondary teachers. *American Educational Research Journal, 31*(3), 645–673.

Cacioppo, J. T., & Berntson, G. G. (2002). Social neuroscience. In J. T. Cacioppo, G. G. Berntson, R. Adolphs, C. S. Carter, R. J. Davidson, M. K. McClintock, S. E. Taylor (Eds.), *Foundations in social neuroscience* (pp. 2–10). Cambridge, MA: MIT Press.

Cacioppo, J. T., & Hawkley, L. C. (2003). Social isolation and health, with an emphasis on underlying mechanisms. *Perspectives in Biology and Medicine, 46*(3), S39–S52.

Cacioppo, J. T., & Hawkley, L. C. (2009). Perceived social isolation and cognition. *Trends in Cognitive Sciences, 13*(10), 447–454.

Cahen, L. S. (1966). *Experimental manipulation of bias in teachers' scoring of subjective tests.* Paper presented at the American Psychological Association, New York, NY.

Calarge, C., Andreasen, N. C., & O'Leary, D. S. (2003). Visualizing how one brain understands another: A PET study of theory of mind. *American Journal of Psychiatry, 160*(11), 1954–1964.

Calcagnetti, D. J., & Schechter, M. D. (1992). Place conditioning reveals the rewarding aspect of social interaction in juvenile rats. *Physiology & Behavior, 51*(4), 667–672.

Calder, A. J., Keane, J., Manly, T., Sprengelmeyer, R., Scott, S., Nimmo-Smith, I., & Young, A. W. (2003). Facial expression recognition across the adult life span. *Neuropsychologia, 41*(2), 195–202.

Caldji, C., Diorio, J., Anisman, H., & Meaney, M. J. (2004). Maternal behavior regulates benzodiazepine/GABAA receptor subunit expression in brain regions associated with fear in BALB/c and C57BL/6 mice. *Neuropsychopharmacology, 29*(7), 1344–1352.

Caldji, C., Diorio, J., & Meaney, M. J. (2000). Variations in maternal care in infancy regulate the development of stress reactivity. *Biological Psychiatry, 48*(12), 1164–1174.

Caldji, C., Diorio, J., & Meaney, M. J. (2003). Variations in maternal care alter GABA(A) receptor subunit expression in brain regions associated with fear. *Neuropsychopharmacology, 28*(11), 1950–1959.

Caldji, C., Tannenbaum, B., Sharma, S., Francis, D., Plotsky, P. M., & Meaney, M. J. (1998). Maternal care during infancy regulates the development of neural systems mediating the expression of fearfulness in the rat. *Proceedings of the National Academy of Sciences of the United States of America, 95*(9), 5335–5340.

Cameron, N. M., Champagne, F. A., Parent, C., Fish, E. W., Ozaki-Kuroda, K., & Meaney, M. J. (2005). The programming of individual differences in defensive responses and reproductive strategies in the rat through variations in maternal care. *Neuroscience and Biobehavioral Reviews, 29*(4–5), 843–865.

Cameron, N. M., Fish, E. W., & Meaney, M. J. (2008). Maternal influences on the sexual behavior and reproductive success of the female rat. *Hormones and Behavior, 54*(1), 178–184.

Campbell, J. (1968). *The hero with a thousand faces.* Princeton, NJ: Princeton University Press.

Campeau, S., Nyhuis, T. J., Sasse, S. K., Day, H. E., & Masini, C. V. (2008). Acute and chronic effects of ferret odor exposure in Sprague-Dawley rats. *Neuroscience and Biobehavioral Reviews, 32*(7), 1277–1286.

Canetti, L., Bachar, E., Galili-Weisstub, E., De-Nour, A. K., & Shalev, A. Y. (1997). Parental bonding and mental health in adolescence. *Adolescence, 32*(126), 381–394.

Cann, A., Calhoun, L. G., & Banks, J. S. (1997). On the role of humor appreciation in interpersonal attraction: It's no joking matter. *International Journal of Humor Research, 10*(1), 77–90.

Cann, A., Holt, K., & Calhoun, L. G. (1999). The roles of humor and sense of humor in responses to stressors. *International Journal of Humor Research, 12*(2), 177–194.

Cannon, R., Lubar, J., Clements, J., Harvey, E., & Baldwin, D. (2007). Practical joking and cingulate cortex: A standardized low-resolution electromagnetic tomography (sLORETA) investigation of practical joking in the cerebral volume. *Journal of Neurotherapy, 11*(4), 51–63.

Cantalupo, C., & Hopkins, W. D. (2001). Asymmetric Broca's areas in great apes. A region of the ape brain in uncannily similar to one linked with speech in humans. *Nature, 414*, 505.

Carlage, C., Andreasen, N. C., & O'Leary, D. S. (2003). Visualizing how one brain understands another: A PET study of theory of mind. *American Journal of Psychiatry, 160*, 1954–1964.

Carney, J. V. (2000). Bullied to death: Perceptions of peer abuse and suicidal behaviour during adolescence. *School Psychology International, 21*(2), 213–223.

Carney, J. V., Hazler, R. J., Oh, I., Hibel, L. C., & Granger, D. A. (2010). The relations between bullying exposures in middle childhood, anxiety, and adrenocortical activity. *Journal of School Violence, 9*(2), 194–211.

Caro, T. M. (1988). Adaptive significance of play: Are we getting closer? *Trends in Ecology & Evolution, 3*(2), 50–54.

Carr, E. H. (1962). *What is history?* New York, NY: Knopf.

Carr, L., Iacoboni, M., Dubeau, M. C., Mazziotta, J. C., & Lenzi, G. L. (2003). Neural mechanisms of empathy in humans: A relay from neural systems for imitation to limbic areas. *Proceedings of the National Academy of Sciences of the United States of America, 100*(9), 5497–5502.

Carro, E., Trejo, J. L., Busiguina, S., & Torres-Aleman, I. (2001). Circulating insulin-like growth factor I mediates the protective effects of physical exercise against brain insults of different etiology and anatomy. *Journal of Neuroscience, 21*(15), 5678–5684.

Carskadon, M. A., Acebo, C., Wolfson, A. R., Tzischinsky, O., & Darley, C. (1997). REM sleep on MSLTS in high school students is related to circadian phase. *Sleep Research, 26*, 705–707.

Carskadon, M. A., Wolfson, A. R., Acebo, C., Tzischinsky, O., & Seifer, R. (1998). Adolescent sleep patterns, circadian timing, and sleepiness at a transition to early school days. *Sleep, 21*(8), 871–881.

Carson, R. L., Templin, T. J., & Weiss, H. M. (2006). *Exploring the episodic nature of teachers' emotions and its relationship to teacher burnout.* Paper presented at the American Education Research Association Annual Convention, San Francisco, CA.

Carswell, S. (1993). The potential for treating neurodegenerative disorders with NGF-inducing compounds. *Experimental Neurology, 124*(1), 36–42.

Casey, B. J., Galvan, A., & Hare, T. A. (2005). Changes in cerebral functional organization during cognitive development. *Current Opinion in Neurobiology, 15*(2), 239–244.

Cash, A. H., El-Mallakh, R. S., Chamberlain, K., Bratton, J. Z., & Li, R. (1997). Structure of music may influence cognition. *Perceptual and Motor Skills, 84*(1), 66.

Cassidy, J., & Asher, S. R. (1992). Loneliness and peer relations in young children. *Child Development, 63*(2), 350–365.

Castelli, F., Glaser, D. E., & Butterworth, B. (2006). Discrete and analogue quantity processing in the parietal lobe: A functional MRI study. *Proceedings of the National Academy of Sciences of the United States of America, 103*(12), 4693–4698.

Cavigelli, S. A., & McClintock, M. K. (2003). Fear of novelty in infant rats predicts adult corticosterone dynamics and an early death. *Proceedings of the National Academy of Sciences of the United States of America, 100*(26), 16131–16136.

Celso, B. G., Ebener, D. J., & Burkhead, E. J. (2003). Humor coping, health status, and life satisfaction among older adults residing in assisted living facilities. *Aging & Mental Health, 7*(6), 438–445.

Chambers, R. A., & Potenza, M. N. (2003). Neurodevelopment, impulsivity, and adolescent gambling. *Journal of Gambling Studies, 19*(1), 53–84.

Chaminade, T., Meltzoff, A., & Decety, J. (2002). Does the end justify the means? A PET exploration of the mechanisms involved in human imitation. *NeuroImage, 15*(2), 318–328.

Champagne, D. L., Bagot, R. C., van Hasselt, F., Ramakers, G., Meaney, M. J., de Kloet, E. R., . . . Krugers, H. (2008). Maternal care and hippocampal plasticity: Evidence for experience-dependent structural plasticity, altered synaptic functioning, and differential responsiveness to glucocorticoids and stress. *Journal of Neuroscience, 28*(23), 6037–6045.

Champagne, F., Diorio, J., Sharma, S., & Meaney, M. J. (2001). Naturally occurring variations in maternal behavior in the rat are associated with differences in estrogen-inducible central oxytocin receptors. *Proceedings of the National Academy of Sciences of the United States of America, 98*, 12736–12741.

Champagne, F. A., Francis, D. D., Mar, A., & Meaney, M. J. (2003). Variations in maternal care in the rat as a mediating influence for the effects of environment on development. *Physiology & Behavior, 79*(3), 359–371.

Champagne, F. A., & Meaney, M. J. (2007). Transgenerational effects of social environment on variations in maternal care and behavioral response to novelty. *Behavioral Neuroscience, 121*(6), 1353–1363.

Champagne, F. A., Weaver, I. C., Diorio, J., Dymov, S., Szyf, M., & Meaney, M. J. (2006). Maternal care associated with methylation of the estrogen receptor-alpha1b promoter and estrogen receptor-alpha expression in the medial preoptic area of female offspring. *Endocrinology, 147*(6), 2909–2915.

Chan, A. S., Ho, Y. C., & Cheung, M. C. (1998). Music training improves verbal memory. *Nature, 396*(6707), 128.

Chang, M. L. (2009). An appraisal perspective of teacher burnout: Examining the emotional work of teachers. *Educational Psychology Review, 21*(3), 193–218.

Charnov, E. L., & Berrigan, D. (2005). Why do female primates have such long lifespans and so few babies? Or life in the slow lane. *Evolutionary Anthropology, 1*(6), 191–194.

Chase, I. D. (1982). Dynamics of hierarchy formation: The sequential development of dominance relationships. *Behaviour, 80*(4), 218–240.

Chase, I. D., Tovey, C., Spangler-Martin, D., & Manfredonia, M. (2002). Individual differences versus social dynamics in the formation of animal dominance hierarchies. *Proceedings of the National Academy of Sciences of the United States of America, 99*(8), 5744–5749.

Cheng, D. T., Knight, D. C., Smith, C. N., & Helmstetter, F. J. (2006). Human amygdala activity during the expression of fear responses. *Behavioral Neuroscience, 120*(6), 1187–1195.

Cheng, Y., Meltzoff, A. N., & Decety, J. (2007). Motivation modulates the activity of the human mirror-neuron system. *Cerebral Cortex, 17*(8), 1979–1986.

Cherkas, L. F., Aviv, A., Valdes, A. M., Hunkin, J. L., Gardner, J. P., Surdulescu, G. L., . . . Spector, T. D. (2006). The effects of social status on biological aging as measured by white-blood-cell telomere length. *Aging Cell, 5*(5), 361–365.

Chia, R., & King, I. W. (1998). The organizational structuring of novelty. Organization, 5(4), 461–478.

Chiao, J. Y., Adams, R. B., Tse, P. U., Lowenthal, L., Richeson, J. A., & Ambady, N. (2008). Knowing who's boss: FMRI and ERP investigations of social dominance perception. *Group Processes & Intergroup Relations, 11*(2), 201–214.

Chiron, C., Jambaque, I., Nabbout, R., Lounes, R., Syrota, A., & Dulac, O. (1997). The right brain hemisphere is dominant in human infants. *Brain, 120*(6), 1057–1065.

Chochon, F., Cohen, L., van de Moortele, P. F., & Dehaene, S. (1999). Differential contributions of the left and right inferior parietal lobules to number processing. *Journal of Cognitive Neuroscience, 11*(6), 617–630.

Chollet, F., DiPiero, V., Wise, R. J., Brooks, D. J., Dolan, R. J., & Frackowiak, R. S. (1991). The functional anatomy of motor recovery after stroke in humans: A study with positron emission tomography. *Annals of Neurology, 29*(1), 63–71.

Christensen, A. J., Edwards, D. L., Wiebe, J. S., Benotsch, E. G., McKelvey, L., Andrews, M., & Lubaroff, D. M. (1996). Effect of verbal self-disclosure on natural killer cell activity: Moderating influence of cynical hostility. *Psychosomatic Medicine, 58*(2), 150–155.

Christensen, H., Henderson, A. S., Griffiths, K., & Levings, C. (1997). Does ageing inevitably lead to declines in cognitive performance? A longitudinal study of elite academics. *Personality and Individual Differences, 23*(1), 67–78.

Christie, W., & Moore, C. (2005). The impact of humor on patients with cancer. *Clinical Journal of Oncology Nursing, 9*(2), 211–218.

Chugani, H. T., Phelps, M. E., & Mazziotta, J. C. (1987). Positron emission tomography study of human brain functional development. *Annals of Neurology, 22*(4), 487–497.

Claesson, K., & Sohlberg, S. (2002). Internalized shame and early interactions characterized by indifference, abandonment and rejection: Replicated findings. *Clinical Psychology & Psychotherapy, 9*(4), 277–284.

Clark, B. R. (1962). *Educating the expert society*. San Francisco, CA: Chandler.

Clark, J. (1989). *Laying down the law*. Washington, DC: Regnery.

Clark, K. B., & Clark, M. K. (1950). Emotional factors in racial identification and preference in negro children. *Journal of Negro Education, 19*(3), 341–350.

Clark, R. (2003). *The Essential 55: An award-winning educator's rules for discovering the successful student in every child*. New York, NY: Hyperion.

Classen, J., Liepert, J., Wise, S. P., Hallett, M., & Cohen, L. G. (1998). Rapid plasticity of human cortical movement representation induced by practice. *Journal of Neurophysiology, 79*(2), 1117–1123.

Clinchy, M., Zanette, L., Boonstra, R., Wingfield, J. C., & Smith, J. N. (2004). Balancing food and predator pressure induces chronic stress in songbirds. *Proceedings of the Royal Society B: Biological Sciences, 271*(1556), 2473–2479.

Clovis, C., Pollock, J., Goodman, R., Impey, S., Dunn, J. Mandel, G., Nestler, E. J. (2005). Epigenetic mechanisms and gene networks in the nervous system. *The Journal of Neuroscience, 25*(45), 10379–10389.

Coan, J. A., Schaefer, H. S., & Davidson, R. J. (2006). Lending a hand: Social regulation of the neural response to threat. *Psychological Science, 17*(12), 1032–1039.

Coates, T. J., & Thoresen, C. E. (1976). Teacher anxiety: A review with recommendations. *Review of Educational Research, 46*(2), 159–184.

Coch, D., & Ansari, D. (2009). Thinking about mechanisms is crucial to connecting neuroscience and education. *Cortex, 45*(4), 546–547.

Coe, C. L., Mendoza, S. P., & Levine, S. (1979). Social status constrains the stress response in the squirrel monkey. *Physiology & Behavior, 23*(4), 633–638.

Cohen, A. A. (2004). Female post-reproductive lifespan: A general mammalian trait. *Biological Reviews of the Cambridge Philosophical Society, 79*(4), 733–750.

Cohen, G. D. (2005). *The mature mind: The positive power of the aging brain*. New York, NY: Basic Books.

Cohen, S. (2004). Social relationships and health. *American Psychologist, 59*(8), 676–684.

Cohen, S., Doyle, W. J., Turner, R., Alper, C. M., & Skoner, D. P. (2003). Sociability and susceptibility to the common cold. *Psychological Science, 14*(5), 389–395.

Cohen, S., & Wills, T. A. (1985). Stress, social support, and the buffering hypothesis. *Psychological Bulletin, 98*(2), 310–357.

Collette, J. C., Millam, J. R., Klasing, K. C., & Wakenell, P. S. (2000). Neonatal handling of Amazon parrots alters the stress response and immune function. *Applied Animal Behaviour Science, 66*(4), 335–349.

Collins, M. (1992). *Ordinary children, extraordinary teachers*. Newburyport, MA: Hampton Roads Publishing.

Colombo, J., & Bundy, R. S. (1983). Infant response to auditory familiarity and novelty. *Infant Behavior and Development, 6*(2–3), 305–311.

Colvis, C. M., Pollock, J. D., Goodman, R. H., Impey, S., Dunn, J., Mandel, G., . . . Nestler, E. J. (2005). Epigenetic mechanisms and gene networks in the nervous system. *Journal of Neuroscience, 25*(45), 10379–10389.

Compton, D. M., Bachman, L. D., Brand, D., & Avet, T. L. (2000). Age-associated changes in cognitive function in highly educated adults: Emerging myths and realities. *International Journal of Geriatric Psychiatry, 15*(1), 75–85.

Conant, J. B. (1959). *The American high school today.* New York, NY: Mc-Graw-Hill.

Conrad, C. D., Lupien, S. J., & McEwen, B. S. (1999). Support for a bimodal role for type II adrenal steroid receptors in spatial memory. *Neurobiology of Learning and Memory, 72*(1), 39–46.

Corbetta, M., & Shulman, G. L. (2002). Control of goal-directed and stimulus-driven attention in the brain. *Nature Reviews Neuroscience, 3*(3), 201–215.

Cornette, L., Dupont, P., Salmon, E., & Orban, G. A. (2001). The neural substrate of orientation working memory. *Journal of Cognitive Neuroscience, 13*(6), 813–828.

Costabile, A., Smith, P. K., Matheson, L., Aston, J., Hunter, T., & Boulton, M. (1991). Cross-national comparison of how children distinguish serious and playful fighting. *Developmental Psychology, 27*(5), 881–887.

Costela, C., Tejedor-Real, P., Mico, J. A., & Gibert-Rahola, J. (1995). Effect of neonatal handling on learned helplessness model of depression. *Physiology & Behavior, 57*(2), 407–410.

Cotman, C. W., & Berchtold, N. C. (2002). Exercise: A behavioral intervention to enhance brain health and plasticity. *Trends in Neurosciences, 25*(6), 295–301.

Cotman, C. W., Berchtold, N. C., & Christie, L. A. (2007). Exercise builds brain health: Key roles of growth factor cascades and inflammation. *Trends in Neurosciences, 30*(9), 464–472.

Cotton, K. (1996). *Affective and social benefits of small-scale schooling.* Retrieved from ERIC database. (ED401088)

Coulson, S., & Van Petten, C. (2007). A special role for the right hemisphere in metaphor comprehension? ERP evidence from hemifield presentation. *Brain Research, 1146,* 128–145.

Coulson, S., & Wu, Y. C. (2005). Right hemisphere activation of joke-related information: An event-related brain potential study. *Journal of Cognitive Neuroscience, 17*(3), 494–506.

Cousins, N. (1979). *Anatomy of an illness as perceived by the patient: Reflections on healing and regeneration.* New York, NY: W. W. Norton.

Coutinho, S. V., Plotsky, P. M., Sablad, M., Miller, J. C., Zhou, H., Bayati, A. I., . . . Mayer, E. A. (2002). Neonatal maternal separation alters stress-induced responses to viscerosomatic nociceptive stimuli in rat. *Gastrointestinal and Liver Physiology, 282*(2), G307–G316.

Covert, M. V., Tangney, J. P., Maddux, J. E., & Heleno, N. M. (2003). Shame-proneness, guilt-proneness, and interpersonal problem solving: A social cognitive analysis. *Journal of Social and Clinical Psychology, 22*(1), 1–12.

Covington, M. V. (1984a). The motive for self-worth. In R. Ames & C. Ames (Eds.), *Research on motivation in education* (pp. 71–113). New York, NY: Academic Press.

Covington, M. V. (1984b). The self-worth theory of achievement motivation: Findings and implications. *Elementary School Journal, 85*(1), 5–20.

Cowan, W. M., & Kandel, E. R. (2001). A brief history of synapses and synaptic transmission. In W. M. Cowan, T. C. Sudhof, & C. F. Stevens (Eds.), *Synapses* (pp. 1–88). Baltimore, MD: Johns Hopkins University Press.

Cozolino, L. J. (2008). *The healthy aging brain: Sustaining attachment, attaining wisdom.* New York, NY: W. W. Norton.

Crabbe, J. C., & Phillips, T. J. (2003). Mother nature meets mother nurture. *Nature Neuroscience, 6*(5), 440–442.

Craig, W. M. (1998). The relationship among bullying, victimization, depression, anxiety and aggression in elementary school children. *Personality and Individual Differences, 24*(1), 123–130.

Craig, W. M., & Harel, Y. (2004). Bullying, physical fighting and victimization. In C. Currie, C. Roberts, A. Morgan, R. Smith, W. Settertobulte, O. Samdal, & B. Rasmussen (Eds.), *Young people's health in context: Health behavior in school-aged children (HBSC) study: International report from the 2001/2002 survey* (pp. 144). Copenhagen, Sweden: World Health Organization.

Craig, W. M., Pepler, D., & Atlas, R. (2000). Observations of bullying in the playground and in the classroom. *School Psychology International, 21*(1), 22–36.

Crane, S., & Iwanicki, E. F. (1983). *The effect of role conflict and role ambiguity on perceived levels of burnout among special education teachers.* Paper presented at the meeting of the American Educational Research Association, Montreal, QC.

Creel, S. (2001). Social dominance and stress hormones. *Trends in Ecology & Evolution, 16*(9), 491–497.

Creel, S. (2005). Dominance, aggression, and glucocorticoid levels in social carnivores. *Journal of Mammalogy, 86*(2), 255–264.

Creel, S., Creel, N. M., Mills, M. G. L., & Monfort, S. L. (1997). Rank and reproduction in cooperatively breeding African wild dogs: Behavioral and endocrine correlates. *Behavioral Ecology, 8*(3), 298–306.

Creel, S., Winnie, J. A., Jr., & Christianson, D. (2009). Glucocorticoid stress hormones and the effect of predation risk on elk reproduction. *Proceedings of the National Academy of Sciences of the United States of America, 106*(30), 12388–12393.

Crick, N. R. (1996). The role of overt aggression, relational aggression, and prosocial behavior in the prediction of children's future social adjustment. *Child Development, 67*(5), 2317–2327.

Crick, N. R., Casas, J. F., & Ku, H. C. (1999). Relational and physical forms of peer victimization in preschool. *Developmental Psychology, 35*(2), 376–385.

Critchley, H. D. (2005). Neural mechanisms of autonomic, affective, and cognitive integration. *Journal of Comparative Neurology, 493*(1), 154–166.

Critchley, H. D., Wiens, S., Rotshtein, P., Ohman, A., & Dolan, R. J. (2004). Neural systems supporting interoceptive awareness. *Nature Neuroscience, 7*(2), 189–195.

Crow, L. (1964). *Public attitudes and expectations as a disturbing variable in experimentation and therapy.* Unpublished paper, Harvard University, Cambridge, MA.

Crowell, J. A., Treboux, D., & Waters, E. (2002). Stability of attachment representations: The transition to marriage. *Developmental Psychology, 38*(4), 467–479.

Cummins, D. D. (1999). Cheater detection is modified by social rank: The impact of dominance on the evolution of cognitive functions. *Ethology and Sociobiology, 20*(4), 229–248.

Cunningham, W. A., Johnson, M. K., Raye, C. L., Chris Gatenby, J., Gore, J. C., & Banaji, M. R. (2004). Separable neural components in the processing of black and white faces. *Psychological Science, 15*(12), 806–813.

Curcio, G., Ferrara, M., & De Gennaro, L. (2006). Sleep loss, learning capacity and academic performance. *Sleep Medicine Reviews, 10*(5), 323–337.

Cushner, F. D., & Friedman, R. J. (1989). Humor and the physician. *Southern Medical Journal, 82*(1), 51–52.

Cutrona, C., Russell, D., & Rose, J. (1986). Social support and adaptation to stress by the elderly. *Psychology and Aging, 1*(1), 47–54.

Czeh, B., Muller-Keuker, J. I., Rygula, R., Abumaria, N., Hiemke, C., Domenici, E., & Fuchs, E. (2007). Chronic social stress inhibits cell proliferation in the adult medial prefrontal cortex: Hemispheric asymmetry and reversal by fluoxetine treatment. *Neuropsychopharmacology, 32*(7), 1490–1503.

Dahl, R. E. (1999). The consequences of insufficient sleep for adolescents: Links between sleep and emotional regulation. *Phi Delta Kappan, 80*(5), 354–359.

Dahl, R. E. (2004). Adolescent brain development: A period of vulnerabilities and opportunities. Keynote address. *Annals of the New York Academy of Sciences, 1021,* 1–22.

Dalla, C., Bangasser, D. A., Edgecomb, C., & Shors, T. J. (2007). Neurogenesis and learning: Acquisition and asymptotic performance predict how many new cells survive in the hippocampus. *Neurobiology of Learning and Memory, 88*(1), 143–148.

Damasio, A. R. (1994). *Descartes' error: Emotion, reason, and the human brain.* New York, NY: Putnam.

Dani, J., Burrill, C., & Demmig-Adams, B. (2005). The remarkable role of nutrition in learning and behaviour. *Nutrition and Food Science, 35*(4), 258–263.

Danso, H. A., & Esses, V. M. (2001). Black experimenters and the intellectual test performance of white participants: The tables are turned. *Journal of Experimental Social Psychology, 37*(2), 158–165.

Danzer, A., Dale, J. A., & Klions, H. L. (1990). Effect of exposure to humorous stimuli on induced depression. *Psychological Reports, 66*(3), 1027–1036.

Darling-Hammond, L. (2001). The challenge of staffing our schools. *Educational Leadership, 58*(8), 12–17.

Darling-Hammond, L., & Sclan, E. M. (1996). Who teaches and why: Dilemma of building a profession for twenty-first-century schools. In J. Sikula (Ed.), *Handbook of research on teacher education* (2nd ed., pp. 67–101). New York, NY: Macmillan.

Darling-Hammond, L., & Sykes, G. (2003). Wanted: A national teacher supply policy for education: The right way to meet the "highly qualified teacher" challenge. *Education Policy Analysis Archives, 11*(33), 1–55.

Davatzikos, C., & Resnick, S. M. (2002). Degenerative age changes in white matter connectivity visualized in vivo using magnetic resonance imaging. *Cerebral Cortex, 12*(7), 767–771.

Davidson, R. J. (2000). Affective style, psychopathology, and resilience: Brain mechanisms and plasticity. *American Psychologist, 55*(11), 1196–1214.

Davidson, R. J., Jackson, D. C., & Kalin, N. H. (2000). Emotion, plasticity, context, and regulation: Perspectives from affective neuroscience. *Psychological Bulletin, 126*(6), 890–909.

Davis, M. (1992). The role of the amygdala in fear and anxiety. *Annual Review of Neuroscience, 15*, 353–375.

Davis, M. (1997). Neurobiology of fear responses: The role of the amygdala. *Journal of Neuropsychiatry and Clinical Neurosciences, 9*(3), 382–402.

Davis, M. (1998). Are different parts of the extended amygdala involved in fear versus anxiety? *Biological Psychiatry, 44*(12), 1239–1247.

Davis, M., Myers, K. M., Chhatwal, J., & Ressler, K. J. (2006). Pharmacological treatments that facilitate extinction of fear: Relevance to psychotherapy. *Journal of the American Society for Experimental NeuroTherapeutics, 3*(1), 82–96.

De Bellis, M. D., Keshavan, M. S., Clark, D. B., Casey, B. J., Giedd, J. N., Boring, A. M., . . . Ryan, N. D. (1999). Developmental traumatology part II: Brain development. *Biological Psychiatry, 45*(10), 1271–1284.

Dehaene, S., Piazza, M., Pinel, P., & Cohen, L. (2003). Three parietal circuits for number processing. *Cognitive Neuropsychology, 20*(3), 487–506.

de Hooge, I. E., Breugelmans, S. M., & Zeelenberg, M. (2008). Not so ugly after all: When shame acts as a commitment device. *Journal of Personality and Social Psychology, 95*(4), 933–943.

de Lange, J. (1993). Assessment in problem-oriented curricula. In N. Webb & A. F. Coxford (Eds.), *Assessment in the mathematics classroom* (pp. 197–208). Reston, VA: National Council of Teachers of Mathematics.

de Vignemont, F., & Singer, T. (2006). The empathic brain: How, when and why? *Trends in Cognitive Sciences, 10*(10), 435–441.

Deak, T., Arakawa, H., Bekkedal, M. Y., & Panksepp, J. (2009). Validation of a novel social investigation task that may dissociate social motivation from exploratory activity. *Behavioural Brain Research, 199*(2), 326–333.

Deaner, S. L., & McConatha, J. T. (1993). The relation of humor to depression and personality. *Psychological Reports, 72*(3), 755–763.

Decety, J., & Chaminade, T. (2003a). Neural correlates of feeling sympathy. *Neuropsychologia, 41*(2), 127–138.

Decety, J., & Chaminade, T. (2003b). When the self represents the other: A new cognitive neuroscience view on psychological identification. *Consciousness and Cognition, 12*(4), 577–596.

Decety, J., & Lamm, C. (2006). Human empathy through the lens of social neuroscience. *The Scientific World Journal, 6*, 1146–1163.

Deci, E., Vallerand, R., Pelletier, L., & Ryan, R. (1991). Motivation and education: The self-determination perspective. *Educational Psychologist, 26*(3–4), 325–346.

Deckers, L., & Devine, J. (1981). Humor by violating an existing expectancy. *Journal of Psychology, 108*(1), 107–110.

del Barrio, C., Martin, E., Montero, I., Gutierrez, H., Barrios, A., & de Dios, M. J. (2008). Bullying and social exclusion in Spanish secondary schools: National trends from 1999 to 2006. *International Journal of Clinical and Health Psychology, 8*(3), 657–677.

Del Bel, E. A., & Guimaraes, F. S. (1997). Social isolation increases cholecystokinin mRNA in the central nervous system of rats. *NeuroReport, 8*(16), 3597–3600.

Delaney, B. H., Newcomb, M., & Dembo, M. H. (1997). *The role of hardiness, efficacy, and humanitarianism in the reduction of educator stress, burnout and illness.* Paper presented at the annual meeting of the American Educational Research Association, Chicago, IL.

deMause, L. (1975). Our forebears made childhood a nightmare. *Psychology Today, 8*, 85–88.

Dembicki, D., & Anderson, J. (1996). Pet ownership may be a factor in improved health of the elderly. *Journal of Nutrition for the Elderly, 15*(3), 15–31.

Denenberg, V. H., & Grota, L. J. (1964). Social-seeking and novelty-seeking behavior as a function of differential rearing histories. *Journal of Abnormal Psychology, 69*, 453–456.

Dennett, D. C. (1991). *Consciousness explained*. Boston, MA: Little, Brown.

Derfler-Rozin, R., Pillutla, M., & Thau, S. (2010). Social reconnection revisited: The effects of social exclusion risk on reciprocity, trust, and general risk-taking. *Organizational Behavior and Human Decision Processes, 112*(2), 140–150.

Derks, P., Bogart, E., & Gillikin, L. (1991). *Neuroelectrical activity and humor*. Paper presented at the 9th International Conference on Humour and Laughter at Brock University, St. Catherines, Canada.

Derryberry, D., & Reed, M. A. (2002). Anxiety-related attentional biases and their regulation by attentional control. *Journal of Abnormal Psychology, 111*(2), 225–236.

Desimone, R. (1991). Face-selective cells in the temporal cortex of monkeys. *Journal of Cognitive Neuroscience, 3*(1), 1–8.

DeSteno, D., Dasgupta, N., Bartlett, M. Y., & Cajdric, A. (2004). Prejudice from thin air: The effect of emotion on automatic intergroup attitudes. *Psychological Science, 15*(5), 319–324.

Dettling, A. C., Feldon, J., & Pryce, C. R. (2002). Early deprivation and behavioral and physiological responses to social separation/novelty in the marmoset. *Pharmacology, Biochemistry, and Behavior, 73*(1), 259–269.

Devereux, P. G., & Ginsburg, G. P. (2001). Sociality effects on the production of laughter. *Journal of General Psychology, 128*(2), 227–240.

Devine, P. G. (1989). Stereotypes and prejudice: Their automatic and controlled components. *Journal of Personality and Social Psychology, 56*(1), 5–18.

DeVries, A. C., Glasper, E. R., & Detillion, C. E. (2003). Social modulation of stress responses. *Physiology & Behavior, 79*(3), 399–407.

DeWall, C. N., & Baumeister, R. F. (2006). Alone but feeling no pain: Effects of social exclusion on physical pain tolerance and pain threshold, affective forecasting, and interpersonal empathy. *Journal of Personality and Social Psychology, 91*(1), 1–15.

Dexter, D., Bijwadia, J., Schilling, D., & Applebaugh, G. (2003). Sleep, sleepiness and school start times: A preliminary study. *Wisconsin Medical Journal, 102*(1), 44–46.

di Pellegrino, G., Fadiga, L., Fogassi, L., Gallese, V., & Rizzolatti, G. (1992). Understanding motor events: A neurophysiological study. *Experimental Brain Research, 91*(1), 176–180.

Diamond, D. M., Bennett, M. C., Fleshner, M., & Rose, G. M. (1992). Inverted-U relationship between the level of peripheral corticosterone and the magnitude of hippocampal primed burst potentiation. *Hippocampus, 2*(4), 421–430.

Diamond, D. M., Campbell, A. M., Park, C. R., Woodson, J. C., Conrad, C. D., Bachstetter, A. D., & Mervis, R. F. (2006). Influence of predator stress on the consolidation versus retrieval of long-term spatial memory and hippocampal spinogenesis. *Hippocampus, 16*(7), 571–576.

Diamond, D. M., Park, C. R., Heman, K. L., & Rose, G. M. (1999). Exposing rats to a predator impairs spatial working memory in the radial arm water maze. *Hippocampus, 9*(5), 542–552.

Diamond, J., & Bond, A. B. (2003). A comparative analysis of social play in birds. *Behaviour, 140*(8–9), 1091–1115.

Diamond, M. C., Krech, D., & Rosenzweig, M. R. (1964). The effects of an enriched environment on the histology of the rat cerebral cortex. *Journal of Comparative Neurology, 123*, 111–120.

Dias, R., Robbins, T. W., & Roberts, A. C. (1996). Dissociation in prefrontal cortex of affective and attentional shifts. *Nature, 380*(6569), 69–72.

Dickerson, S. S., Kemeny, M. E., Aziz, N., Kim, K. H., & Fahey, J. L. (2004). Immunological effects of induced shame and guilt. *Psychosomatic Medicine, 66*(1), 124–131.

Diego, M. A., Field, T., Hernandez-Reif, M., Shaw, J. A., Rothe, E. M., Castellanos, D., & Mesner, L. (2002). Aggressive adolescents benefit from massage therapy. *Adolescence, 37*(147), 597–607.

Diego, M. A., Field, T., Hernandez-Reif, M., Shaw, K., Friedman, L., & Ironson, G. (2001). HIV adolescents show improved immune function following massage therapy. *International Journal of Neuroscience, 106*(1–2), 35–45.

Dielenberg, R. A., & McGregor, I. S. (2001). Defensive behavior in rats towards predatory odors: A review. *Neuroscience and Biobehavioral Reviews, 25*(7–8), 597–609.

Dijk, C., de Jong, P. J., & Peters, M. L. (2009). The remedial value of blushing in the context of transgressions and mishaps. *Emotion, 9*(2), 287–291.

Dill, E. J., Vernberg, E. M., Fonagy, P., Twemlow, S. W., & Gamm, B. K. (2004). Negative affect in victimized children: The roles of social withdrawal, peer rejection, and attitudes toward bullying. *Journal of Abnormal Child Psychology, 32*(2), 159–173.

Dillon, K. M., Minchoff, B., & Baker, K. H. (1985). Positive emotional states and enhancement of the immune system. *International Journal of Psychiatry in Medicine, 15*(1), 13–18.

Diorio, J., & Meaney, M. J. (2007). Maternal programming of defensive responses through sustained effects on gene expression. *Journal of Psychiatry & Neuroscience, 32*(4), 275–284.

Dolcos, F., & McCarthy, G. (2006). Brain systems mediating cognitive interference by emotional distraction. *Journal of Neuroscience, 26*(7), 2072–2079.

Domes, G., Rothfischer, J., Reichwald, U., & Hautzinger, M. (2005). Inverted-U function between salivary cortisol and retrieval of verbal memory after hydrocortisone treatment. *Behavioral Neuroscience, 119*(2), 512–517.

Doran, S. M., Van Dongen, H. P., & Dinges, D. F. (2001). Sustained attention performance during sleep deprivation: Evidence of state instability. *Archives Italiennes de Biologie, 139*(3), 253–267.

Douglas, R. J. (1967). The hippocampus and behavior. *Psychological Bulletin, 67*(6), 416–422.

Doyon, C., Gilmour, K. M., Trudeau, V. L., & Moon, T. W. (2003). Corticotropin-releasing factor and neuropeptide Y mRNA levels are elevated in the preoptic area of socially subordinate rainbow trout. *General and Comparative Endocrinology, 133*(2), 260–271.

Dranovsky, A., & Hen, R. (2006). Hippocampal neurogenesis: Regulation by stress and antidepressants. *Biological Psychiatry, 59*(12), 1136–1143.

Drea, C. M. (1996). Aggression decreases as play emerges in infant spotted hyaenas: Preparation for joining the clan. *Animal Behaviour, 51*(6), 1323–1336.

Due, P., Holstein, B. E., Lynch, B., Diderichsen, F., Gabhain, S. N., Scheidt, P., & Currie, C. (2005). Bullying and symptoms among school-aged children: International comparative cross sectional study in 28 countries. *European Journal of Public Health, 15*(2), 128–132.

Dunbar, R. (1992). Neocortex size as a constraint on group size in primates. *Journal of Human Evolution, 22*(6), 469–493.

Duncan, C. P., Nelson, J. E., & Frontczak, N. T. (1984). The effect of humor on advertising comprehension. *Advances in Consumer Research, 11*, 432–437.

Dunham, J. (1977). The effects of disruptive behavior on teachers. *Educational Review, 19*(3), 181–187.

Dussault, M., Deaudelin, C., Royer, N., & Loiselle, F. (1999). Professional isolation and occupational stress in teachers. *Psychological Reports, 84*(3), 943–946.

Duthie, S. J., Whalley, L. J., Collins, A. R., Leaper, S., Berger, K., & Deary, I. J. (2002). Homocysteine, B vitamin status, and cognitive function in the elderly. *American Journal of Clinical Nutrition, 75*(5), 908–913.

Dutton, D. G., van Ginkel, C., & Starzomski, A. (1995). The role of shame and guilt in the intergenerational transmission of abusiveness. *Violence and Victims, 10*(2), 121–131.

Duzel, E., Bunzeck, N., Guitart-Masip, M., & Duzel, S. (2010). Novelty-related motivation of anticipation and exploration by dopamine (NOMAD): Implications for healthy aging. *Neuroscience and Biobehavioral Reviews, 34*(5), 660–669.

Dwivedi, Y., Rizavi, H. S., Conley, R. R., Roberts, R. C., Tamminga, C. A., & Pandey, G. N. (2003). Altered gene expression of brain-derived neurotrophic factor and receptor tyrosine kinase B in postmortem brain of suicide subjects. *Archives of General Psychiatry, 60*(8), 804–815.

Eales, L. A. (1985). Song learning in zebra finches: Some effects of song model availability on what is learnt and when. *Animal Behaviour, 33*(4), 1293–1300.

Edelman, G. M. (1989). *The remembered present: A biological theory of consciousness.* New York, NY: Basic Books.

Edens, J. L., Larkin, K. T., & Abel, J. L. (1992). The effect of social support and physical touch on cardiovascular reactions to mental stress. *Journal of Psychosomatic Research, 36*(4), 371–381.

Edin, F., Macoveanu, J., Olesen, P., Tegner, J., & Klingberg, T. (2007). Stronger synaptic connectivity as a mechanism behind development of working memory–related brain activity during childhood. *Journal of Cognitive Neuroscience, 19*(5), 750–760.

Edwards, C. A. (1994). Leadership in groups of school-age girls. *Developmental Psychology, 30*(6), 920–927.

Egan, S. K., & Perry, D. G. (1998). Does low self-regard invite victimization? *Developmental Psychology, 34*(2), 299–309.

Eibl-Eibesfeldt, I. (2007). *Human ethology.* New Brunswick, NJ: Aldine Transaction.

Eichenbaum, H. (1992). The hippocampal system and declarative memory in animals. *Journal of Cognitive Neuroscience, 4*(3), 217–231.

Eisenberger, N. I., Jarcho, J. M., Lieberman, M. D., & Naliboff, B. D. (2006). An experimental study of shared sensitivity to physical pain and social rejection. *Pain, 126*(1–3), 132–138.

Eisenberger, N. I., Lieberman, M. D., & Williams, K. D. (2003). Does rejection hurt? An fMRI study of social exclusion. *Science, 302*(5643), 290–292.

El Hage, W., Griebel, G., & Belzung, C. (2006). Long-term impaired memory following predatory stress in mice. *Physiology & Behavior, 87*(1), 45–50.

Elbert, T., Flor, H., Birbaumer, N., Knecht, S., Hampson, S., Larbig, W., & Taub, E. (1994). Extensive reorganization of the somatosensory cortex in adult humans after nervous system injury. *NeuroReport, 5*(18), 2593–2597.

Elbert, T., Pantev, C., Wienbruch, C., Rockstroh, B., & Taub, E. (1995). Increased cortical representation of the fingers of the left hand in string players. *Science, 270*(5234), 305–307.

Elder, J. L., & Pederson, D. R. (1978). Preschool children's use of objects in symbolic play. *Child Development, 49*(2), 500–504.

Elinoff, M. J., Chafouleas, S. M., & Sassu, K. A. (2004). Bullying: Considerations for defining and intervening in school settings. *Psychology in the Schools, 41*(8), 887–897.

Eliot, L. (1999). *What's going on in there? How the brain and mind develop in the first five years of life*. New York, NY: Bantam.

Elliott, R., Agnew, Z., & Deakin, J. F. (2008). Medial orbitofrontal cortex codes relative rather than absolute value of financial rewards in humans. *European Journal of Neuroscience, 27*(9), 2213–2218.

Elliott, R., Friston, K. J., & Dolan, R. J. (2000). Dissociable neural responses in human reward systems. *Journal of Neuroscience, 20*(16), 6159–6165.

Ellis, A. (1962). *Reason and emotion in psychotherapy*. Secaucus, NJ: Citadel Press.

Ely, D. L., & Henry, J. P. (1978). Neuroendocrine response patterns in dominant and subordinate mice. *Hormones and Behavior, 10*(2), 156–169.

Eng, P. M., Rimm, E. B., Fitzmaurice, G., & Kawachi, I. (2002). Social ties and change in social ties in relation to subsequent total and cause-specific mortality and coronary heart disease incidence in men. *American Journal of Epidemiology, 155*(8), 700–709.

Engh, A. L., Beehner, J. C., Bergman, T. J., Whitten, P. L., Hoffmeier, R. R., Seyfarth, R. M., & Cheney, D. L. (2006). Female hierarchy instability, male immigration and infanticide increase glucocorticoid levels in female chacma baboons. *Animal Behaviour, 71*(5), 1227–1237.

Entwisle, D. R., & Hayduk, L. A. (1978). *Too great expectations: The academic outlook of young children*. Baltimore, MD: Johns Hopkins University Press.

Eriksson, P. S., Perfilieva, E., Bjork-Eriksson, T., Alborn, A. M., Nordborg, C., Peterson, D. A., & Gage, F. H. (1998). Neurogenesis in the adult human hippocampus. Nature Medicine, 4(11), 1313–1317.

Erraji-Benchekroun, L., Underwood, M. D., Arango, V., Galfalvy, H., Pavlidis, P., Smyrniotopoulos, P., . . . Sibille, E. (2005). Molecular aging in human prefrontal cortex is selective and continuous throughout adult life. *Biological Psychiatry, 57*(5), 549–558.

Escalante, J. (1990). The Jaime Escalante math program. *Journal of Negro Education, 59*(3), 407–423.

Esch, T., & Stefano, G. B. (2005). The neurobiology of love. *Neuro Endocrinology Letters, 26*(3), 175–192.

Espelage, D. L., Bosworth, K., & Simon, T. R. (2000). Examining the social context of bullying behaviors in early adolescence. *Journal of Counseling & Development, 78*(3), 326–333.

Etchison, M., & Kleist, D. M. (2000). Review of narrative therapy: Research and utility. *The Family Journal, 8*(1), 61–66.

Evans, S. J., Choudary, P. V., Neal, C. R., Li, J. Z., Vawter, M. P., Tomita, H., . . . Akil, H. (2004). Dysregulation of the fibroblast growth factor system in major depression. *Proceedings of the National Academy of Sciences of the United States of America, 101*(43), 15506–15511.

Fabel, K., Fabel, K., Tam, B., Kaufer, D., Baiker, A., Simmons, N., . . . Palmer, T. D. (2003). VEGF is necessary for exercise-induced adult hippocampal neurogenesis. *European Journal of Neuroscience, 18*(10), 2803–2812.

Fadiga, L., Craighero, L., Buccino, G., & Rizzolatti, G. (2002). Speech listening specifically modulates the excitability of tongue muscles: A TMS study. *European Journal of Neuroscience, 15*(2), 399–402.

Fadiga, L., Fogassi, L., Pavesi, G., & Rizzolatti, G. (1995). Motor facilitation during action observation: A magnetic stimulation study. *Journal of Neurophysiology, 73*(6), 2608–2611.

Farber, B. A. (1984). Stress and burnout in suburban teachers. *Journal of Educational Research, 77*(6), 325–331.

Farber, B. A., & Miller, J. (1981). Teacher burnout: A psychoeducational perspective. *Teachers College Record, 83*(2), 235–243.

Farmer, J., Zhao, X., van Praag, H., Wodtke, K., Gage, F. H., & Christie, B. R. (2004). Effects of voluntary exercise on synaptic plasticity and gene expression in the dentate gyrus of adult male Sprague–Dawley rats in vivo. *Neuroscience, 124*(1), 71–79.

Fein, S., & Spencer, S. J. (1997). Prejudice as self-image maintenance: Affirming the self through derogating others. *Journal of Personality and Social Psychology, 73*(1), 31–44.

Fekkes, M., Pijpers, F. I., Fredriks, A. M., Vogels, T., & Verloove-Vanhorick, S. P. (2006). Do bullied children get ill, or do ill children get bullied? A prospective cohort study on the relationship between bullying and health-related symptoms. *Pediatrics, 117*(5), 1568–1574.

Fekkes, M., Pijpers, F. I. M., & Verloove-Vanhorick, S. P. (2005). Bullying: Who does what, when and where? Involvement of children, teachers and parents in bullying behavior. *Health Education Research, 20*(1), 81–91.

Feldman, R., Greenbaum, C. W., Mayes, L. C., & Erlich, S. H. (1997). Change in mother-infant interactive behavior: Relations to change in the mother, the infant, and the social context. *Infant Behavior & Development, 20*(2), 151–164.

Feldman, R., Greenbaum, C. W., & Yirmiya, N. (1999). Mother-infant affect synchrony as an antecedent of the emergence of self-control. *Developmental Psychology, 35*(1), 223–231.

Fellin, T., Pascual, O., & Haydon, P. G. (2006). Astrocytes coordinate synaptic networks: Balanced excitation and inhibition. *Physiology, 21*, 208–215.

Ferguson, T. J., Stegge, H., & Damhuis, I. (1991). Children's understanding of guilt and shame. *Child Development, 62*(4), 827–839.

Ferrari, P. F., Gallese, V., Rizzolatti, G., & Fogassi, L. (2003). Mirror neurons responding to the observation of ingestive and communicative mouth actions in the monkey ventral premotor cortex. *European Journal of Neuroscience, 17*(8), 1703–1714.

Fias, W., Lammertyn, J., Caessens, B., & Orban, G. A. (2007). Processing of abstract ordinal knowledge in the horizontal segment of the intraparietal sulcus. *Journal of Neuroscience, 27*(33), 8952–8956.

Fias, W., Lammertyn, J., Reynvoet, B., Dupont, P., & Orban, G. A. (2003). Parietal representation of symbolic and nonsymbolic magnitude. *Journal of Cognitive Neuroscience, 15*(1), 47–56.

Field, T. (2000). Infant massage therapy. In C. H. Zeanah Jr. (Ed.), *Handbook of infant mental health* (2nd ed., pp. 494–500). New York, NY: Guilford.

Field, T. (2002). Violence and touch deprivation in adolescents. *Adolescence, 37*(148), 735–749.

Field, T., Grizzle, N., Scafidi, F., Abrams, S., Richardson, S., Kuhn, C., & Schanberg, S. (1996). Massage therapy for infants of depressed mothers. *Infant Behavior & Development, 19*(1), 107–112.

Field, T. M., Woodson, R., Greenberg, R., & Cohen, D. (1982). Discrimination and imitation of facial expression by neonates. *Science, 218*(4568), 179–181.

Figueiredo, H. F., Bodie, B. L., Tauchi, M., Dolgas, C. M., & Herman, J. P. (2003). Stress integration after acute and chronic predator stress: Differential activation of central stress circuitry and sensitization of the hypothalamo-pituitary-adrenocortical axis. *Endocrinology, 144*(12), 5249–5258.

Fine, H. (2007, June 4). *Unsentimental education: Steve Barr, founder and chief executive of charter school company Green Dot, has become a major reformer within the L.A. Unified School District. He's encountered some resistance.* Retrieved from http://www.allbusiness.com/north-america/united-states-california-metro-areas/4502238–1.html

Finn, J. D. (1972). Expectations and the educational environment. *Review of Educational Research, 42*(3), 387–410.

Fiorillo, C. D., Tobler, P. N., & Schultz, W. (2003). Discrete coding of reward probability and uncertainty by dopamine neurons. *Science, 299*(5614), 1898–1902.

Fischer, K. W. (1987). Relations between brain and cognitive development. *Child Development, 58*(3), 623–632.

Fischer, K. W., & Daley, S. G. (2006). Connecting cognitive science and neuroscience to education: Potentials and pitfalls in inferring executive processes. In L. Meltzer (Ed.), *Understanding executive function: Implications and opportunities for the classroom* (pp. 55–72). New York, NY: Guilford.

Fish, E. W., Shahrokh, D., Bagot, R., Caldji, C., Bredy, T., Szyf, M., & Meaney, M. J. (2004). Epigenetic programming of stress responses through variations in maternal care. *Annals of the New York Academy of Sciences, 1036,* 167–180.

Fisher, S., Cole, J. O., Rickels, K., & Ulenhuth, E. H. (1964). Drug-set interaction: The effect of expectations on drug response in outpatients. In P. B. Bradley, F. Fliigel, & P. Hoch (Eds.), *Neuropsychopharmacology* (pp. 149–156). New York, NY: Elsevier.

Fleming, A. S., Kraemer, G. W., Gonzalez, A., Lovic, V., Rees, S., & Melo, A. (2002). Mothering begets mothering: The transmission of behavior and its neurobiology across generations. *Pharmacology, Biochemistry, and Behavior, 73*(1), 61–75.

Flinn, M. V. (2006). Evolution and ontogeny of stress response to social challenges in the human child. *Developmental Review, 26*(2), 138–174.

Fode, K. L. (1960). *The effect of non-visual and non-verbal interaction on experimenter bias* (Unpublished master's thesis). University of North Dakota, Grand Forks, ND.

Fonagy, P. (1991). The capacity for understanding mental states: The reflective self in parent and child and its significance for security of attachment. *Infant Mental Health Journal, 12*(3), 201–218.

Fonagy, P., Steele, H., & Steele, M. (1991). Maternal representations of attachment during pregnancy predict the organization of infant-mother attachment at one year of age. *Child Development, 62*(5), 891–905.

Fonagy, P., Steele, M., Steele, H., Moran, G. S., & Higgitt, A. C. (1991). The capacity to understand mental states: The reflective self in parent and child and its significance for security of attachment. *Infant Mental Health Journal, 12,* 201–218.

Forabosco, G. (1992). Cognitive aspects of the humor process: The concept of incongruity. *International Journal of Humor Research, 5*(1–2), 45–68.

Ford, M. B., & Collins, N. L. (2010). Self-esteem moderates neuroendocrine and psychological responses to interpersonal rejection. *Journal of Personality and Social Psychology, 98*(3), 405–419.

Forero, R., McLellan, L., Rissel, C., & Bauman, A. (1999). Bullying behaviour and psychosocial health among school students in New South Wales, Australia: Cross sectional survey. *British Medical Journal, 319*(7206), 344–348.

Fowler, C. D., Liu, Y., Ouimet, C., & Wang, Z. (2002). The effects of social environment on adult neurogenesis in the female prairie vole. *Journal of Neurobiology, 51*(2), 115–128.

Fowler, W. J., Jr. (1995). School size and student outcomes. *Advances in Educational Productivity, 5,* 3–26.

Fowler, W. J., Jr., & Walberg, H. J. (1991). School size, characteristics, and outcomes. *Educational Evaluation and Policy Analysis, 13*(2), 189–202.

Fox, A. S., Oakes, T. R., Shelton, S. E., Converse, A. K., Davidson, R. J., & Kalin, N. H. (2005). Calling for help is independently modulated by brain systems underlying goal-directed behavior and threat perception. *Proceedings of the National Academy of Sciences of the United States of America, 102*(11), 4176–4179.

Fox, H. E., White, S. A., Kao, M. H., & Fernald, R. D. (1997). Stress and dominance in a social fish. *Journal of Neuroscience, 17*(16), 6463–6469.

Fox, S., & Stallworth, L. E. (2005). Racial/ethnic bullying: Exploring links between bullying and racism in the U.S. workplace. *Journal of Vocational Behavior, 66*(3), 438–456.

Francis, D. D., Caldji, C., Champagne, F., Plotsky, P. M., & Meaney, M. J. (1999). The role of corticotropin-releasing factor–norepinephrine systems in mediating the effects of early experience on the development of behavioral and endocrine responses to stress. *Biological Psychiatry, 46*(9), 1153–1166.

Francis, D. D., Diorio, J., Plotsky, P. M., & Meaney, M. J. (2002). Environmental enrichment reverses the effects of maternal separation on stress reactivity. *Journal of Neuroscience, 22*(18), 7840–7843.

Franco, O. H., Burger, H., Lebrun, C. E., Peeters, P. H., Lamberts, S. W., Grobbee, D. E., & Van Der Schouw, Y. T. (2005). Higher dietary intake of lignans is associated with better cognitive performance in postmenopausal women. *Journal of Nutrition, 135*(5), 1190–1195.

Frank, J. D. (1963). *Persuasion and healing: A comparative study of psychotherapy*. New York, NY: Schocken.

Frecknall, P. (1994). Good humor: A qualitative study of the uses of humor in everyday life. *Psychology: A Journal of Human Behavior, 31*(1), 12–21.

Fredrickson, B. L. (2001). The role of positive emotions in positive psychology: The broaden-and-build theory of positive emotions. *American Psychologist, 56*(3), 218–226.

Fredrickson, B. L., & Branigan, C. (2005). Positive emotions broaden the scope of attention and thought-action repertoires. *Cognition and Emotion, 19*(3), 313–332.

Freeman, E. W., Weiss, E., & Brown, J. L. (2004). Examination of the interrelationships of behavior, dominance status, and ovarian activity in captive Asian and African elephants. *Zoo Biology, 23*(5), 431–448.

Freudenberger, H. J. (1974). Staff burnout. *Journal of Social Issues, 30*, 159–164.

Freund, H. J. (2001). The parietal lobe as a sensorimotor interface: A perspective from clinical and neuroimaging data. *NeuroImage, 14*(1), S142–S146.

Frey, K. S., Hirschstein, M. K., Snell, J. L., Edstrom, L. V. S., MacKenzie, E. P., & Broderick, C. J. (2005). Reducing playground bullying and supporting beliefs: An experimental trial of the Steps to Respect program. *Developmental Psychology, 41*(3), 479–491.

Frey, S., & Petrides, M. (2000). Orbitofrontal cortex: A key prefrontal region for encoding information. *Proceedings of the National Academy of Sciences of the United States of America, 97*(15), 8723–8727.

Fricchione, G., & Stefano, G. B. (2005). Placebo neural systems: Nitric oxide, morphine and the dopamine brain reward and motivation circuitries. *Medical Science Monitor, 11*(5), MS54–MS65.

Friedman, I. A. (1995). Student behavior patterns contributing to teacher burnout. *Journal of Educational Research, 88*(5), 281–289.

Friedman, I. A. (2003). Self-efficacy and burnout in teaching: The importance of interpersonal-relations efficacy. *Social Psychology of Education, 6*(3), 191–215.

Friedman, I. A., & Farber, B. A. (1992). Professional self-concept as a predictor of teacher burnout. *Journal of Educational Research, 86*(1), 28–35.

Frisone, D. F., Frye, C. A., & Zimmerberg, B. (2002). Social isolation stress during the third week of life has age-dependent effects on spatial learning in rats. *Behavioural Brain Research, 128*(2), 153–160.

Fry, W. F., Jr. (1984). *Learning with humor.* Paper presented at the annual meeting of the International Conference on Humor, Tel Aviv, Israel.

Fry, W. F., Jr. (1986). Humor, physiology, and the aging process. In L. Nahemow, K. A. McCluskey-Fawecett, & P. E. McGhee (Eds.), *Humor and aging* (pp. 81–98). Orlando, FL: Academic.

Fry, W. F., Jr. (1992). The physiologic effects of humor, mirth, and laughter. *Journal of the American Medical Association, 267*(13), 1857–1858.

Fry, W. F., Jr. (1994). The biology of humor. *International Journal of Humor Research, 7*(2), 111–126.

Fry, W. F., & Rader, C. (1977). The respiratory components of mirthful laughter. *Journal of Biological Psychology, 19*(2), 39–50.

Fry, W. F., Jr., & Savin, W. M. (1988). Mirthful laughter and blood pressure. *International Journal of Humor Research, 1*(1), 49–62.

Fry, W. F., Jr., & Stoft, P. E. (1971). Mirth and oxygen saturation levels of peripheral blood. *Psychotherapy and Psychosomatics, 19*(1), 76–84.

Frymier, A. B., Wanzer, M. B., & Wojtaszczyk, A. M. (2008). Assessing students' perceptions of inappropriate and appropriate teacher humor. *Communication Education, 57*(2), 266–288.

Fuchs, E., & Flugge, G. (2002). Social stress in tree shrews: Effects on physiology, brain function, and behavior of subordinate individuals. *Pharmacology, Biochemistry, and Behavior, 73*(1), 247–258.

Fujikawa, T., Soya, H., Fukuoka, H., Alam, K. S., Yoshizato, H., McEwen, B. S., & Nakashima, K. (2000). A biphasic regulation of receptor mRNA expressions for growth hormone, glucocorticoid and mineralocorticoid in the rat dentate gyrus during acute stress. *Brain Research, 874*(2), 186–193.

Funk, D., & Amir, S. (2000). Circadian modulation of fos responses to odor of the red fox, a rodent predator, in the rat olfactory system. *Brain Research, 866*(1–2), 262–267.

Fuster, J. M. (1996). Frontal lobe and the cognitive foundation of behavioral action. In A. R. Damasio, H. Damasio, & Y. Christen (Eds.), *Neurobiology of decision-making* (pp. 47–61). Berlin: Springer-Verlag.

Fuster, J. M. (1997). *The prefrontal cortex: Anatomy, physiology, and neuropsychology of the frontal lobe.* Philadelphia: Lippincott-Raven.

Gallagher, M., McMahan, R. W., & Schoenbaum, G. (1999). Orbitofrontal cortex and representation of incentive value in associative learning. *Journal of Neuroscience, 19*(15), 6610–6614.

Gallese, V. (2001). The "shared manifold" hypothesis: From mirror neurons to empathy. *Journal of Consciousness Studies, 8*(5/7), 33–50.

Gallese, V., Fadiga, L., Fogassi, L., & Rizzolatti, G. (1996). *Action recognition in the premotor cortex. Brain,* 119(2), 593–609.

Gallese, V., & Goldman, A. (1998). Mirror neurons and the simulation theory of mind-reading. *Trends in Cognitive Sciences, 2*(12), 493–501.

Gallese, V., Keysers, C., & Rizzolatti, G. (2004). A unifying view of the basis of social cognition. *Trends in Cognitive Sciences, 8*(9), 396–403.

Galli, R. L., Shukitt-Hale, B., Youdim, K. A., & Joseph, J. A. (2002). Fruit polyphenolics and brain aging: Nutritional interventions targeting age-related neuronal and behavioral deficits. *Annals of the New York Academy of Sciences, 959,* 128–132.

Gamble, J., & Cristol, D. (2002). Drop-catch behaviour is play in herring gulls, Larus argentatus. *Animal Behaviour, 63*(2), 339–345.

Gardner, R., Jr. (1997). Sociophysiology as the basic science of psychiatry. *Theoretical Medicine, 18*(4), 335–356.

Gardner, W. L., Pickett, C. L., & Brewer, M. B. (2000). Social exclusion and selective memory: How the need to belong influences memory for social events. *Personality and Social Psychology Bulletin, 26*(4), 486–496.

Gardner, W. L., Pickett, C. L., Jefferis, V., & Knowles, M. (2005). On the outside looking in: Loneliness and social monitoring. *Personality & Social Psychology Bulletin, 31*(11), 1549–1560.

Garner, R. L. (2006). Humor in pedagogy: How ha-ha can lead to aha! *College Teaching, 54*(1), 177–180.

Garoflos, E., Stamatakis, A., Pondiki, S., Apostolou, A., Philippidis, H., & Stylianopoulou, F. (2007). Cellular mechanisms underlying the effect of a single exposure to neonatal handling on neurotrophin-3 in the brain of 1-day-old rats. *Neuroscience, 148*(2), 349–358.

Garoflos, E., Stamatakis, A., Rafrogianni, A., Pondiki, S., & Stylianopoulou, F. (2008). Neonatal handling on the first postnatal day leads to increased maternal behavior and fos levels in the brain of the newborn rat. *Developmental Psychobiology, 50*(7), 704–713.

Garrity, T. F., Stallones, L., Marx, M. B., & Johnson, T. P. (1989). Pet ownership and attachment as supportive factors in the health of the elderly. *Anthrozoos, 3*, 35–44.

Garza, A. A., Ha, T. G., Garcia, C., Chen, M. J., & Russo-Neustadt, A. A. (2004). Exercise, antidepressant treatment, and BDNF mRNA expression in the aging brain. *Pharmacology, Biochemistry, and Behavior, 77*(2), 209–220.

Gauthier, I., Tarr, M. J., Moylan, J., Skudlarski, P., Gore, J. C., & Anderson, A. W. (2000). The fusiform "face area" is part of a network that processes faces at the individual level. *Journal of Cognitive Neuroscience, 12*(3), 495–504.

Gazelle, H., & Druhen, M. J. (2009). Anxious solitude and peer exclusion predict social helplessness, upset affect, and vagal regulation in response to behavioral rejection by a friend. *Developmental Psychology, 45*(4), 1077–1096.

Ge, Y., Grossman, R. I., Babb, J. S., Rabin, M. L., Mannon, L. J., & Kolson, D. L. (2002). Age-related total gray matter and white matter changes in normal adult brain, part I: Volumetric MR imaging analysis. *American Journal of Neuroradiology, 23*(8), 1327–1333.

Gehring, W. J., Karpinski, A., & Hilton, J. L. (2003). Thinking about interracial interactions. *Nature Neuroscience, 6*(12), 1241–1243.

Gehring, W. J., & Willoughby, A. R. (2002). The medial frontal cortex and the rapid processing of monetary gains and losses. *Science, 295*(5563), 2279–2282.

Gerin, W., Pieper, C., Levy, R., & Pickering, T. G. (1992). Social support in social interaction: A moderator of cardiovascular reactivity. *Psychosomatic Medicine, 54*(3), 324–336.

Geuze, E., Vermetten, E., & Bremner, J. D. (2005). MR-based in vivo hippocampal volumetrics: 2. Findings in neuropsychiatric disorders. *Molecular Psychiatry, 10*(2), 160–184.

Gianaros, P. J., Horenstein, J. A., Hariri, A. R., Sheu, L. K., Manuck, S. B., Matthews, K. A., & Cohen, S. (2008). Potential neural embedding of parental social standing. *Social Cognitive and Affective Neuroscience, 3*(2), 91–96.

Giannakopoulos, P., Hof, P. R., Michel, J. P., Guimon, J., & Bouras, C. (1997). Cerebral cortex pathology in aging and Alzheimer's disease: A quantitative survey of large hospital-based geriatric and psychiatric cohorts. *Brain Research Reviews, 25*(2), 217–245.

Gick, M. L., & Holyoak, K. J. (1983). Schema induction and analogical transfer. *Cognitive Psychology, 15*(1), 1–38.

Giedd, J. N. (2004). Structural magnetic resonance imaging of the adolescent brain. *Annals of the New York Academy of Sciences, 1021*, 77–85.

Giedd, J. N., Rumsey, J. M., Castellanos, F. X., Rajapakse, J. C., Kaysen, D., Vaituzis, A. C., . . . Rapoport, J. L. (1996). A quantitative MRI study of the corpus callosum in children and adolescents. *Developmental Brain Research, 91*(2), 274–280.

Gilbert, P., & Gerlsma, C. (1999). Recall of shame and favouritism in relation to psychopathology. *British Journal of Clinical Psychology, 38*(4), 357–373.

Gilbert, P., & Miles, J. N. (2000). Sensitivity to social put-down: Its relationship to perceptions of social rank, shame, social anxiety, depression, anger and self-other blame. *Personality and Individual Differences, 29*(4), 757–774.

Gilbertson, M. W., Shenton, M. E., Ciszewski, A., Kasai, K., Lasko, N. B., Orr, S. P., & Pitman, R. K. (2002). Smaller hippocampal volume predicts pathologic vulnerability to psychological trauma. *Nature Neuroscience, 5*(11), 1242–1247.

Glenn, E. W. (1993). The adaptive value of humor and laughter. *Ethology and Sociobiology, 14*(2), 141–169.

Glickman, C. D., & Tamashiro, R. T. (1982). A comparison of first-year, fifth-year, and former teachers on efficacy, ego development, and problem solving. *Psychology in the Schools, 19*(4), 558–562.

Glover, D., Gough, G., Johnson, M., & Cartwright, N. (2000). Bullying in 25 secondary schools: Incidence, impact and intervention. *Educational Research, 42*(2), 141–156.

Goel, V., & Dolan, R. J. (2001). The functional anatomy of humor: Segregating cognitive and affective components. *Nature Neuroscience, 4*(3), 237–238.

Gogtay, N., Giedd, J. N., Lusk, L., Hayashi, K. M., Greenstein, D., Vaituzis, A. C., . . . Thompson, P. M. (2004). Dynamic mapping of human cortical development during childhood through early adulthood. *Proceedings of the National Academy of Sciences of the United States of America, 101*(21), 8174–8179.

Golby, A. J., Gabrieli, J. D., Chiao, J. Y., & Eberhardt, J. L. (2001). Differential responses in the fusiform region to same-race and other-race faces. *Nature Neuroscience, 4*(8), 845–850.

Gold, Y. (1985). The relationship of six personal and life history variables to standing on three dimensions of the Maslach burnout inventory in a sample of elementary and junior high school teachers. *Educational and Psychological Measurement, 45*(2), 377–387.

Goldberg, E., Podell, K., & Lovell, M. (1994). Lateralization of frontal lobe functions and cognitive novelty. *Journal of Neuropsychiatry and Clinical Neurosciences, 6*(4), 371–378.

Goldman, P. S. (1971). Functional development of the prefrontal cortex in early life and the problem of neuronal plasticity. *Experimental Neurology, 32*(3), 366–387.

Goldman, P. S., & Galkin, T. W. (1978). Prenatal removal of frontal association cortex in the fetal rhesus monkey: Anatomical and functional consequences in postnatal life. *Brain Research, 152*(3), 451–485.

Goldstein, J. H. (1976). Theoretical notes on humor. *Journal of Communication, 26*(3), 104–112.

Golub, M. S., Sassenrath, E. N., & Goo, G. P. (1979). Plasma cortisol levels and dominance in peer groups of rhesus monkey weanlings. *Hormones and Behavior, 12*(1), 50–59.

Gonzalez, M. A. (1997). Study of the relationship of stress, burnout, hardiness, and social support in urban, secondary school teachers. *Dissertation Abstracts International Section A: Humanities and Social Sciences, 58*(6), 2000.

Good, C. D., Johnsrude, I., Ashburner, J., Henson, R. N., Friston, K. J., & Frackowiak, R. S. (2001). Cerebral asymmetry and the effects of sex and handedness on brain structure: A voxel-based morphometric analysis of 465 normal adult human brains. *NeuroImage, 14*(3), 685–700.

Good, T. L. (1980). Classroom expectations: Teacher–pupil interactions. In J. McMillan (Ed.), *The social psychology of school learning* (pp. 79–122). New York, NY: Academic Press.

Goodfellow, L. M. (2003). The effects of therapeutic back massage on psychophysiologic variables and immune function in spouses of patients with cancer. *Nursing Research, 52*(5), 318–328.

Goodheart, A. (1994). *Laughter therapy: How to laugh about everything in your life that isn't really funny*. Santa Barbara, CA: Less Stress Press.

Goodman, J. B. (1992). Laughing matters: Taking your job seriously and yourself lightly. *Journal of the American Medical Association, 267*(13), 1858.

Goodman, V. B. (1980). *Urban teacher stress: A critical literature review*. Retrieved from ERIC database. (ED221611)

Gordon, N. S., Burke, S., Akil, H., Watson, S. J., & Panksepp, J. (2003). Socially-induced brain "fertilization": Play promotes brain-derived neurotrophic factor transcription in the amygdala and dorsolateral frontal cortex in juvenile rats. *Neuroscience Letters, 341*(1), 17–20.

Gordon, N. S., Kollack-Walker, S., Akil, H., & Panksepp, J. (2002). Expression of c-fos gene activation during rough and tumble play in juvenile rats. *Brain Research Bulletin, 57*(5), 651–659.

Goswami, U. (2006). Neuroscience and education: From research to practice? *Nature Reviews Neuroscience, 7*(5), 406–411.

Gottfried, A. E. (1990). Academic intrinsic motivation in young elementary school children. *Journal of Educational Psychology, 82*(3), 525–538.

Gottfried, J. A., & Dolan, R. J. (2004). Human orbitofrontal cortex mediates extinction learning while accessing conditioned representations of value. *Nature Neuroscience, 7*(10), 1144–1152.

Gould, E. (2007). How widespread is adult neurogenesis in mammals? *Nature Reviews Neuroscience, 8*(6), 481–488.

Gould, E., McEwen, B. S., Tanapat, P., Galea, L. A., & Fuchs, E. (1997). Neurogenesis in the dentate gyrus of the adult tree shrew is regulated by psychosocial stress and NMDA receptor activation. *Journal of Neuroscience, 17*(7), 2492–2498.

Gould, E., Reeves, A. J., Graziano, M. S., & Gross, C. G. (1999). Neurogenesis in the neocortex of adult primates. *Science, 286*(5439), 548–552.

Gould, E., Woolley, C. S., Frankfurt, M., & McEwen, B. S. (1990). Gonadal steroids regulate dendritic spine density in hippocampal pyramidal cells in adulthood. *Journal of Neuroscience, 10*(4), 1286–1291.

Grafton, S. T., Arbib, M. A., Fadiga, L., & Rizzolatti, G. (1996). Localization of grasp representations in humans by positron emission tomography. 2. Observation compared with imagination. *Experimental Brain Research, 112*(1), 103–111.

Graham, S., & Juvonen, J. (1998). Self-blame and peer victimization in middle school: An attributional analysis. *Developmental Psychology, 34*(3), 587–599.

Grant, R., Condon, B., Lawrence, A., Hadley, D. M., Patterson, J., Bone, I., & Teasdale, G. M. (1987). Human cranial CSF volumes measured by MRI: Sex and age influences. *Magnetic Resonance Imaging, 5*(6), 465–468.

Gray, J. R., Braver, T. S., & Raichle, M. E. (2002). Integration of emotion and cognition in the lateral prefrontal cortex. *Proceedings of the National Academy of Sciences of the United States of America, 99*(6), 4115–4120.

Greenglass, E. R., Burke, R. J., & Konarski, R. (1997). The impact of social support on the development of burnout in teachers: Examination of a model. *Work and Stress, 11*(3), 267–278.

Greenglass, E., Fiksenbaum, L., & Burke, R. J. (1996). Components of social support, buffering effects and burnout: Implications for psychological functioning. *Anxiety, Stress & Coping, 9*(3), 185–197.

Greenough, W. T. (1987). Experience effects on the developing and mature brain: Dendritic branching and synaptogenesis. In N. A. Krasnegor, E. M. Blass, M. A. Hofer, & W. P. Smotherman (Eds.), *Perinatal development: A psychobiological perspective* (pp. 195–221). Orlando, FL: Academic Press.

Green-Reese, S., Johnson, D. J., & Campbell, W. A. (1991). Teacher job satisfaction and teacher job stress: School size, age and teaching experience. *Education, 112*(2), 247–252.

Greenspan, S. I., & Shanker, S. (2004). *The first idea: How symbols, language, and intelligence evolved from our early primate ancestors to modern humans.* Cambridge, MA: Da Capo Press.

Greenwald, D. F., & Harder, D. W. (1998). Domains of shame: Evolutionary, cultural and psychotherapeutic aspects. In P. Gilbert & B. Andrews (Eds.), *Shame: Interpersonal behavior, psychopathology and culture* (pp. 225–245). New York, NY: Oxford University Press.

Greenwood, A. K., & Fernald, R. D. (2004). Social regulation of the electrical properties of gonadotropin-releasing hormone neurons in a cichlid fish (Astatotilapia burtoni). *Biology of Reproduction, 71*(3), 909–918.

Grefkes, C., & Fink, G. R. (2005). The functional organization of the intraparietal sulcus in humans and monkeys. *Journal of Anatomy, 207*(1), 3–17.

Grieve, S. M., Clark, C. R., Williams, L. M., Peduto, A. J., & Gordon, E. (2005). Preservation of limbic and paralimbic structures in aging. *Human Brain Mapping, 25*(4), 391–401.

Griffith, J., Steptoe, A., & Cropley, M. (1999). An investigation of coping strategies associated with job stress in teachers. *British Journal of Educational Psychology, 69*(4), 517–531.

Griffiths, T. D., Rees, G., Rees, A., Green, G. G., Witton, C., Rowe, D., . . . Frackowiak, R. S. (1998). Right parietal cortex is involved in the perception of sound movement in humans. *Nature Neuroscience, 1*(1), 74–79.

Grippo, A. J., Lamb, D. G., Carter, C. S., & Porges, S. W. (2007). Social isolation disrupts autonomic regulation of the heart and influences negative affective behaviors. *Biological Psychiatry, 62*(10), 1162–1170.

Gritz, R. M., & Theobald, N. D. (1996). The effects of school district spending priorities on length of stay in teaching. *Journal of Human Resources, 31*(3), 477–512.

Gross, C. G. (2000). Neurogenesis in the adult brain: Death of a dogma. *Nature Reviews Neuroscience, 1*(1), 67–73.

Gruenewald, T. L., Kemeny, M. E., Aziz, N., & Fahey, J. L. (2004). Acute threat to the social self: Shame, social self-esteem, and cortisol activity. *Psychosomatic Medicine, 66*(6), 915–924.

Gruwell, E. (2007). *Teach with your heart: Lessons I learned from the Freedom Writers: A memoir.* New York, NY: Broadway.

Gruwell, E., & Freedom Writers. (2007). *The Freedom Writers diary: How a teacher and 150 teens used writing to change themselves and the world around them.* New York, NY: Broadway.

Guglielmi, R. S., & Tatrow, K. (Spring 1998). Occupational stress, burnout, and health in teachers: A methodological and theoretical analysis. *Review of Educational Research, 68*(1), 61–99.

Gundel, H., Lopez-Sala, A., Ceballos-Baumann, A. O., Deus, J., Cardoner, N., Marten-Mittag, B., . . . Pujol, J. (2004). Alexithymia correlates with the size of the right anterior cingulate. *Psychosomatic Medicine, 66*(1), 132–140.

Gunning-Dixon, F. M., Head, D., McQuain, J., Acker, J. D., & Raz, N. (1998). Differential aging of the human striatum: A prospective MR imaging study. *American Journal of Neuroradiology, 19*(8), 1501–1507.

Gusnard, D. A., Akbudak, E., Shulman, G. L., & Raichle, M. E. (2001). Medial prefrontal cortex and self-referential mental activity: Relation to a default mode of brain function. *Proceedings of the National Academy of Sciences of the United States of America, 98*(7), 4259–4264.

Guttmann, C. R., Jolesz, F. A., Kikinis, R., Killiany, R. J., Moss, M. B., Sandor, T., & Albert, M. S. (1998). White matter changes with normal aging. *Neurology, 50*(4), 972–978.

Guzowski, J. F., Setlow, B., Wagner, E. K., & McGaugh, J. L. (2001). Experience-dependent gene expression in the rat hippocampus after spatial learning: A comparison of the immediate-early genes arc, c-fos, and zif268. *Journal of Neuroscience, 21*(14), 5089–5098.

Haberman, M. (1995). The dimensions of excellence in programs preparing teachers for urban poverty schools. *Peabody Journal of Education, 70*(2), 24–43.

Halassa, M. M., Fellin, T., & Haydon, P. G. (2007). The tripartite synapse: Roles for gliotransmission in health and disease. *Trends in Molecular Medicine, 13*(2), 54–63.

Halbesleben, J. R. B., & Buckley, M. R. (2004). Burnout in organizational life. *Journal of Management, 30*(6), 859–879.

Halgren, E., Dale, A. M., Sereno, M. I., Tootell, R. B., Marinkovic, K., & Rosen, B. R. (1999). Location of human face-selective cortex with respect to retinotopic areas. *Human Brain Mapping, 7*(1), 29–37.

Hall, J., Thomas, K. L., & Everitt, B. J. (2000). Rapid and selective induction of BDNF expression in the hippocampus during contextual learning. *Nature Neuroscience, 3*(6), 533–535.

Hampes, W. P. (1992). Relation between intimacy and humor. Psychological Reports, 71(1), 127–130.

Hampes, W. P. (1999). The relationship between humor and trust. *International Journal of Humor Research, 12*(3), 253–260.

Handa, R. J., Nunley, K. M., & Bollnow, M. R. (1993). Induction of c-fos mRNA in the brain and anterior pituitary gland by a novel environment. *NeuroReport, 4*(9), 1079–1082.

Hane, A. A., & Fox, N. A. (2006). Ordinary variations in maternal caregiving influence human infants' stress reactivity. *Psychological Science, 17*(6), 550–556.

Hanfmann, E. (1935). Social structure of a group of kindergarten children. *American Journal of Orthopsychiatry, 5*(4), 407–410.

Hannikainen, M. (2001). Playful actions as a sign of togetherness in day care centres. *International Journal of Early Years Education, 9*(2), 125–134.

Hanson, B. S., Isacsson, S. O., Janzon, L., Lindell, S. E., & Rastam, L. (1988). Social anchorage and blood pressure in elderly men—a population study. *Journal of Hypertension, 6*(6), 503–510.

Hanushek, E. (2002). Publicly provided education. In A. J. Auerbach & M. Feldstein (Eds.), *The handbook of public economics*. Amsterdam, The Netherlands: Elsevier Science.

Happe, F. G., Winner, E., & Brownell, H. (1998). The getting of wisdom: Theory of mind in old age. *Developmental Psychology, 34*(2), 358–362.

Hardingham, G. E., & Bading, H. (2003). The yin and yang of NMDA receptor signaling. *Trends in Neurosciences, 26*(2), 81–89.

Hareli, S., Shomrat, N., & Hess, U. (2009). Emotional versus neutral expressions and perceptions of social dominance and submissiveness. *Emotion, 9*(3), 378–384.

Hargreaves, A. (1994). *Changing teachers, changing times: Teachers' work and culture in the postmodern age*. London, England: Cassell.

Hariri, A. R., Bookheimer, S. Y., & Mazziotta, J. C. (2000). Modulating emotional responses: Effects of a neocortical network on the limbic system. *NeuroReport, 11*(1), 43–48.

Harlow, H. F., & Suomi, S. J. (1971). Social recovery by isolation-reared monkeys. *Proceedings of the National Academy of Sciences of the United States of America, 68*(7), 1534–1538.

Harrison, Y., & Horne, J. A. (1999). One night of sleep loss impairs innovative thinking and flexible decision making. *Organizational Behavior and Human Decision Processes, 78*(2), 128–145.

Harrison, Y., & Horne, J. A. (2000). The impact of sleep deprivation on decision making: A review. *Journal of Experimental Psychology: Applied, 6*(3), 236–249.

Hart, A., & Morry, M. (1996). Nonverbal behavior, race, and attitude attributions. *Journal of Experimental Social Psychology, 32*(2), 165–179.

Hart, A. J., & Morry, M. M. (1997). Trait inferences based on racial and behavioral cues. *Basic and Applied Social Psychology, 19*(1), 33–48.

Hart, A. J., Whalen, P. J., Shin, L. M., McInerney, S. C., Fischer, H., & Rauch, S. L. (2000). Differential response in the human amygdala to racial outgroup vs. ingroup face stimuli. *NeuroReport, 11*(11), 2351–2355.

Harter, S. (1982). The perceived competence scale for children. *Child Development, 53*(1), 87–97.

Harter, S. (1990). Causes, correlates, and the functional role of global self-worth: A life-span perspective. In R. J. Sternberg & J. Kolligian (Eds.), *Competence considered* (pp. 67–97). New Haven, CT: Yale University Press.

Hass, R. G., Katz, I., Rizzo, N., Bailey, J., & Eisenstadt, D. (1991). Cross-racial appraisal as related to attitude ambivalence and cognitive complexity. *Personality and Social Psychology Bulletin, 17*(1), 83–92.

Hasselmo, M. E., Rolls, E. T., & Baylis, G. C. (1989). The role of expression and identity in the face-selective responses of neurons in the temporal visual cortex of the monkey. *Behavioural Brain Research, 32*(3), 203–18.

Hawkins, D. L., Pepler, D. J., & Craig, W. M. (2001). Naturalistic observations of peer interventions in bullying. *Social Development, 10*(4), 512–527.

Hawley, P. H. (1999). The ontogenesis of social dominance: A strategy-based evolutionary perspective. *Developmental Review, 19*(1), 97–132.

Hay, C., & Meldrum, R. (2010). Bullying victimization and adolescent self-harm: Testing hypotheses from general strain theory. *Journal of Youth and Adolescence, 39*(5), 446–459.

Hayashi, M., Yamashita, A., & Shimizu, K. (1997). Somatostatin and brain-derived neurotrophic factor mRNA expression in the primate brain: Decreased levels of mRNAs during aging. *Brain Research, 749*(2), 283–289.

Hayashi, T., Urayama, O., Kawai, K., Hayashi, K., Iwanaga, S., Ohta, M., . . . Murakami, K. (2006). Laughter regulates gene expression in patients with type 2 diabetes. *Psychotherapy and Psychosomatics, 75*(1), 62–65.

Head, D., Snyder, A. Z., Girton, L. E., Morris, J. C., & Buckner, R. L. (2005). Frontal-hippocampal double dissociation between normal aging and Alzheimer's disease. *Cerebral Cortex, 15*(6), 732–739.

Hebb, D. O. (1949). *The organization of behavior: A neuropsychological theory.* New York, NY: John Wiley.

Hechinger, G., & Hechinger, F. M. (1967). *Teen-age tyranny.* Greenwich, CT: Fawcett.

Heft, H. (1989). Affordances and the body: An intentional analysis of Gibson's ecological approach to visual perception. *Journal for the Theory of Social Behaviour, 19*(1), 1–30.

Heimer, L., & Van Hoesen, G. W. (2006). The limbic lobe and its output channels: Implications for emotional functions and adaptive behavior. *Neuroscience and Biobehavioral Reviews, 30*(2), 126–147.

Heiser, M., Iacoboni, M., Maeda, F., Marcus, J., & Mazziotta, J. C. (2003). The essential role of Broca's area in imitation. *European Journal of Neuroscience, 17*(5), 1123–1128.

Hellemans, K. G., Benge, L. C., & Olmstead, M. C. (2004). Adolescent enrichment partially reverses the social isolation syndrome. *Developmental Brain Research, 150*(2), 103–115.

Henderson, D., & Henderson, T. (1996). *Texas teachers: Moonlighting and morale: 1980–1996.* Retrieved from ERIC database. (ED398179)

Hennessy, M. B., Mendoza, S. P., Mason, W. A., & Moberg, G. P. (1995). Endocrine sensitivity to novelty in squirrel monkeys and titi monkeys: Species differences in characteristic modes of responding to the environment. *Physiology & Behavior, 57*(2), 331–338.

Henry, R. R., Satz, P., & Saslow, E. (1984). Early brain damage and the ontogenesis of functional asymmetry. In C. R. Almli & S. Finger (Eds.), *Early brain damage, volume 1: Research orientations and clinical observations* (pp. 253–275). New York, NY: Academic Press.

Henson, R. N., Shallice, T., & Dolan, R. J. (1999). Right prefrontal cortex and episodic memory retrieval: A functional MRI test of the monitoring hypothesis. *Brain : A Journal of Neurology, 122*(7), 1367–1381.

Herberholz, J., McCurdy, C., & Edwards, D. H. (2007). Direct benefits of social dominance in juvenile crayfish. *Biological Bulletin, 213*(1), 21–27.

Hermes, G. L., Delgado, B., Tretiakova, M., Cavigelli, S. A., Krausz, T., Conzen, S. D., & McClintock, M. K. (2009). Social isolation dysregulates endocrine and behavioral stress while increasing malignant burden of spontaneous mammary tumors. *Proceedings of the National Academy of Sciences of the United States of America, 106*(52), 22393–22398.

Hernandez-Reif, M., Ironson, G., Field, T., Hurley, J., Katz, G., Diego, M., . . . Burman, I. (2004). Breast cancer patients have improved immune and neuroendocrine functions following massage therapy. *Journal of Psychosomatic Research, 57*(1), 45–52.

Herschkowitz, N., Kagan, J., & Zilles, K. (1997). Neurobiological bases of behavioral development in the first year. *Neuropediatrics, 28*(6), 296–306.

Hess, Y. D., & Pickett, C. L. (2010). Social rejection and self- versus other-awareness. *Journal of Experimental Social Psychology, 46*(2), 453–456.

Hesse, E. (1999). The adult attachment interview: Historical and current perspectives. In J. Cassidy & P. R. Shaver (Eds.), *Handbook of attachment: Theory, research, and clinical applications* (pp. 395–433). New York, NY: Guilford.

Ho, Y. C., Cheung, M. C., & Chan, A. S. (2003). Music training improves verbal but not visual memory: Cross-sectional and longitudinal explorations in children. *Neuropsychology, 17*(3), 439–450.

Hodge, C. J., Jr., & Boakye, M. (2001). Biological plasticity: The future of science in neurosurgery. *Neurosurgery, 48*(1), 2–16.

Hodges, E. V., Boivin, M., Vitaro, F., & Bukowski, W. M. (1999). The power of friendship: Protection against an escalating cycle of peer victimization. *Developmental Psychology, 35*(1), 94–101.

Hodges, E. V., & Perry, D. G. (1999). Personal and interpersonal antecedents and consequences of victimization by peers. *Journal of Personality and Social Psychology, 76*(4), 677–685.

Hoel, H., & Cooper, C. L. (2000). *Destructive conflict and bullying at work.* Manchester, England: School of Management, University of Manchester, Institute of Science and Technology.

Hofer, M. A. (1984). Relationships as regulators: A psychobiologic perspective on bereavement. *Psychosomatic Medicine, 46*(3), 183–197.

Hofer, M. A. (1987). Early social relationships: A psychobiologist's view. *Child Development, 58*(3), 633–647.

Hofferth, S. L., & Sandberg, J. F. (2001). How American children spend their time. *Journal of Marriage and Family, 63,* 295–308.

Hol, T., Van den Berg, C. L., Van Ree, J. M., & Spruijt, B. M. (1999). Isolation during the play period in infancy decreases adult social interactions in rats. *Behavioural Brain Research, 100*(1–2), 91–97.

Hole, G. (1991). The effects of social deprivation on levels of social play in the laboratory rat rattus norvegicus. *Behavioural Processes, 25*(1), 41–53.

Holekamp, K. E., & Smale, L. (1998). Dispersal status influences hormones and behavior in the male spotted hyena. *Hormones and Behavior, 33*(3), 205–216.

Holliday, S. G., & Chandler, M. J. (1986). *Wisdom: Explorations in adult competence.* New York, NY: Karger.

Holloway, K. S., & Suter, R. B. (2004). Play deprivation without social isolation: Housing controls. *Developmental Psychobiology, 44*(1), 58–67.

Homberg, J. R., Schiepers, O. J., Schoffelmeer, A. N., Cuppen, E., & Vanderschuren, L. J. (2007). Acute and constitutive increases in central serotonin levels reduce social play behaviour in peri-adolescent rats. *Psychopharmacology, 195*(2), 175–182.

Hood, K. E., Dreschel, N. A., & Granger, D. A. (2003). Maternal behavior changes after immune challenge of neonates with developmental effects on adult social behavior. *Developmental Psychobiology, 42*(1), 17–34.

Hornik, R., Risenhoover, N., & Gunnar, M. (1987). The effects of maternal positive, neutral, and negative affective communications on infant responses to new toys. *Child Development, 58*(4), 937–944.

Horowitz, R. A. (1979). Effects of the open classroom. In H. J. Walberg (Ed.), *Educational environments and effects* (pp. 275–292). Berkeley, CA: McCutchan.

Houbre, B., Tarquinio, C., & Lanfranchi, J. B. (2010). Expression of self-concept and adjustment against repeated aggressions: The case of a longitudinal study on school bullying. *European Journal of Psychology of Education, 25*(1), 105–123.

House, J. S., Landis, K. R., & Umberson, D. (1988). Social relationships and health. *Science, 241*(4865), 540–545.

Hsu, F. C., Zhang, G. J., Raol, Y. S., Valentino, R. J., Coulter, D. A., & Brooks-Kayal, A. R. (2003). Repeated neonatal handling with maternal separation permanently alters hippocampal GABAA receptors and behavioral stress responses. *Proceedings of the National Academy of Sciences of the United States of America, 100*(21), 12213–12218.

Huang, Z. J., Kirkwood, A., Pizzorusso, T., Porciatti, V., Morales, B., Bear, M. F., . . . Tonegawa, S. (1999). BDNF regulates the maturation of inhibition and the critical period of plasticity in mouse visual cortex. *Cell, 98*(6), 739–755.

Hubbs, A., Millar, J., & Wiebe, J. (2000). Effect of brief exposure to a potential predator on cortisol concentrations in female Columbian ground squirrels (*spermophilus columbianus*). *Canadian Journal of Zoology, 78*, 578–587.

Huberman, A. M., Grounauer, M. M., & Marti, J. (1993). *The lives of teachers*. New York, NY: Teachers College Press.

Hugenberg, K., & Bodenhausen, G. V. (2003). Facing prejudice: Implicit prejudice and the perception of facial threat. *Psychological Science, 14*(6), 640–643.

Humphreys, A., & Einon, D. (1981). Play as a reinforcer for maze-learning in juvenile rats. *Animal Behaviour, 29*(1), 259–270.

Hurley, R. A., Taber, K. H., Zhang, J., & Hayman, L. A. (1999). Neuropsychiatric presentation of multiple sclerosis. *Journal of Neuropsychiatry and Clinical Neurosciences, 11*(1), 5–7.

Hurren, B. L. (2006). The effects of principals' humor on teachers' job satisfaction. *Educational Studies, 32*(4), 373–385.

Husain, M., & Nachev, P. (2007). Space and the parietal cortex. *Trends in Cognitive Sciences, 11*(1), 30–36.

Hutchison, W. D., Davis, K. D., Lozano, A. M., Tasker, R. R., & Dostrovsky, J. O. (1999). Pain-related neurons in the human cingulate cortex. *Nature Neuroscience, 2*(5), 403–405.

Huttenlocher, P. R. (1994). Synaptogenesis in human cerebral cortex. In G. Dawson & K. W. Fischer (Eds.), *Human behavior and the developing brain* (pp. 137–152). New York, NY: Guilford.

Iacoboni, M., Koski, L. M., Brass, M., Bekkering, H., Woods, R. P., Dubeau, M. C., . . . Rizzolatti, G. (2001). Reafferent copies of imitated actions in the right superior temporal cortex. *Proceedings of the National Academy of Sciences of the United States of America, 98*(24), 13995–13999.

Iacoboni, M., Lieberman, M. D., Knowlton, B. J., Molnar-Szakacs, I., Moritz, M., Throop, C. J., & Fiske, A. P. (2004). Watching social interactions produces dorsomedial prefrontal and medial parietal BOLD fMRI signal increases compared to a resting baseline. *NeuroImage, 21*(3), 1167–1173.

Iacoboni, M., Woods, R. P., Brass, M., Bekkering, H., Mazziotta, J. C., & Rizzolatti, G. (1999). Cortical mechanisms of human imitation. *Science, 286*(5449), 2526–2528.

Ickes, B. R., Pham, T. M., Sanders, L. A., Albeck, D. S., Mohammed, A. H., & Granholm, A. C. (2000). Long-term environmental enrichment leads to regional increases in neurotrophin levels in rat brain. *Experimental Neurology, 164*(1), 45–52.

Iglowstein, I., Jenni, O. G., Molinari, L., & Largo, R. H. (2003). Sleep duration from infancy to adolescence: Reference values and generational trends. *Pediatrics, 111*(2), 302–307.

Ikemoto, S., & Panksepp, J. (1992). The effects of early social isolation on the motivation for social play in juvenile rats. *Developmental Psychobiology, 25*(4), 261–274.

Immordino-Yang, M. H., & Damasio, A. (2007). We feel, therefore we learn: The relevance of affective and social neuroscience to education. *Mind, Brain, and Education, 1*(1), 3–10.

Ince, P. G. (2001). Pathological correlates of late-onset dementia in a multi-centre, community-based population in England and Wales. *Lancet, 357*(9251), 169–175.

Introini-Collison, I., & McGaugh, J. L. (1987). Naloxone and beta-endorphine alter the effects of post-training epinephrine on retention of an inhibitory avoidance response. *Psychopharmacology, 92*, 229–235.

Isaac, M. R., Walker, J. M., & Williams, A. W. (1994). Group size and the voluntary provision of public goods: Experimental evidence utilizing large groups. *Journal of Public Economics, 54*, 1–36.

Isaacson, R. L., Yongue, B., & McClearn, D. (1978). Dopamine agonists: Their effect on locomotion and exploration. *Behavioral Biology, 23*(2), 163–179.

Isenbarger, L., & Zembylas, M. (2006). The emotional labour of caring in teaching. *Teaching and Teacher Education, 22*(1), 120–134.

Isovich, E., Engelmann, M., Landgraf, R., & Fuchs, E. (2001). Social isolation after a single defeat reduces striatal dopamine transporter binding in rats. *European Journal of Neuroscience, 13*(6), 1254–1256.

Issa, F. A., Adamson, D. J., & Edwards, D. H. (1999). Dominance hierarchy formation in juvenile crayfish procambarus clarkii. *Journal of Experimental Biology, 202*(24), 3497–3506.

Ito, T. A., Thompson, E., & Cacioppo, J. T. (2004). Tracking the time course of social perception: The effects of racial cues on event-related brain potentials. *Personality & Social Psychology Bulletin, 30*(10), 1267–1280.

Ito, T. A., & Urland, G. R. (2003). Race and gender on the brain: Electro-cortical measures of attention to the race and gender of multiply categorizable individuals. *Journal of Personality and Social Psychology, 85*(4), 616–626.

Ivanovic, D. M., Leiva, B. P., Perez, H. T., Inzunza, N. B., Almagià, A. F., Toro, T. D., . . . Bosch, E. O. (2000). Long-term effects of severe undernutrition during the first year of life on brain development and learning in Chilean high-school graduates. *Nutrition, 16*(11–12), 1056–1063.

Iwaniuk, A. N., Nelson, J. E., & Pellis, S. M. (2001). Do big-brained animals play more? Comparative analyses of play and relative brain size in mammals. *Journal of Comparative Psychology, 115*(1), 29–41.

Iwase, M., Ouchi, Y., Okada, H., Yokoyama, C., Nobezawa, S., Yoshikawa, E., . . . Watanabe, Y. (2002). Neural substrates of human facial expression of pleasant emotion induced by comic films: A PET study. *NeuroImage, 17*(2), 758–768.

Izard, C. E. (1991). Infant cardiac activity: Developmental changes and relations with attachment. *Developmental Psychology, 27*(3), 432–439.

Izquierdo, L. A., Viola, H., Barros, D. M., Alonso, M., Vianna, M. R., Furman, M., . . . Izquierdo, I. (2001). Novelty enhances retrieval: Molecular mechanisms involved in rat hippocampus. *European Journal of Neuroscience, 13*(7), 1464–1467.

Jablonska, B., Gierdalski, M., Kossut, M., & Skangiel-Kramska, J. (1999). Partial blocking of NMDA receptors reduces plastic changes induced by short-lasting classical conditioning in the SI barrel cortex of adult mice. Cerebral Cortex, 9(3), 222–231.

Jack, C. R., Dickson, D. W., Parisi, J. E., Xu, Y. C., Cha, R. H., O'Brien, P. C., . . . Petersen, R. C. (2002). Antemortem MRI findings correlate with hippocampal neuropathology in typical aging and dementia. *Neurology, 58*(5), 750–757.

Jackson, P. L., & Decety, J. (2004). Motor cognition: A new paradigm to study self-other interactions. *Current Opinion in Neurobiology, 14*(2), 259–263.

Jackson, S. E. (1983). Participation in decision making as a strategy for reducing job–related strain. *Journal of Applied Psychology, 68*(1), 3–19.

Jacobs, B., Driscoll, L., & Schall, M. (1997). Life-span dendritic and spine changes in areas 10 and 18 of human cortex: A quantitative Golgi study. *Journal of Comparative Neurology, 386*(4), 661–680.

Jacobs, B., Schall, M., & Scheibel, A. B. (1993). A quantitative dendritic analysis of Wernicke's area in humans. II. gender, hemispheric, and environmental factors. *Journal of Comparative Neurology, 327*(1), 97–111.

Jacobs, B. L., van Praag, H., & Gage, F. H. (2000). Depression and the birth and death of brain cells. *American Scientist, 88*, 340–345.

Jacobson, L. (1966). *Explorations of variations in education achievement among Mexican children, grades one to six.* (Unpublished doctoral dissertation). University of California at Berkeley, Berkeley, CA.

Janssen, I., Craig, W. M., Boyce, W. F., & Pickett, W. (2004). Associations between overweight and obesity with bullying behaviors in school-aged children. *Pediatrics, 113*(5), 1187–1194.

Jason, G. W., & Pajurkova, E. M. (1992). Failure of metacontrol: Breakdown in behavioural unity after lesion of the corpus callosum and inferomedial frontal lobes. *Cortex, 28*(2), 241–260.

Jeannerod, M., Arbib, M. A., Rizzolatti, G., & Sakata, H. (1995). Grasping objects: The cortical mechanisms of visuomotor transformation. *Trends in Neurosciences, 18*(7), 314–320.

Jellema, T., Baker, C. I., Wicker, B., & Perrett, D. I. (2000). Neural representation for the perception of the intentionality of actions. *Brain and Cognition, 44*(2), 280–302.

Jellema, T., Maassen, G., & Perrett, D. I. (2004). Single cell integration of animate form, motion and location in the superior temporal cortex of the macaque monkey. *Cerebral Cortex, 14*(7), 781–790.

Jenkins, S., & Calhoun, J. F. (1991). Teacher stress: Issues and intervention. *Psychology in the Schools, 28*(1), 60–70.

Jennings, P. A., & Greenberg, M. T. (2009). The prosocial classroom: Teacher social and emotional competence in relation to student and classroom outcomes. *Review of Educational Research, 79*(1), 491–525.

Jensen, A. R. (1969). How much can we boost IQ and scholastic achievement? *Harvard Educational Review, 39*, 1–123.

Jernigan, T. L., Archibald, S. L., Fennema-Notestine, C., Gamst, A. C., Stout, J. C., Bonner, J., & Hesselink, J. R. (2001). Effects of age on tissues and regions of the cerebrum and cerebellum. *Neurobiology of Aging, 22*(4), 581–594.

Ji, J., & Maren, S. (2007). Hippocampal involvement in contextual modulation of fear extinction. *Hippocampus, 17*(9), 749–758.

Johansson, B. B. (2000). Brain plasticity and stroke rehabilitation: The Willis lecture. *Stroke: A Journal of Cerebral Circulation, 31*(1), 223–230.

Johnson, H., Thompson, M., Wilkinson, S., Walsh, L., Balding, J., & Wright, V. (2002). Vulnerability to bullying: Teacher-reported conduct and emotional problems, hyperactivity, peer relationship difficulties, and prosocial behaviour in primary school children. *Educational Psychology, 22*(5), 553–556.

Johnson, L. (2005). *Teaching outside the box: How to grab your students by their brains.* San Francisco: Jossey-Bass.

Johnson, M. (1987). *The body in the mind: The bodily basis of meaning, imagination, and reason.* Chicago: University of Chicago Press.

Johnstone, T., van Reekum, C. M., Urry, H. L., Kalin, N. H., & Davidson, R. J. (2007). Failure to regulate: Counterproductive recruitment of top-down prefrontal-subcortical circuitry in major depression. *Journal of Neuroscience, 27*(33), 8877–8884.

Jolles, J., Rompabarendregt, J., & Gispen, W. (1979). Novelty and grooming behavior in the rat. *Behavioral and Neural Biology, 25*(4), 563–572.

Jones, N. A., & Field, T. (1999). Massage and music therapies attenuate frontal EEG asymmetry in depressed adolescents. *Adolescence, 34*(135), 529–534.

Jonides, J., Schumacher, E. H., Smith, E. E., Koeppe, R. A., Awh, E., Reuter-Lorenz, P. A., . . . Willis, C. R. (1998). The role of parietal cortex in verbal working memory. *Journal of Neuroscience, 18*(13), 5026–5034.

Jost, J. T. (2003). Social inequality and the reduction of ideological dissonance on behalf of the system: Evidence of enhanced system justification among the disadvantaged. *European Journal of Social Psychology, 33*(1), 13–36.

Jussim, L., Eccles, J., & Madon, S. (1996). Social perception, social stereotypes, and teacher expectations: Accuracy and the quest for the powerful self-fulfilling prophecy. In M. P. Zanna (Ed.), *Advances in experimental social psychology* (pp. 281–388). San Diego, CA: Academic Press.

Jussim, L., Smith, A., Madon, S., & Palumbo, P. (1998). Teacher expectations. *Expectations in the Classroom, 7,* 1–48.

Juvonen, J., Graham, S., & Schuster, M. A. (2003). Bullying among young adolescents: The strong, the weak, and the troubled. *Pediatrics, 112*(6), 1231–1237.

Kabuki, Y., Mizobe, Y., Yamada, S., & Furuse, M. (2009). Dietary L-tyrosine alleviates the behavioral alterations induced by social isolation stress in mice. *Brain Research Bulletin, 80*(6), 389–396.

Kalin, N. H., Shelton, S. E., Davidson, R. J., & Kelley, A. E. (2001). The primate amygdala mediates acute fear but not the behavioral and physiological components of anxious temperament. *Journal of Neuroscience, 21*(6), 2067–2074.

Kalinichev, M., Easterling, K. W., Plotsky, P. M., & Holtzman, S. G. (2002). Long-lasting changes in stress-induced corticosterone response and anxiety-like behaviors as a consequence of neonatal maternal separation in Long-Evans rats. *Pharmacology, Biochemistry, and Behavior, 73*(1), 131–140.

Kalisch, R., Korenfeld, E., Stephan, K. E., Weiskopf, N., Seymour, B., & Dolan, R. J. (2006). Context-dependent human extinction memory is mediated by a ventromedial prefrontal and hippocampal network. *Journal of Neuroscience, 26*(37), 9503–9511.

Kaltiala-Heino, R. (1999). Bullying, depression, and suicidal ideation in Finnish adolescents: School survey. *British Medical Journal, 319*(7206), 348–351.

Kaltiala-Heino, R., Rimpela, M., Rantanen, P., & Rimpela, A. (2000). Bullying at school—an indicator of adolescents at risk for mental disorders. *Journal of Adolescence, 23*(6), 661–674.

Kamarck, T. W., Manuck, S. B., & Jennings, J. R. (1990). Social support reduces cardiovascular reactivity to psychological challenge: A laboratory model. *Psychosomatic Medicine, 52*(1), 42–58.

Kamitakahara, H., Monfils, M. H., Forgie, M. L., Kolb, B., & Pellis, S. M. (2007). The modulation of play fighting in rats: Role of the motor cortex. *Behavioral Neuroscience, 121*(1), 164–176.

Kampe, K. K., Frith, C. D., Dolan, R. J., & Frith, U. (2001). Reward value of attractiveness and gaze. *Nature, 413*(6856), 589–602.

Kanarek, R. (1997). Psychological effects of snacks and altered meal frequency. *British Journal of Nutrition, 77*, 105–118.

Kandel, E. R., & Squire, L. R. (2000). Neuroscience: Breaking down scientific barriers to the study of brain and mind. *Science, 290*(5494), 1113–1120.

Kang, H., & Schuman, E. M. (1995). Long-lasting neurotrophin-induced enhancement of synaptic transmission in the adult hippocampus. *Science, 267*(5204), 1658–1662.

Kaplan, H. S., & Robson, A. J. (2002). The emergence of humans: The co-evolution of intelligence and longevity with intergenerational transfers. *Proceedings of the National Academy of Sciences of the United States of America, 99*(15), 10221–10226.

Kaplan, R. M., & Pascoe, G. C. (1977). Humorous lectures and humorous examples: Some effects upon comprehension and retention. *Journal of Educational Psychology, 69*(1), 61–65.

Karasek, R. A., Jr. (1979). Job demands, job decision latitude, and mental strain: Implications for job redesign. *Administrative Science Quarterly, 24*(2), 285–308.

Karmiloff-Smith, A., Klima, E., Bellugi, U., Grant, J., & Baron-Cohen, S. (1995). Is there a social module? Language, face processing, and theory of mind in individuals with Williams syndrome. *Journal of Cognitive Neuroscience, 7*(2), 196–208.

Karni, A., Meyer, G., Jezzard, P., Adams, M. M., Turner, R., & Ungerleider, L. G. (1995). Functional MRI evidence for adult motor cortex plasticity during motor skill learning. *Nature, 377*(6545), 155–158.

Karten, Y. J., Olariu, A., & Cameron, H. A. (2005). Stress in early life inhibits neurogenesis in adulthood. *Trends in Neurosciences, 28*(4), 171–172.

Kats, L. B., & Dill, L. M. (1998). The scent of death: Chemosensory assessment of predation risk by prey animals. *Ecoscience, 5*(3), 361–394.

Katz, L. C., & Shatz, C. J. (1996). Synaptic activity and the construction of cortical circuits. *Science, 274*(5290), 1133–1138.

Katz, R. J., & Gelbart, J. (1978). Endogenous opiates and behavioral responses to environmental novelty. *Behavioral Biology, 24*(3), 338–348.

Katzman, R., Aronson, M., Fuld, P., Kawas, C., Brown, T., Morgenstern, H., . . . Ooi, W. L. (1989). Development of dementing illnesses in an 80-year-old volunteer cohort. *Annals of Neurology, 25*(4), 317–324.

Kaufman, G. (1974). The meaning of shame: Toward a self-affirming identity. *Journal of Counseling Psychology, 21*(6), 568–574.

Keating, C. F., & Heltman, K. R. (1994). Dominance and deception in children and adults: Are leaders the best misleaders? *Personality and Social Psychology Bulletin, 20*(3), 312–321.

Kegan, R. (2000). What "form" transforms?: A constructive-developmental perspective on transformational learning. In J. Mezirow (Ed.), *Learning as transformation: Critical perspectives on a theory in progress.* (pp. 35–52). San Francisco, CA: Jossey-Bass.

Kellaris, J. J., & Cline, T. W. (2007). Humor and ad memorability: On the contributions of humor expectancy, relevancy, and need for humor. *Psychology and Marketing, 24*(6), 497–509.

Kelley, A. E., Schochet, T., & Landry, C. F. (2004). Risk taking and novelty seeking in adolescence: Introduction to part I. *Annals of the New York Academy of Sciences, 1021*, 27–32.

Kelly, A., Mullany, P. M., & Lynch, M. A. (2000). Protein synthesis in entorhinal cortex and long-term potentiation in dentate gyrus. *Hippocampus, 10*(4), 431–437.

Kemp, A., & Manahan-Vaughan, D. (2004). Hippocampal long-term depression and long-term potentiation encode different aspects of novelty acquisition. *Proceedings of the National Academy of Sciences of the United States of America, 101*(21), 8192–8197.

Kempermann, G., Kuhn, H. G., & Gage, F. H. (1998). Experience-induced neurogenesis in the senescent dentate gyrus. *Journal of Neuroscience, 18*(9), 3206–3212.

Kennard, M. A. (1955). The cingulate gyrus in relation to consciousness. *Journal of Nervous and Mental Disease, 121*(1), 34–39.

Kennedy, P. M. (1989). *The rise and fall of the great powers: Economic change and military conflict from 1500 to 2000.* New York, NY: Vintage.

Kerr, D. S., Huggett, A. M., & Abraham, W. C. (1994). Modulation of hippocampal long-term potentiation and long-term depression by corticosteroid receptor activation. *Psychobiology, 22*(2), 123–133.

Kessler, R. C., Berglund, P., Demler, O., Jin, R., Koretz, D., Merikangas, K. R., . . . Wang, P. S. (2003). The epidemiology of major depressive disorder: Results from the national comorbidity survey replication (NCS-R). *Journal of the American Medical Association, 289*(23), 3095–3105.

Kher, N., Molstad, S., & Donahue, R. (1999). Using humor in the college classroom to enhance teaching effectiveness in "dread courses." *College Student Journal, 33*(3), 400–406.

Kiecolt-Glaser, J. K., McGuire, L., Robles, T. F., & Glaser, R. (2002). Psychoneuroimmunology and psychosomatic medicine: Back to the future. *Psychosomatic Medicine, 64*(1), 15–28.

Kiecolt-Glaser, J. K., Ricker, D., George, J., Messick, G., Speicher, C. E., Garner, W., & Glaser, R. (1984). Urinary cortisol levels, cellular immunocompetency, and loneliness in psychiatric inpatients. *Psychosomatic Medicine, 46*(1), 15–23.

Kilgard, M. P., & Merzenich, M. M. (1998). Cortical map reorganization enabled by nucleus basalis activity. *Science, 279*(5357), 1714–1718.

Kim, J. J., & Diamond, D. M. (2002). The stressed hippocampus, synaptic plasticity and lost memories. *Nature Reviews Neuroscience, 3*(6), 453–462.

Kim, Y. S., Koh, Y. J., & Leventhal, B. L. (2004). Prevalence of school bullying in Korean middle school students. *Archives of Pediatrics & Adolescent Medicine, 158*(8), 737–741.

Kimble, D. P. (1968). Hippocampus and internal inhibition. *Psychological Bulletin, 70*(5), 285–295.

Kintsch, W., & Bates, E. (1977). Recognition memory for statements from a classroom lecture. *Journal of Experimental Psychology: Human Learning and Memory, 3*(2), 150–159.

Kirkwood, A., Rozas, C., Kirkwood, J., Perez, F., & Bear, M. F. (1999). Modulation of long-term synaptic depression in visual cortex by acetylcholine and norepinephrine. *Journal of Neuroscience, 19*(5), 1599–1609.

Kirschbaum, C., Wolf, O. T., May, M., Wippich, W., & Hellhammer, D. H. (1996). Stress- and treatment-induced elevations of cortisol levels associated with impaired declarative memory in healthy adults. *Life Sciences, 58*(17), 1475–1483.

Kitchigina, V., Vankov, A., Harley, C., & Sara, S. J. (1997). Novelty-elicited, noradrenaline-dependent enhancement of excitability in the dentate gyrus. *European Journal of Neuroscience, 9*(1), 41–47.

Klahr, D., & Carver, S. M. (1988). Cognitive objectives in a LOGO debugging curriculum: Instruction, learning, and transfer. *Cognitive Psychology, 20*(3), 362–404.

Kling, A., & Steklis, H. D. (1976). A neural substrate for affiliative behavior in nonhuman primates. *Brain, Behavior and Evolution, 13*(2–3), 216–238.

Knight, R. T. (1996). Contribution of human hippocampal region to novelty detection. *Nature, 383*(6597), 256–259.

Knight, R. T., & Grabowecky, M. (1995). Escape from linear time: Prefrontal cortex and conscious experience. In M. S. Gazzaniga (Ed.), *The cognitive neurosciences* (pp. 1357–1371). Cambridge, MA: MIT Press.

Knox, S. S., & Uvnas-Moberg, K. (1998). Social isolation and cardiovascular disease: An atherosclerotic pathway? *Psychoneuroendocrinology, 23*(8), 877–890.

Knutson, B., Burgdorf, J., & Panksepp, J. (1998). Anticipation of play elicits high-frequency ultrasonic vocalizations in young rats. *Journal of Comparative Psychology, 112*(1), 65–73.

Kochenderfer, B. J., & Ladd, G. W. (1997). Victimized children's responses to peers' aggression: Behaviors associated with reduced versus continued victimization. *Development and Psychopathology, 9*(1), 59–73.

Koechlin, E., Ody, C., & Kouneiher, F. (2003). The architecture of cognitive control in the human prefrontal cortex. *Science, 302*(5648), 1181–1185.

Koestner, R., & Zuckerman, M. (1994). Causality orientations, failure, and achievement. *Journal of Personality, 62*(3), 321–346.

Kolb, B., & Gibb, R. (1991). Environmental enrichment and cortical injury: Behavioral and anatomical consequences of frontal cortex lesions. *Cerebral Cortex, 1*(2), 189–198.

Kolb, B., & Gibb, R. (2002). Frontal lobe plasticity and behavior. In T. Donald & T. Robert (Eds.), *Principles of frontal lobe function* (pp. 541–556). New York, NY: Oxford University Press.

Kolb, B., & Whishaw, I. Q. (1998). Brain plasticity and behavior. *Annual Review of Psychology, 49*, 43–64.

Kollack-Walker, S., Watson, S. J., & Akil, H. (1997). Social stress in hamsters: Defeat activates specific neurocircuits within the brain. *Journal of Neuroscience, 17*(22), 8842–8855.

Konert, E. (1997). *Relationship among middle-school teacher burnout, stress, job satisfaction and coping styles.* (Unpublished doctoral dissertation). Wayne State University, Detroit, MI.

Korte, S. M., Koolhaas, J. M., Wingfield, J. C., & McEwen, B. S. (2005). The Darwinian concept of stress: Benefits of allostasis and costs of allostatic load and the trade-offs in health and disease. *Neuroscience and Biobehavioral Reviews, 29*(1), 3–38.

Kosten, T. A., Lee, H. J., & Kim, J. J. (2007). Neonatal handling alters learning in adult male and female rats in a task-specific manner. *Brain Research, 1154*, 144–153.

Kowalski, R., & Limber, S. (2007). Electronic bullying among middle school students. *Journal of Adolescent Health, 41*(6), S22–S30.

Kozorovitskiy, Y., & Gould, E. (2004). Dominance hierarchy influences adult neurogenesis in the dentate gyrus. *Journal of Neuroscience, 24*(30), 6755–6759.

Krebs, R. M., Schott, B. H., & Duzel, E. (2009). Personality traits are differentially associated with patterns of reward and novelty processing in the human substantia nigra/ventral tegmental area. *Biological Psychiatry, 65*(2), 103–110.

Krill, A., & Platek, S. M. (2009). In-group and out-group membership mediates anterior cingulate activation to social exclusion. *Frontiers in Evolutionary Neuroscience, 1*, 1.

Kringelbach, M. L. (2005). The human orbitofrontal cortex: Linking reward to hedonic experience. *Nature Reviews Neuroscience, 6*(9), 691–702.

Kroger, J. K., Sabb, F. W., Fales, C. L., Bookheimer, S. Y., Cohen, M. S., & Holyoak, K. J. (2002). Recruitment of anterior dorsolateral prefrontal cortex in human reasoning: A parametric study of relational complexity. *Cerebral Cortex, 12*(5), 477–485.

Krueger, F., Moll, J., Zahn, R., Heinecke, A., & Grafman, J. (2007). Event frequency modulates the processing of daily life activities in human medial prefrontal cortex. *Cerebral Cortex, 17*(10), 2346–2353.

Krugers, H. J., Douma, B. R., Andringa, G., Bohus, B., Korf, J., & Luiten, P. G. (1997). Exposure to chronic psychosocial stress and corticosterone in the rat: Effects on spatial discrimination learning and hippocampal protein kinase cgamma immunoreactivity. *Hippocampus, 7*(4), 427–436.

Krugers, H. J., Goltstein, P. M., van der Linden, S., & Joels, M. (2006). Blockade of glucocorticoid receptors rapidly restores hippocampal CA1 synaptic plasticity after exposure to chronic stress. *European Journal of Neuroscience, 23*(11), 3051–3055.

Kruman, I. I., Kumaravel, T. S., Lohani, A., Pedersen, W. A., Cutler, R. G., Kruman, Y., . . . Mattson, M. P. (2002). Folic acid deficiency and homocysteine impair DNA repair in hippocampal neurons and sensitize them to amyloid toxicity in experimental models of Alzheimer's disease. *Journal of Neuroscience, 22*(5), 1752–1762.

Kuhlmann, S., Piel, M., & Wolf, O. T. (2005). Impaired memory retrieval after psychosocial stress in healthy young men. *Journal of Neuroscience, 25*(11), 2977–2982.

Kuhn, C. C. (1994). The stages of laughter. *Journal of Nursing Jocularity, 4*(2), 34–35.

Kuhn, C. M., & Schanberg, S. M. (1998). Responses to maternal separation: Mechanisms and mediators. *International Journal of Developmental Neuroscience, 16*(3–4), 261–270.

Kukolja, J., Schlapfer, T. E., Keysers, C., Klingmuller, D., Maier, W., Fink, G. R., & Hurlemann, R. (2008). Modeling a negative response bias in the human amygdala by noradrenergic-glucocorticoid interactions. *Journal of Neuroscience, 28*(48), 12868–12876.

Kumpulainen, K., Rasanen, E., Henttonen, I., Almqvist, F., & Kresanov, K. (1998). Bullying and psychiatric symptoms among elementary school-age children. *Child Abuse & Neglect, 22*(7), 705–717.

Kuperminc, G., Leadbeater, B., Emmons, C., & Blatt, S. (1997). Perceived school climate and difficulties in the social adjustment of middle school students. *Applied Developmental Science, 1*(2), 76–88.

Kuppens, S., Grietens, H., Onghena, P., Michiels, D., & Subramanian, S. V. (2008). Individual and classroom variables associated with relational aggression in elementary-school aged children: A multilevel analysis. *Journal of School Psychology, 46*(6), 639–660.

Kurzban, R., & Leary, M. R. (2001). Evolutionary origins of stigmatization: The functions of social exclusion. *Psychological Bulletin, 127*(2), 187–208.

Kyriacou, C. (1987). Teacher stress and burnout: An international review. *Educational Research, 29*(2), 146–152.

Kytta, M. (2002). Affordances of children's environments in the context of cities, small towns, suburbs and rural villages in Finland and Belarus. *Journal of Environmental Psychology, 22*(1–2), 109–123.

Labouvie-Vief, G. (1990). Wisdom as integrated thought: Historical and developmental perspectives. In R. J. Sternberg (Ed.), *Wisdom: Its nature, origins, and development* (pp. 52–83). New York, NY: Cambridge University Press.

Lachmann, F. M., & Beebe, B. A. (1996). Three principles of salience in the organization of the patient-analyst interaction. *Psychoanalytic Psychology, 13*(1), 1–22.

Ladd, C. O., Thrivikraman, K. V., Huot, R. L., & Plotsky, P. M. (2005). Differential neuroendocrine responses to chronic variable stress in adult Long-Evans rats exposed to handling-maternal separation as neonates. *Psychoneuroendocrinology, 30*(6), 520–533.

Ladd, G. W., Herald-Brown, S. L., & Reiser, M. (2008). Does chronic classroom peer rejection predict the development of children's classroom participation during the grade school years? *Child Development, 79*(4), 1001–1015.

LaFontana, K. M., & Cillessen, A. H. (2002). Children's perceptions of popular and unpopular peers: A multimethod assessment. *Developmental Psychology, 38*(5), 635–647.

Lakoff, G. (1990). *Women, fire, and dangerous things: What categories reveal about the mind.* Chicago: University of Chicago Press.

Lamude, K. G., Scudder, J., & Furno-Lamude, D. (1992). The relationship of student resistance strategies in the classroom to teacher burnout and teacher type-A behavior. *Journal of Social Behavior & Personality, 7*(4), 597–610.

Langer, E. J., Bashner, R. S., & Chanowitz, B. (1985). Decreasing prejudice by increasing discrimination. *Journal of Personality and Social Psychology, 49*(1), 113–120.

Larson, R. (1978). Thirty years of research on the subjective well-being of older Americans. *Journal of Gerontology, 33*(1), 109–125.

Lau, F. C., Shukitt-Hale, B., & Joseph, J. A. (2005). The beneficial effects of fruit polyphenols on brain aging. *Neurobiology of Aging, 26*(S1), 128–132.

Le Carret, N., Lafont, S., Mayo, W., & Fabrigoule, C. (2003). The effect of education on cognitive performances and its implication for the constitution of the cognitive reserve. *Developmental Neuropsychology, 23*(3), 317–337.

Leary, M. R., Kowalski, R. M., Smith, L., & Phillips, S. (2003). Teasing, rejection, and violence: Case studies of the school shootings. *Aggressive Behavior, 29*(3), 202–214.

Leasure, J. L., & Decker, L. (2009). Social isolation prevents exercise-induced proliferation of hippocampal progenitor cells in female rats. *Hippocampus, 19*(10), 907–912.

Lebrecht, S., Pierce, L. J., Tarr, M. J., & Tanaka, J. W. (2009). Perceptual other-race training reduces implicit racial bias. *PloS One, 4*(1), e4215. doi:10.1371/journal.pone.0004215

LeDoux, J. E. (1986). Sensory systems and emotion: A model of affective processing. *Integrative Psychiatry, 4*, 237–243.

LeDoux, J. E. (1994). Emotion, memory and the brain. *Scientific American, 270*(6), 50–57.

LeDoux, J. (2003). The self: Clues from the brain. *Annals of the New York Academy of Sciences, 1001*, 295–304.

Lefcourt, H. M., Davidson-Katz, K., & Kueneman, K. (1990). Humor and immune-system functioning. *International Journal of Humor Research, 3*(3), 305–322.

Lefcourt, H. M., & Thomas, S. (1998). Humor and stress revisited. In W. Ruch (Ed.), *The sense of humor: Explorations of a personality characteristic* (pp. 179–202). Berlin, Germany: Morton de Gruyter.

Leff, S. S., Kupersmidt, J. B., Patterson, C., & Power, T. J. (1999). Factors influencing teacher predictions of peer bullying and victimization. *School Psychology Review, 28*, 505–517.

Leithwood, K., Leonard, L., & Sharratt, L. (1998). Conditions fostering organizational learning in schools. *Educational Administration Quarterly, 34*(2), 243–276.

Lemaire, V., Aurousseau, C., Le Moal, M., & Abrous, D. N. (1999). Behavioural trait of reactivity to novelty is related to hippocampal neurogenesis. *The European Journal of Neuroscience, 11*(11), 4006–4014.

Lemer, C., Dehaene, S., Spelke, E., & Cohen, L. (2003). Approximate quantities and exact number words: Dissociable systems. *Neuropsychologia, 41*(14), 1942–1958.

Lepore, S. J., Allen, K. A., & Evans, G. W. (1993). Social support lowers cardiovascular reactivity to an acute stressor. *Psychosomatic Medicine, 55*(6), 518–524.

Leslie, F. M., Loughlin, S. E., Wang, R., Perez, L., Lotfipour, S., & Belluzzia, J. D. (2004). Adolescent development of forebrain stimulant responsiveness: Insights from animal studies. *Annals of the New York Academy of Sciences, 1021*, 148–159.

Leventopoulos, M., Ruedi-Bettschen, D., Knuesel, I., Feldon, J., Pryce, C. R., & Opacka-Juffry, J. (2007). Long-term effects of early life deprivation on brain glia in Fischer rats. *Brain Research, 1142*, 119–126.

Levesque, J., Eugene, F., Joanette, Y., Paquette, V., Mensour, B., Beaudoin, G., . . . Beauregard, M. (2003). Neural circuitry underlying voluntary suppression of sadness. *Biological Psychiatry, 53*(6), 502–510.

Levine, J. D., Gordon, N. C., & Fields, H. L. (1978). The mechanism of placebo analgesia. *The Lancet, 312*(8091), 654–657.

Levine, S. (1967). Physiological and behavioral effects of infantile stimulation. *Physiology and Behavior, 2*(1), 55–59.

Levitov, I., & Wangberg, E. (1983). Identifying factors of teacher stress and dissatisfaction. *Thrust, 12*, 20–21.

Lev-Wiesel, R., Nuttman-Shwartz, O., & Sternberg, R. (2006). Peer rejection during adolescence: Psychological long-term effects—a brief report. *Journal of Loss & Trauma, 11*(2), 131–142.

Lewis, J. M. (2000). Repairing the bond in important relationships: A dynamic for personality maturation. *American Journal of Psychiatry, 157*(9), 1375–1378.

Li, N. P., & Balliet, D. (2009). Emotional expression of capacity and trustworthiness in humor and in social dilemmas. *Behavioral and Brain Sciences, 32*(5), 396–397.

Liberman, A. M., & Mattingly, I. G. (1985). The motor theory of speech perception revised. *Cognition, 21*(1), 1–36.

Lickel, B., Schmader, T., Curtis, M., Scarnier, M., & Ames, D. (2005). Vicarious shame and guilt. *Group Processes & Intergroup Relations, 8*(2), 145–157.

Lieberman, M. D., Eisenberger, N. I., Crockett, M. J., Tom, S. M., Pfeifer, J. H., & Way, B. M. (2007). Putting feelings into words: Affect labeling disrupts amygdala activity in response to affective stimuli. *Psychological Science, 18*(5), 421–428.

Lieberman, M. D., Hariri, A., Jarcho, J. M., Eisenberger, N. I., & Bookheimer, S. Y. (2005). An fMRI investigation of race-related amygdala activity in African-American and Caucasian-American individuals. *Nature Neuroscience, 8*(6), 720–722.

Liechty, R. D. (1987). Humor and the surgeon. *Archives of Surgery, 122*(5), 519–522.

Lien, L., Green, K., Welander-Vatn, A., & Bjertness, E. (2009). Mental and somatic health complaints associated with school bullying between 10th and 12th grade students: Results from cross sectional studies in Oslo, Norway. *Clinical Practice and Epidemiology in Mental Health, 5*, 6.

Lihoreau, M., Brepson, L., & Rivault, C. (2009). The weight of the clan: Even in insects, social isolation can induce a behavioural syndrome. *Behavioural Processes, 82*(1), 81–84.

Lim, J., & Dinges, D. F. (2008). Sleep deprivation and vigilant attention. *Annals of the New York Academy of Sciences, 1129*(1), 305–322.

Lindsay, P. (1982). The effect of high school size on student participation, satisfaction, and attendance. *Educational Evaluation and Policy Analysis, 4*(1), 57–65.

Linton, S. J., Hellsing, A. L., Halme, T., & Akerstedt, K. (1994). The effects of ergonomically designed school furniture on pupils' attitudes, symptoms and behaviour. *Applied Ergonomics, 25*(5), 299–304.

Linville, P. W., & Jones, E. E. (1980). Polarized appraisals of out-group members. *Journal of Personality and Social Psychology, 38*(5), 689–703.

Liu, D., Diorio, J., Day, J. C., Francis, D. D., & Meaney, M. J. (2000). Maternal care, hippocampal synaptogenesis and cognitive development in rats. *Nature Neuroscience, 3*(8), 799–806.

Liu, D., Diorio, J., Tannenbaum, B., Caldji, C., Francis, D., Freedman, A., . . . Meaney, M. J. (1997). Maternal care, hippocampal glucocorticoid receptors, and hypothalamic-pituitary-adrenal responses to stress. *Science, 277*(5332), 1659–1662.

Lloyd, E. L. (1938). The respiratory mechanism of laughter. *Journal of General Psychology, 10*, 179–189.

Lomax, R. G., & Moosavi, S. A. (2002). Using humor to teach statistics: Must they be orthogonal? *Understanding Statistics, 1*(2), 113–130.

Lopez, F. G., Gover, M. R., Leskela, J., Sauer, E. M., Schirmer, L., & Wyssmann, J. (1997). Attachment styles, shame, guilt, and collaborative problem-solving orientations. *Personal Relationships, 4*(2), 187–199.

Lopez, O. (1995). *The effect of the relationship between classroom student diversity and teacher capacity on student performance*. Retrieved from ERIC database. (ED386423)

Lordi, B., Patin, V., Protais, P., Mellier, D., & Caston, J. (2000). Chronic stress in pregnant rats: Effects on growth rate, anxiety and memory capabilities of the offspring. *International Journal of Psychophysiology, 37*(2), 195–205.

Lortie, D. C. (1975). *Schoolteacher: A sociological study*. Chicago: University of Chicago Press.

Lotan, R. A., & Ben-Ari, R. (1994). Complex instructions. In Y. Rich & R. Ben-Ari (Eds.), *Shitot hora'a lekita hahetrogenit* [*Instructional strategies for heterogeneous classes*] (pp. 189–216). Even Yehuda, Israel: Reches.

Lou, H. C., Luber, B., Crupain, M., Keenan, J. P., Nowak, M., Kjaer, T. W., . . . Lisanby, S. H. (2004). Parietal cortex and representation of the mental self. *Proceedings of the National Academy of Sciences of the United States of America, 101*(17), 6827–6832.

Lou, H. C., Nowak, M., & Kjaer, T. W. (2005). The mental self. *Progress in Brain Research, 150,* 197–204.

Lu, S. T., Hamalainen, M. S., Hari, R., Ilmoniemi, R. J., Lounasmaa, O. V., Sams, M., & Vilkman, V. (1991). Seeing faces activates three separate areas outside the occipital visual cortex in man. *Neuroscience, 43*(2–3), 287–290.

Lukkes, J. L., Watt, M. J., Lowry, C. A., & Forster, G. L. (2009). Consequences of post-weaning social isolation on anxiety behavior and related neural circuits in rodents. *Frontiers in Behavioral Neuroscience, 3,* 18.

Lumsden, L. (1998). *Teacher morale.* Retrieved from ERIC database. (ED422601)

Luna, B., & Sweeney, J. A. (2004). The emergence of collaborative brain function: fMRI studies of the development of response inhibition. *Annals of the New York Academy of Sciences, 1021,* 296–309.

Lund, I., Ge, Y., Yu, L. C., Uvnas-Moberg, K., Wang, J., Yu, C., . . . Lundeberg, T. (2002). Repeated massage-like stimulation induces long-term effects on nociception: Contribution of oxytocinergic mechanisms. *European Journal of Neuroscience, 16*(2), 330–338.

Lundqvist, L. O., & Dimberg, U. (1995). Facial expressions are contagious. *Journal of Psychophysiology, 9*(3), 203–211.

Lupien, S. J., de Leon, M., de Santi, S., Convit, A., Tarshish, C., Nair, N. P., . . . Meaney, M. J. (1998). Cortisol levels during human aging predict hippocampal atrophy and memory deficits. *Nature Neuroscience, 1*(1), 69–73.

Lupien, S. J., & McEwen, B. S. (1997). The acute effects of corticosteroids on cognition: Integration of animal and human model studies. *Brain Research Reviews, 24*(1), 1–27.

Luttwak, E., & Horowitz, D. (1975). *The Israeli army.* New York, NY: Harper & Row.

Lutwak, N., & Ferrari, J. R. (1997). Understanding shame in adults: Retrospective perceptions of parental bonding during childhood. *Journal of Nervous and Mental Disease, 185*(10), 595–598.

Ma, X. (2002). Bullying in middle school: Individual and school characteristics of victims and offenders. *School Effectiveness and School Improvement, 13*(1), 63–89.

Ma, X., & Macmillan, R. B. (1999). Influences of workplace conditions on teachers' job satisfaction. *Journal of Educational Research, 93*(1), 39–47.

Maccari, S., Piazza, P. V., Kabbaj, M., Barbazanges, A., Simon, H., & Le Moal, M. (1995). Adoption reverses the long-term impairment in glucocorticoid feedback induced by prenatal stress. *Journal of Neuroscience, 15*(1), 110–116.

Macdonald, G., & Leary, M. R. (2005). Why does social exclusion hurt? The relationship between social and physical pain. *Psychological Bulletin, 131*(2), 202–223.

Machne, X., & Segundo, J. P. (1956). Unitary responses to afferent volleys in amygdaloid complex. *Journal of Neurophysiology, 19*(3), 232–240.

MacIver, D. J., Stipek, D. J., & Daniels, D. H. (1991). Explaining within-semester changes in student effort in junior high school and senior high school courses. *Journal of Educational Psychology, 83*(2), 201–211.

MacLean, P. D. (1985). Brain evolution relating to family, play, and the separation call. *Archives of General Psychiatry, 42*(4), 405–417.

Macrae, C. N., Moran, J. M., Heatherton, T. F., Banfield, J. F., & Kelley, W. M. (2004). Medial prefrontal activity predicts memory for self. *Cerebral Cortex, 14*(6), 647–654.

Madden, T. J., & Weinberger, M. G. (1982). The effects of humor on attention in magazine advertising. *Journal of Advertising, 11*(3), 8–14.

Maddi, S. R., & Hess, M. J. (1992). Personality hardiness and success in basketball. *International Journal of Sport Psychology, 23*(4), 360–368.

Maddi, S. R., & Kobasa, S. C. (1984). *The hardy executive: Health under stress.* Homewood, IL: Dow Jones-Irwin.

Madon, S., Jussim, L., & Eccles, J. (1997). In search of the powerful self-fulfilling prophecy. *Journal of Personality and Social Psychology, 72*(4), 791–809.

Maguire, E. A., Burgess, N., Donnett, J. G., Frackowiak, R. S., Frith, C. D., & O'Keefe, J. (1998). Knowing where and getting there: A human navigation network. *Science, 280*(5365), 921–924.

Maguire, E. A., Woollett, K., & Spiers, H. J. (2006). London taxi drivers and bus drivers: A structural MRI and neuropsychological analysis. *Hippocampus, 16*(12), 1091–1101.

Maier, S. F., Amat, J., Baratta, M. V., Paul, E., & Watkins, L. R. (2006). Behavioral control, the medial prefrontal cortex, and resilience. *Dialogues in Clinical Neuroscience, 8*(4), 397–406.

Main, M. (1993). Discourse, prediction, and the recent studies in attachment: Implications for psychoanalysis. *Journal of the American Psychoanalytic Association, 41,* 209–244.

Main, M., & Goldwyn, R. (1998). *Adult attachment scoring and classification system.* Unpublished manuscript, University of California at Berkeley, Berkeley, CA.

Main, M., Kaplan, N., & Cassidy, J. (1985). Security in infancy, childhood, and adulthood: A move to the level of representation. *Monographs of the Society for Research in Child Development, 50*(2), 66–104.

Malenka, R. C., & Siegelbaum, S. A. (2001). Synaptic plasticity: Diverse targets and mechanisms for regulating synaptic efficacy. In W. M. Cowan, T. C. Sudhof, & C. F. Stevens (Eds.), *Synapses* (pp. 393–453). Baltimore, MD: Johns Hopkins University Press.

Maletic-Savatic, M., Malinow, R., & Svoboda, K. (1999). Rapid dendritic morphogenesis in CA1 hippocampal dendrites induced by synaptic activity. *Science, 283*(5409), 1923–1927.

Malloy, P., Bihrle, A., Duffy, J., & Cimino, C. (1993). The orbitomedial frontal syndrome. *Archives of Clinical Neuropsychology, 8*(3), 185–201.

Malpass, R. S., & Kravitz, J. (1969). Recognition for faces of own and other race. *Journal of Personality and Social Psychology, 13*(4), 330–334.

Manahan-Vaughan, D., & Braunewell, K. H. (1999). Novelty acquisition is associated with induction of hippocampal long-term depression. *Proceedings of the National Academy of Sciences of the United States of America, 96*(15), 8739–8744.

Maner, J. K., DeWall, C. N., Baumeister, R. F., & Schaller, M. (2007). Does social exclusion motivate interpersonal reconnection? Resolving the "porcupine problem." *Journal of Personality and Social Psychology, 92*(1), 42–55.

Mann, D. (1996). Serious play. *Teachers College Record, 97*(3), 446–469.

Marais, L., van Rensburg, S. J., van Zyl, J. M., Stein, D. J., & Daniels, W. M. (2008). Maternal separation of rat pups increases the risk of developing depressive-like behavior after subsequent chronic stress by altering corticosterone and neurotrophin levels in the hippocampus. *Neuroscience Research, 61*(1), 106–112.

Marci, C. D., Ham, J., Moran, E., & Orr, S. P. (2007). Physiologic correlates of perceived therapist empathy and social-emotional process during psychotherapy. *Journal of Nervous and Mental Disease, 195*(2), 103–111.

Marr, D. (1971). Simple memory: A theory for archicortex. *Philosophical Transactions of the Royal Society of London: Series B, Biological Sciences, 262*(841), 23–81.

Marsh, H. W. (1992). Content specificity of relations between academic achievement and academic self-concept. *Journal of Educational Psychology, 84*(1), 35–42.

Marsh, H. W., Balla, J. R., & McDonald, R. P. (1988). Goodness-of-fit indexes in confirmatory factor analysis: The effect of sample size. *Psychological Bulletin, 103*(3), 391–410.

Marsh, H. W., & Yeung, A. S. (1997a). Causal effects of academic self-concept on academic achievement: Structural equation models of longitudinal data. *Journal of Educational Psychology, 89*(1), 41–54.

Marsh, H. W., & Yeung, A. S. (1997b). Coursework selection: Relations to academic self-concept and achievement. *American Educational Research Journal, 34*(4), 691–720.

Marshuetz, C., Smith, E. E., Jonides, J., DeGutis, J., & Chenevert, T. L. (2000). Order information in working memory: fMRI evidence for parietal and prefrontal mechanisms. *Journal of Cognitive Neuroscience, 12*(S2), 130–144.

Martin, A. (1999). Automatic activation of the medial temporal lobe during encoding: Lateralized influences of meaning and novelty. *Hippocampus, 9*(1), 62–70.

Martin, R. A., Kuiper, N. A., Olinger, L. J., & Dance, K. A. (1993). Humor, coping with stress, self-concept, and psychological well-being. *International Journal of Humor Research, 6*(1), 89–104.

Maslach, C. (1976). Burned-out. *Human Behavior, 5*, 16–22.

Maslach, C., & Jackson, S. E. (1981). The measurement of experienced burnout. *Journal of Occupational Behaviour, 2*, 99–113.

Maslach, C., Schaufeli, W. B., & Leiter, M. P. (2001). Job burnout. *Annual Review of Psychology, 52*, 397–422.

Masten, C. L., Eisenberger, N. I., Borofsky, L. A., Pfeifer, J. H., McNealy, K., Mazziotta, J. C., & Dapretto, M. (2009). Neural correlates of social exclusion during adolescence: Understanding the distress of peer rejection. *Social Cognitive and Affective Neuroscience, 4*(2), 143–157.

Masten, C. L., Eisenberger, N. I., Pfeifer, J. H., & Dapretto, M. (2010). Witnessing peer rejection during early adolescence: Neural correlates of empathy for experiences of social exclusion. *Social Neuroscience, 5*(5–6), 496–507.

Mateer, C. A., & Kerns, K. A. (2000). Capitalizing on neuroplasticity. *Brain and Cognition, 42*(1), 106–109.

Matsumoto, K., & Tanaka, K. (2004). The role of the medial prefrontal cortex in achieving goals. *Current Opinion in Neurobiology, 14*(2), 178–185.

Matthiesen, S. B., & Einarsen, S. (2001). MMPI-2 configurations among victims of bullying at work. *European Journal of Work and Organizational Psychology, 10*(4), 467–484.

Matthiesen, S. B., & Einarsen, S. (2004). Psychiatric distress and symptoms of PTSD among victims of bullying at work. *British Journal of Guidance and Counselling, 32*(3), 335–356.

Mattson, M. P. (2003). Gene-diet interactions in brain aging and neurodegenerative disorders. *Annals of Internal Medicine, 139*(S2), 441–444.

Mattson, M. P., Kruman, I. I., & Duan, W. (2002). Folic acid and homocysteine in age-related disease. *Ageing Research Reviews, 1*(1), 95–111.

Matzel, L. D., Townsend, D. A., Grossman, H., Han, Y. R., Hale, G., Zappulla, M., . . . Kolata, S. (2006). Exploration in outbred mice covaries with general learning abilities irrespective of stress reactivity, emotionality, and physical attributes. *Neurobiology of Learning and Memory, 86*(2), 228–240.

May, R. (1953) *Man's search for himself.* New York, NY: W. W. Norton.

Mayer, R. E., Bove, W., Bryman, A., Mars, R., & Tapangco, L. (1996). When less is more: Meaningful learning from visual and verbal summaries of science textbook lessons. *Journal of Educational Psychology, 88*(1), 64–73.

Mazur, A. (1985). A biosocial model of status in face-to-face primate groups. *Social Forces, 64*(2), 377–402.

Mazur, P. J., & Lynch, M. D. (1989). Differential impact of administrative, organizational, and personality factors on teacher burnout. *Teaching and Teacher Education, 5*(4), 337–353.

McCarthy, G. (1995). Functional neuroimaging of memory. *The Neuroscientist, 1*(3), 155–163.

McClelland, D. C., & Cheriff, A. D. (1997). The immunoenhancing effects of humor on secretory IgA end resistance to respiratory infections. *Psychology & Health, 12*(3), 329–344.

McCormick, J. (1997). Occupational stress of teachers: Biographical differences in a large school system. *Journal of Educational Administration, 35*(1), 18–38.

McCormick, J. A., Lyons, V., Jacobson, M. D., Noble, J., Diorio, J., Nyirenda, M., . . . Chapman, K. E. (2000). 5'-heterogeneity of glucocorticoid receptor messenger RNA is tissue specific: Differential regulation of variant transcripts by early-life events. *Molecular Endocrinology, 14*(4), 506–517.

McCowan, B., Marino, L., Vance, E., Walke, L., & Reiss, D. (2000). Bubble ring play of bottlenose dolphins (Tursiops truncatus): Implications for cognition. *Journal of Comparative Psychology, 114*(1), 98–106.

McDaniel, M. A., Waddill, P. J., & Einstein, G. O. (1988). A contextual account of the generation effect: A three-factor theory. *Journal of Memory and Language, 27*(5), 521–536.

McGaugh, J. L. (2004). The amygdala modulates the consolidation of memories of emotionally arousing experiences. *Annual Review of Neuroscience, 27*, 1–28.

McGaugh, J. L., Introini-Collison, I. B., Cahill, L. F., Castellano, C., Dalmaz, C., Parent, M. B., & Williams, C. L. (1993). Neuromodulatory systems and memory storage: Role of the amygdala. *Behavioural Brain Research, 58*(1–2), 81–90.

McGowan, P. O., Sasaki, A., D'Alessio, A. C., Dymov, S., Labonte, B., Szyf, M., . . . Meaney, M. J. (2009). Epigenetic regulation of the glucocorticoid receptor in human brain associates with childhood abuse. *Nature Neuroscience, 12*(3), 342–348.

McGowan, P. O., Sasaki, A., Huang, T. C., Unterberger, A., Suderman, M., Ernst, C., . . . Szyf, M. (2008). Promoter-wide hypermethylation of the ribosomal RNA gene promoter in the suicide brain. *PloS One, 3*(5), e2085. doi:10.1371/journal.pone.0002085

McGray, D. (2009). The instigator. *The New Yorker, 85*(13), 66.

McGregor, I. S., Schrama, L., Ambermoon, P., & Dielenberg, R. A. (2002). Not all "predator odours" are equal: Cat odour but not 2,4,5 trimethylthiazoline (TMT; fox odour) elicits specific defensive behaviours in rats. *Behavioural Brain Research, 129*(1–2), 1–16.

McGuire, P. K., Paulesu, E., Frackowiak, R. S., & Frith, C. D. (1996). Brain activity during stimulus independent thought. *NeuroReport, 7*(13), 2095–2099.

McGurk, H., & MacDonald, J. (1976). Hearing lips and seeing voices. Nature, 264(5588), 746–748.

McIntyre, T. C. (1984). The relationship between locus of control and teacher burnout. *British Journal of Educational Psychology, 54*(2), 235–238.

McKittrick, C. R., Magarinos, A. M., Blanchard, D. C., Blanchard, R. J., McEwen, B. S., & Sakai, R. R. (2000). Chronic social stress reduces dendritic arbors in CA3 of hippocampus and decreases binding to serotonin transporter sites. *Synapse, 36*(2), 85–94.

McKown, C., & Weinstein, R. S. (2002). Modeling the role of child ethnicity and gender in children's differential response to teacher expectations. *Journal of Applied Social Psychology, 32*(1), 159–184.

McNicholas, J., Gilbey, A., Rennie, A., Ahmedzai, S., Dono, J. A., & Ormerod, E. (2005). Pet ownership and human health: A brief review of evidence and issues. *British Medical Journal, 331*(7527), 1252–1254.

Meaney, M. J., Aitken, D. H., van Berkel, C., Bhatnagar, S., & Sapolsky, R. M. (1988). Effect of neonatal handling on age-related impairments associated with the hippocampus. *Science, 239*(4841), 766–768.

Meaney, M. J., Aitken, D. H., Viau, V., Sharma, S., & Sarrieau, A. (1989). Neonatal handling alters adrenocortical negative feedback sensitivity and hippocampal type II glucocorticoid receptor binding in the rat. *Neuroendocrinology, 50*(5), 597–604.

Meaney, M. J., Diorio, J., Francis, D., Weaver, S., Yau, J., Chapman, K., & Seckl, J. R. (2000). Postnatal handling increases the expression of cAMP-inducible transcription factors in the rat hippocampus: The effects of thyroid hormones and serotonin. *Journal of Neuroscience, 20*(10), 3926–3935.

Meaney, M. J., Diorio, J., Francis, D., Widdowson, J., LaPlante, P., Caldji, C., . . . Plotsky, P. M. (1996). Early environmental regulation of forebrain glucocorticoid receptor gene expression: Implications for adrenocortical responses to stress. *Developmental Neuroscience, 18*(1–2), 61–72.

Meaney, M. J., Mitchell, J. B., Aitken, D. H., Bhatnagar, S., Bodnoff, S. R., Iny, L. J., & Sarrieau, A. (1991). The effects of neonatal handling on the development of the adrenocortical response to stress: Implications for neuropathology and cognitive deficits in later life. *Psychoneuroendocrinology, 16*(1–3), 85–103.

Meaney, M. J., & Szyf, M. (2005). Maternal care as a model for experience-dependent chromatin plasticity? *Trends in Neurosciences, 28*(9), 456–463.

Mearns, J., & Cain, J. E. (2003). Relationships between teachers' occupational stress and their burnout and distress: Roles of coping and negative mood regulation expectancies. *Anxiety, Stress & Coping, 16*(1), 71–82.

Medeiros, A. L. D., Mendes, D. B. F., Lima, P. F., & Araujo, J. F. (2001). The relationships between sleep-wake cycle and academic performance in medical students. *Biological Rhythm Research, 32*(2), 263–270.

Mednick, S., Nakayama, K., Cantero, J. L., Atienza, M., Levin, A. A., Pathak, N., & Stickgold, R. (2002). The restorative effect of naps on perceptual deterioration. *Nature Neuroscience, 5*(7), 677–681.

Mednick, S., Nakayama, K., & Stickgold, R. (2003). Sleep-dependent learning: A nap is as good as a night. *Nature Neuroscience, 6*(7), 697–698.

Meece, J. L., Blumenfeld, P. C., & Hoyle, R. H. (1988). Students' goal orientations and cognitive engagement in classroom activities. *Journal of Educational Psychology, 80*(4), 514–523.

Meehan, C. L., & Mench, J. A. (2002). Environmental enrichment affects the fear and exploratory responses to novelty of young Amazon parrots. *Applied Animal Behaviour Science, 79*(1), 75–88.

Meltzoff, A. N. (1995). Understanding the intentions of others: Re-enactment of intended acts by 18-month-old children. *Developmental Psychology, 31*(5), 838–850.

Meltzoff, A. N., Kuhl, P. K., Movellan, J., & Sejnowski, T. J. (2009). Foundations for a new science of learning. *Science, 325*(5938), 284–288.

Meltzoff, A. N., & Moore, M. K. (1992). Early imitation within a functional framework: The importance of person identity, movement, and development. *Infant Behavior & Development, 15*(4), 479–505.

Menard, J. L., Champagne, D. L., & Meaney, M. J. (2004). Variations of maternal care differentially influence "fear" reactivity and regional patterns of cFos immunoreactivity in response to the shock-probe burying test. *Neuroscience, 129*(2), 297–308.

Merten, D. E. (1997). The meaning of meanness: Popularity, competition, and conflict among junior high school girls. *Sociology of Education, 70*(3), 175–191.

Mesches, M. H., Fleshner, M., Heman, K. L., Rose, G. M., & Diamond, D. M. (1999). Exposing rats to a predator blocks primed burst potentiation in the hippocampus in vitro. *Journal of Neuroscience, 19*(14), RC18.

Mesulam, M. M. (1987). Involutional and developmental implications of age-related neuronal changes: In search of an engram for wisdom. *Neurobiology of Aging, 8*(6), 581–583.

Mesulam, M. M. (1998). From sensation to cognition. *Brain, 121*(6), 1013–1052.

Mettke-Hofmann, C., Winkler, H., & Leisler, B. (2002). The significance of ecological factors for exploration and neophobia in parrots. *Ethology, 108*(3), 249–272.

Meyer, M., Baumann, S., Wildgruber, D., & Alter, K. (2007). How the brain laughs: Comparative evidence from behavioral, electrophysiological and neuroimaging studies in human and monkey. *Behavioural Brain Research, 182*(2), 245–260.

Michel, G. F., & Moore, C. L. (1995). *Developmental psychobiology: An interdisciplinary science*. Cambridge, MA: MIT Press.

Miech, R. A., & Elder, G. H., Jr. (1996). The service ethic and teaching. *Sociology of Education, 69*(3), 237–253.

Milad, M. R., Orr, S. P., Pitman, R. K., & Rauch, S. L. (2005). Context modulation of memory for fear extinction in humans. *Psychophysiology, 42*(4), 456–464.

Milad, M. R., & Quirk, G. J. (2002). Neurons in medial prefrontal cortex signal memory for fear extinction. *Nature, 420*(6911), 70–74.

Milad, M. R., Vidal-Gonzalez, I., & Quirk, G. J. (2004). Electrical stimulation of medial prefrontal cortex reduces conditioned fear in a temporally specific manner. *Behavioral Neuroscience, 118*(2), 389–394.

Milgram, S. (1983). *Obedience to authority*. New York, NY: Harper Perennial.

Milligan, K., Atkinson, L., Trehub, S. E., Benoit, D., & Poulton, L. (2003). Maternal attachment and the communication of emotion through song. *Infant Behavior & Development, 26*(1), 1–13.

Mills, R. S. L. (2003). Possible antecedents and developmental implications of shame in young girls. *Infant and Child Development, 12*(4), 329–349.

Mills, R. S. L., Imm, G. P., Walling, B. R., & Weiler, H. A. (2008). Cortisol reactivity and regulation associated with shame responding in early childhood. *Developmental Psychology, 44*(5), 1369–1380.

Milsum, J. H. (1985). A model of the eustress system for health/illness. *Behavioral Science, 30*(4), 179–186.

Minagawa-Kawai, Y., Matsuoka, S., Dan, I., Naoi, N., Nakamura, K., & Kojima, S. (2009). Prefrontal activation associated with social attachment: Facial-emotion recognition in mothers and infants. *Cerebral Cortex, 19*(2), 284–292.

Mineka, S., & Cook, M. (1993). Mechanisms involved in the observational conditioning of fear. *Journal of Experimental Psychology: General, 122*(1), 23–38.

Mirenowicz, J., & Schultz, W. (1994). Importance of unpredictability for reward responses in primate dopamine neurons. *Journal of Neurophysiology, 72*(2), 1024–1027.

Mirescu, C., Peters, J. D., & Gould, E. (2004). Early life experience alters response of adult neurogenesis to stress. *Nature Neuroscience, 7*(8), 841–846.

Mitchell, J. P., Banaji, M. R., & Macrae, C. N. (2005). The link between social cognition and self-referential thought in the medial prefrontal cortex. *Journal of Cognitive Neuroscience, 17*(8), 1306–1315.

Mitchell, J. P., Macrae, C. N., & Banaji, M. R. (2006). Dissociable medial prefrontal contributions to judgments of similar and dissimilar others. *Neuron, 50*(4), 655–663.

Mobbs, D., Greicius, M. D., Abdel-Azim, E., Menon, V., & Reiss, A. L. (2003). Humor modulates the mesolimbic reward centers. *Neuron, 40*(5), 1041–1048.

Moerman, D. E., & Jonas, W. B. (2002). Deconstructing the placebo effect and finding the meaning response. *Annals of Internal Medicine, 136*(6), 471–476.

Molko, N., Cachia, A., Rivière, D., Mangin, J., Bruandet, M., Le Bihan, D., . . . Dehaene, S. (2003). Functional and structural alterations of the intraparietal sulcus in a developmental dyscalculia of genetic origin. *Neuron, 40*(4), 847–858.

Molteni, R., Barnard, R. J., Ying, Z., Roberts, C. K., & Gómez-Pinilla, F. (2002). A high-fat, refined sugar diet reduces hippocampal brain-derived neurotrophic factor, neuronal plasticity, and learning. *Neuroscience, 112*(4), 803–814.

Monfils, M. H., Cowansage, K. K., & LeDoux, J. E. (2007). Brain-derived neurotrophic factor: Linking fear learning to memory consolidation. *Molecular Pharmacology, 72*(2), 235–237.

Montag-Sallaz, M., Welzl, H., Kuhl, D., Montag, D., & Schachner, M. (1999). Novelty-induced increased expression of immediate-early genes c-fos and arg 3.1 in the mouse brain. *Journal of Neurobiology, 38*(2), 234–246.

Montgomery, C., & Rupp, A. A. (2005). A meta-analysis for exploring the diverse causes and effects of stress in teachers. *Canadian Journal of Education, 28*(3), 458–486.

Moore, G. T. (1986). Effects of the spatial definition of behavior settings on children's behavior: A quasi-experimental field study. *Journal of Environmental Psychology, 6*(3), 205–231.

Moran, J. M., Wig, G. S., Adams, R. B., Jr, Janata, P., & Kelley, W. M. (2004). Neural correlates of humor detection and appreciation. *NeuroImage, 21*(3), 1055–1060.

Morgan, D., Grant, K. A., Gage, H. D., Mach, R. H., Kaplan, J. R., Prioleau, O., . . . Nader, M. A. (2002). Social dominance in monkeys: Dopamine D2 receptors and cocaine self-administration. *Nature Neuroscience, 5*(2), 169–174.

Morgan, M. A., Romanski, L. M., & LeDoux, J. E. (1993). Extinction of emotional learning: Contribution of medial prefrontal cortex. *Neuroscience Letters, 163*(1), 109–113.

Moriceau, S., & Sullivan, R. M. (2004). Corticosterone influences on mammalian neonatal sensitive-period learning. *Behavioral Neuroscience, 118*(2), 274–281.

Morkes, J., Kernal, H. K., & Nass, C. (1999). Effects of humor in task-oriented human-computer interaction and computer-mediated communication: A direct test of SRCT theory. *Human-Computer Interaction, 14*(4), 395–435.

Morley-Fletcher, S., Rea, M., Maccari, S., & Laviola, G. (2003). Environmental enrichment during adolescence reverses the effects of prenatal stress on play behaviour and HPA axis reactivity in rats. *European Journal of Neuroscience, 18*(12), 3367–3374.

Morris, J. S., Ohman, A., & Dolan, R. J. (1998). Conscious and unconscious emotional learning in the human amygdala. *Nature, 393*(6684), 467–470.

Morris, J. S., Ohman, A., & Dolan, R. J. (1999). A subcortical pathway to the right amygdala mediating "unseen" fear. *Proceedings of the National Academy of Sciences of the United States of America, 96*(4), 1680–1685.

Morrison, B. (2006). School bullying and restorative justice: Toward a theoretical understanding of the role of respect, pride, and shame. *Journal of Social Issues, 62*(2), 371–392.

Morrison, J. H., & Hof, P. R. (2003). Changes in cortical circuits during aging. *Clinical Neuroscience Research, 2*(5–6), 294–304.

Morrow, B. A., Redmond, A. J., Roth, R. H., & Elsworth, J. D. (2000). The predator odor, TMT, displays a unique, stress-like pattern of dopaminergic and endocrinological activation in the rat. *Brain Research, 864*(1), 146–151.

Morton, L. L., Vesco, R., Williams, N. H., & Awender, M. A. (1997). Student teacher anxieties related to class management, pedagogy, evaluation, and staff relations. *British Journal of Educational Psychology, 67*(1), 69–89.

Mosley, J. C. (1999). Influence of social dominance on habitat selection by free-ranging ugulates. In K. L. Launchbaugh, J. C. Mosley, & K. D. Sanders (Eds.), *Grazing behavior of livestock and wildlife* (pp. 109–118). Moscow, ID: Idaho Forest, Wildlife and Range Experiment Station Bulletin 70.

Mountcastle, V. B. (1995). The parietal system and some higher brain functions. *Cerebral Cortex, 5*(5), 377–390.

Myers, J. J., & Sperry, R. W. (1985). Interhemispheric communication after section of the forebrain commissures. *Cortex, 21*(2), 249–260.

Myers, W. A., Churchill, J. D., Muja, N., & Garraghty, P. E. (2000). Role of NMDA receptors in adult primate cortical somatosensory plasticity. *Journal of Comparative Neurology, 418*(4), 373–382.

Nachmias, M., Gunnar, M., Mangelsdorf, S., Parritz, R. H., & Buss, K. (1996). Behavioral inhibition and stress reactivity: The moderating role of attachment security. *Child Development, 67*(2), 508–522.

Nagahama, Y., Okada, T., Katsumi, Y., Hayashi, T., Yamauchi, H., Oyanagi, C., . . . Shibasaki, H. (2001). Dissociable mechanisms of attentional control within the human prefrontal cortex. *Cerebral Cortex, 11*(1), 85–92.

Nagahara, A. H., & Handa, R. J. (1997). Age-related changes in c-fos mRNA induction after open-field exposure in the rat brain. *Neurobiology of Aging, 18*(1), 45–55.

Nakamura, S., Sadato, N., Oohashi, T., Nishina, E., Fuwamoto, Y., & Yonekura, Y. (1999). Analysis of music–brain interaction with simultaneous measurement of regional cerebral blood flow and electroencephalogram beta rhythm in human subjects. *Neuroscience Letters, 275*(3), 222–226.

Nanda, S. A., Qi, C., Roseboom, P. H., & Kalin, N. H. (2008). Predator stress induces behavioral inhibition and amygdala somatostatin receptor 2 gene expression. *Genes, Brain, and Behavior, 7*(6), 639–648.

Nansel, T. R., Overpeck, M., Pilla, R. S., Ruan, W. J., Simons-Morton, B., & Scheidt, P. (2001). Bullying behaviors among US youth: Prevalence and association with psychosocial adjustment. *Journal of the American Medical Association, 285*(16), 2094–2100.

Nasrallah, H. A. (1985). The unintegrated right cerebral hemispheric consciousness as alien intruder: A possible mechanism for Schneiderian delusions in schizophrenia. *Comprehensive Psychiatry, 26*(3), 273–282.

Nedergaard, M., Ransom, B., & Goldman, S. A. (2003). New roles for astrocytes: Redefining the functional architecture of the brain. *Trends in Neurosciences, 26*(10), 523–530.

Neeper, S. A., Gomez-Pinilla, F., Choi, J., & Cotman, C. (1995). Exercise and brain neurotrophins. *Nature, 373*(6510), 109.

Neeper, S. A., Gomez-Pinilla, F., Choi, J., & Cotman, C. W. (1996). Physical activity increases mRNA for brain-derived neurotrophic factor and nerve growth factor in rat brain. *Brain Research, 726*(1–2), 49–56.

Nelson, E. E., Leibenluft, E., McClure, E. B., & Pine, D. S. (2005). The social re-orientation of adolescence: A neuroscience perspective on the process and its relation to psychopathology. *Psychological Medicine, 35*(2), 163–174.

Nelson, E. E., & Panksepp, J. (1998). Brain substrates of infant-mother attachment: Contributions of opioids, oxytocin, and norepinephrine. *Neuroscience and Biobehavioral Reviews, 22*(3), 437–452.

Nelson, J. (2008). Laugh and the world laughs with you: An attachment perspective on the meaning of laughter in psychotherapy. *Clinical Social Work Journal, 36*(1), 41–49.

Nelson, K. (1993). The psychological and social origins of autobiographical memory. *Psychological Science, 4*(1), 7–14.

Nelson, P. B., & Soli, S. (2000). Acoustical barriers to learning: Children at risk in every classroom. *Language, Speech and Hearing Services in Schools, 31*(4), 356–361.

Neumann, I. D. (2008). Brain oxytocin: A key regulator of emotional and social behaviours in both females and males. *Journal of Neuroendocrinology, 20*(6), 858–865.

Newcomer, J. W., Craft, S., Hershey, T., Askins, K., & Bardgett, M. E. (1994). Glucocorticoid-induced impairment in declarative memory performance in adult humans. *Journal of Neuroscience, 14*(4), 2047–2053.

Newcomer, J. W., Selke, G., Melson, A. K., Hershey, T., Craft, S., Richards, K., & Alderson, A. L. (1999). Decreased memory performance in healthy humans induced by stress-level cortisol treatment. *Archives of General Psychiatry, 56*(6), 527–533.

Newman, E. A. (2003). New roles for astrocytes: Regulation of synaptic transmission. *Trends in Neurosciences, 26*(10), 536–542.

Newman, S. D., Carpenter, P. A., Varma, S., & Just, M. A. (2003). Frontal and parietal participation in problem solving in the Tower of London: fMRI and computational modeling of planning and high-level perception. *Neuropsychologia, 41*(12), 1668–1682.

Newman-Carlson, D., & Horne, A. M. (2004). Bully busters: A psychoeducational intervention for reducing bullying behavior in middle school students. *Journal of Counseling and Development, 82*(3), 259.

Nezu, A. M., Nezu, C. M., & Blissett, S. E. (1988). Sense of humor as a moderator of the relation between stressful events and psychological distress: A prospective analysis. *Journal of Personality and Social Psychology, 54*(3), 520–525.

Nilsson, L., Mohammed, A. K., Henriksson, B. G., Folkesson, R., Winblad, B., & Bergstrom, L. (1993). Environmental influence on somatostatin levels and gene expression in the rat brain. *Brain Research, 628*(1–2), 93–98.

Nimchinsky, E. A., Gilissen, E., Allman, J. M., Perl, D. P., Erwin, J. M., & Hof, P. R. (1999). A neuronal morphologic type unique to humans and great apes. *Proceedings of the National Academy of Sciences of the United States of America, 96*(9), 5268–5273.

Nimchinsky, E. A., Vogt, B. A., Morrison, J. H., & Hof, P. R. (1995). Spindle neurons of the human anterior cingulate cortex. *Journal of Comparative Neurology, 355*(1), 27–37.

Nishina, A., & Juvonen, J. (2005). Daily reports of witnessing and experiencing peer harassment in middle school. *Child Development, 76*(2), 435–450.

Nishitani, N., & Hari, R. (2000). Temporal dynamics of cortical representation for action. *Proceedings of the National Academy of Sciences of the United States of America, 97*(2), 913–918.

Nishitani, N., & Hari, R. (2002). Viewing lip forms: Cortical dynamics. *Neuron, 36*(6), 1211–1220.

Nishitani, N., Schurmann, M., Amunts, K., & Hari, R. (2005). Broca's region: From action to language. *Physiology, 20*(1), 60–69.

Nitschke, J. B., Nelson, E. E., Rusch, B. D., Fox, A. S., Oakes, T. R., & Davidson, R. J. (2004). Orbitofrontal cortex tracks positive mood in mothers viewing pictures of their newborn infants. *NeuroImage, 21*(2), 583–592.

Noble, K. G., Norman, M. F., & Farah, M. J. (2005). Neurocognitive correlates of socioeconomic status in kindergarten children. *Developmental Science, 8*(1), 74–87.

Nobre, A. C., Coull, J. T., Frith, C. D., & Mesulam, M. M. (1999). Orbitofrontal cortex is activated during breaches of expectation in tasks of visual attention. *Nature Neuroscience, 2*(1), 11–12.

Nolte, J. (2008). *The human brain: An introduction to its functional anatomy* (6th ed.). St. Louis, MO: Mosby.

Nomura, M., Iidaka, T., Kakehi, K., Tsukiura, T., Hasegawa, T., Maeda, Y., & Matsue, Y. (2003). Frontal lobe networks for effective processing of ambiguously expressed emotions in humans. *Neuroscience Letters, 348*(2), 113–116.

Novick, L. R., & Holyoak, K. J. (1991). Mathematical problem solving by analogy. *Journal of Experimental Psychology: Learning, Memory, and Cognition, 17*(3), 398–415.

Núñez, J. F., Ferré, P., García, E., Escorihuela, R. M., Fernández-Teruel, A., & Tobeña, A. (1995). Postnatal handling reduces emotionality ratings and accelerates two-way active avoidance in female rats. *Physiology & Behavior, 57*(5), 831–835.

Nusbaum, A. O., Tang, C. Y., Buchsbaum, M. S., Wei, T. C., & Atlas, S. W. (2001). Regional and global changes in cerebral diffusion with normal aging. *American Journal of Neuroradiology, 22*(1), 136–142.

Nuttin, J. M. J. (1996). *The illusion of attitude change: Towards a response contagion theory of persuasion.* New York, NY: Cornell University Press.

Nwokah, E. E., Hsu, H., Dobrowolska, O., & Fogel, A. (1994). The development of laughter in mother-infant communication: Timing parameters and temporal sequences. *Infant Behavior and Development, 17*(1), 23–35.

Nyberg, L., Petersson, K. M., Nilsson, L. G., Sandblom, J., Aberg, C., & Ingvar, M. (2001). Reactivation of motor brain areas during explicit memory for actions. *NeuroImage, 14*(2), 521–528.

Oatley, K. (1992). Integrative action of narrative. In D. J. Stein & J. E. Young (Eds.), *Cognitive science and clinical disorders* (pp. 151–172). New York, NY: Academic Press.

Oberheim, N. A., Wang, X., Goldman, S., & Nedergaard, M. (2006). Astrocytic complexity distinguishes the human brain. *Trends in Neurosciences, 29*(10), 547–553.

Ochs, E., & Capps, L. (2001). *Living narrative: Creating lives in everyday storytelling.* Cambridge, MA: Harvard University Press.

Ochsner, K. N., Ray, R. D., Cooper, J. C., Robertson, E. R., Chopra, S., Gabrieli, J. D., & Gross, J. J. (2004). For better or for worse: Neural systems supporting the cognitive down- and up-regulation of negative emotion. *NeuroImage, 23*(2), 483–499.

O'Connell, J. F., Hawkes, K., & Blurton Jones, N. G. (1999). Grandmothering and the evolution of homo erectus. *Journal of Human Evolution, 36*(5), 461–485.

O'Connell, W. E. (1960). The adaptive functions of wit and humor. *Journal of Abnormal and Social Psychology, 61*, 263–270.

O'Doherty, J. P. (2004). Reward representations and reward-related learning in the human brain: Insights from neuroimaging. *Current Opinion in Neurobiology, 14*(6), 769–776.

O'Doherty, J. P., Deichmann, R., Critchley, H. D., & Dolan, R. J. (2002). Neural responses during anticipation of a primary taste reward. *Neuron, 33*(5), 815–826.

O'Doherty, J. P., Kringelbach, M. L., Rolls, E. T., Hornak, J., & Andrews, C. (2001). Abstract reward and punishment representations in the human orbitofrontal cortex. *Nature Neuroscience, 4*(1), 95–102.

O'Donnell, D., Larocque, S., Seckl, J. R., & Meaney, M. J. (1994). Postnatal handling alters glucocorticoid, but not mineralocorticoid messenger RNA expression in the hippocampus of adult rats. *Molecular Brain Research, 26*(1–2), 242–248.

Ohman, A., Carlsson, K., Lundqvist, D., & Ingvar, M. (2007). On the unconscious subcortical origin of human fear. *Physiology & Behavior, 92*(1–2), 180–185.

Ohnishi, T., Moriguchi, Y., Matsuda, H., Mori, T., Hirakata, M., Imabayashi, E., . . . Uno, A. (2004). The neural network for the mirror system and mentalizing in normally developed children: An fMRI study. *NeuroReport, 15*(9), 1483–1487.

O'Kane, G., Insler, R. Z., & Wagner, A. D. (2005). Conceptual and perceptual novelty effects in human medial temporal cortex. *Hippocampus, 15*(3), 326–332.

O'Keefe, J., & Nadel, L. (1978). *The hippocampus as a cognitive map.* New York, NY: Oxford University Press.

Olausson, H., Lamarre, Y., Backlund, H., Morin, C., Wallin, B. G., Starck, G., . . . Bushnell, M. C. (2002). Unmyelinated tactile afferents signal touch and project to insular cortex. *Nature Neuroscience, 5*(9), 900–904.

Oliff, H. S., Berchtold, N. C., Isackson, P., & Cotman, C. W. (1998). Exercise-induced regulation of brain-derived neurotrophic factor (BDNF) transcripts in the rat hippocampus. *Molecular Brain Research, 61*(1–2), 147–153.

Olsson, A., Ebert, J. P., Banaji, M. R., & Phelps, E. A. (2005). The role of social groups in the persistence of learned fear. *Science, 309*(5735), 785–787.

Olweus, D. (1991). Bully/victim problems among schoolchildren: Basic facts and effects of a school-based intervention program. In D. Pepler & K. Rubin (Eds.), *Development and treatment of childhood aggression* (pp. 411–448). Hillsdale, NJ: Erlbaum.

O'Neil, R., Welsh, M., Parke, R. D., Wang, S., & Strand, C. (1997). A longitudinal assessment of the academic correlates of early peer acceptance and rejection. *Journal of Clinical Child Psychology, 26*(3), 290–303.

Ongur, D., & Price, J. L. (2000). The organization of networks within the orbital and medial prefrontal cortex of rats, monkeys and humans. *Cerebral Cortex, 10*(3), 206–219.

Ono, T., Nishijo, H., & Uwano, T. (1995). Amygdala role in conditioned associative learning. *Progress in Neurobiology, 46*(4), 401–422.

Onozawa, K., Glover, V., Adams, D., Modi, N., & Kumar, R. C. (2001). Infant massage improves mother–infant interaction for mothers with postnatal depression. *Journal of Affective Disorders, 63*(1–3), 201–207.

Onyango, P. O., Gesquiere, L. R., Wango, E. O., Alberts, S. C., & Altmann, J. (2008). Persistence of maternal effects in baboons: Mother's dominance rank at son's conception predicts stress hormone levels in subadult males. *Hormones and Behavior, 54*(2), 319–324.

Orban, G. A., Sunaert, S., Todd, J. T., Van Hecke, P., & Marchal, G. (1999). Human cortical regions involved in extracting depth from motion. *Neuron, 24*(4), 929–940.

Orpinas, P., Horne, A. M., & Staniszewski, D. (2003). School bullying: Changing the problem by changing the school. *School Psychology Review, 32*(3), 431–444.

Orr, G., Rao, G., Houston, F. P., McNaughton, B. L., & Barnes, C. A. (2001). Hippocampal synaptic plasticity is modulated by theta rhythm in the fascia dentata of adult and aged freely behaving rats. *Hippocampus, 11*(6), 647–654.

O'Sullivan, M., Jones, D. K., Summers, P. E., Morris, R. G., Williams, S. C., & Markus, H. S. (2001). Evidence for cortical "disconnection" as a mechanism of age-related cognitive decline. *Neurology, 57*(4), 632–638.

Ottenbacher, K. J., Muller, L., Brandt, D., Heintzelman, A., Hojem, P., & Sharpe, P. (1987). The effectiveness of tactile stimulation as a form of early intervention: A quantitative evaluation. *Journal of Developmental and Behavioral Pediatrics, 8*(2), 68–76.

Overholser, J. C. (1992). Sense of humor when coping with life stress. *Personality and Individual Differences, 13*(7), 799–804.

Ovtscharoff, W., Jr., & Braun, K. (2001). Maternal separation and social isolation modulate the postnatal development of synaptic composition in the infralimbic cortex of octodon degus. *Neuroscience, 104*(1), 33–40.

Pagnoni, G., Zink, C. F., Montague, P. R., & Berns, G. S. (2002). Activity in human ventral striatum locked to errors of reward prediction. *Nature Neuroscience, 5*(2), 97–98.

Pakkenberg, B., & Gundersen, H. J. (1997). Neocortical neuron number in humans: Effect of sex and age. *Journal of Comparative Neurology, 384*(2), 312–320.

Palmer, P. (1998). *The courage to teach: Exploring the inner landscape of a teacher's life.* San Francisco: Jossey-Bass.

Panksepp, J. (1998). *Affective neuroscience: The foundation of human and animal emotions.* New York, NY: Oxford University Press.

Panksepp, J. (2007a). Can play diminish ADHD and facilitate the construction of the social brain? *Journal of the Canadian Academy of Child and Adolescent Psychiatry, 16*(2), 57–66.

Panksepp, J. (2007b). Neuroevolutionary sources of laughter and social joy: Modeling primal human laughter in laboratory rats. *Behavioural Brain Research, 182*(2), 231–244.

Panksepp, J., & Beatty, W. W. (1980). Social deprivation and play in rats. *Behavioral and Neural Biology, 30*(2), 197–206.

Panksepp, J., Herman, B. H., Vilberg, T., Bishop, P., & DeEskinazi, F. G. (1980). Endogenous opioids and social behavior. *Neuroscience and Biobehavioral Reviews, 4*(4), 473–487.

Panksepp, J., Najam, N., & Soares, F. (1979). Morphine reduces social cohesion in rats. *Pharmacology, Biochemistry, and Behavior, 11*(2), 131–134.

Pariente, J., White, P., Frackowiak, R. S. J., & Lewith, G. (2005). Expectancy and belief modulate the neuronal substrates of pain treated by acupuncture. *NeuroImage, 25*(4), 1161–1167.

Park, C. R., Campbell, A. M., Woodson, J. C., Smith, T. P., Fleshner, M., & Diamond, D. M. (2006). Permissive influence of stress in the expression of a U-shaped relationship between serum corticosterone levels and spatial memory errors in rats. *Dose-Response, 4*(1), 55–74.

Park, C. R., Zoladz, P. R., Conrad, C. D., Fleshner, M., & Diamond, D. M. (2008). Acute predator stress impairs the consolidation and retrieval of hippocampus-dependent memory in male and female rats. *Learning & Memory,* *15*(4), 271–280.

Park, D. C., Welsh, R. C., Marshuetz, C., Gutchess, A. H., Mikels, J., Polk, T. A., . . . Taylor, S. F. (2003). Working memory for complex scenes: Age differences in frontal and hippocampal activations. *Journal of Cognitive Neuroscience, 15*(8), 1122–1134.

Parkhurst, J. T., & Asher, S. R. (1992). Peer rejection in middle school: Subgroup differences in behavior, loneliness, and interpersonal concerns. *Developmental Psychology, 28*(2), 231–241.

Parkin, A. J. (1997). Human memory: Novelty, association and the brain. *Current Biology, 7*(12), R768–R769.

Parrott, W. G., & Gleitman, H. (1989). Infants' expectations in play: The joy of peek-a-boo. *Cognition & Emotion, 3*(4), 291–311.

Parsons, C. G., Stoffler, A., & Danysz, W. (2007). Memantine: An NMDA receptor antagonist that improves memory by restoration of homeostasis in the glutamatergic system—too little activation is bad, too much is even worse. *Neuropharmacology, 53*(6), 699–723.

Parsons, L. M., Fox, P. T., Downs, J. H., Glass, T., Hirsch, T. B., Martin, C. C., . . . Lancaster, J. L. (1995). Use of implicit motor imagery for visual shape discrimination as revealed by PET. *Nature, 375*(6526), 54–58.

Pascual-Leone, A., Wassermann, E. M., Grafman, J., & Hallett, M. (1996). The role of the dorsolateral prefrontal cortex in implicit procedural learning. Experimental Brain Research, 107(3), 479–485.

Paskind, H. A. (1932). Effects of laughter on muscle tone. *Archives of Neurological Psychiatry, 28*, 623–628.

Pasupathi, M., & Staudinger, U. M. (2001). Do advanced moral reasoners also show wisdom? Linking moral reasoning and wisdom-rleated knowledge and judgment. *International Journal of Behavioral Development, 25*(5), 401–415.

Patchin, J. W., & Hinduja, S. (2006). Bullies move beyond the schoolyard: A preliminary look at cyberbullying. *Youth Violence and Juvenile Justice, 4*(2), 148–169.

Patterson, C. J., Vaden, N. A., & Kupersmidt, J. B. (1991). Family background, recent life events and peer rejection during childhood. *Journal of Social and Personal Relationships, 8*(3), 347–361.

Paulhus, D. L., Wehr, P., Harms, P. D., & Strasser, D. I. (2002). Use of exemplar surveys to reveal implicit types of intelligence. *Personality and Social Psychology Bulletin, 28*(8), 1051–1062.

Paulson, J. F., Buermeyer, C., & Nelson-Gray, R. O. (2005). Social rejection and ADHD in young adults: An analogue experiment. *Journal of Attention Disorders, 8*(3), 127–135.

Paus, T., Zijdenbos, A., Worsley, K., Collins, D. L., Blumenthal, J., Giedd, J. N., . . . Evans, A. C. (1999). Structural maturation of neural pathways in children and adolescents: In vivo study. *Science, 283*(5409), 1908–1911.

Pavlides, C., Watanabe, Y., Magarinos, A. M., & McEwen, B. S. (1995). Opposing roles of type I and type II adrenal steroid receptors in hippocampal long-term potentiation. *Neuroscience, 68*(2), 387–394.

Payne, B. K. (2001). Prejudice and perception: The role of automatic and controlled processes in misperceiving a weapon. *Journal of Personality and Social Psychology, 81*(2), 181–192.

Pearce, J. M. (2004). Some neurological aspects of laughter. European Neurology, 52(3), 169–171.

Peers, P. V., Ludwig, C. J., Rorden, C., Cusack, R., Bonfiglioli, C., Bundesen, C., . . . Duncan, J. (2005). Attentional functions of parietal and frontal cortex. *Cerebral Cortex, 15*(10), 1469–1484.

Peigneux, P., Laureys, S., Delbeuck, X., & Maquet, P. (2001). Sleeping brain, learning brain. the role of sleep for memory systems. *NeuroReport, 12*(18), A111–A124.

Pellegrini, A. D. (2002). Bullying, victimization, and sexual harassment during the transition to middle school. *Educational Psychologist, 37*(3), 151–163.

Pellegrini, A. D. (2003). Perceptions and functions of play and real fighting in early adolescence. *Child Development, 74*(5), 1522–1533.

Pellegrini, A. D., & Bartini, M. (2001). Dominance in early adolescent boys: Affiliative and aggressive dimensions and possible functions. *Merrill-Palmer Quarterly, 47*(1), 142–163.

Pellegrini, A. D., Dupuis, D., & Smith, P. K. (2007). Play in evolution and development. *Developmental Review, 27*(2), 261–276.

Pellis, S. M. (1993). Sex and the evolution of play fighting: A review and model based on the behavior of muriod rodents. *Journal of Play Therapy and Research, 1,* 55–75.

Pellis, S. M., Hastings, E., Shimizu, T., Kamitakahara, H., Komorowska, J., Forgie, M. L., & Kolb, B. (2006). The effects of orbital frontal cortex damage on the modulation of defensive responses by rats in playful and nonplayful social contexts. *Behavioral Neuroscience, 120*(1), 72–84.

Pellis, S. M., & Iwaniuk, A. N. (1999). The problem of adult play fighting: A comparative analysis of play and courtship in primates. *Ethology, 105*(9), 783–806.

Pellis, S. M., & Iwaniuk, A. N. (2000). Comparative analyses of the role of postnatal development on the expression of play fighting. *Developmental Psychobiology, 36*(2), 136–147.

Pellis, S. M., & Iwaniuk, A. N. (2002). Brain system size and adult–adult play in primates: A comparative analysis of the roles of the non-visual neocortex and the amygdala. *Behavioural Brain Research, 134*(1–2), 31–39.

Pellis, S. M., & Pellis, V. C. (1991). Role reversal changes during the ontogeny of play fighting in male rats: Attack vs. defense. *Aggressive Behavior, 17*(3), 179–189.

Pelphrey, K. A., Mitchell, T. V., McKeown, M. J., Goldstein, J., Allison, T., & McCarthy, G. (2003). Brain activity evoked by the perception of human walking: Controlling for meaningful coherent motion. *Journal of Neuroscience, 23*(17), 6819–6825.

Pencea, V., Bingaman, K. D., Wiegand, S. J., & Luskin, M. B. (2001). Infusion of brain-derived neurotrophic factor into the lateral ventricle of the adult rat leads to new neurons in the parenchyma of the striatum, septum, thalamus, and hypothalamus. *Journal of Neuroscience, 21*(17), 6706–6717.

Penman, R., Meares, R., Baker, K., & Milgrom-Friedman, J. (1983). Synchrony in mother-infant interaction: A possible neurophysiological base. *British Journal of Medical Psychology, 56*(1), 1–7.

Pennebaker, J. W. (1997). Writing about emotional experiences as a therapeutic process. *Psychological Science, 8*(3), 162–166.

Pennebaker, J. W., & Beall, S. K. (1986). Confronting a traumatic event: Toward an understanding of inhibition and disease. *Journal of Abnormal Psychology, 95*(3), 274–281.

Pennebaker, J. W., Kiecolt-Glaser, J. K., & Glaser, R. (1988). Disclosure of traumas and immune function: Health implications for psychotherapy. *Journal of Consulting and Clinical Psychology, 56*(2), 239–245.

Pepler, D. J., Craig, W. M., Connolly, J. A., Yuile, A., McMaster, L., & Jiang, D. (2006). A developmental perspective on bullying. *Aggressive Behavior, 32*(4), 376–384.

Pereira, M. E. (1995). Development and social dominance among group-living primates. *American Journal of Primatology, 37*(2), 143–175.

Perez-Chada, D., Perez-Lloret, S., Videla, A. J., Cardinali, D., Bergna, M. A., Fernandez-Acquier, M., . . . Drake, C. (2007). Sleep-disordered breathing and daytime sleepiness are associated with poor academic performance in teenagers. a study using the pediatric daytime sleepiness scale (PDSS). *Sleep, 30*(12), 1698–1703.

Perez-Gonzalez, D., Malmierca, M. S., & Covey, E. (2005). Novelty detector neurons in the mammalian auditory midbrain. *European Journal of Neuroscience, 22*(11), 2879–2885.

Pérez-Jaranay, J. M., & Vives, F. (1991). Electrophysiological study of the response of medial prefrontal cortex neurons to stimulation of the basolateral nucleus of the amygdala in the rat. *Brain Research, 564*(1), 97–101.

Perrot-Sinal, T., Ossenkopp, K. P., & Kavaliers, M. (2000). Influence of a natural stressor (predator odor) on locomotor activity in the meadow vole (Microtus pennsylvanicus): Modulation by sex, reproductive condition and gonadal hormones. *Psychoneuroendocrinology, 25*(3), 259–276.

Perry, D. G., Kusel, S. J., & Perry, L. C. (1988). Victims of peer aggression. *Developmental Psychology, 24*(6), 807–814.

Peters, Y. M., & O'Donnell, P. (2005). Social isolation rearing affects prefrontal cortical response to ventral tegmental area stimulation. *Biological Psychiatry, 57*(10), 1205–1208.

Petitto, L. A., Zatorre, R. J., Gauna, K., Nikelski, E. J., Dostie, D., & Evans, A. C. (2000). Speech-like cerebral activity in profoundly deaf people processing sign languages: Implications for the neural basis of human language. *Proceedings of the National Academy of Sciences of the United States of America, 97*(25), 13961–13966.

Petrella, J. R., Townsend, B. A., Jha, A. P., Ziajko, L. A., Slavin, M. J., Lustig, C., . . . Doraiswamy, P. M. (2005). Increasing memory load modulates regional brain activity in older adults as measured by fMRI. *Journal of Neuropsychiatry and Clinical Neurosciences, 17*(1), 75–83.

Petrides, M. (2007). The orbitofrontal cortex: Novelty, deviation from expectation, and memory. *Annals of the New York Academy of Sciences, 1121,* 33–53.

Petrides, M., Alivisatos, B., & Frey, S. (2002). Differential activation of the human orbital, mid-ventrolateral, and mid-dorsolateral prefrontal cortex during the processing of visual stimuli. *Proceedings of the National Academy of Sciences of the United States of America, 99*(8), 5649–5654.

Petrie, K. J., Booth, R. J., & Pennebaker, J. W. (1998). The immunological effects of thought suppression. *Journal of Personality and Social Psychology, 75*(5), 1264–1272.

Petrie, K. J., Booth, R. J., Pennebaker, J. W., Davison, K. P., & Thomas, M. G. (1995). Disclosure of trauma and immune response to a hepatitis B vaccination program. *Journal of Consulting and Clinical Psychology, 63*(5), 787–792.

Petrovic, P., Dietrich, T., Fransson, P., Andersson, J., Carlsson, K., & Ingvar, M. (2005). Placebo in emotional processing—induced expectations of anxiety relief activate a generalized modulatory network. *Neuron, 46*(6), 957–969.

Pettit, G. S., Bakshi, A., Dodge, K. A., & Coie, J. D. (1990). The emergence of social dominance in young boys' play groups: Developmental differences and behavior correlates. *Developmental Psychology, 26*(6), 1017–1025.

Pezdek, K., & Miceli, L. (1982). Life-span differences in memory integration as a function of processing time. *Developmental Psychology, 18*(3), 485–490.

Pfefferbaum, A., Adalsteinsson, E., & Sullivan, E. V. (2005). Frontal circuitry degradation marks healthy adult aging: Evidence from diffusion tensor imaging. *NeuroImage, 26*(3), 891–899.

Pfefferbaum, A., Mathalon, D. H., Sullivan, E. V., Rawles, J. M., Zipursky, R. B., & Lim, K. O. (1994). A quantitative magnetic resonance imaging study of changes in brain morphology from infancy to late adulthood. *Archives of Neurology, 51*(9), 874–887.

Pfefferbaum, A., Sullivan, E. V., Hedehus, M., Lim, K. O., Adalsteinsson, E., & Moseley, M. (2000). Age-related decline in brain white matter anisotropy measured with spatially corrected echo-planar diffusion tensor imaging. *Magnetic Resonance in Medicine, 44*(2), 259–268.

Pfeifer, D. L. (1992). *Humor and aging: A comparison between a younger and older group.* (Doctoral dissertation). Retrieved from Dissertation Abstracts.

Pfrieger, F. W., & Barres, B. A. (1996). New views on synapse-glia interactions. *Current Opinion in Neurobiology, 6*(5), 615–621.

Pham, K., Nacher, J., Hof, P. R., & McEwen, B. S. (2003). Repeated restraint stress suppresses neurogenesis and induces biphasic PSA-NCAM expression in the adult rat dentate gyrus. *European Journal of Neuroscience, 17*(4), 879–886.

Pham, T. M., Soderstrom, S., Henriksson, B. G., & Mohammed, A. H. (1997). Effects of neonatal stimulation on later cognitive function and hippocampal nerve growth factor. *Behavioural Brain Research, 86*(1), 113–120.

Phelps, E. A. (2006). Emotion and cognition: Insights from studies of the human amygdala. *Annual Review of Psychology, 57,* 27–53.

Phelps, E. A., & Anderson, A. K. (1997). Emotional memory: What does the amygdala do? *Current Biology, 7*(5), R311–R314.

Phelps, E. A., Delgado, M. R., Nearing, K. I., & LeDoux, J. E. (2004). Extinction learning in humans: Role of the amygdala and vmPFC. *Neuron, 43*(6), 897–905.

Phelps, E. A., O'Connor, K. J., Cunningham, W. A., Funayama, E. S., Gatenby, J. C., Gore, J. C., & Banaji, M. R. (2000). Performance on indirect measures of race evaluation predicts amygdala activation. *Journal of Cognitive Neuroscience, 12*(5), 729–738.

Phelps, E. A., O'Connor, K. J., Gatenby, J. C., Gore, J. C., Grillon, C., & Davis, M. (2001). Activation of the left amygdala to a cognitive representation of fear. *Nature Neuroscience, 4*(4), 437–441.

Phelps, E. A., & Thomas, L. A. (2003). Race, behavior, and the brain: The role of neuroimaging in understanding complex social behaviors. *Political Psychology, 24*(4), 747–758.

Phillips, D. P., Ruth, T. E., & Wagner, L. M. (1993). Psychology and survival. *Lancet, 342*(8880), 1142–1145.

Pierce, C. M. B., & Molloy, G. N. (1990). Psychological and biographical differences between secondary school teachers experiencing high and low levels of burnout. *British Journal of Educational Psychology, 60*(1), 37–51.

Pihlajamaki, M., Tanila, H., Hanninen, T., Kononen, M., Mikkonen, M., Jalkanen, V., . . . Soininen, H. (2003). Encoding of novel picture pairs activates the perirhinal cortex: An fMRI study. *Hippocampus, 13*(1), 67–80.

Pihlajamaki, M., Tanila, H., Kononen, M., Hanninen, T., Hamalainen, A., Soininen, H., & Aronen, H. J. (2004). Visual presentation of novel objects and new spatial arrangements of objects differentially activates the medial temporal lobe subareas in humans. *European Journal of Neuroscience, 19*(7), 1939–1949.

Pines, A. M. (2003). Teacher burnout: A psychodynamic existential perspective. *Educational Administration Abstracts, 38*(2), 121–140.

Platek, S. M., Critton, S. R., Myers, T. E., & Gallup, G. G. (2003). Contagious yawning: The role of self-awareness and mental state attribution. *Cognitive Brain Research, 17*(2), 223–227.

Ploj, K., Roman, E., Bergstrom, L., & Nylander, I. (2001). Effects of neonatal handling on nociceptin/orphanin FQ and opioid peptide levels in female rats. *Pharmacology, Biochemistry, and Behavior, 69*(1–2), 173–179.

Plotsky, P. M., & Meaney, M. J. (1993). Early, postnatal experience alters hypothalamic corticotropin-releasing factor (CRF) mRNA, median eminence CRF content and stress-induced release in adult rats. *Molecular Brain Research, 18*(3), 195–200.

Pohorecky, L. A., Skiandos, A., Zhang, X., Rice, K. C., & Benjamin, D. (1999). Effect of chronic social stress on delta-opioid receptor function in the rat. *Journal of Pharmacology and Experimental Therapeutics, 290*(1), 196–206.

Poirier, F. E., & Smith, E. O. (1974). Socializing functions of primate play. *American Zoologist, 14*(1), 275–287.

Polley, D. B., Chen-Bee, C. H., & Frostig, R. D. (1999). Two directions of plasticity in the sensory-deprived adult cortex. *Neuron, 24*(3), 623–637.

Popescu, A. T., Saghyan, A. A., & Pare, D. (2007). NMDA-dependent facilitation of corticostriatal plasticity by the amygdala. *Proceedings of the National Academy of Sciences of the United States of America, 104*(1), 341–346.

Porges, S. W., Doussard-Roosevelt, J. A., & Maiti, A. K. (1994). Vagal tone and the physiological regulation of emotion. *Monographs of the Society for Research in Child Development, 59*(2–3), 167–186.

Porges, S. W., Doussard-Roosevelt, J. A., Portales, A. L., & Greenspan, S. I. (1996). Infant regulation of the vagal "brake" predicts child behavior problems: A psychobiological model of social behavior. *Developmental Psychobiology, 29*(8), 697–712.

Posner, M. I. (1988). Structures and function of selective attention. In T. Boll & B. K. Bryant (Eds.), *Clinical neuropsychology and brain function: Research, measurement, and practice, the master lecture series* (pp. 173–202). Washington, DC: American Psychological Association.

Post, R. M., & Weiss, S. R. (1997). Emergent properties of neural systems: How focal molecular neurobiological alterations can affect behavior. *Development and Psychopathology, 9*(4), 907–929.

Price, J. L., Carmichael, S. T., & Drevets, W. C. (1996). Networks related to the orbital and medial prefrontal cortex: A substrate for emotional behavior? *Progress in Brain Research, 107*, 523–536.

Prickaerts, J., Koopmans, G., Blokland, A., & Scheepens, A. (2004). Learning and adult neurogenesis: Survival with or without proliferation? *Neurobiology of Learning and Memory, 81*(1), 1–11.

Provine, R. R. (1992). Contagious laughter: Laughter is a sufficient stimulus for laughs and smiles. *Bulletin of the Psychonometric Society, 30*(1), 1–4.

Provine, R. R. (2010). Laughter punctuates speech: Linguistic, social and gender contexts of laughter. *Ethology, 95*(4), 291–298.

Pruessner, J. C., Baldwin, M. W., Dedovic, K., Renwick, R., Mahani, N. K., Lord, C., . . . Lupien, S. (2005). Self-esteem, locus of control, hippocampal volume, and cortisol regulation in young and old adulthood. *NeuroImage, 28*(4), 815–826.

Purves, D., & Lichtman, J. W. (1980). Elimination of synapses in the developing nervous system. *Science, 210*(4466), 153–157.

Purves, D., & Voyvodic, J. T. (1987). Imaging mammalian nerve cells and their connections over time in living animals. *Trends in Neurosciences, 10*(10), 398–404.

Puts, D. A., Gaulin, S. J. C., & Verdolini, K. (2006). Dominance and the evolution of sexual dimorphism in human voice pitch. *Evolution and Human Behavior, 27*(4), 283–296.

Quartz, K., & TEP Research Group (2003). Too angry to leave: Supporting new teachers' commitment to transform urban schools. *Journal of Teacher Education, 54*(2), 99–111.

Quine, L. (1999). Workplace bullying in NHS community trust: Staff questionnaire survey. *British Medical Journal, 318*(7178), 228–232.

Quine, L. (2001). Workplace bullying in nurses. *Journal of Health Psychology, 6*(1), 73–84.

Quine, L. (2002). Workplace bullying in junior doctors: Questionnaire survey. *British Medical Journal, 324*(7342), 878–879.

Quirk, G. J., & Beer, J. S. (2006). Prefrontal involvement in the regulation of emotion: Convergence of rat and human studies. *Current Opinion in Neurobiology, 16*(6), 723–727.

Quirk, G. J., Likhtik, E., Pelletier, J. G., & Pare, D. (2003). Stimulation of medial prefrontal cortex decreases the responsiveness of central amygdala output neurons. *Journal of Neuroscience, 23*(25), 8800–8807.

Quirk, G. J., & Mueller, D. (2008). Neural mechanisms of extinction learning and retrieval. *Neuropsychopharmacology, 33*(1), 56–72.

Radecki, D. T., Brown, L. M., Martinez, J., & Teyler, T. J. (2005). BDNF protects against stress-induced impairments in spatial learning and memory and LTP. *Hippocampus, 15*(2), 246–253.

Rainnie, D. G., Bergeron, R., Sajdyk, T. J., Patil, M., Gehlert, D. R., & Shekhar, A. (2004). Corticotrophin releasing factor-induced synaptic plasticity in the amygdala translates stress into emotional disorders. *Journal of Neuroscience, 24*(14), 3471–3479.

Rajapakse, J. C., Giedd, J. N., Rumsey, J. M., Vaituzis, A. C., Hamburger, S. D., & Rapoport, J. L. (1996). Regional MRI measurements of the corpus callosum: A methodological and developmental study. *Brain & Development, 18*(5), 379–388.

Ramachandran, V. S., Rogers-Ramachandran, D., & Stewart, M. (1992). Perceptual correlates of massive cortical reorganization. *Science, 258*(5085), 1159–1160.

Rampersaud, G. C., Pereira, M. A., Girard, B. L., Adams, J., & Metzl, J. D. (2005). Breakfast habits, nutritional status, body weight, and academic performance in children and adolescents. *Journal of the American Dietetic Association, 105*(5), 743–760.

Rampon, C., Jiang, C. H., Dong, H., Tang, Y. P., Lockhart, D. J., Schultz, P. G., . . . Hu, Y. (2000). Effects of environmental enrichment on gene expression in the brain. *Proceedings of the National Academy of Sciences of the United States of America, 97*(23), 12880–12884.

Ranganath, C., & Rainer, G. (2003). Neural mechanisms for detecting and remembering novel events. *Nature Reviews Neuroscience, 4*(3), 193–202.

Rao, V. R., & Finkbeiner, S. (2007). NMDA and AMPA receptors: Old channels, new tricks. *Trends in Neurosciences, 30*(6), 284–291.

Rau, V., & Fanselow, M. S. (2007). Neurobiological and neuroethological perspectives on fear and anxiety. In L. J. Kirmayer, R. Lemelson, & M. Barad (Eds.), *Understanding trauma: Integrating biological, clinical, and cultural perspectives* (pp. 27–40). New York, NY: Cambridge University Press.

Ray, J. C., & Sapolsky, R. M. (1992). Styles of male social behavior and their endocrine correlates among high-ranking wild baboons. *American Journal of Primatology, 28*(4), 231–250.

Raywind, M. A. (1994). Alternative schools: The state of the art. *Educational Leadership, 52*(1), 26–31.

Raz, N., Gunning, F. M., Head, D., Dupuis, J. H., McQuain, J., Briggs, S. D., . . . Acker, J. D. (1997). Selective aging of the human cerebral cortex observed in vivo: Differential vulnerability of the prefrontal gray matter. *Cerebral Cortex*, 7(3), 268–282.

Raz, N., Gunning-Dixon, F., Head, D., Williamson, A., & Acker, J. D. (2001). Age and sex differences in the cerebellum and the ventral pons: A prospective MR study of healthy adults. *American Journal of Neuroradiology*, 22(6), 1161–1167.

Raz, N., Rodrigue, K. M., Head, D., Kennedy, K. M., & Acker, J. D. (2004). Differential aging of the medial temporal lobe: A study of a 5-year change. *Neurology*, 62(3), 433–438.

Raz, N., Rodrigue, K. M., Kennedy, K. M., Head, D., Gunning-Dixon, F., & Acker, J. D. (2003). Differential aging of the human striatum: Longitudinal evidence. *American Journal of Neuroradiology*, 24(9), 1849–1856.

Rees, S. L., Steiner, M., & Fleming, A. S. (2006). Early deprivation, but not maternal separation, attenuates rise in corticosterone levels after exposure to a novel environment in both juvenile and adult female rats. *Behavioural Brain Research*, 175(2), 383–391.

Reeve, J. (2002). Self-determination theory applied to educational settings. In E. L. Deci & R. M. Ryan (Eds.), *The handbook of self-determination research* (pp. 183–203). Rochester, NY: University of Rochester Press.

Reeve, J., Bolt, E., & Cai, Y. (1999). Autonomy-supportive teachers: How they teach and motivate students. *Journal of Educational Psychology*, 91(3), 537–548.

Reid, D. K., Stoughton, E. H., & Smith, R. (2006). The humorous construction of disability: "Stand-up" comedians in the United States. *Disability & Society*, 21(6), 629–643.

Relyea, R. A. (2004). Synergistic impacts of malathion and predatory stress on six species of North American tadpoles. *Environmental Toxicology and Chemistry*, 23(4), 1080–1084.

Remington, R. (2002). Calming music and hand massage with agitated elderly. *Nursing Research*, 51(5), 317–323.

Resnick, S. M., Goldszal, A. F., Davatzikos, C., Golski, S., Kraut, M. A., Metter, E. J., . . . Zonderman, A. B. (2000). One-year age changes in MRI brain volumes in older adults. *Cerebral Cortex*, 10(5), 464–472.

Resnick, S. M., Pham, D. L., Kraut, M. A., Zonderman, A. B., & Davatzikos, C. (2003). Longitudinal magnetic resonance imaging studies of older adults: A shrinking brain. *Journal of Neuroscience*, 23(8), 3295–3301.

Ressler, K. J., Rothbaum, B. O., Tannenbaum, L., Anderson, P., Graap, K., Zimand, E., . . . Davis, M. (2004). Cognitive enhancers as adjuncts to psychotherapy: Use of D-cycloserine in phobic individuals to facilitate extinction of fear. *Archives of General Psychiatry*, 61(11), 1136–1144.

Rezai, K., Andreasen, N. C., Alliger, R., Cohen, G., Swayze, V., & O'Leary, D. S. (1993). The neuropsychology of the prefrontal cortex. *Archives of Neurology, 50*(6), 636–642.

Rhodes, J. S., van Praag, H., Jeffrey, S., Girard, I., Mitchell, G. S., Garland, T., Jr., & Gage, F. H. (2003). Exercise increases hippocampal neurogenesis to high levels but does not improve spatial learning in mice bred for increased voluntary wheel running. *Behavioral Neuroscience, 117*(5), 1006–1016.

Ribeiro, S., Gervasoni, D., Soares, E. S., Zhou, Y., Lin, S. C., Pantoja, J., . . . Nicolelis, M. A. (2004). Long-lasting novelty-induced neuronal reverberation during slow-wave sleep in multiple forebrain areas. *PLoS Biology, 2*(1), E24. doi:10.1371/journal.pbio.0020024

Rich, V. L., & Rich, A. R. (1987). Personality hardiness and burnout in female staff nurses. *Journal of Nursing Scholarship, 19*(2), 63–66.

Richards, M., & Deary, I. J. (2005). A life course approach to cognitive reserve: A model for cognitive aging and development? *Annals of Neurology, 58*(4), 617–622.

Richerson, P. J., & Boyd, R. (1998). The evolution of human ultra-sociality. In I. Eibl-Eibisfeldt & F. Salter (Eds.), *Indoctrinability, ideology, and warfare: Evolutionary perspectives* (pp. 71–96). New York, NY: Berghahn.

Richeson, J. A., Baird, A. A., Gordon, H. L., Heatherton, T. F., Wyland, C. L., Trawalter, S., & Shelton, J. N. (2003). An fMRI investigation of the impact of interracial contact on executive function. *Nature Neuroscience, 6*(12), 1323–1328.

Richeson, J. A., Trawalter, S., & Shelton, J. N. (2005). African Americans' implicit racial attitudes and the depletion of executive function after interracial interactions. *Social Cognition, 23*(4), 336–352.

Rigby, K. (1994). Psychosocial functioning in families of Australian adolescent schoolchildren involved in bully/victim problems. *Journal of Family Therapy, 16*(2), 173–187.

Rigby, K. (1997). What children tell us about bullying in schools. Children Australia, 22(2), 28–34.

Rigby, K. (2000). Effects of peer victimization in schools and perceived social support on adolescent well-being. *Journal of Adolescence, 23*(1), 57–68.

Rigby, K. (2003). Consequences of bullying in schools. Canadian Journal of Psychiatry, 48(9), 583–590.

Rilling, J., Gutman, D., Zeh, T., Pagnoni, G., Berns, G., & Kilts, C. (2002). A neural basis for social cooperation. *Neuron, 35*(2), 395–405.

Rivers, I. (2001). The bullying of sexual minorities at school: Its nature and long-term correlates. *Educational and Child Psychology, 18*, 32–46.

Rivers, I. (2004). Recollections of bullying at school and their long-term implications for lesbians, gay, men, and bisexuals. *Crisis, 25*(4), 1–7.

Rivers, J. J., & Josephs, R. A. (2010). Dominance and health. In A. Guinote & T. K. Vescio (Eds.), *The social psychology of power* (pp. 87–112). New York, NY: Guilford.

Rizzolatti, G., & Arbib, M. A. (1998). Language within our grasp. *Trends in Neurosciences, 21*(5), 188–194.

Rizzolatti, G., Fadiga, L., Fogassi, L., & Gallese, V. (1999). Resonance behaviors and mirror neurons. *Archives Italiennes de Biologie, 137*(2–3), 85–100.

Rizzolatti, G., Fadiga, L., Gallese, V., & Fogassi, L. (1996). Premotor cortex and the recognition of motor actions. *Cognitive Brain Research, 3*(2), 131–141.

Rizzolatti, G., & Sinigaglia, C. (2008). *Mirrors in the brain: How our minds share actions and emotions*. New York, NY: Oxford University Press.

Roberts, G. (1996). Why individual vigilance declines as group size increases. *Animal Behaviour, 51*, 1077–1086.

Rodseth, L., Wrangham, R. W., Harrigan, A. M., & Smuts, B. B. (1991). The human community as a primate society. *Current Anthropology, 32*(3), 221–254.

Rogers, R. G. (1987). Is bigger better? Fact or fad concerning school district organization. *Spectrum, 5*(4), 36–39.

Rollefson, M. (April, 1990). *Teacher turnover: Patterns of entry to and exit from teaching*. Paper presented at the annual meeting of the American Educational Research Association, Boston, MA.

Rolls, E. T., O'Doherty, J., Kringelbach, M. L., Francis, S., Bowtell, R., & McGlone, F. (2003). Representations of pleasant and painful touch in the human orbitofrontal and cingulate cortices. *Cerebral Cortex, 13*(3), 308–317.

Roozendaal, B. (2000). Glucocorticoids and the regulation of memory consolidation. *Psychoneuroendocrinology, 25*(3), 213–238.

Rose, M. R. (1991). Evolutionary biology of aging. New York, NY: Oxford University Press.

Rosebook, P. H., Nanda, S. A., Bakshi, V. P., Trentani, A., Newman, S. M., & Kalin, N. H. (2007). Predator threat induces behavioral inhibition, pituitary-adrenal activation and changes in amygdala CRF-binding protein gene expression. *Psychoneuroendocrinology, 32*, 44–55.

Rosen, J. B., Adamec, R. E., & Thompson, B. L. (2005). Expression of egr-1 (zif268) mRNA in select fear-related brain regions following exposure to a predator. *Behavioural Brain Research, 162*(2), 279–288.

Rosenberg, D. R., & Lewis, D. A. (1995). Postnatal maturation of the dopaminergic innervation of monkey prefrontal and motor cortices: A tyrosine hydroxylase immunohistochemical analysis. *Journal of Comparative Neurology, 358*(3), 383–400.

Rosenberg, L. (1991). A qualitative investigation of the use of humor by emergency personnel as a strategy for coping with stress. *Journal of Emergency Nursing, 17*(4), 197–202.

Rosenholtz, S. J. (1989). Workplace conditions that affect teacher quality and commitment: Implications for teacher induction programs. *Elementary School Journal, 89*(4), 421–439.

Rosenzweig, M. R. (2001). Learning and neural plasticity over the life span. In P. Gold & W. Greenough (Eds.), *Memory consolidation: Essays in honor of James L. McGaugh* (pp. 275–294). Washington, DC: American Psychological Association.

Rossi, E. L. (1993). *The psychobiology of mind-body healing : New concepts of therapeutic hypnosis.* New York, NY: W. W. Norton.

Rothbart, M. K., Taylor, S. B., & Tucker, D. M. (1989). Right-sided facial asymmetry in infant emotional expression. *Neuropsychologia, 27*(5), 675–687.

Rowe, J. W., & Kahn, R. L. (1997). Successful aging. *The Gerontologist, 37*(4), 433–440.

Rowe, R., Maughan, B., Worthman, C. M., Costello, E. J., & Angold, A. (2004). Testosterone, antisocial behavior, and social dominance in boys: Pubertal development and biosocial interaction. *Biological Psychiatry, 55*(5), 546–552.

Roy, W. (1974). *The effect of a group dynamic approach to student teaching on cohesiveness, dogmatism, pupil control ideology and perceived problems.* (Unpublished doctoral dissertation). University of Wisconsin, Milwaukee, WI.

Ruby, P., & Decety, J. (2001). Effect of subjective perspective taking during simulation of action: A PET investigation of agency. *Nature Neuroscience, 4*(5), 546–550.

Rudd, W. G. A., & Wiseman, S. (1962). Sources of dissatisfaction among a group of teachers. *British Journal of Educational Psychology, 32*(P3), 275–291.

Rushworth, M. F., Krams, M., & Passingham, R. E. (2001). The attentional role of the left parietal cortex: The distinct lateralization and localization of motor attention in the human brain. *Journal of Cognitive Neuroscience, 13*(5), 698–710.

Russell, D. W., & Cutrona, C. E. (1991). Social support, stress, and depressive symptoms among the elderly: Test of a process model. *Psychology and Aging, 6*(2), 190–201.

Rutishauser, U., Mamelak, A. N., & Schuman, E. M. (2006). Single-trial learning of novel stimuli by individual neurons of the human hippocampus-amygdala complex. *Neuron, 49*(6), 805–813.

Sachser, N., Durschlag, M., & Hirzel, D. (1998). Social relationships and the management of stress. *Psychoneuroendocrinology, 23*(8), 891–904.

Salat, D. H., Tuch, D. S., Greve, D. N., van der Kouwe, A. J., Hevelone, N. D., Zaleta, A. K., . . . Dale, A. M. (2005). Age-related alterations in white matter microstructure measured by diffusion tensor imaging. *Neurobiology of Aging, 26*(8), 1215–1227.

Salmivalli, C., Lagerspetz, K., Bjorkqvist, K., Osterman, K., & Kaukiainen, A. (1996). Bullying as a group process: Participant roles and their relations to social status within the group. *Aggressive Behavior, 22*(1), 1–15.

Samson, A. C., Hempelmann, C. F., Huber, O., & Zysset, S. (2009). Neural substrates of incongruity-resolution and nonsense humor. *Neuropsychologia, 47*(4), 1023–1033.

Sanchez, M. M., Aguado, F., Sanchez-Toscano, F., & Saphier, D. (1995). Effects of prolonged social isolation on responses of neurons in the bed nucleus of the stria terminalis, preoptic area, and hypothalamic paraventricular nucleus to stimulation of the medial amygdala. *Psychoneuroendocrinology, 20*(5), 525–541.

Sander, K., & Scheich, H. (2001). Auditory perception of laughing and crying activates human amygdala regardless of attentional state. *Cognitive Brain Research, 12*(2), 181–198.

Sander, K., & Scheich, H. (2005). Left auditory cortex and amygdala, but right insula dominance for human laughing and crying. *Journal of Cognitive Neuroscience, 17*(10), 1519–1531.

Sands, J., & Creel, S. (2004). Social dominance, aggression and faecal glucocorticoid levels in a wild population of wolves, *Canis lupus. Animal Behaviour, 67*(3), 387–396.

Sandstrom, M. J., & Coie, J. D. (1999). A developmental perspective on peer rejection: Mechanisms of stability and change. *Child Development, 70*(4), 955–966.

Santillan-Doherty, A. M., Cortes-Sotres, J., Arenas-Rosas, R. V., Marquez-Arias, A., Cruz, C., Medellin, A., . . . Diaz, J. L. (2010). Novelty-seeking temperament in captive stumptail macaques (*Macaca arctoides*) and spider monkeys (*Ateles geoffroyi*). *Journal of Comparative Psychology, 124*(2), 211–218.

Sapolsky, R. M. (1990). Stress in the wild. *Scientific American, 262*(1), 116–123.

Sapolsky, R. M. (2004). Mothering style and methylation. *Nature Neuroscience, 7*(8), 791–792.

Sapolsky, R. M. (2005). The influence of social hierarchy on primate health. *Science, 308*(5722), 648–652.

Sapolsky, R. M., Alberts, S. C., & Altmann, J. (1997). Hypercortisolism associated with social subordinance or social isolation among wild baboons. *Archives of General Psychiatry, 54*(12), 1137–1143.

Sapolsky, R. M., Uno, H., Rebert, C. S., & Finch, C. E. (1990). Hippocampal damage associated with prolonged glucocorticoid exposure in primates. *Journal of Neuroscience, 10*(9), 2897–2902.

Sarason, S. B. (1974). *The psychological sense of community: Perspectives for community psychology.* San Francisco: Jossey-Bass.

Sarrieau, A., Dussaillant, M., Sapolsky, R. M., Aitken, D. H., Olivier, A., Lal, S., . . . Meaney, M. J. (1988). Glucocorticoid binding sites in human temporal cortex. *Brain Research, 442*(1), 157–160.

Sauseng, P., Klimesch, W., Schabus, M., & Doppelmayr, M. (2005). Fronto-parietal EEG coherence in theta and upper alpha reflect central executive functions of working memory. *International Journal of Psychophysiology, 57*(2), 97–103.

Saxe, R. R., Whitfield-Gabrieli, S., Scholz, J., & Pelphrey, K. A. (2009). Brain regions for perceiving and reasoning about other people in school-aged children. *Child Development, 80*(4), 1197–1209.

Scarmeas, N., Zarahn, E., Anderson, K. E., Honig, L. S., Park, A., Hilton, J., . . . Stern, Y. (2004). Cognitive reserve-mediated modulation of positron emission tomographic activations during memory tasks in Alzheimer disease. *Archives of Neurology, 61*(1), 73–78.

Schaaf, M. J., De Kloet, E. R., & Vreugdenhil, E. (2000). Corticosterone effects on BDNF expression in the hippocampus. implications for memory formation. *Stress, 3*(3), 201–208.

Schacter, D. L. (1992). Priming and multiple memory systems: Perceptual mechanisms of implicit memory. *Journal of Cognitive Neuroscience, 4*(3), 244–256.

Schaefer, S. M., Jackson, D. C., Davidson, R. J., Aguirre, G. K., Kimberg, D. Y., & Thompson-Schill, S. L. (2002). Modulation of amygdalar activity by the conscious regulation of negative emotion. *Journal of Cognitive Neuroscience, 14*(6), 913–921.

Schaie, K. W., & Willis, S. L. (1986). Can decline in adult intellectual functioning be reversed? *Developmental Psychology, 22*(2), 223–232.

Schall, J. D. (2001). Neural basis of deciding, choosing and acting. *Nature Reviews Neuroscience, 2*(1), 33–42.

Schaller, M., Park, J. H., & Mueller, A. (2003). Fear of the dark: Interactive effects of beliefs about danger and ambient darkness on ethnic stereotypes. *Personality and Social Psychology Bulletin, 29*(5), 637–649.

Scheuerlein, A., Van't Hof, T. J., & Gwinner, E. (2001). Predators as stressors? Physiological and reproductive consequences of predation risk in tropical stonechats (*Saxicola torquata axillaris*). *Proceedings of the Royal Society B: Biological Sciences, 268*(1476), 1575–1582.

Schmader, T., & Lickel, B. (2006). The approach and avoidance function of guilt and shame emotions: Comparing reactions to self-caused and other-caused wrongdoing. *Motivation and Emotion, 30*(1), 42–55.

Schmand, B., Smit, J. H., Geerlings, M. I., & Lindeboom, J. (1997). The effects of intelligence and education on the development of dementia: A test of the brain reserve hypothesis. *Psychological Medicine, 27*(6), 1337–1344.

Schmidt, S., Nachtigall, C., Wuethrich-Martone, O., & Strauss, B. (2002). Attachment and coping with chronic disease. *Journal of Psychosomatic Research, 53*(3), 763–773.

Schmidt, S. R. (1994). Effects of humor on sentence memory. *Journal of Experimental Psychology: Learning, Memory, and Cognition, 20*(4), 953–967.

Schmidt, S. R., & Williams, A. R. (2001). Memory for humorous cartoons. *Memory & Cognition, 29*(2), 305–311.

Schmithorst, V. J., & Holland, S. K. (2004). The effect of musical training on the neural correlates of math processing: A functional magnetic resonance imaging study in humans. *Neuroscience Letters, 354*(3), 193–196.

Schnohr, C., & Niclasen, B. V. (2006). Bullying among Greenlandic schoolchildren: Development since 1994 and relations to health and health behaviour. *International Journal of Circumpolar Health, 65*(4), 305–312.

Schore, A. N. (1994). *Affect regulation and the origin of the self: The neurobiology of emotional development.* Hillsdale, NJ: Lawrence Erlbaum.

Schore, A. N. (2001). Minds in the making: Attachment, the self-organizing brain, and developmentally-oriented psychoanalytic psychotherapy. *British Journal of Psychotherapy, 17,* 299–328.

Schore, J., & Schore, A. (2008). Modern attachment theory: The central role of affect regulation in development and treatment. *Clinical Social Work Journal, 36*(1), 9–20.

Schrott, L. M. (1997). Effect of training and environment on brain morphology and behavior. *Acta Paediatrica Supplement, 422,* 45–47.

Schrott, L. M., Denenberg, V. H., Sherman, G. F., Waters, N. S., Rosen, G. D., & Galaburda, A. M. (1992). Environmental enrichment, neocortical ectopias, and behavior in the autoimmune NZB mouse. *Developmental Brain Research, 67*(1), 85–93.

Schultz, W. (1998). Predictive reward signal of dopamine neurons. *Journal of Neurophysiology, 80*(1), 1–27.

Schultz, W., Apicella, P., Scarnati, E., & Ljungberg, T. (1992). Neuronal activity in monkey ventral striatum related to the expectation of reward. *Journal of Neuroscience, 12*(12), 4595–4610.

Schultz, W., Dayan, P., & Montague, P. R. (1997). A neural substrate of prediction and reward. *Science, 275*(5306), 1593–1599.

Schunk, D. H. (1983). Ability versus effort attributional feedback: Differential effects on self-efficacy and achievement. *Journal of Educational Psychology, 75*(6), 848–856.

Schunk, D. H., & Cox, P. D. (1986). Strategy training and attributional feedback with learning disabled students. *Journal of Educational Psychology, 78*(3), 201–209.

Schunk, D. H., & Ertmer, P. A. (1999). Self-regulatory processes during computer skill acquisition: Goal and self-evaluative influences. *Journal of Educational Psychology, 91*(2), 251–260.

Schunk, D. H., & Hanson, A. R. (1985). Peer models: Influence on children's self-efficacy and achievement. *Journal of Educational Psychology, 77*(3), 313–322.

Schunk, D. H., Hanson, A. R., & Cox, P. D. (1987). Peer-model attributes and children's achievement behaviors. *Journal of Educational Psychology, 79*(1), 54–61.

Schunk, D. H., & Swartz, C. W. (1993). Goals and progress feedback: Effects on self-efficacy and writing achievement. *Contemporary Educational Psychology, 18*(3), 337–354.

Schuz, A. (1978). Some facts and hypotheses concerning dendritic spines and learning. In M. Braizer & H. Petsche (Eds.), *Architectonics of the cerebral cortex* (pp. 129–135). New York, NY: Raven.

Schwab, R. L., Jackson, S. E., & Schuler, R. S. (1986). Educator burnout: Sources and consequences. *Educational Research Quarterly, 10*(3), 14–30.

Schwartz, C., Meisenhelder, J. B., Ma, Y., & Reed, G. (2003). Altruistic social interest behaviors are associated with better mental health. *Psychosomatic Medicine, 65*(5), 778–785.

Schwarz, M., Blumberg, S., & Susswein, A. J. (1998). Social isolation blocks the expression of memory after training that a food is inedible in aplysia fasciata. *Behavioral Neuroscience, 112*(4), 942–951.

Schweinsburg, A. D., Nagel, B. J., & Tapert, S. F. (2005). fMRI reveals alteration of spatial working memory networks across adolescence. *Journal of the International Neuropsychological Society, 11*(5), 631–644.

Seeman, T. E. (1996). Social ties and health: The benefits of social integration. *Annals of Epidemiology, 6*(5), 442–451.

Segrin, C. (2003). Age moderates the relationship between social support and psychosocial problems. Human Communication Research, 29(3), 317–342.

Seitz, R. J., Nickel, J., & Azari, N. P. (2006). Functional modularity of the medial prefrontal cortex: Involvement in human empathy. *Neuropsychology, 20*(6), 743–751.

Semmer, N. (1996). Individual differences, work stress, and health. In M. J. Schabracqu, J. A. M. Winnubst, & C. L. Cooper (Eds.), *Handbook of work and health psychology* (pp. 51–86). Chichester, England: Wiley.

Sergent, J. (1986). Subcortical coordination of hemisphere activity in commissurotomized patients. *Brain, 109*(2), 357–369.

Sergent, J. (1990). Furtive incursions into bicameral minds: Integrative and coordinating role of subcortical structures. *Brain, 113*(2), 537–568.

Shabanov, P. D., Lebedev, A. A., & Nozdrachev, A. A. (2004). Social isolation syndrome in rats. *Proceedings of the Academy of Sciences of the USSR, 395,* 99–102.

Shammi, P., & Stuss, D. T. (1999). Humour appreciation: A role of the right frontal lobe. *Brain, 122*(4), 657–666.

Shapiro, A. K. (1960). Attitudes toward the use of placebos in treatment. *Journal of Nervous and Mental Disease, 130,* 200–211.

Shatz, C. J. (1990). Impulse activity and the patterning of connections during CNS development. *Neuron, 5*(6), 745–756.

Shavelson, R. J., & Bolus, R. (1982). Self concept: The interplay of theory and methods. *Journal of Educational Psychology, 74*(1), 3–17.

Shelton, J. N., Richeson, J. A., Salvatore, J., & Trawalter, S. (2005). Ironic effects of racial bias during interracial interactions. *Psychological Science, 16*(5), 397–402.

Sheriff, M. J., Krebs, C. J., & Boonstra, R. (2009). The sensitive hare: Sublethal effects of predator stress on reproduction in snowshoe hares. *Journal of Animal Ecology, 78*(6), 1249–1258.

Sherman, K. M. (1998). Healing with humor. *Seminars in Perioperative Nursing, 7*(2), 128–137.

Sherry, D. F., Jacobs, L. F., & Gaulin, S. J. (1992). Spatial memory and adaptive specialization of the hippocampus. *Trends in Neurosciences, 15*(8), 298–303.

Sherry, D. F., & Schacter, D. L. (1987). The evolution of multiple memory systems. *Psychological Review, 94*(4), 439–454.

Shields, A., & Cicchetti, D. (2001). Parental maltreatment and emotion dysregulation as risk factors for bullying and victimization in middle childhood. *Journal of Clinical Child Psychology, 30*(3), 349–363.

Shimada, S., & Hiraki, K. (2006). Infant's brain responses to live and televised action. *NeuroImage, 32*(2), 930–939.

Shin, L. M., Rauch, S. L., & Pitman, R. K. (2006). Amygdala, medial prefrontal cortex, and hippocampal function in PTSD. *Annals of the New York Academy of Sciences, 1071,* 67–79.

Shinskey, J. L., & Munakata, Y. (2010). Something old, something new: A developmental transition from familiarity to novelty preferences with hidden objects. *Developmental Science, 13*(2), 378–384.

Shmuelof, L., & Zohary, E. (2006). A mirror representation of others' actions in the human anterior parietal cortex. *Journal of Neuroscience, 26*(38), 9736–9742.

Shye, D., Mullooly, J. P., Freeborn, D. K., & Pope, C. R. (1995). Gender differences in the relationship between social network support and mortality: A longitudinal study of an elderly cohort. *Social Science & Medicine, 41*(7), 935–947.

Sidanius, J., Levin, S., Federico, C., & Pratto, F. (2001). Legitimizing Ideologies: The social dominance approach. In J. T. Jost & B. Major (Eds.), *The psychology of legitimacy: Emerging perspectives on ideology, justice, and intergroup relations* (pp. 307–331). New York, NY: Cambridge University Press.

Siegel, D. J. (2012a). *The developing mind: How relationships and the brain interact to shape who we are* (2nd ed.). New York, NY: Guilford.

Siegel, D. J. (2012b). *Pocket guide to interpersonal neurobiology*. New York, NY: Norton.

Sih, A., Bell, A. M., & Kerby, J. L. (2004). Two stressors are far deadlier than one. *Trends in Ecology & Evolution, 19*(6), 274–276.

Simpson, J. R., Drevets, W. C., Snyder, A. Z., Gusnard, D. A., & Raichle, M. E. (2001). Emotion-induced changes in human medial prefrontal cortex: II. During anticipatory anxiety. *Proceedings of the National Academy of Sciences of the United States of America, 98*(2), 688–693.

Singer, J. L., & Lythcott, M. A. (2002). Fostering school achievement and creativity through sociodramatic play in the classroom. *Research in the Schools, 9*(2), 43–52.

Singer, T., Seymour, B., O'Doherty, J., Kaube, H., Dolan, R. J., & Frith, C. D. (2004). Empathy for pain involves the affective but not sensory components of pain. *Science, 303*(5661), 1157–1162.

Sirevaag, A. M., & Greenough, W. T. (1988). A multivariate statistical summary of synaptic plasticity measures in rats exposed to complex, social and individual environments. *Brain Research, 441*(1–2), 386–392.

Siviy, S. M., & Harrison, K. A. (2008). Effects of neonatal handling on play behavior and fear towards a predator odor in juvenile rats (*Rattus norvegicus*). *Journal of Comparative Psychology, 122*(1), 1–8.

Skaalvik, E. M. (1997a). Issues in research on self-concept. In M. Maehr & P. Pintrich (Eds.), *Advances in motivation and achievement* (pp. 51–97). New York, NY: JAI Press.

Skaalvik, E. M. (1997b). Self-enhancing and self-defeating ego orientation: Relations with task and avoidance orientation, achievement, self-perceptions, and anxiety. *Journal of Educational Psychology, 89*(1), 71–81.

Skaalvik, E. M. (1998). *Self-enhancing and self-defeating ego-orientation: Relations with task and avoidance goals, achievement, and self perceptions.* Unpublished manuscript.

Skaalvik, E. M., & Hagtvet, K. A. (1990). Academic achievement and self-concept: An analysis of causal predominance in a developmental perspective. *Journal of Personality and Social Psychology, 58*(2), 292–307.

Skaalvik, E. M., & Rankin, R. J. (1995). A test of the Internal/External Frame of Reference Model at different levels of math and verbal self-perception. *American Educational Research Journal, 32*(1), 161–184.

Skaalvik, E. M., & Rankin, R. J. (1996). *Studies of academic self-concept using a Norwegian modification of the SDQ*. Unpublished manuscript.

Skaalvik, E. M., & Skaalvik, S. (2000). *Math and verbal achievement, motivation, anxiety, and study behavior: A study of relations in a developmental perspective*. Unpublished manuscript.

Skaalvik, E. M., & Vals, H. (1999). *Achievement and self-concept in mathematics and verbal arts: A study of relations*. Unpublished manuscript.

Skinner, E. A., Wellborn, J. G., & Connell, J. P. (1990). What it takes to do well in school and whether I've got it: A process model of perceived control and children's engagement and achievement in school. *Journal of Educational Psychology, 82*(1), 22–32.

Slaughter, V., Dennis, M. J., & Pritchard, M. (2002). Theory of mind and peer acceptance in preschool children. *British Journal of Developmental Psychology, 20*(4), 545–564.

Sluckin, A. M., & Smith, P. K. (1977). Two approaches to the concept of dominance in preschool children. *Child Development, 48*(3), 917–923.

Smith, D. G., Davis, R. J., Gehlert, D. R., & Nomikos, G. G. (2006). Exposure to predator odor stress increases efflux of frontal cortex acetylcholine and monoamines in mice: Comparisons with immobilization stress and reversal by chlordiazepoxide. *Brain Research, 1114*(1), 24–30.

Smith, L. K., Fantella, S. L. N., & Pellis, S. M. (1999). Playful defensive responses in adult male rats depend on the status of the unfamiliar opponent. *Aggressive Behavior, 25*(2), 141–152.

Smith, P. K. (1982). Does play matter? Functional and evolutionary aspects of animal and human play. *Behavioral and Brain Sciences, 5*, 139–184.

Smith, P. K. (1991). The silent nightmare: Bullying and victimization in school peer groups. *The Psychologist, 4*, 243–248.

Smith, P. K., & Lewis, K. (1985). Rough-and-tumble play, fighting, and chasing in nursery school children. *Ethology and Sociobiology, 6*(3), 175–181.

Smith, P. K., & Shu, S. (2000). What good schools can do about bullying: Findings from a survey in English schools after a decade of research and action. *Childhood, 7*(2), 193–212.

Smith, R. H., Webster, J. M., Parrott, W. G., & Eyre, H. L. (2002). The role of public exposure in moral and nonmoral shame and guilt. *Journal of Personality and Social Psychology, 83*(1), 138–159.

Smylie, M. A. (1999). Teacher stress in a time of reform. In R. Vandenberghe & A. M. Huberman (Eds.), *Understanding and preventing teacher burnout: A sourcebook of international research and practice* (pp. 59–84). New York, NY: Cambridge University Press.

Smythe, J. W., Rowe, W. B., & Meaney, M. J. (1994). Neonatal handling alters serotonin (5-HT) turnover and 5-HT2 receptor binding in selected brain regions: Relationship to the handling effect on glucocorticoid receptor expression. *Developmental Brain Research, 80*(1–2), 183–189.

Somerville, L. H., Heatherton, T. F., & Kelley, W. M. (2006). Anterior cingulate cortex responds differentially to expectancy violation and social rejection. *Nature Neuroscience, 9*(8), 1007–1008.

Sommer, K. L., & Baumeister, R. F. (2002). Self-evaluation, persistence, and performance following implicit rejection: The role of trait self-esteem. *Personality and Social Psychology Bulletin, 28*(7), 926–938.

Song, C. K., Johnstone, L. M., Schmidt, M., Derby, C. D., & Edwards, D. H. (2007). Social domination increases neuronal survival in the brain of juvenile crayfish *Procambarus clarkii. Journal of Experimental Biology, 210*(8), 1311–1324.

Sontheimer, H. (1995). Glial influences on neuronal signaling. *The Neuroscientist, 1*(3), 123–126.

Sourander, A., Helstela, L., Helenius, H., & Piha, J. (2000). Persistence of bullying from childhood to adolescence—A longitudinal 8-year follow-up study. *Child Abuse & Neglect, 24*(7), 873–881.

Sowell, E. R., Thompson, P. M., Holmes, C. J., Jernigan, T. L., & Toga, A. W. (1999). In vivo evidence for post-adolescent brain maturation in frontal and striatal regions. *Nature Neuroscience, 2*(10), 859–861.

Sowell, E. R., Thompson, P. M., Welcome, S. E., Henkenius, A. L., Toga, A. W., & Peterson, B. S. (2003). Cortical abnormalities in children and adolescents with attention-deficit hyperactivity disorder. *Lancet, 362,* 1699–1707.

Sowell, E. R., Trauner, D. A., Gamst, A., & Jernigan, T. L. (2002). Development of cortical and subcortical brain structures in childhood and adolescence: A structural MRI study. *Developmental Medicine and Child Neurology, 44*(1), 4–16.

Spangler, G., & Grossmann, K. E. (1993). Biobehavioral organization in securely and insecurely attached infants. *Child Development, 64*(5), 1439–1450.

Spangler, G., & Schieche, M. (1998). Emotional and adrenocortical responses of infants to the strange situation: The differential function of emotional expression. *International Journal of Behavioural Development, 22*(4), 681–706.

Spear, L. P. (2000). The adolescent brain and age-related behavioral manifestations. *Neuroscience and Biobehavioral Reviews, 24*(4), 417–463.

Spinka, M., Newberry, R. C., & Bekoff, M. (2001). Mammalian play: Training for the unexpected. *Quarterly Review of Biology, 76*(2), 141–168.

Spitzer, S. B., Llabre, M. M., Ironson, G. H., Gellman, M. D., & Schneiderman, N. (1992). The influence of social situations on ambulatory blood pressure. *Psychosomatic Medicine, 54*(1), 79–86.

Spotts, H. E., Weinberger, M. G., & Parsons, A. L. (1997). Assessing the use and impact of humor on advertising effectiveness: A contingency approach. *Journal of Advertising, 26*(3), 17–32.

Spriggs, A. L., Iannotti, R. J., Nansel, T. R., & Haynie, D. L. (2007). Adolescent bullying involvement and perceived family, peer and school relations: Commonalities and differences across race/ethnicity. *Journal of Adolescent Health, 41*(3), 283–293.

Squire, L. R. (1987). *Memory and brain.* New York, NY: Oxford University Press.

Stadler, C., Feifel, J., Poustka, F., Rohrmann, S., & Vermeiren, R. (2010). Peer-victimization and mental health problems in adolescents: Are parental and school support protective? *Child Psychiatry and Human Development, 41*(4), 371–386.

Staff, R. T., Murray, A. D., Deary, I. J., & Whalley, L. J. (2004). What provides cerebral reserve? *Brain, 127*(5), 1191–1199.

Stamatakis, A., Pondiki, S., Kitraki, E., Diamantopoulou, A., Panagiotaropoulos, T., Raftogianni, A., & Stylianopoulou, F. (2008). Effect of neonatal handling on adult rat spatial learning and memory following acute stress. *Stress, 11*(2), 148–159.

Stansfield, K. H., & Kirstein, C. L. (2006). Effects of novelty on behavior in the adolescent and adult rat. *Developmental Psychobiology, 48*(1), 10–15.

Staudinger, U. M. (1999). Older and wiser? Integrating results on the relationship between age and wisdom-related performance. *International Journal of Behavioural Development, 23*(3), 641–664.

Staudinger, U. M., & Baltes, P. B. (1996). Interactive minds: A facilitative setting for wisdom-related performance? *Journal of Personality and Social Psychology, 71*(4), 746–762.

Staudinger, U. M., Maciel, A. G., Smith, J., & Baltes, P. B. (1998). What predicts wisdom-related performance? A first look at personality, intelligence, and facilitative experiential contexts. *European Journal of Personality, 12*(1), 1–17.

Steinberg, L. (2008). A social neuroscience perspective on adolescent risk-taking. *Developmental Review, 28*(1), 78–106.

Stennett, R. G. (1957). The relationship of performance level to level of arousal. *Journal of Experimental Psychology, 54*(1), 54–61.

Stern, Y., Alexander, G. E., Prohovnik, I., & Mayeux, R. (1992). Inverse relationship between education and parietotemporal perfusion deficit in Alzheimer's disease. *Annals of Neurology, 32*(3), 371–375.

Stern, Y., Alexander, G. E., Prohovnik, I., Stricks, L., Link, B., Lennon, M. C., & Mayeux, R. (1995). Relationship between lifetime occupation and parietal flow: Implications for a reserve against Alzheimer's disease pathology. *Neurology, 45*(1), 55–60.

Stern, Y., Habeck, C., Moeller, J., Scarmeas, N., Anderson, K. E., Hilton, H. J., . . . van Heertum, R. (2005). Brain networks associated with cognitive reserve in healthy young and old adults. *Cerebral Cortex, 15*(4), 394–402.

Sternberg, R. J. (1990). *Wisdom: Its nature, origins, and development.* New York, NY: Cambridge University Press.

Sterr, A., Muller, M. M., Elbert, T., Rockstroh, B., Pantev, C., & Taub, E. (1998a). Changed perceptions in Braille readers. Nature, 391(6663), 134–135.

Sterr, A., Muller, M. M., Elbert, T., Rockstroh, B., Pantev, C., & Taub, E. (1998b). Perceptual correlates of changes in cortical representation of fingers in blind multifinger Braille readers. *Journal of Neuroscience, 18*(11), 4417–4423.

Stiles, J. (2000). Neural plasticity and cognitive development. *Developmental Neuropsychology, 18*(2), 237–272.

Stillman, T. F., Baumeister, R. F., Lambert, N. M., Crescioni, A. W., Dewall, C. N., & Fincham, F. D. (2009). Alone and without purpose: Life loses meaning following social exclusion. *Journal of Experimental Social Psychology, 45*(4), 686–694.

Stipek, D. J. (1977). *Changes during first grade in children's social-motivational development.* (Doctoral dissertation). Yale University, New Haven, CT.

Stockdale, M. S., Hangaduambo, S., Duys, D., Larson, K., & Sarvela, P. D. (2002). Rural elementary students', parents', and teachers' perceptions of bullying. *American Journal of Health Behavior, 26*(4), 266–277.

Stouten, J., De Cremer, D., & van Dijk, E. (2009). When being disadvantaged grows into vengeance: The effects of asymmetry of interest and social rejection in social dilemmas. *European Journal of Social Psychology, 39*(4), 526–539.

Stranahan, A. M., Khalil, D., & Gould, E. (2006). Social isolation delays the positive effects of running on adult neurogenesis. *Nature Neuroscience, 9*(4), 526–533.

Strange, B. A., & Dolan, R. J. (2004). Beta-adrenergic modulation of emotional memory–evoked human amygdala and hippocampal responses. *Proceedings of the National Academy of Sciences of the United States of America, 101*(31), 11454–11458.

Straube, T., Korz, V., & Frey, J. U. (2003). Bidirectional modulation of long-term potentiation by novelty-exploration in rat dentate gyrus. *Neuroscience Letters, 344*(1), 5–8.

Strauss, R. S., & Pollack, H. A. (2003). Social marginalization of overweight children. *Archives of Pediatrics & Adolescent Medicine, 157*(8), 746–752.

Strayer, F., & Trudel, M. (1984). Developmental changes in the nature and function of social dominance among young children. *Ethology and Sociobiology, 5*(4), 279–295.

Strick, M., van Baaren, R. B., Holland, R. W., & van Knippenberg, A. (2009). Humor in advertisements enhances product liking by mere association. *Journal of Experimental Psychology: Applied, 15*(1), 35–45.

Stuewig, J., & McCloskey, L. A. (2005). The relation of child maltreatment to shame and guilt among adolescents: Psychological routes to depression and delinquency. *Child Maltreatment, 10*(4), 324–336.

Sugden, K., Arseneault, L., Harrington, H., Moffitt, T. E., Williams, B., & Caspi, A. (2010). Serotonin transporter gene moderates the development of emotional problems among children following bullying victimization. *Journal of the American Academy of Child and Adolescent Psychiatry, 49*(8), 830–840.

Sullivan, E. V., Deshmukh, A., Desmond, J. E., Lim, K. O., & Pfefferbaum, A. (2000). Cerebellar volume decline in normal aging, alcoholism, and Korsakoff's syndrome: Relation to ataxia. *Neuropsychology, 14*(3), 341–352.

Sullivan, E. V., Marsh, L., Mathalon, D. H., Lim, K. O., & Pfefferbaum, A. (1995). Age-related decline in MRI volumes of temporal lobe gray matter but not hippocampus. *Neurobiology of Aging, 16*(4), 591–606.

Sullivan, H. S. (1947). *Conceptions of modern psychiatry: The first William Alanson White memorial lectures.* Washington, DC: William Alanson White Psychiatric Foundation.

Sullivan, R. M., Wilson, D. A., & Leon, M. (1989). Norepinephrine and learning-induced plasticity in infant rat olfactory system. *Journal of Neuroscience, 9*(11), 3998–4006.

Sutton, R. (2004). Emotional regulation goals and strategies of teachers. *Social Psychology of Education, 7*(4), 379–398.

Sutton, R. E., & Wheatley, K. F. (2003). Teachers' emotions and teaching: A review of the literature and directions for future research. *Educational Psychology Review, 15*(4), 327–358.

Svebak, S. (1982). The effect of mirthfulness upon amount of discordant right-left occipital EEG alpha. *Motivation and Emotion, 6*(2), 133–147.

Swain, R. A., Harris, A. B., Wiener, E. C., Dutka, M. V., Morris, H. D., Theien, B. E., . . . Greenough, W. T. (2003). Prolonged exercise induces angiogenesis and increases cerebral blood volume in primary motor cortex of the rat. *Neuroscience, 117*(4), 1037–1046.

Sweeting, H., & West, P. (2001). Being different: Correlates of the experience of teasing and bullying at age 11. *Research Papers in Education, 16*(3), 225–246.

Szyf, M., McGowan, P., & Meaney, M. J. (2008). The social environment and the epigenome. *Environmental and Molecular Mutagenesis, 49*(1), 46–60.

Szyf, M., Weaver, I. C., Champagne, F. A., Diorio, J., & Meaney, M. J. (2005). Maternal programming of steroid receptor expression and phenotype through DNA methylation in the rat. *Frontiers in Neuroendocrinology, 26*(3–4), 139–162.

Szyf, M., Weaver, I. C., & Meaney, M. (2007). Maternal care, the epigenome and phenotypic differences in behavior. *Reproductive Toxicology, 24*(1), 9–19.

Tabibnia, G., & Lieberman, M. D. (2007). Fairness and cooperation are rewarding: Evidence from social cognitive neuroscience. *Annals of the New York Academy of Sciences, 1118*, 90–101.

Taghzouti, K., Simon, H., & Le Moal, M. (1986). Disturbances in exploratory behavior and functional recovery in the Y and radial mazes following dopamine depletion of the lateral septum. *Behavioral and Neural Biology, 45*(1), 48–56.

Takahashi, K., Iwase, M., Yamashita, K., Tatsumoto, Y., Ue, H., Kuratsune, H., . . . Takeda, M. (2001). The elevation of natural killer cell activity induced by laughter in a crossover designed study. *International Journal of Molecular Medicine, 8*(6), 645–650.

Takahashi, L. K., Nakashima, B. R., Hong, H., & Watanabe, K. (2005). The smell of danger: A behavioral and neural analysis of predator odor-induced fear. *Neuroscience and Biobehavioral Reviews, 29*(8), 1157–1167.

Takahashi, M., & Bordia, P. (2000). The concept of wisdom: A cross-cultural comparison. *International Journal of Psychology, 35*(1), 1–9.

Takahashi, M., & Inoue, T. (2009). The effects of humor on memory for nonsensical pictures. *Acta Psychologica, 132*(1), 80–84.

Takahashi, M., & Overton, W. (2002). Wisdom: A culturally inclusive developmental perspective. *International Journal of Behavioral Development, 26*(3), 269–277.

Takahashi, T., Ikeda, K., Ishikawa, M., Tsukasaki, T., Nakama, D., Tanida, S., & Kameda, T. (2004). Social stress-induced cortisol elevation acutely impairs social memory in humans. *Neuroscience Letters, 363*(2), 125–130.

Talbot, J. A., Talbot, N. L., & Tu, X. (2004). Shame-proneness as a diathesis for dissociation in women with histories of childhood sexual abuse. *Journal of Traumatic Stress, 17*(5), 445–448.

Tanaka, J. W., & Pierce, L. J. (2009). The neural plasticity of other-race face recognition. *Cognitive, Affective & Behavioral Neuroscience, 9*(1), 122–131.

Tanapat, P., Hastings, N. B., Rydel, T. A., Galea, L. A., & Gould, E. (2001). Exposure to fox odor inhibits cell proliferation in the hippocampus of adult rats via an adrenal hormone-dependent mechanism. *Journal of Comparative Neurology, 437*(4), 496–504.

Tang, A. C., Akers, K. G., Reeb, B. C., Romeo, R. D., & McEwen, B. S. (2006). Programming social, cognitive, and neuroendocrine development by early exposure to novelty. *Proceedings of the National Academy of Sciences of the United States of America, 103*(42), 15716–15721.

Tang, A. C., Reeb, B. C., Romeo, R. D., & McEwen, B. S. (2003). Modification of social memory, hypothalamic-pituitary-adrenal axis, and brain asymmetry by neonatal novelty exposure. *Journal of Neuroscience, 23*(23), 8254–8260.

Tang, A. C., & Zou, B. (2002). Neonatal exposure to novelty enhances long-term potentiation in CA1 of the rat hippocampus. *Hippocampus, 12*(3), 398–404.

Tang, Y., Nyengaard, J. R., Pakkenberg, B., & Gundersen, H. J. (1997). Age-induced white matter changes in the human brain: A stereological investigation. *Neurobiology of Aging, 18*(6), 609–615.

Tang, Y. P., Shimizu, E., Dube, G. R., Rampon, C., Kerchner, G. A., Zhuo, M., . . . Tsien, J. Z. (1999). Genetic enhancement of learning and memory in mice. *Nature, 401*(6748), 63–69.

Tangney, J. P., Wagner, P., & Gramzow, R. (1992). Proneness to shame, proneness to guilt, and psychopathology. *Journal of Abnormal Psychology, 101*(3), 469–478.

Tanji, J., & Hoshi, E. (2001). Behavioral planning in the prefrontal cortex. *Current Opinion in Neurobiology, 11*(2), 164–170.

Tapper, D. (1995). *Swimming upstream: The first-year experiences of teachers working in New York city public schools.* Retrieved from ERIC database. (ED460085)

Taris, T. W., Horn, J. E. V., Schaufeli, W. B., & Schreurs, P. J. G. (2004). Inequity, burnout and psychological withdrawal among teachers: A dynamic exchange model. *Anxiety, Stress & Coping, 17*(1), 103–122.

Taylor, A. R. (1989). Predictors of peer rejection in early elementary grade: Roles of problem behavior, academic achievement, and teacher preference. *Journal of Clinical Child Psychology, 18*(4), 360–365.

Taylor, J. G. (2001). The central role of the parietal lobes in consciousness. *Consciousness and Cognition, 10*(3), 379–417.

Taylor, R. D., Casten, R., Flickinger, S. M., Roberts, D., & Fulmore, C. D. (1994). Explaining the school performance of African-American adolescents. *Journal of Research on Adolescence, 4*(1), 21–44.

Teasdale, J. D., Howard, R. J., Cox, S. G., Ha, Y., Brammer, M. J., Williams, S. C., & Checkley, S. A. (1999). Functional MRI study of the cognitive generation of affect. *American Journal of Psychiatry, 156*(2), 209–215.

Tehrani, N. (2004). Bullying: A source of chronic post traumatic stress? *British Journal of Guidance and Counselling, 32*(3), 357–366.

Teicher, M. H., Andersen, S. L., & Hostetter, J. C., Jr. (1995). Evidence for dopamine receptor pruning between adolescence and adulthood in striatum but not nucleus accumbens. *Developmental Brain Research, 89*(2), 167–172.

Teicher, M. H., Dumont, N. L., Ito, Y., Vaituzis, C., Giedd, J. N., & Andersen, S. L. (2004). Childhood neglect is associated with reduced corpus callosum area. *Biological Psychiatry, 56*(2), 80–85.

Tejedor-Real, P., Costela, C., & Gibert-Rahola, J. (1998). Neonatal handling reduces emotional reactivity and susceptibility to learned helplessness: Involvement of catecholaminergic systems. *Life Sciences, 62*(1), 37–50.

ten Cate, C. (1989). Behavioral development: Toward understanding processes. In P. P. G. Bateson & P. Klopfer (Eds.), *Perspectives in ethology* (pp. 243–269). New York, NY: Plenum.

Thomas, P. D., Goodwin, J. M., & Goodwin, J. S. (1985). Effect of social support on stress-related changes in cholesterol level, uric acid level, and immune function in an elderly sample. *American Journal of Psychiatry, 142*(6), 735–737.

Thompson, P. M., Giedd, J. N., Woods, R. P., MacDonald, D., Evans, A. C., & Toga, A. W. (2000). Growth patterns in the developing brain detected by using continuum mechanical tensor maps. *Nature, 404*(6774), 190–193.

Thor, D. H., & Holloway, W. R. (1983). Play-solicitation behavior in juvenile male and female rats. *Animal Learning & Behavior, 11*(2), 173–178.

Thorndike, R. L. (1968). Reviews: Rosenthal, Robert, and Jacobson, Lenore. Pygmalion in the classroom. *American Educational Research Journal, 5*(4), 708–711.

Thorson, J. A. (1985). A funny thing happened on the way to the morgue: Some thoughts on humor and death, and a taxonomy of the humor associated with death. *Death Studies, 9*(3), 201–216.

Tillich, P. (1952). *The courage to be.* New Haven, CT: Yale University Press.

Tisserand, D. J., van Boxtel, M. P., Pruessner, J. C., Hofman, P., Evans, A. C., & Jolles, J. (2004). A voxel-based morphometric study to determine individual differences in gray matter density associated with age and cognitive change over time. *Cerebral Cortex, 14*(9), 966–973.

Tomasi, T. B. (1976). *The immune system of secretions.* Englewood Cliffs, NJ: Prentice-Hall.

Torasdotter, M., Metsis, M., Henriksson, B. G., Winblad, B., & Mohammed, A. H. (1998). Environmental enrichment results in higher levels of nerve growth factor mRNA in the rat visual cortex and hippocampus. *Behavioural Brain Research, 93*(1–2), 83–90.

Tough, P. *Whatever it takes: Geoffrey Canada's quest to change Harlem and America.* New York: Houghton Mifflin Harcourt, 2009.

Tran, A. H., Uwano, T., Kimura, T., Hori, E., Katsuki, M., Nishijo, H., & Ono, T. (2008). Dopamine D1 receptor modulates hippocampal representation plasticity to spatial novelty. *Journal of Neuroscience, 28*(50), 13390–13400.

Trejo, J. L., Carro, E., & Torres-Aleman, I. (2001). Circulating insulin-like growth factor I mediates exercise-induced increases in the number of new neurons in the adult hippocampus. *Journal of Neuroscience, 21*(5), 1628–1634.

Tremblay, L., & Schultz, W. (1999). Relative reward preference in primate orbitofrontal cortex. *Nature, 398*(6729), 704–708.

Tremblay, R. E., Schaal, B., Boulerice, B., Arseneault, L., Soussignan, R. G., Paquette, D., & Laurent, D. (1998). Testosterone, physical aggression, dominance, and physical development in early adolescence. *International Journal of Behavioural Development, 22*(4), 753–777.

Trojan, S., & Pokorny, J. (1999). Theoretical aspects of neuroplasticity. *Physiological Research, 48*(2), 87–97.

Trouilloud, D., Sarrazin, P., Bressoux, P., & Bois, J. (2006). Relation between teachers' early expectations and students' later perceived competence in physical education classes: Autonomy-supportive climate as a moderator. *Journal of Educational Psychology, 98*(1), 75–86.

Trouilloud, D. O., Sarrazin, P. G., Martinek, T. J., & Guillet, E. (2002). The influence of teacher expectations on student achievement in physical education classes: Pygmalion revisited. *European Journal of Social Psychology, 32*(5), 591–607.

Tsatsoulis, A., & Fountoulakis, S. (2006). The protective role of exercise on stress system dysregulation and comorbidities. *Annals of the New York Academy of Sciences, 1083*(1), 196–213.

Tsoory, M. M., Vouimba, R. M., Akirav, I., Kavushansky, A., Avital, A., & Richter-Levin, G. (2008). Amygdala modulation of memory-related processes in the hippocampus: Potential relevance to PTSD. *Progress in Brain Research, 167*, 35–51.

Tuboly, G., Benedek, G., & Horvath, G. (2009). Selective disturbance of pain sensitivity after social isolation. *Physiology & Behavior, 96*(1), 18–22.

Tulving, E., Markowitsch, H. J., Craik, F. E., Habib, R., & Houle, S. (1996). Novelty and familiarity activations in PET studies of memory encoding and retrieval. *Cerebral Cortex, 6*(1), 71–79.

Turner, C. A., Calvo, N., Frost, D. O., Akil, H., & Watson, S. J. (2008). The fibroblast growth factor system is downregulated following social defeat. *Neuroscience Letters, 430*(2), 147–150.

Twemlow, S. W., Fonagy, P., & Sacco, F. C. (2004). The role of the bystander in the social architecture of bullying and violence in schools and communities. *Annals of the New York Academy of Sciences, 1036*, 215–232.

Twenge, J. M., Baumeister, R. F., Tice, D. M., & Stucke, T. S. (2001). If you can't join them, beat them: Effects of social exclusion on aggressive behavior. *Journal of Personality and Social Psychology, 81*(6), 1058–1069.

Twenge, J. M., Zhang, L., Catanese, K. R., Dolan-Pascoe, B., Lyche, L. F., & Baumeister, R. F. (2007). Replenishing connectedness: Reminders of social activity reduce aggression after social exclusion. *British Journal of Social Psychology, 46*(1), 205–224.

Tye, B. B., & O'Brien, L. (2002). Why are experienced teachers leaving the profession? *Phi Delta Kappan, 84*(1), 24–32.

Tyrka, A. R., Wier, L., Price, L. H., Ross, N., Anderson, G. M., Wilkinson, C. W., & Carpenter, L. L. (2008). Childhood parental loss and adult hypothalamic-pituitary-adrenal function. *Biological Psychiatry, 63*(12), 1147–1154.

Uauy, R., & Dangour, A. D. (2006). Nutrition in brain development and aging: Role of essential fatty acids. *Nutrition Reviews, 64*(S2), S24–S33.

Uchino, B. N., Cacioppo, J. T., & Kiecolt-Glaser, J. K. (1996). The relationship between social support and physiological processes: A review with emphasis on underlying mechanisms and implications for health. *Psychological Bulletin, 119*(3), 488–531.

Uddin, L. Q., Kaplan, J. T., Molnar-Szakacs, I., Zaidel, E., & Iacoboni, M. (2005). Self-face recognition activates a frontoparietal "mirror" network in the right hemisphere: An event-related fMRI study. *NeuroImage, 25*, 926–935.

Uhlmann, E., Dasgupta, N., Elgueta, A., Greenwald, A. G., & Swanson, J. (2002). Subgroup prejudice based on skin color among Hispanics in the United States and Latin America. *Social Cognition, 20*(3), 198–226.

Ulrich, R. S. (1984). View through a window may influence recovery from surgery. *Science, 224*(4647), 420–421.

Unnever, J., & Cornell, D. (2003). Bullying, self-control, and ADHD. *Journal of Interpersonal Violence, 18*(2), 129–147.

Uysal, N., Tugyan, K., Kayatekin, B. M., Acikgoz, O., Bagriyanik, H. A., Gonenc, S., . . . Semin, I. (2005). The effects of regular aerobic exercise in adolescent period on hippocampal neuron density, apoptosis and spatial memory. *Neuroscience Letters, 383*(3), 241–245.

Vaillancourt, T., DeCatanzaro, D., Duku, E., & Muir, C. (2009). Androgen dynamics in the context of children's peer relations: An examination of the links between testosterone and peer victimization. *Aggressive Behavior, 35*(1), 103–113.

Vaillancourt, T., DeCatanzaro, D., Schmidt, L. A., Duku, E., Macmillan, H., & Muir, C. (2008). Variation in hypothalamic-pituitary-adrenal axis activity among bullied and non-bullied children. *Aggressive Behavior, 34*(3), 294–305.

Vaina, L. M., Solomon, J., Chowdhury, S., Sinha, P., & Belliveau, J. W. (2001). Functional neuroanatomy of biological motion perception in humans. *Proceedings of the National Academy of Sciences of the United States of America, 98*(20), 11656–11661.

Vallee, M., MacCari, S., Dellu, F., Simon, H., Le Moal, M., & Mayo, W. (1999). Long-term effects of prenatal stress and postnatal handling on age-related glucocorticoid secretion and cognitive performance: A longitudinal study in the rat. *European Journal of Neuroscience, 11*(8), 2906–2916.

Vallee, M., Mayo, W., Dellu, F., Le Moal, M., Simon, H., & Maccari, S. (1997). Prenatal stress induces high anxiety and postnatal handling induces low anxiety in adult offspring: Correlation with stress-induced corticosterone secretion. *Journal of Neuroscience, 17*(7), 2626–2636.

van den Berg, C. L., Hol, T., Van Ree, J. M., Spruijt, B. M., Everts, H., & Koolhaas, J. M. (1999). Play is indispensable for an adequate development of coping with social challenges in the rat. *Developmental Psychobiology, 34*(2), 129–138.

van der Wal, M. F., de Wit, C. A., & Hirasing, R. A. (2003). Psychosocial health among young victims and offenders of direct and indirect bullying. *Pediatrics, 111*(6), 1312–1317.

van Horn, J. E., Schaufeli, W. B., & Enzmann, D. (1999). Teacher burnout and lack of reciprocity. *Journal of Applied Social Psychology, 29*(1), 91–108.

Van Opstal, F., Verguts, T., Orban, G. A., & Fias, W. (2008). A hippocampal-parietal network for learning an ordered sequence. *NeuroImage, 40*(1), 333–341.

Van Petten, C., Plante, E., Davidson, P. S., Kuo, T. Y., Bajuscak, L., & Glisky, E. L. (2004). Memory and executive function in older adults: Relationships with temporal and prefrontal gray matter volumes and white matter hyperintensities. *Neuropsychologia, 42*(10), 1313–1335.

van Praag, H., Shubert, T., Zhao, C., & Gage, F. H. (2005). Exercise enhances learning and hippocampal neurogenesis in aged mice. *Journal of Neuroscience, 25*(38), 8680–8685.

Vanderschuren, L. J., Niesink, R. J., & Van Ree, J. M. (1997). The neurobiology of social play behavior in rats. *Neuroscience and Biobehavioral Reviews, 21*(3), 309–326.

Vandervoort, D. (1999). Quality of social support in mental and physical health. *Current Psychology, 18*(2), 205–222.

Vartia, M. A. (2001). Consequences of workplace bullying with respect to the well-being of its targets and the observers of bullying. *Scandinavian Journal of Work, Environment & Health, 27*(1), 63–69.

Vaynman, S., Ying, Z., & Gomez-Pinilla, F. (2003). Interplay between brain-derived neurotrophic factor and signal transduction modulators in the regulation of the effects of exercise on synaptic-plasticity. *Neuroscience, 122*(3), 647–657.

Vaynman, S., Ying, Z., & Gomez-Pinilla, F. (2004). Hippocampal BDNF mediates the efficacy of exercise on synaptic plasticity and cognition. *European Journal of Neuroscience, 20*(10), 2580–2590.

Vecchio, R. P., Justin, J. E., & Pearce, C. L. (2009). The influence of leader humor on relationships between leader behavior and follower outcomes. *Journal of Managerial Issues, 21*(2), 171–194.

Veenstra, R., Lindenberg, S., Munniksma, A., & Dijkstra, J. K. (2010). The complex relation between bullying, victimization, acceptance, and rejection: Giving special attention to status, affection, and sex differences. *Child Development, 81*(2), 480–486.

Vernadakis, A. (1996). Glia-neuron intercommunications and synaptic plasticity. *Progress in Neurobiology, 49*(3), 185–214.

Vernadine, T. (1997). *What research says about administrators' management style, effectiveness, and teacher morale.* Retrieved from ERIC database. (ED411569)

Verstynen, T., Tierney, R., Urbanski, T., & Tang, A. (2001). Neonatal novelty exposure modulates hippocampal volumetric asymmetry in the rat. *NeuroReport, 12*(14), 3019–3022.

Viola, H., Furman, M., Izquierdo, L. A., Alonso, M., Barros, D. M., de Souza, M. M., . . . Medina, J. H. (2000). Phosphorylated cAMP response element-binding protein as a molecular marker of memory processing in rat hippocampus: Effect of novelty. *Journal of Neuroscience, 20*(23), RC112.

Virgin, C. E., Jr., & Sapolsky, R. M. (1997). Styles of male social behavior and their endocrine correlates among low-ranking baboons. *American Journal of Primatology, 42*(1), 25–39.

Vogeley, K., May, M., Ritzl, A., Falkai, P., Zilles, K., & Fink, G. R. (2004). Neural correlates of first-person perspective as one constituent of human self-consciousness. *Journal of Cognitive Neuroscience, 16*(5), 817–827.

Vogt, B. A. (2005). Pain and emotion interactions in subregions of the cingulate gyrus. *Nature Reviews Neuroscience, 6*(7), 533–544.

von Bonin, G. (1963). *The evolution of the human brain.* Chicago: University of Chicago Press.

Voss, L. D., & Mulligan, J. (2000). Bullying in school: Are short pupils at risk? questionnaire study in a cohort. *British Medical Journal, 320*(7235), 612–613.

Vyas, A., Bernal, S., & Chattarji, S. (2003). Effects of chronic stress on dendritic arborization in the central and extended amygdala. *Brain Research, 965*(1–2), 290–294.

Vyas, A., & Chattarji, S. (2004). Modulation of different states of anxiety-like behavior by chronic stress. *Behavioral Neuroscience, 118*(6), 1450–1454.

Wager, T. D., Phan, K. L., Liberzon, I., & Taylor, S. F. (2003). Valence, gender, and lateralization of functional brain anatomy in emotion: A meta-analysis of findings from neuroimaging. *NeuroImage, 19*(3), 513–531.

Wager, T. D., Rilling, J. K., Smith, E. E., Sokolik, A., Casey, K. L., Davidson, R. J., . . . Cohen, J. D. (2004). Placebo-induced changes in fMRI in the anticipation and experience of pain. *Science, 303*(5661), 1162–1167.

Wagner, A. D., Shannon, B. J., Kahn, I., & Buckner, R. L. (2005). Parietal lobe contributions to episodic memory retrieval. *Trends in Cognitive Sciences, 9*(9), 445–453.

Wahlund, L. O., Almkvist, O., Basun, H., & Julin, P. (1996). MRI in successful aging, a 5-year follow-up study from the eighth to ninth decade of life. *Magnetic Resonance Imaging, 14*(6), 601–608.

Walden, L. M., & Beran, T. N. (2010). Attachment quality and bullying behavior in school-aged youth. *Canadian Journal of School Psychology, 25*(1), 5–18.

Walden, T. A., & Ogan, T. A. (1988). The development of social referencing. *Child Development, 59*(5), 1230–1240.

Walker, M. P., Brakefield, T., Morgan, A., Hobson, J. A., & Stickgold, R. (2002). Practice with sleep makes perfect: Sleep-dependent motor skill learning. *Neuron, 35*(1), 205–211.

Walker, P. M., & Tanaka, J. W. (2003). An encoding advantage for own-race versus other-race faces. *Perception, 32*(9), 1117–1125.

Wallace, D. L., Han, M. H., Graham, D. L., Green, T. A., Vialou, V., Iniguez, S. D., . . . Nestler, E. J. (2009). CREB regulation of nucleus accumbens excitability mediates social isolation-induced behavioral deficits. *Nature Neuroscience, 12*(2), 200–209.

Walsh, R. N., Budtz-Olsen, O. E., Penny, J. E., & Cummins, R. A. (1969). The effects of environmental complexity on the histology of the rat hippocampus. *Journal of Comparative Neurology, 137*(3), 361–366.

Wanisch, K., Tang, J., Mederer, A., & Wotjak, C. T. (2005). Trace fear conditioning depends on NMDA receptor activation and protein synthesis within the dorsal hippocampus of mice. *Behavioural Brain Research, 157*(1), 63–69.

Wanzer, M. B., Frymier, A. B., & Irwin, J. (2010). An explanation of the relationship between instructor humor and student learning: Instructional humor processing theory. *Communication Education, 59*(1), 1–18.

Watanabe, Y., Gould, E., & McEwen, B. S. (1992). Stress induces atrophy of apical dendrites of hippocampal CA3 pyramidal neurons. *Brain Research, 588*(2), 341–345.

Watson, D., Clark, L. A., & Harkness, A. R. (1994). Structures of personality and their relevance to psychopathology. *Journal of Abnormal Psychology, 103*(1), 18–31.

Watson, K. K., Matthews, B. J., & Allman, J. M. (2007). Brain activation during sight gags and language-dependent humor. *Cerebral Cortex, 17*(2), 314–324.

Wear, D., Aultman, J. M., Zarconi, J., & Varley, J. D. (2009). Derogatory and cynical humour directed towards patients: Views of residents and attending doctors. *Medical Education, 43*(1), 34–41.

Weaver, I. C., Cervoni, N., Champagne, F. A., D'Alessio, A. C., Sharma, S., Seckl, J. R., . . . Meaney, M. J. (2004). Epigenetic programming by maternal behavior. *Nature Neuroscience, 7*(8), 847–854.

Weaver, I. C., Champagne, F. A., Brown, S. E., Dymov, S., Sharma, S., Meaney, M. J., & Szyf, M. (2005). Reversal of maternal programming of stress responses in adult offspring through methyl supplementation: Altering epigenetic marking later in life. *Journal of Neuroscience, 25*(47), 11045–11054.

Weaver, I. C., D'Alessio, A. C., Brown, S. E., Hellstrom, I. C., Dymov, S., Sharma, S., . . . Meaney, M. J. (2007). The transcription factor nerve growth factor-inducible protein a mediates epigenetic programming: Altering epigenetic marks by immediate-early genes. *Journal of Neuroscience, 27*(7), 1756–1768.

Weaver, I. C., Grant, R. J., & Meaney, M. J. (2002). Maternal behavior regulates long-term hippocampal expression of BAX and apoptosis in the offspring. *Journal of Neurochemistry, 82*(4), 998–1002.

Weaver, I. C., Meaney, M. J., & Szyf, M. (2006). Maternal care effects on the hippocampal transcriptome and anxiety-mediated behaviors in the offspring that are reversible in adulthood. *Proceedings of the National Academy of Sciences of the United States of America, 103*(9), 3480–3485.

Weaver, S. A., Aherne, F. X., Meaney, M. J., Schaefer, A. L., & Dixon, W. T. (2000). Neonatal handling permanently alters hypothalamic-pituitary-adrenal axis function, behaviour, and body weight in boars. *Journal of Endocrinology, 164*(3), 349–359.

Weinstein, R. S., Marshall, H. H., Brattesani, K. A., & Middlestadt, S. E. (1982). Student perceptions of differential teacher treatment in open and traditional classrooms. *Journal of Educational Psychology, 74*(5), 678–692.

Weinstein, R. S., & Middlestadt, S. E. (1979). Student perceptions of teacher interactions with male high and low achievers. *Journal of Educational Psychology, 71*(4), 421–431.

Weisberg, J., & Sagie, A. (1999). Teachers' physical, mental, and emotional burnout: Impact on intention to quit. *Journal of Psychology, 133*(3), 333–339.

Weiss, I. C., Pryce, C. R., Jongen-Relo, A. L., Nanz-Bahr, N. I., & Feldon, J. (2004). Effect of social isolation on stress-related behavioural and neuroendocrine state in the rat. *Behavioural Brain Research, 152*(2), 279–295.

Weller, A., & Feldman, R. (2003). Emotion regulation and touch in infants: The role of cholecystokinin and opioids. *Peptides, 24*(5), 779–788.

Wells, M., & Jones, R. (2000). Childhood parentification and shame-proneness: A preliminary study. *American Journal of Family Therapy, 28*(1), 19–27.

West, M. J. (1993). Regionally specific loss of neurons in the aging human hippocampus. *Neurobiology of Aging, 14*(4), 287–293.

Whalley, L. J., & Deary, I. J. (2001). Longitudinal cohort study of childhood IQ and survival up to age 76. *British Medical Journal, 322*(7290), 819.

Whalley, L. J., Deary, I. J., Appleton, C. L., & Starr, J. M. (2004). Cognitive reserve and the neurobiology of cognitive aging. *Ageing Research Reviews, 3*(4), 369–382.

Wheeler, M. E., & Fiske, S. T. (2005). Controlling racial prejudice: Social-cognitive goals affect amygdala and stereotype activation. *Psychological Science, 16*(1), 56–63.

Whishaw, I. Q., Gharbawie, O. A., Clark, B. J., & Lehmann, H. (2006). The exploratory behavior of rats in an open environment optimizes security. *Behavioural Brain Research, 171*(2), 230–239.

White, M. (2007). Maps of narrative practice. New York, NY: W. W. Norton.

Whiteman, J. L., Young, J. C., & Fisher, M. L. (1985). Teacher burnout and the perception of student behavior. *Education, 105*(3), 299–305.

Wiens, S. (2006). Subliminal emotion perception in brain imaging: Findings, issues, and recommendations. *Progress in Brain Research, 156*, 105–121.

Wigfield, A., Eccles, J. S., Yoon, K. S., Harold, R. D., Arbreton, A. J. A., Freedman-Doan, C., & Blumenfeld, P. C. (1997). Change in children's competence beliefs and subjective task values across the elementary school years: A 3-year study. *Journal of Educational Psychology, 89*(3), 451–469.

Wild, B., Erb, M., & Bartels, M. (2001). Are emotions contagious? Evoked emotions while viewing emotionally expressive faces: Quality, quantity, time course and gender differences. *Psychiatry Research, 102*(2), 109–124.

Wild, B., Rodden, F. A., Grodd, W., & Ruch, W. (2003). Neural correlates of laughter and humour. *Brain, 126*(10), 2121–2138.

Wilkowski, B. M., Robinson, M. D., & Friesen, C. K. (2009). Gaze-triggered orienting as a tool of the belongingness self-regulation system. *Psychological Science, 20*(4), 495–501.

Williams, D. E., & Schaller, K. A. (1993). Peer persuasion: A study of children's dominance strategies. *Early Child Development and Care, 88*, 31–41.

Williams, L. M., Kemp, A. H., Felmingham, K., Barton, M., Olivieri, G., Peduto, A., . . . Bryant, R. A. (2006). Trauma modulates amygdala and medial prefrontal responses to consciously attended fear. *NeuroImage, 29*(2), 347–357.

Willis, M. W., Ketter, T. A., Kimbrell, T. A., George, M. S., Herscovitch, P., Danielson, A. L., . . . Post, R. M. (2002). Age, sex and laterality effects on cerebral glucose metabolism in healthy adults. *Psychiatry Research, 114*(1), 23–37.

Willower, D. J., Hoy, W. K., & Eidell, T. L. (1967). The counselor and the school as a social organization. *Personnel and Guidance Journal, 46*(3), 228–234.

Winick, M., Meyer, K. K., & Harris, R. C. (1975). Malnutrition and environmental enrichment by early adoption. *Science, 190*(4220), 1173–1175.

Winnicott, D. W. (1962). *The child and the family: First relationships.* London, England: Tavistock.

Wittemyer, G., Getz, W., Vollrath, F., & Douglas-Hamilton, I. (2007). Social dominance, seasonal movements, and spatial segregation in African elephants: A contribution to conservation behavior. *Behavioral Ecology and Sociobiology, 61*(12), 1919–1931.

Wittmann, B. C., Daw, N. D., Seymour, B., & Dolan, R. J. (2008). Striatal activity underlies novelty-based choice in humans. *Neuron, 58*(6), 967–973.

Wolf, N., Gales, M., Shane, E., & Shane, M. (2001). The developmental trajectory from amodal perception to empathy and communication: The role of mirror neurons in this process. *HPSI Psychoanalytic Inquiry, 21*(1), 94–112.

Wolfson, A. R., & Carskadon, M. A. (1998). Sleep schedules and daytime functioning in adolescents. *Child Development, 69*(4), 875–887.

Wolkove, N., Elkholy, O., Baltzan, M., & Palayew, M. (2007). Sleep and aging: 2. Management of sleep disorders in older people. *Canadian Medical Association Journal, 176*(10), 1449–1454.

Wolpert, D. M., Goodbody, S. J., & Husain, M. (1998). Maintaining internal representations: The role of the human superior parietal lobe. *Nature Neuroscience, 1*(6), 529–533.

Wood-Gush, D., & Vestergaard, K. (1991). The seeking of novelty and its relation to play. *Animal Behaviour, 42*(4), 599–606.

Woodson, J. C., Macintosh, D., Fleshner, M., & Diamond, D. M. (2003). Emotion-induced amnesia in rats: Working memory-specific impairment, corticosterone-memory correlation, and fear versus arousal effects on memory. *Learning & Memory, 10*(5), 326–336.

Woolfolk, A. E., Rosoff, B., & Hoy, W. K. (1990). Teachers' sense of efficacy and their beliefs about managing students. *Teaching and Teacher Education, 6*(2), 137–148.

Wooten, P. (1996). Humor: An antidote for stress. *Holistic Nursing Practice, 10*(2), 49–56.

Wroblewski, E. E., Schumacher-Stankey, J. C., Pusey, A. E., Murray, C. M., Keele, B. F., & Hahn, B. H. (2009). Male dominance rank and reproductive success in chimpanzees, *Pan troglodytes schweinfurthii. Animal Behaviour, 77*(4), 873–885.

Yamaguchi, S., Hale, L. A., D'Esposito, M., & Knight, R. T. (2004). Rapid prefrontal-hippocampal habituation to novel events. *Journal of Neuroscience, 24*(23), 5356–5363.

Yau, J. L., Olsson, T., Morris, R. G., Meaney, M. J., & Seckl, J. R. (1995). Glucocorticoids, hippocampal corticosteroid receptor gene expression and antidepressant treatment: Relationship with spatial learning in young and aged rats. *Neuroscience, 66*(3), 571–581.

Ybarra, M. L. (2004). Linkages between depressive symptomatology and Internet harassment among young regular Internet users. *Psychology & Behavior, 7*(2), 247–257.

Ybarra, M. L., Dienerwest, M., & Leaf, P. (2007). Examining the overlap in Internet harassment and school bullying: Implications for school intervention. *Journal of Adolescent Health, 41*(6), S42–S50.

Ybarra, M. L., & Mitchell, K. J. (2004). Youth engaging in online harassment: Associations with caregiver-child relationships, Internet use, and personal characteristics. *Journal of Adolescence, 27*(3), 319–336.

Yerkes, R. M., & Dodson, J. D. (1908). The relation of strength of stimulus to rapidity of habit-formation. *Journal of Comparative Neurology and Psychology, 18*(5), 459–482.

Yoder, M. A., & Haude, R. H. (1995). Sense of humor and longevity: Older adults' self-ratings compared with ratings for deceased siblings. *Psychological Reports, 76*(3), 945–946.

Youngs, B. B. (1978). Anxiety and stress—how they affect teachers, teaching. *NASSP Bulletin, 62*(421), 78–83.

Yovetich, N. A., Dale, J. A., & Hudak, M. A. (1990). Benefits of humor in reduction of threat-induced anxiety. *Psychological Reports, 66*(1), 51–58.

Zald, D. H., & Kim, S. W. (2001). The orbitofrontal cortex. In S. P. Salloway, P. F. Malloy, & J. D. Duffy (Eds.), *The frontal lobes and neuropsychiatric illness* (pp. 33–69). Washington, DC: American Psychiatric Press.

Zaslav, M. R. (1998). Shame-related states of mind in psychotherapy. *Journal of Psychotherapy Practice and Research, 7*(2), 154–166.

Zhang, F., & Labouvie-Vief, G. (2004). Stability and fluctuation in adult attachment style over a 6-year period. *Attachment & Human Development, 6*(4), 419–437.

Zhang, J., Niaura, R., Todaro, J., McCaffery, J., Shen, B., Spiro, A., & Ward, K. (2005). Suppressed hostility predicted hypertension incidence among middle-aged men: The normative aging study. *Journal of Behavioral Medicine, 28*(5), 443–454.

Zhang, J. X., Cao, C., Gao, H., Yang, Z. S., Sun, L., Zhang, Z. B., & Wang, Z. W. (2003). Effects of weasel odor on behavior and physiology of two hamster species. *Physiology & Behavior, 79*(4–5), 549–552.

Zhang, L. X., Levine, S., Dent, G., Zhan, Y., Xing, G., Okimoto, D., . . . Smith, M. A. (2002). Maternal deprivation increases cell death in the infant rat brain. *Developmental Brain Research, 133*(1), 1–11.

Zhao, L., Chen, Q., & Diaz Brinton, R. (2002). Neuroprotective and neurotrophic efficacy of phytoestrogens in cultured hippocampal neurons. *Experimental Biology and Medicine, 227*(7), 509–519.

Zhu, X. O., Brown, M. W., McCabe, B. J., & Aggleton, J. P. (1995). Effects of the novelty or familiarity of visual stimuli on the expression of the immediate early gene c-fos in rat brain. *Neuroscience, 69*(3), 821–829.

Zhu, X. O., & Waite, P. M. (1998). Cholinergic depletion reduces plasticity of barrel field cortex. *Cerebral Cortex, 8*(1), 63–72.

Ziegler, J. (1995). Immune system may benefit from the ability to laugh. *Journal of the National Cancer Institute, 87*(5), 342–343.

Zillmann, D., Williams, B. R., Bryant, J., Boynton, K. R., & Wolf, M. A. (1980). Acquisition of information from educational television programs as a function of differently paced humorous inserts. *Journal of Educational Psychology, 72*(2), 170–180.

Zimmerman, F. J., Glew, G. M., Christakis, D. A., & Katon, W. (2005). Early cognitive stimulation, emotional support, and television watching as predictors of subsequent bullying among grade-school children. *Archives of Pediatrics & Adolescent Medicine, 159*(4), 384–388.

Ziv, A. (1976). Facilitating effects of humor on creativity. *Journal of Educational Psychology, 68*(3), 318–322.

Zoladz, P. R., Conrad, C. D., Fleshner, M., & Diamond, D. M. (2008). Acute episodes of predator exposure in conjunction with chronic social instability as an animal model of post-traumatic stress disorder. *Stress, 11*(4), 259–281.

Zola-Morgan, S. M., & Squire, L. R. (1990). The primate hippocampal formation: Evidence for a time-limited role in memory storage. *Science, 250*(4978), 288–290.

Index